JACK STRAW was born in Buckhurst Hill in 1946. Brought up in Loughton, he studied law at Leeds University and practised at the bar before becoming an MP in 1979. He served as Home Secretary, Foreign Secretary and Leader of the House of Commons during Tony Blair's premiership and Secretary of State for Justice and Lord Chancellor under Gordon Brown. Married with two children, he lives in London and his Blackburn constituency.

'Straw has an ear for anecdote and quotation, and is honest about his difficult early life; self-justifying, but also self-aware about his record, including as Foreign Secretary during the Iraq war'

Books of the Year, *Independent on Sunday*

'One of the best memoirs of a contemporary Labour politician, the Gromyko of his generation, even if at times he carefully navigates round some political and personal issues'   Iain Dale, www.iaindale.com

'The big beast of this year's memoirs . . . an acerbic, plain-spoken, often self-mocking account of Straw's progress up the greasy pole'

Robert McCrum, Books of the Year, *Observer*

'This book is no dull ministerial CV. One of Straw's virtues as a politician was that he was one of the few interviewees who would, at 8.10 a.m. on the *Today* programme, answer the questions and engage in the argument. No surprise, then, that he is a good writer, with a nice line in understated wit . . . You might think, after all the memoirs of the New Labour years, that it would be hard to add much that is new. Yet each different voice adds a different perspective, and this is one of the best and most distinctive. Straw has ensured that he will go down in history as more than a footnote'

Sunday

'Crafted with literary elegance – erudite, forensic and fascinating. Always a consummate politician – possessed of "guile and low cunning", as his old ministerial boss Barbara Castle memorably put it – his book is a tour de force through the fluctuating fortunes of the Labour party from the mid-1960s to the 2010 election defeat . . . Some memoirs by former Labour politicians generated headlines and big serialization fees – promptly to disappear, quickly remaindered. This book will stand the test of time. Straw's account of Labour's journeys in and out of power over nearly five decades is a must for serious students of government and politics'

Peter Hain, *Observer*

JACK STRAW

LAST MAN STANDING

MEMOIRS OF A POLITICAL SURVIVOR

PAN BOOKS

First published 2012 by Macmillan
First published in paperback 2013 by Pan Books
an imprint of Pan Macmillan, a division of Macmillan Publishers Limited
Pan Macmillan, 20 New Wharf Road, London N1 9RR
Basingstoke and Oxford
Associated companies throughout the world
www.panmacmillan.com

ISBN 978-1-4472-2276-7

Typeset by Ellipsis Digital Limited, Glasgow
Printed and bound by CPI Group (UK) Ltd, Croydon

Visit **www.panmacmillan.com** to read more about all our books
and to buy them. You will also find features, author interviews and
news of any author events, and you can sign up for e-newsletters
so that you're always first to hear about our new releases.

It is not the critic who counts: not the man who points out how the strong man stumbles or where the doer of deeds could have done better. The credit belongs to the man who is actually in the arena, whose face is marred by dust and sweat and blood, who strives valiantly, who errs and comes up short again and again, because there is no effort without error or shortcoming, but who knows the great enthusiasms, the great devotions, who spends himself for a worthy cause; who, at the best, knows, in the end, the triumph of high achievement, and who, at the worst, if he fails, at least he fails while daring greatly, so that his place shall never be with those cold and timid souls who knew neither victory nor defeat.

THEORDORE ROOSEVELT, 26th President of the United States (1901–1909); 'Citizenship in a Republic', speech at the Sorbonne, Paris, 23 April 1910

For Alice

CONTENTS

INTRODUCTION

I love politics, Parliament, my Blackburn constituency.

I've been an MP for thirty-three years, at the time of writing. Every day that I see the wondrous mellow stone of the Palace of Westminster my spirits are lifted. Inside the building, I marvel at its inspiration, its combination of the spiritual and the temporal which makes our lives worthwhile.

In this book I seek to honour the practice of the building – of politics in a democratic society – and reflect on my luck that I have been part of that practice for so long. Politics should be a high calling – the means by which we make difficult, sometimes nigh-impossible decisions without resort to violence and bloodshed. In our country, it's rooted in the representation of *communes* – the old-French root of 'Commons' – where our first duty is to speak for the people of a defined community.

British politics is hard. It can be self-serving, petty. In reputation, politicians rank near the bottom, with journalists, estate agents – and bankers. The pressures can be relentless; the toll on one's family oppressive; the brickbats frequent (and the material reward less than for many journalists, estate agents, and certainly bankers). I still think it's great. I can think of no other way in which I could have spent my working life that would have brought such setbacks and frustrations, but such satisfactions. Holding high office for thirteen years is an extraordinary privilege. So too is serving on the back benches – where, after a thirty-year interval on the front bench, I'm much enjoying the wider freedoms I have to think, and to take action, especially on my constituents' behalf.

Some may think that my progress was pre-ordained, onwards and upwards at every point. In prospect, it wasn't like that at all. (It is for very few, whether they're born with a silver spoon in their mouth, or a plastic one.) I've been lucky, but part of that luck I've made. I want to tell my story. I want to celebrate politics, spell out why it can make such a difference to people's lives and draw some of the lessons that I've learnt for those facing the daily grind of political decision-making.

'The further back I look, the further forward I can see,' wrote Winston Churchill.

I was alive to the politics of the time in which I was living from a very early age. I have been a voracious reader of histories, and biographies of all kinds. In writing this book I have sought to place what I was doing in the context of wider events and trends. The absence of memory is one of the greatest dangers that our society, and our politics, faces today.

I am blessed with a very retentive memory, but in writing a book of this kind it is rash indeed to rely on that alone. Since school I have built up a large archive of records and papers – so large that it fills our basement and my study in our Blackburn home. I have retained all my engagement diaries. I have never systematically kept a personal diary, but I have on occasions kept notes of key incidents and events. For my thirteen years in government I have had access to my Ministerial papers. Hansard, newspapers, political biographies, and other open sources have proved invaluable. Wherever the written record has been inadequate I have sought corroboration from others. Every effort has been made to ensure the factual accuracy of this book. All errors, misstatements and misjudgements, are mine.

Because this book spans six and a half decades, I have had to be highly selective. Some of the most difficult decisions have been over what to omit. I made the judgement that it was better to cover fewer issues and events, but in depth, rather than simply skim the surface of many more. As well as trying to ground my narrative in a wider historical setting, I have also endeavoured to convey what it all felt like at the time.

This book, as with everything I have achieved in my life, would not have been possible without the encouragement, help, and support of many people.

My first debt of gratitude goes to my mother, Joan Ormston, a lioness of a woman who brought up her family of five, single-handed, in straitened circumstances, and was relentless in seeking the best for her children. In her nineties, and frail, she nonetheless was as alert as ever until a month ago, when she suffered a stroke. Fortunately she was able to read the first two chapters, on my childhood, before this – and offer some corrections; as did her surviving brother, my uncle Norman, and his wife Beryl, to whom many thanks.

I was closest in age, and in my experience of childhood, to my elder sister Suzy (two years my senior). Tragically, Suzy (otherwise extremely fit) collapsed in late September 2011 from a burst aorta, and died ten days later. My three other siblings – Ed, Will and Helen – have been very supportive, and I am very grateful to them, as I am to Patrick Carter, my oldest and closest friend.

Mark Mitchell, also a lifelong friend whom I met on my first day at Leeds University, commented in much detail on our time there and in the National Union of Students (NUS). Margaret Wallis, Valerie Hardwick, and her sister Daphne Barry, who each worked at the NUS, were very helpful, as were Nicholas Riddell and Anne Page in respect of our time together on Islington Council.

In Blackburn, some of those who were involved in my selection as the town's Labour candidate thirty five-years ago, or who came on the scene shortly after that, are still active. We have, as it were, grown up together. These include: Phil Riley and his partner Ann Parker, Bill (now

Sir Bill) and Anne Taylor, Andy Kay, Sylvia Liddle, Mike Madigan, Adam (now Lord) Patel, Tom (now Lord) Taylor, John Roberts, his partner Kate Hollern (now council leader), Akhtar Hussain, Mohammed Khan, Ibby Master, Maureen Bateson and many many others. It has been a remarkable journey for us all, and I could have done very little without their help and encouragement. That also applies to my staff in Blackburn – Anne Higginson, who ran my office for twenty-one years from 1983, and now Damian Talbot, Annette Murphy, Pat Maudsley and Mumtaz Patel.

I was blessed, too, with dedicated and expert staff in London before, and during my time in the Shadow Cabinet – my PAs, Jenny Hall, Janet Anderson (later MP Darwen and Rossendale), Judy Ray and Sue Peters; researchers Richard Margrave, Ben Lucas and Alex Cole – and Ed Owen. Ed came to work with me in 1993. When I became Home Secretary in 1997 he served as my special adviser, staying until 2005, to be succeeded by Mark Davies. On the policy side, my special advisers in the Home Office were Norman (now Lord) Warner and Justin Russell; in the FCO, Michael (now Lord) Williams, Brian Donnelly and Malcolm Chalmers; and in the Leader's Office and the Ministry of Justice, Declan McHugh.

One of the great joys of being a member of the Shadow Cabinet, and the real one, was that of leading, and binding together, a team – which I sought to do partly through regular weekly team meetings, with all the ministers working with me, my parliamentary private secretaries (PPS's), and the relevant staff in the Party HQ and the Leader's Office. I am very grateful to all of them; in particular my many highly able ministers, not all of whom, unfortunately, due to the constraints of my narrative, I have been able to name. PPSs are in many ways the unsung heroes of our system – their inclusion by the Whips Office as part of the 'Payroll Vote' (whose loyalty, or at least whose presence in the correct division lobby, is not in question) mocks them, for unlike ministers they receive no additional pay for their work. Especial thanks, therefore, to Paddy Tipping, Colin Pickthall, Mark Hendrick, Mike Hall and Sadiq Khan, who served me with great loyalty and assiduity, and who often had the unenviable task of telling me what I didn't particularly want to hear. So too did George Howarth, who worked with me as a Home Office minister for two years, but who has been a close friend and confidant for over twenty-five years.

No minister is likely to be effective – or survive too long – unless there is a close relationship of trust between them, their special advisers, their Private Office, their permanent secretaries, and departmental civil servants. Through my experience as a special adviser, and especially through my marriage to Alice Perkins, a career civil servant for thirty-four years, I perhaps had a better understanding of this official tribe than some. I was exceptionally well served by my principal private secretaries – Ken Sutton and Hilary Jackson in the Home Office; Simon McDonald, Geoffrey Adams and Peter Hayes in the Foreign and Commonwealth Office; Stephen Hillcoat in the Leader's Office and Antonia Romeo and Alison Blackburne in the Ministry of Justice. I have, where needed, drawn on their recollections, as I have other members of my Private Offices – in the Home Office Clare Sumner, Mara Goldstein, Stephen Harrison and David Redhouse; in the FCO, Mark Sedwill, Jonathan Sinclair, Kara Owen, Caroline Wilson, Irfan Siddiq and my FCO press secretary, John Williams, who gave invaluable help; and in the Ministry of Justice, Rebecca Ellis.

Many others have commented on sections of this book in draft. These include Michael Ancram, Michael Portillo, Mike O'Brien, Sir David Omand and Malcolm Brindred. Doreen Lawrence commented on Chapter Ten about the inquiry into the murder of her son Stephen. Professor David Sugarman, Professor of Law in the University of Lancaster, has written extensively on the extradition of General Augusto Pinochet (Chapter Eleven), and was very generous with his time and expertise. Professor Francesca Klug, Professorial Research Fellow at the London School of Economics, and Professor Robert Hazell, Head of the Constitution Unit at University College, London, provided great assistance with Chapter Twelve. Robert, his colleague Meg Russell, and Peter

Riddell, formerly of *The Times*, now heading up the Institute for Government, were also very helpful in respect of my ideas for strengthening Cabinet governance. Former US Secretary of State Colin Powell was as ever extremely generous with his time and comments. Throughout my time in Parliament, I have relied heavily on the House of Commons Library, as I have for this book: on its lending, its reference and especially its brilliant Research Division. I am particularly grateful to Oonagh Gay, and Christine Gillie and many other staff there. I am also grateful to the current Private Offices and the records management teams in the Home Office, Foreign Office and Ministry of Justice.

I wrote every word of this book, but the task would have been far more difficult without the extraordinary effort of two people who have worked alongside me throughout – Deborah Crewe and Dan Sleat. Deborah was a fast-stream civil servant who served in the Cabinet Office (with my wife Alice), and in the Home Office and Ministry of Justice, and who (happily for me) decided on a career change. Exceptionally bright, well-organized (and tidy), with great command of English, she has worked tirelessly, co-ordinating the many comments on sections, knocking them into shape, doing the first edits – and so keeping me to my deadlines that she earned the title of 'Ms S D' (Slave Driver). Dan has been my Commons' Researcher since October 2010. An expert in international relations, he has an insatiable appetite for work, and has spent days on background research, fact-checking and much else besides, in addition to his job of assisting me with my parliamentary duties. The title was his inspiration, to great relief all round, especially from the publishers. We three have enjoyed each other's good humour too.

It was my literary agent, Georgina Capel, of Capel and Land, who first suggested that I write this book, gently but firmly had me revise my outline into something presentable, and encouraged me in many ways throughout this book's gestation. I am very grateful to her, and to her husband, the publisher Anthony Cheetham, who gave me sage advice at a critical juncture. I am equally grateful to the team at

Macmillan: to Philippa McEwan, to Harriet Sanders, to Tania Wilde, to my copy-editor, David Milner, and above all to my ever-professional editor, Georgina Morley.

I have often quipped that I would never marry an MP, still less a busy minister; I am not certain I would volunteer to have an MP and cabinet minister as a Dad, either. To Alice, to William and to Charlotte, the words 'thanks' or 'gratitude' scarcely convey the depth of what I feel towards them. I have been an MP for the whole of my children's lives, and became Home Secretary when they were teenagers. They have each commented on many of the chapters, and given me such love and support.

Alice has been my soul-mate and life partner for thirty-six years; she has lived with me through all but the first three chapters of this book. Unable (by law) to take any active part in my constituency or other parliamentary work, she is, nonetheless, one of the sharpest observers of the political scene I know, and has an intimate understanding of the highways and byways of the British government system. I have learnt so much from her; many have been the occasions when she has saved me from the inevitable consequences of a rash course on which I was about to embark. Alice has read and commented on every chapter of this book. She has also had to live with me whilst this book took me over in a way which neither I, nor she, ever anticipated. The book is dedicated to her, with love and so many thanks.

Enoch Powell claimed in his biography of Joseph Chamberlain, 'All political lives, unless they are cut off in midstream at a happy juncture, end in failure, because that is the nature of politics and of human affairs.'[1] I dispute this dismal commentary, this received wisdom about British politics. All political lives have to come to an end – and, from high office, abruptly – but that's not because politicians, and the institutions they have moulded, are all failures; it's because we are all flesh and blood, and because we all live in a democracy.

Jack Straw, *August 2012*

ONE

My Mother, Your Father

'My mother has just married your father,' Reg announced.

It was late April 1967; three weeks to the Final examinations for my law degree at Leeds University. I'd had a great time. It was the Sixties. But, as my day of judgement approached, I was (temporarily) regretting that I had spent too much time on student politics, trying to impress women, and generally enjoying myself, and not enough on my studies.

The Parkinson Building on Woodhouse Lane is the most imposing building at Leeds University, and sits at the top of a hill half a mile north of the city centre. For me, it was not only imposing but intimidating, its dominant presence a constant reproach that I should have spent my time there, in the Brotherton Library, rather than a hundred yards away in the Student Union building.

As I climbed the stone steps to the front entrance, my mind was on the finer points of the law of contract when I saw Reg Gratton approach. Reg had been editor of *Union News*, the well-produced and popular student newspaper, and as a student politician anxious for good coverage I knew him, although he was not a close friend. We had occasionally had a drink together, but nothing more.

'Hi, Jack,' he greeted me.

I mumbled a 'Good morning' in reply, and we passed.

I was some paces towards the doors to the library itself when I heard a tentative, then an imperative: 'Jack, Jack.'

I turned and walked back to Reg, who was now nervously shifting from foot to foot.

'Jack, there's something I've been meaning to tell you.'

'What's that, Reg?' I asked, thinking that he might be about to impart some inner detail of the running of *Union News*, or gossip about some adversary.

'There's something I've got to tell you.'

'Tell me, Reg, please.'

There was a long pause. Then he told me that his mother had just married my father.

My parents had parted when I was ten. I was now twenty. I had not seen or heard of my father in the intervening decade, except via reports from my mother complaining about the late arrival of the required maintenance payments. These were seventeen shillings and sixpence (87½p) for each of their five children, due in cash in a registered envelope every other Tuesday. I knew from this that my father was still alive, but nothing more.

'We'd better go and have a coffee,' I suggested.

In a café across the road from the library, the story unfolded. Reg had been sending home copies of *Union News*. His proud mother had been showing them to her husband. He had noticed reports about a Jack Straw, and gradually worked out that this young man was his son.

Through Reg I remade contact with my father. So did my siblings. We were all reconciled by the time of his death in March 2002.

Walter Arthur Whitaker Straw was born in March 1917, in the pit village Worsbrough Dale, just outside Barnsley, South Yorkshire. His father was a railway carpenter, his mother the local midwife. When he was two years old, his father died in the great flu epidemic that killed even more people than had lost their lives in the First World War. Two of his sisters died shortly after, leaving him in the care of his mother, ground down and ill-tempered, and his elder sister Dorothy, whom he claimed was continuously unpleasant towards him.

My father was a bright child, and in 1928 won a scholarship to the Barnsley and District Holgate Grammar School. But in 1930, when he was thirteen, his mother made a decision that, though taken for the best of reasons, was to mar the rest of his life. She had had enough of the grime, deprivation and choking atmosphere of a pit village, and took a post as the district midwife in Woodford Green, Essex, on the edge of East London.

Woodford Green was – and still is – a pleasant leafy suburb close to Epping Forest, staunchly Conservative in outlook. Winston Churchill was the area's Member of Parliament from 1924 until he stood down in the 1964 general election.

Arthur (as he was always known) transferred to nearby Wanstead County High School. He said, in the graphic terms he always used, that for quality of life, moving south was the difference between 'heaven and hell'. The 1929 slump wreaked devastation on the industrial and mining areas of the north, but the south largely escaped its impact.

However, class and accent mattered much more than today, and my father had a rasping South Yorkshire accent, which he never lost. Despite being able to buy a small house, his mother was much less well off than the parents of his classmates. The combination led to him feeling like a social outcast: 'Sometimes I felt treated like a n*****,' he claimed. A preoccupying self-pity became one of his most enduring, and least attractive, characteristics.

Four years after Arthur left school and started work as an industrial chemist aged eighteen, the Second World War began. It changed everyone's lives and it changed British society. But my father's war was very different from that of his contemporaries.

October 2000, Wandsworth Jail, South London; one of the forbidding Victorian 'model' prisons built in the shape of a star the better to control the prisoners. I was on one of my (many) routine jail visits as Home Secretary, on this occasion to the Vulnerable Prisoners Wing, the euphemism for sex-offenders, who for their own safety have to be kept separate from other prisoners. One of the inmates started complaining to me in extravagant terms about the food and the facilities, about how he could get a shower only twice a week. Impatiently I turned to him and said: 'Listen, pal, it's a great deal better than when my father was here.'

'Oh, was your father the governor here, then?'

'No,' I replied, 'he was on your side of the cell door during the war, and conditions here were horrible.'

'Thieving, violence, or sex?' asked the inmate.

'None of those,' I replied. 'He was a conscientious objector. He'd refused his call-up.'

'Blimey, you mean he sort of chose to come here? Wouldn't it have been easier if he'd got called up, and dodged the fighting? Plenty did.'

It was a good question, but I was never clear about the origins of my father's pacifism. In the thirties there were plenty of people who profoundly believed that passive resistance to tyranny was a better alternative than the carnage of war. The weak-willed George Lansbury, Labour's leader from soon after the party's catastrophic defeat in 1931 until his brutal (and necessary) despatch by the great trade unionist Ernest Bevin in 1935, was also a leading pacifist. There was not a family in the land who had not been touched by the bloodshed of the First World War, who had not lost a father, son, or brother – the British Cabinet included. Prime Minister Neville Chamberlain's attempts in 1938 to 'appease' Adolf Hitler were much acclaimed at the time.

In the 1914–18 war conscientious objectors were pretty brutally treated. The arrangements for them had improved by 1939, but the penalties for refusing to fight were still high. My father was sentenced to several months. He served most of it in Wandsworth, but towards the end of his sentence was transferred to Exeter. His journey there was the only time, he claimed, that he ever travelled first class on the railway – handcuffed to a prison warder.

On their release, 'conshies' like my father were put to work with prisoners of war, in his case as a land worker in East Anglia, hedging, ditching and digging turnips and sugar beet. Later in the war he returned to work as an industrial chemist, living with his mother in Woodford Green.

As for my mother, her family also had its share of hardship, fairly typical for the times. But instead of sinking into self-pity, as my father did, she determined to do better for herself and the next generation.

One dismal February evening in 2011 I was waiting on a near-deserted platform at Westminster Underground station to go home. My fedora was pulled down low, in the hope that I could read my newspaper in peace. From the corner of my eye I noticed two well-dressed women in their mid-twenties coming towards me, engaged in close debate.

'There, I told you. It is him.'

'It is you, Mr Straw, isn't it? What a surprise, to see you on the Tube.'

'Well,' I replied, 'this is where I work; and even folk like me have homes to go to.'

'I've got to ask you something, Mr Straw.' I abandoned my newspaper, and expected the question to be about the cuts, Iraq, or even football.

'Your mother's a Gilbey, isn't she? My family is too. My dad says that your side of the family took all the money out of the gin firm established by our forebears.'

Would that this had been true.

In the nineteenth century, two brothers, Walter and Alfred Gilbey, had indeed established a gin distillery – W&A Gilbey. The firm prospered. Walter was the driving force. In a romantic Victorian fable of upward social mobility, he later laid out Rotten Row, the carriage drive around Hyde Park, and was knighted by Queen Victoria. In the version I was told, Alfred, was the ne'er-do-well and spent more time drinking the firm's product than he did selling it. Social mobility in the nineteenth century was a ruthless two-way street. Alfred's fortunes went into a fast decline. Pensioned off from the firm, he went to live in Loughton, in Essex. However, although this fable was what we all believed, it does not appear to be correct. The family is related in some way to the founders of the gin company, although I am not clear how. But there is one certainty, as I explained to the young women on the Westminster Underground platform. None of the firm's money went to my side of the family.

The Gilbey forebear of mine had a walk-on part in the long-running nineteenth-century drama of Epping Forest. Its retelling to me, by my mother's father, helped form the beginnings of my political convictions. Above all, it helped me to understand whose side I was on.

Today, Loughton is a London suburb at the eastern end of the Central Line, but it is still surrounded on almost three sides by the wonderful, mysterious Epping Forest, my childhood playground. Since 1878 it has been administered as a public park by the Corporation of the City of London, for 'the recreation and enjoyment of the public'.[1] But it would not be there at all were it not for the heroic efforts of a group of agricultural labourers who took on the landowners and won.

The ordinary residents of the surrounding parishes had for centuries enjoyed two key rights over the common land of the forest: the right to graze their livestock and, critically, the right of 'lopping' – to take wood from the forest, provided the tree itself was left alive. But by 1865 the lord of the manor, John Whitaker Maitland (who conveniently doubled as the rector), had enclosed virtually the whole of the parish's boundaries within the forest – over 1,300 acres – for his own use. In November 1865, one of the parishioners, Thomas Willingale, having exercised his lopping rights, was summoned to appear at the local magistrates' court to answer criminal charges of injuring trees. The chairman of the Bench was the same John Whitaker Maitland. Even he must have had a modicum of shame about the extraordinary conflict of interest involved, and the charges were dismissed. But in the following March further, similar charges were brought against members of Willingale's family. All were found guilty, and served seven days in prison.

The die was then cast. Having Willingale as an adversary was one misfortune for Maitland and his fellow squires; facing the enmity of some very wealthy, Nonconformist Radicals who had happened to settle in the area was their second.

The political history of the nineteenth century is inexplicable without an understanding not just of the conflicts between social classes, but also of those within them, including within what Marxists simplistically referred to as 'the ruling class'.

Many of those who made their money from trade, commerce and manufacturing were deeply hostile to what they saw as the narrow, antediluvian attitudes of the Tory squirearchy. This was a confessional divide as much as a political divide – indeed the one was often inseparable from the other. Great Quaker families like the Frys, Guerneys, Barclays, and their relations (not Quakers) the Buxtons, made their country homes in the area.

Willingale and his associates decided that the only way to determine once and for all the rights of the parishioners was to take legal action. But this was complicated, and so expensive as to be utterly beyond their meagre resources. The Commons Preservation Society, of which local resident Edward North Buxton was a member, stepped in with financial and professional support.

The case proceeded with a pace resonant of *Bleak House*. But for the commoners – and their descendants – it had a much happier ending than Charles Dickens' dismal story. After a twenty-one day hearing, the Master of the Rolls gave judgement in their favour, with excoriation for their opponents. The Rev. John Whitaker Maitland, a pillar of society and Anglican clergyman, and all the other lords of the manors around the forest (one a Queen's Counsel) were said by the judge to have 'taken what did not belong to them . . . and have endeavoured to support their title by a large amount of false evidence'.

This court victory was followed by an Act of Parliament making the forest effectively a national park, with the City Corporation in charge, a role they have carried out in an exemplary way ever since. The lopping rights were commuted to a cash payment to all the commoners (the grazing rights remain). A village hall – Lopping Hall – was built with additional compensation, and is still in use as a public hall in the centre of Loughton.

This remarkable David and Goliath story stayed with me. Had it not been for the victory of Thomas Willingale and his associates, my forebear included, the home town of my childhood would have been a completely different, and much less pleasant place.

My secondary school had a Local History Prize. I decided to enter for it, with an essay about aspects of this fight for the forest. During the Easter holidays in 1961 I spent hours in the Essex Record Office in Chelmsford studying the papers they had about it, including a complete set of John Whitaker Maitland's court documents.

In the margin of one page of these documents, Maitland had written: 'Why should a twenty-five shilling [£1.25] a week labourer be allowed to sue me, the lord of the manor?' That single sentence taught me volumes about the attitude of those in power when they were challenged.

My grandfather was born in a wooden cottage close to the forest in 1896 and went to the newly established Board School in nearby Staples Road. All his six children, my mother included, would go to the same school, as would I and two of my four siblings.

Granddad left school at the age of thirteen and became a butcher's boy with Bosworth's Butchers (which sadly closed in 2011), driving cattle from the main market in Bishop's Stortford the thirteen miles to their slaughter and sale in Loughton. He joined up when the war came, and was one of the lucky few to return more or less physically unscathed from the carnage around him.* He lost a toe from shrapnel, and developed claustrophobia after being buried alive when a sandbank behind which he had taken cover was hit by shells and collapsed.

---

* He served in the Essex Regiment before becoming part of the Machine Gun Corps later in the war.

The woman who was to become his wife, my maternal grandmother, was called, eccentrically, 'Olive Bill'. Her parents were east European Jewish émigrés who had come to the UK in the late 1880s. Little is known about their provenance. The family's surname 'Bill' was almost certainly an anglicized version of their German or Yiddish name. My nana's father was a silversmith. They lived in the East End, on the City Road.

When Nana was about nine and her younger sister Lil was eight, disaster struck the family. Their father died, then, within months, their mother, leaving them orphaned. They were sent to a Methodist orphanage in Bristol, austere in the extreme. The inmates were allowed out on the downs for one day each year. What Judaism either girl had was duly knocked out of them for a 'higher' religion.

As for many women in similar circumstances, it was the First World War that provided Nana with a degree of emancipation. With so many men in uniform, women were to take jobs previously reserved for men. She was sent to work in the vast munitions factory at Waltham Abbey, and found digs a few miles away, in Loughton – where she met, and later married, Granddad.

The couple had six children: my mother, Joan, the eldest, born in 1921, then five sons, born in quick succession over the next decade. One other child died when very young.

Granddad managed to get a secure job as a night mechanic in the Loughton Bus Garage – one which he was to keep until he died in 1955, aged fifty-nine. He was a bright man, full of ideas and initiative. He was very fond of me, his first grandson. I was close to him, and greatly admired him. His politics, like his wife's, had been formed in the hard school of experience. Both had suffered from the rigid class system – and he knew, not least from the fight for the forest in which his own forebears had played a part, about the brazen injustices which those in power were ever ready to perpetrate unless they could be met with some equal force. At the bus garage he formed a branch of the then Transport and General Workers' Union (the 'T&G', now Unite), and became its shop steward. He later became one of the key lay allies of the T&G's general secretary, Ernest Bevin, who served in the wartime Cabinet as minister for labour, and in the post-war Labour government as Foreign Secretary.

Granddad, with Bevin's encouragement, won a scholarship to Ruskin College, Oxford, but illness and money worries meant that he could not take it up. He was one of many 'aristocrats' of the trades union movement in that period; towering figures, exceptionally well read, but denied the opportunities and education for which they so relentlessly fought.

My mother, Joan Sylvia Gilbey, his eldest daughter, and the apple of his eye, was more fortunate. In 1931 she won a scholarship to Loughton County High School and was bright enough to go to university. But that was out of the question. Instead, just as the Second War was to begin, she got a place at a teacher training college, with a loan provided by the London County Council (LCC). After qualifying as a nursery/infant teacher she worked in a succession of the residential nurseries established in the countryside by the LCC to take children who had been evacuated from the East End during the Blitz.

My mother had been appalled by her father's experience in the First War, and his accounts of the terrible suffering that this war had inflicted. Now, with her brothers facing conscription to fight the Second War, she became a pacifist, and joined the Peace Pledge Union. On leave back in Loughton she would go to the Coffee Club at the Buckhurst Hill Congregational Church – where, in 1943, she met my father.

I was the second child of this union – born in August 1946. Their first, Susan, was born in early July 1944.

For years my parents told us that they had married in January 1943. One day, when she was about ten and I was eight, Suzy (as she was always known) rushed in to tell me that she had been rifling through some of our parents' drawers, and had found their marriage certificate. The wedding had in fact taken place in January 1944. Suzy had been conceived out of wedlock. Common enough today – but then such a thing could bring shame on the whole family, especially families believing themselves to be 'respectable'.

Suzy's discovery explained the only surviving wedding photograph. Just four people were present – the bride and groom, looking bemused, and my mother's parents, her father looking as black as thunder. Our father's mother, a tyrant at the best of times, expressed her disapproval at this shotgun marriage by boycotting the whole event.

After the war my father got a job in the City of London as a clerk at a marine insurers and the family moved into 10A Victoria Road, Buckhurst Hill, the ground floor of a Victorian house directly opposite the Underground station.

We were lucky to have a two-bedroomed flat, given the intense shortage of housing in the immediate post-war period. There was a bath in the scullery, under boards, with an 'Ascot geyser' – a gas water heater – which sounded as though it was going to explode every time it was used, and an outside lavatory in the small back garden.

A third child – my brother Edward (Ed) – arrived in January 1949.

My mother secured a teaching post at a private school – Oaklands – on the edge of Loughton, a short bus ride away. She was paid £70 a term, but the fees for her children were waived, so that's where Suzy and I first went to school.

This period was the happiest of my childhood. The tensions that were soon to tear my parents' relationship apart were not really noticeable, although in retrospect I can see that they were there. I cannot recall, for example, any occasion where I witnessed any tenderness between our parents – but at such an early age I had no means of comparison. Even then, I was a precocious child, anxious for an audience. Aged four, I stood on a chair in the kitchen, and shouted 'All peoples be quiet,' as I sought to harangue those in the room.

The family was immersed in the strong Nonconformist community in Buckhurst Hill; every Sunday, without fail, we attended the Congregational Church. Despite their relatively low incomes, my parents were able to save enough for a deposit to put down on a semi

– which in those days would have cost between £2,000 and £3,000. My mother was utterly determined to see her children get on in life, to have the chances denied completely to her father and his generation, and in some ways to her too.

Then the fissures began to appear. My father spent quite a chunk of their savings on a car – a 1932 Armstrong Siddeley – and my mother became pregnant with her fourth child – William – who was born in April 1953. Previously our parents had been able to contain their anger with each other until we children were out of earshot. They could do so no longer. Eruptions could occur at any time, with my father complaining that the pregnancy arose from an immaculate conception in which he had played no part (he had – we all look like him), and my mother counter-charging that he was self-absorbed, selfish, immature, and had spent their money on a car which they could not afford and did not work.

The flat was cramped enough for a family of five. There was simply no space for a sixth, so my parents applied to the local council for rehousing. Out went their dreams of their own house in a respectable neighbourhood. In came the reality of 101 Pyrles Lane, a three-bedroomed maisonette on the first and second floors of a block of flats on a new council estate at the wrong end of Loughton. We moved there in November 1952. The move itself took place during a London smog so bad it had even extended to the suburbs. It persisted for days. Visibility was down to a few yards. The smog seemed to sum up my feelings at the time. I had lost all the certainties in my small world.

Across the road from '101', the Labour-controlled LCC had built one of its many large housing estates on the edge of London. In the main, these were houses, with gardens. But these were for 'their' people – East Enders whose homes had been bombed flat by the Nazis. The responsibility for housing locals fell to the Chigwell Urban District Council – Tory to the core, and with an approach that echoed that of Edwin Chadwick, the architect of the Poor Law Amendment Act 1834, who established the Victorian workhouses on the principle of 'less eligibility' – i.e. that conditions outside the workhouse should always be better than those inside.

Similarly Chigwell Council seemed to have decided that conditions living in council housing should always be worse than those in the private housing sector. For the same money, and land, the council could easily have built proper houses with gardens. They chose instead to put noisy families with children above ground-floor flats for the elderly and couples without children – separated only by a concrete floor. There were strips outside as 'gardens'. Heating for the kitchen boiler, and the fire in the sitting room (there was no heating for the bedrooms whatever) was by coke and coal. The coal bunkers had been placed inside the maisonette, on the first floor, between the kitchen and living room.

The complaints from the coalmen that they had to take 50 kg sacks of coal up a narrow internal staircase were vitriolic. The walls up the stairs were decorated with black stripes from the sacks. The whole house was filled with coal dust for days after a delivery. We could smell it, and chew it.

All the tenants were in the same boat. My mother got them organized and they bombarded the council with protests. After many months new bunkers were built outside our front doors.

My mother had had to give up her job at Oaklands, so Suzy and I moved to our grandfather's old school, Staples Road Primary. I was put in the final year of the Infants. I exchanged a small class, and lots of space, for a cramped classroom with fifty-four other children, in the charge of a single teacher. She was good, but control required that we were only rarely allowed to leave our desks, which were attached to the benches on which we sat.

Despite the lack of facilities, Staples Road was a remarkably advanced and relaxed place – a far cry from the regime under which my grandfather had suffered fifty years before. There was no uniform, all the classes were mixed-ability. The sloping playground was entirely concrete, so I learnt little in the way of cricket or football. There was no playing field. But there was, directly opposite, the forest.

We were all under parental instructions never to go into the forest alone. There were as many, if not more, 'dirty old men' of all ages (now called paedophiles) lurking in the forest in those days as there are now. But we were never banned; nor would a ban have had any effect. Such men were encountered by us, promising payment to go into the bushes with them. We'd tell them to push off, with fruity language if needs be. In our minds, it was simply a hazard to be dealt with, little different from falling into the bogs in the bomb craters which abounded in the forest, or getting bruised when one's tree-climbing did not go according to plan.

In the summer term at Staples Road we were all allowed into the forest at lunchtime, and we observed an imaginary boundary imposed by the teachers about 200 yards (roughly speaking) into the forest. After school, we roamed far and wide and came to no harm.

On 2 June 1953, the Queen's Coronation took place in Westminster Abbey and was marked not only by a public holiday: every child in Essex was given a copy of a booklet called *Royalty in Essex* by the county council.

The Coronation provided a great boost for the sales of televisions. We did not get one until I left home for university in 1964, but the people next door to my grandparents – Mr and Mrs Rosser – had purchased one, and we were invited round to watch. The Rossers' son, Roger – nicknamed 'Happy' because of his cheerful disposition – was, like me, six and a half – and my best friend. We spent hours, days, together playing in the forest, or wandering around Loughton town centre. The year before the Coronation we had caused consternation to our parents when we were so absorbed in an escapade that we had clean forgotten to go home for our lunch. The police were called. We were found by a friendly constable on a bicycle, by the Crown in Loughton, just after Happy had won a penny from me – we'd had a bet as to who would be the first to put some horse dung we had found in the road in our mouths.

Happy and I dutifully sat down with all the loyal parents, grandparents and older children round the flickering television set. Then the most intense boredom set in. We had seen quite enough of people in fancy clothes walking up and down, sitting, kneeling, standing, carrying sticks and offering pots, and certainly did not begin to comprehend the finer details of the ceremony. So, after an hour, we took off to the forest, not returning until late afternoon – by which time the Queen had been crowned, and it was all over.

I loved the forest. It had a peace and serenity about it, which, sadly, was not the case at home. The four and a half years that my parents spent together in 101 were dismal and unsettling for everyone in the family. It would be a rare evening that our parents did not row about something. Sounds bounced off the concrete floor, chairs screeched as they were moved. Noisy disputes in our kitchen were punctuated by repeated knocks from the flat below as the occupier banged a broom handle in a desperate and usually unsuccessful attempt to secure some respite.

It was when we children had gone to bed that the really serious arguments between our parents would kick off. I shared a small bedroom with my two brothers. There was a bunk on one side of the room, a bed the other. It was directly above the kitchen. So we'd hear the rows, the trading of insults, the pots being slammed down on the draining board, cupboard doors slammed.

In a ground-floor flat at the end of the next block lived Stan and Pat Wythe. They were lower middle class too, and like my parents did not particularly enjoy the fact they had come to live on a council estate. Stan was a librarian. Pat had been a teacher, until she had contracted polio, which had left her severely disabled. They became close family friends, a relationship reinforced by the fact that they had a television, which we would go and watch on a Saturday night. The Wythes wanted children, but could not have any, so we became their surrogate family. My brother Ed, then aged four, became so attached to Stan that he began to call him 'Pa', a term which the rest of us children then adopted. I never asked my father what he thought of this. But it was clear that it was one factor, of many, that reinforced the social isolation that had been a feature of his life from the moment that his mother had moved her family from South Yorkshire.

Another strong factor in that isolation was the attitude of his brothers-in-law. My mother's eldest brother lived in Scotland, but the other four brothers lived locally. One, Roy, had had a leg amputated and was invalided out of the Royal Marines. (Astonishingly, he worked for most of his life as a telephone linesman, shinning up telegraph poles.) The other three were plumbers. They had all served in the forces and thought little of 'conshies'. My mother looked out for her brothers, and they for her – and her children. Our childhood would have been significantly more difficult but for the support they, and their wives, gave us.

In late 1955 relations between my mother and my father went from unpleasant to horrible. The arguments and bickering were constant. And then, one particular evening, something strange, and very frightening, happened.

Our primary school, Staples Road, was just a quarter of a mile from our grandparents' house – though my grandfather had tragically died of cancer in May 1955, we'd frequently go to Nana's after school for tea, and sometimes our mother would come and collect us for the bus ride home. On this occasion the two youngest children, my brothers Ed and William (aged six and two), had been collected by our mother. Suzy and I must have separately been playing with friends in the area. I got back to Nana's, and went, unannounced, to play behind a corrugated-roofed shed at the back of the house.

Two of my uncles, Derrick and Don, had 'called in' to see their mother. There was nothing unusual about that. They lived locally. But then my father turned up on his bicycle. He had agreed to collect the younger children, though they had already left.

Nana's back garden was up some steps. The house had been built into a hill so I had a good vantage point down the side of the house. I had a sixth sense that something nasty was about to happen, and so stayed put, hidden but all-seeing.

Derrick and Don came from the back door to meet my father. An argument began. I couldn't catch all of it, but I later learnt that their ire was up because they'd heard from my mother that my father had disputed my brother William's paternity (he was then, and is now, a dead ringer for my father). The argument went on. Then, suddenly, my two uncles shoved my father against the pebble-dash wall of the side of the house. Don held him. Derrick smashed his fist into my father's face, with a force and anger I had never witnessed before. His mouth started to bleed. Half a tooth fell on to the ground and he began to weep.

All three went into the house. I came out of my hiding place and followed them in. 'You weren't supposed to be here, John,' said Don. I might have been only nine, but I'd worked that out for myself.

My sister Suzy then emerged, from the next-door neighbour's. It was not until 2011 that I learnt from her that she had witnessed the whole incident through a gap in the neighbour's fence.

We went home, the three of us, with my father pushing his bicycle.

That was a Friday. At around lunchtime the following day most of the family were out somewhere. I smelt gas, lots of it. I went into the kitchen, and found my father slumped over the table. The oven door was open, the gas taps were on, pouring out gas. I quickly turned them all off.

In those days all gas supplies were 'town gas', which unlike natural gas was very poisonous. Gassing was one of the most common methods of suicide in the fifties, though because the father of a friend of ours had gassed himself, I knew that most suicides put their heads into the oven, to ensure that their end came as quickly as possible.

I went and found my mother and told her what had happened. She stormed into the kitchen, and told my father that if he was intending to take his life, not to involve the children. It was the beginning of the end for my parents' marriage.

The arguments went on, not least over money. One Sunday there was just enough for our bus fare to church, and a penny each for the collection, but that was it. My mother had no more money, so we'd have to walk the four miles back after the service. We did – and as it happened had a great time fooling around on what was otherwise a tranquil Sunday lunchtime.

In June 1956 my mother and her four children were all in the kitchen of 101. She was ironing, the rest of us reading (and intermittently tormenting each other), when she suddenly announced that she had something important to tell us. She was pregnant, again. The baby was due to be born in mid-January 1957.

My reaction to this news was one of rage. Rage that there'd be even more noise in the house, rage that there'd be even less money to go round, but rage at the gods rather than at my mother and father, thanks to a fundamental misunderstanding I had about where babies came from.

My mother had indeed explained the facts of life to us, as soon as we'd put the direct question to her. She had described the mechanics of sexual intercourse accurately. My error (not hers), however, was to believe that intercourse took place once, when a couple married. After that it was pot luck how many children then arrived. There had been no outward signs of affection between my parents for years, so the idea of any sexual attraction was quite beyond my comprehension. I was very struck that many of my friends came from smaller families, and that, in consequence, their parents were happy and had enough money. The only rational explanation for the regular arrival of siblings in the Straw family was therefore fate, and ill-luck.

On 8 January 1957 we got back from school to be told by our father that we now had a baby sister – Helen. My mother had easy pregnancies, and all but her first child at home. My father made us bacon and eggs for tea – something so unusual that I can still see him at the cooker, frying pan in hand. My anger dissolved as soon as I saw and held my new sister, and we became very close.

But only a short while after she had given birth to Helen, my mother decided that life under the same roof as my father was impossible. He would have to leave. Divorce was very difficult then. Its grounds were restricted principally to adultery (not relevant), or physical violence. There had been that, but proof was difficult, the process expensive. In any event, my mother shared the prevailing social aversion to divorce, which was especially strong in the Nonconformist communities. Instead, she decided to get a 'non-cohabitation order' from the magistrates' court, to require my father to move out.

All this coincided with preparations for me to take the 11-plus, which would determine the type of secondary school I was to attend. The school system in our area, as in almost the whole of the country, was based on the 'tripartite' divisions laid down in the 1944 Education Act, of grammar, technical and secondary modern schools.

My elder sister Suzy had passed her 11-plus in 1955, and was, as our mother had done, attending Loughton County High School. Our friend and neighbour Pat Wythe had given her extra tuition for the exam. Pat now did the same for me, taking me through English grammar, arithmetic and much else, with great thoroughness.

Because of the turmoil at home, it was decided that I should go to stay with church friends in Buckhurst Hill – John and Joyce Marsh. Theirs was a 'normal' family – two parents who seemed to like each other, two children, a proper house, in which even I was given my own room. I stayed there for weeks, returning home for lessons with Pat, and sometimes at weekends.

Each time I came home, I could feel the tension in the air the moment I walked through the door. I was given strict instructions not to look under the rug in the sitting room where my mother was concealing from my father her notes for the court case. Of course, both Suzy and I did look, but we put them back.

I happened to be at home for one of the many visits which the Rev. Johnson, the Congregational Church minister, was making to see my mother. My father could present a very good front to others and was friendly with many in the church, including the Rev. Johnson. The minister did not want a marital break-up amongst his flock, and was quite determined to avoid this.

When the first hearing on my mother's application for a non-cohabitation order came up in the Epping Magistrates' Court, the Rev. Johnson appeared as a witness for my father. He convinced the court that with a little more time, he could save the marriage. The court accepted this, and adjourned the hearing for two months. My mother was not only upset, but incandescent, breathing fire about the magistrates, all of whom were well known to the Gilbey family.

It seemed there was to be no respite from the tension at home. Add to that, living in a cramped house, sharing a small bedroom with two younger brothers, and a baby sister teething in my parents' adjacent room, and I could see that there would not be much chance for me to study at home. I had borrowed Anthony Buckeridge's 'Jennings and Darbishire' books from the church's well-stocked library and loved them. The life described seemed idyllic, peaceful and fun compared to mine. So I decided that what I would really like to do was to go away to a boarding school.

Alongside the 'tripartite' system of state secondary schools, there were also 'direct grant' schools. These were independent schools, like St Paul's, Highgate, Manchester Grammar and, in Essex, Bancroft's (in Woodford), Chigwell and Brentwood. In return for taking a significant proportion of pupils from the list of successful 11-plus examinees, the schools were assured an income stream, as the Ministry of Education paid the tuition fees of these children 'direct'. In practice these schools took the highest achieving 11-plus candidates, often running their own entrance examination as well.

Many of these schools took boarders as well as day boys, and Essex County Council provided a very limited number of boarding scholarships each year and I was entered for these scholarships too. Brentwood had the best academic record in the county, and was inaccessible by public transport from Loughton for any day boy. My mother and I made this my first choice, with Bancroft's second.

The 11-plus was a nightmare for many children. Its results were so crucial in determining future life chances that many of my school friends were offered prizes, like new bicycles, for success, which only made their neurosis worse. In contrast, I felt no terror whatever about the exams. I was lucky enough to have a great facility for maths, and had been well tutored in the other subjects by Pat Wythe. I assumed I would pass, and knew that if I did well enough I would get the scholarships I was seeking.

The exam itself was held at Buckhurst Hill County High School one wet day in late February 1957. Most of my school mates were brought in by coach from Loughton. Since the Marshes' house was only down the road from the school, I walked. The exam was fine for me, though I remember looking around the hall to see friends in deep distress and despair.

The results came through when I was still staying at the Marshes' house. My brother Ed passed me a letter of congratulations from my father in the playground at break. He had evidently not been told by my mother that Brentwood was my first choice as he had added kindly, 'Now to Bancroft's, let's hope!'

My mother took me to Brentwood for my entrance examination and interview – a long and tedious series of bus journeys. I was put into my best clothes, and constantly lectured on the way by my mother that I had to remember to shake the headmaster's hand with my right hand. One of the many eccentric habits that Baden-Powell had decreed for the scouting movement was that we should shake with our left hands. As an assiduous member of the 28th Epping Forest Cubs I used only my left.

But I remembered the lecture, shook hands with my right hand, took the examination, and answered the head's questions. Soon after, we had letters from Brentwood to say I'd been accepted, and from the county council to say I'd been awarded a boarding scholarship. I was all set to taste the world of Jennings and Darbishire.

One day I returned from the Marshes' to be told that my father had gone. At the adjourned hearing the court had finally granted the non-cohabitation order, requiring him to leave.

My mother and my siblings were pretty jubilant and I was expected to feel the same. Instead, I felt a mixture of numbness and anger. I knew that in truth life at home with my father would be impossible. He had been violent to my mother, on occasions to my sister Suzy, and brutally off-hand with my brother Ed. On our father's birthday in spring 1956 Ed had spent his pocket money to buy him a special cup and saucer. Seeing it, my father had demanded 'What's this?' and, when it was explained, had pushed it away and left the room. But he had always been OK with me, and he was my father. Most of all I was angry that the others were making assumptions about what I would feel.

My father returned to 101 just once – to collect his box of tools – but was not allowed in the house. I spoke to him outside. He moved into digs, with church friends, in Woodford Green.

The court had provided that he should have access to us, but like many women in the same situation, then and now, my mother was pretty determined to make this as difficult as possible. Suzy, Ed, and I met him on Whitsun bank holiday 1957. The rendezvous was a bus stop by Buckhurst Hill cricket ground. We spent an excruciating hour walking through the forest, listening to a monologue from our father in which he sought to explain how and why he had been the victim of a monstrous injustice by our mother, and the Gilbey family.

I would hear nothing more of him until that extraordinary encounter with Reg Gratton in late April 1967 just before my Finals. He might as well have died. There was no further access. I could forgive him that, given my mother's hostility to the idea. What was far less forgivable was that he could not even manage a card on our birthdays. Whoever else was to blame for his marital problems, it wasn't his children.

My last term at Staples Road Primary School was lovely. All the exams were over, our fates decided. At Easter our class went on a week's trip to the Newlands Valley in the Lake District. I'd been desperate to visit the area ever since I'd devoured Arthur Ransom's 'Swallows and Amazons' series. I was not disappointed. I fell in love with the Lakes.

MY MOTHER, YOUR FATHER

There was also a great boat trip around the Royal Docks in Newham – now the site of London City Airport, then a grimy but fascinating working dock.

When term ended, I said goodbye to close chums. But no one else was going to Brentwood. I never saw them again.

TWO

Boaters and Boiler Suits

'Sorry lads, there's no tea this morning,' Wilson, the head of house, announced. Slippers, fished out from beside the beds, went flying in his direction.

This was 'One Dorm', bedroom of the six senior boys of Otway House, Brentwood School, on Monday 13 May 1963. We, as sixteen- and seventeen-year-old boys, governed the lives of the others in the house by bells, rotas – and punishments.

Each weekday, the senior boy on 'getting-up duty' had the prior responsibility of going down to his day study, putting the kettle on the gas ring in the corner, and making mugs of tea for the dormitory. It was a Monday, so it was Wilson's turn.

'I'm very sorry. The gas is off.'

'Then turn it on, you twerp.'

'I can't. Robertson's dead. On the floor of the Three Study. Gassed himself.'*

The levity stopped immediately. We were all instantly wide awake. I could smell the unmistakable, acrid odour of town gas and saw my father, head in hands at the kitchen table.

We filed downstairs to wash and shave in the changing room, all

---

* Wilson and Robertson are not their real names.

passing the Three Study, the one that I shared with three other senior boys. It was a tiny room – no more than about seven feet square. The windows and door were wide open, to clear the gas. An ambulance man was going through the motions of artificial respiration, without the least conviction that it would work. Robertson's face was puffed up and sweaty. This was the first time I had seen anyone dead. I wondered to myself whether everyone who was dead looked like that.

Robertson was fifteen. In a boarding house renowned for its musical talent – the housemaster was director of music – Robertson was the most talented musician of all, a brilliant pianist. He had the most extraordinary ability to play even the most complicated of pieces by ear. But he frequently got himself into trouble by failing to complete various 'fatigues' laid down for him on one or other rota. The previous evening, I and another senior boy had upbraided him for a yet further catalogue of punishments.

I've often wondered whether this – wholly routine – talking-to had in any way tipped Robertson over the edge. I'll never know. What we did learn pretty quickly was that the reason Robertson gave in the note he left was about something quite else. He believed that he was gay – 'queer' in the brutal parlance of the time. He knew that there was not a single person in authority with whom he could safely discuss his feelings. Not his parents – his father was a senior officer in the services – and certainly not the headmaster, nor any assistant master. So he chose the only route out of his desperation, loneliness and guilt – and killed himself. That, he evidently judged, was far better than the shame and humiliation that would befall him and his family if his love, or simple passion, for another human being who happened to be male was ever found out. He knew for certain that such exposure would mean his expulsion from the school, and public excoriation.

In his biography of Harold Macmillan, D. R. Thorpe describes the pervasive atmosphere of the Eton that Macmillan attended as 'homoerotic'; 'like many public schools at the time, a hothouse of seething passion'.[1]

Brentwood wasn't Eton; and this was half a century later. But

Thorpe's description applies as much to life in a mid-century boarding house of a direct grant school as it does to that in Britain's leading public school at the beginning of the last century.

A great deal had changed in the intervening period. Two world wars, the wind-down of empire, cars, planes, radios and television, the welfare state, all meant that in many respects Britain was a different place. But not much had changed in respect of public attitudes to homosexual behaviour. That revolution in attitudes is far more recent than is often imagined.

Homosexuality was still a serious criminal offence. In the fifties, enforcement of the law had been significantly strengthened. In 1938, for example, there had been just 316 prosecutions for homosexual indecency (consent was no defence); but by 1955 the equivalent number had reached 2,322. This increase followed a campaign led by the then Home Secretary David Maxwell Fyfe that homosexuality was a great and growing evil.[2] The law was amended in 1967. The change in social attitudes between the early and late sixties was very rapid.

The law in the early sixties did not stop men, or boys, from having sexual feelings for each other. It never had. It never could. Rather, it suppressed, and sometimes perverted, these feelings. It overlay the sexual excitement of encounters with the guilt of doing something 'wrong' and the risks of being found out.

At Brentwood, 'experimentation' between pubescent boys was treated as an internal 'problem' – if its endemic practice were ever to come to the attention of the masters in a way that required them to act. It never ever did in my time at the school. On the other hand, sexual activity involving a senior boy (ill-defined for these purposes, but in practice over the age of fifteen or sixteen) would always lead to expulsion. Not that this 'rule' was ever written down. Denial was the order of the day. Everyone knew what went on, and no one knew.

It was a beautiful July evening in 1962, nearly a year before Robertson killed himself in preference to facing expulsion and disgrace. The setting sun was catching the bay windows of the house library, and the lawn outside. 'Lighten our darkness, we beseech thee O Lord, and by thy great mercy defend us from all perils and dangers of this night,' intoned our housemaster, Dr Edgar Brice, as he did at evening prayers every weekday evening. (Fifty years on, I can still repeat the Collects by heart.) But this Evening Prayers was different. For the only time that I can recall, the headmaster, C. Ralph Alison, was to address the house.

We all knew why. Two senior boys, one from another boarding house, the other from ours, had been found engaging in homosexual activities. The matter had come to the attention of the headmaster in a bizarre way. The boy from our house was from a very rich family and had lent the other boy money, which he couldn't repay. As a result he was forced to redeem his debt in the form of regular assignations behind the cricket pavilion. He got fed up with this arrangement and went to the head to complain, naively believing that he would be treated as a less-than-willing victim. But, victim or not, he had still been a participant. Alison was a courteous man, ready to engage in discussion, decent, caring, and in many ways rather liberal; but he was also a man of his time and had taken the view that if homosexuality was a crime outside the school, it had to be treated as a crime within the school too. Both boys were to be expelled.

We all listened in silence as the head explained his decision. As he was leaving the house after the assembly, I caught up with him, saying that I thought he had made a profound mistake. Surely, I asked, homosexuality should be seen as a personal problem, not as something to punish? His approach would not eliminate homosexual practices, which – in case he didn't know – were common in our school. What his approach would do, however, was to ensure that those who had this 'problem' would bottle it up; they would never be able to speak to anyone in authority for fear that they would be dealt with as he had just dealt with these two boys. Who knows, I asked, what could be the consequences of such an approach on these unhappy individuals?

Sadly, it took only ten months to find out.

The people who ran the school were familiar with death in a way in which my generation, and every subsequent one, is not. They had all been through one war; some through two. Almost all of them had seen death at close quarters. Yet they were profoundly ill-prepared for the impact of Robertson's suicide. At all costs the truth of what had been behind the suicide had to be suppressed. The whole school was warned that on no account should we say anything to the press (in the improbable event of any of us being asked). The funeral was held; with the most peremptory of inquests on Thursday 16 May – four days after his death. There was a note, said the coroner, 'in which he [Robertson] expresses great unhappiness and some fearful burden on his mind and hints at some irregular practices but doesn't say what it is'.[3] It was the main story in the local papers. The father commented that his son 'had great respect for his headmaster, his housemaster, his music master and the school chaplain, I think we could say that he loved them and that he felt the shame would let them down'.[4] The waters closed over.

The refusal to face the truth did nothing to heal the profound trauma that everyone in the school suffered – especially those most directly affected, in my boarding house.

The key adults on whom we should have been able to rely seemed paralysed by shock (and maybe guilt too). In many ways, it was as if the house, and the school, suffered a collective nervous breakdown.

All this happened three weeks before my A levels were to begin. These days there would be offers of counselling, letters to exam boards, extra tuition. We were simply expected to cope, to pretend that nothing had happened.

My five and a half terms in the sixth form had been a golden period for me. I'd flowered. In a highly competitive environment, I'd come joint top in my subjects in mock A levels and similar grades were expected of me in the real exams. In the event, Robertson's suicide knocked me for six. I got three Ds.

*

My career at Brentwood had begun nearly six years before, on 19 September 1957.

In the summer holidays, my mother and I had taken the long bus journey to Brentwood to visit the school shop. There, at the astonishing cost of £30 (three times the average weekly wage) I was kitted out – two grey serge suits (one for Sundays only), a blazer and flannels for the Trinity (summer) Term, grey socks, grey shirts, house tie, cap, endless items of sports kit – and scores of Cash's name tapes bearing the legend 'STRAW Ot 46'.

All this, a tin tuck-box on which I'd painted my name, and much more, was packed into a trunk, and despatched in advance by British Road Services (fee 3/6d – 17½p), to await my arrival.

For this first evening away, we were to go by car – driven by our neighbour Stan Wythe. I said goodbye to my brothers and sisters, took a last look around our maisonette, and off we set.

We arrived around 6 p.m. It is the smells that most stick in my memory – of the turpentine from the thick layers of polish that had been applied to the common-room table, and every floor surface; of disinfectant; and of the maroon carbolic soap that wafted from the changing room.

This was Otway House, term-time home for forty-two boys.* It was a large, late-Victorian family house to which a much larger austere wing had been attached in the twenties. On the ground floor was the common room, changing room with twelve basins, two baths and two showers, a boot room, three day studies for the senior boys, three lavatories, and the 'stoke hole' with the coke boilers for heating and hot water, and a huge pile of coke. On the two upper floors were five of the house's six dormitories, and the matron's rooms. The original part of the building contained the housemaster's quarters, the house library, and the junior dormitory, the 'Six Dorm'.

---

* Named after George Otway, the school's first master, on its foundation in 1557.

The ethos of the house, and school, was one of muscular Christianity. Open windows were a requirement regardless of the weather. There was no heating in the dormitories, except in the senior boys' coveted One Dorm; no dormitory door could ever be closed, except again the door to the One Dorm.

As someone who had shared a very small bedroom with two brothers, I'd only ever known communal living. It was not until I was nineteen that I had a bedroom to myself. For those who'd enjoyed such luxury, the total absence of any privacy must have come as a shock.

Seniority determined almost everything – the location of one's bed, where one stood in house assembly, where one sat in the dining hall, one's position in the roll call. I was the youngest boy in the house, and therefore the most junior.

In the Six Dorm we each had an iron bedstead, a chair, some hanging space and a drawer. From my bed I could look down the long corridor, with the three most senior dormitories on it – the One Dorm at the far end. As a result, I had to keep 'cave' – watching out for prefects patrolling to detect those who were talking after lights-out. Our lights went off at 8.45 p.m.; Five Dorm's at 9 p.m.; Four Dorm's at 9.15 p.m., and so on. Only the One Dorm, whose occupants controlled the rest of us, could suit themselves.

My first term at Brentwood lived up to all my expectations of boarding-school life, which had been drawn in their entirety from Jennings and Darbishire. There were, however, many aspects of life at Brentwood which had not featured in those rose-tinted volumes, and for which I was wholly unprepared.

One of attractions of the life described by Anthony Buckeridge, I can now see, was the happy and constructive adult/child relationships on which his narrative was founded. In Otway, the housemaster, Edgar Brice, was kind and thoroughly pleasant; so was his wife. But what mattered most for Brice was music. He lived for it. As the school's director of music, he led the chapel choir, was the chapel organist, conducted the school orchestra, and ran the town's choral society as well. A strict rota of music practices was enforced for those many members of the house (me included) who played a musical instrument. Beyond that, he was a distant figure, leaving us almost exclusively under the control of the senior boys. Whether life was tolerable, or not, depended on the personality of the head of house, and the level of collective sadism of the One Dorm.

The fatigues and duties that so caught out poor Robertson led inevitably to every junior boy in the house piling up punishments. No talking after lights, no talking in prep, no running in the corridors, no eating in public outside the tuck-shop square, no gym kit on the floor of the changing room, no fighting, no lateness – the list of prohibitions was endless; above all 'no cheek' – speaking in an impertinent way to a senior boy.

The punishment system was carefully ritualized. Miscreants were normally required to stand outside the relevant prefect's study straight after breakfast – and would then be issued with their punishment. 'Drills', detentions, and 'pages' were the most frequent. Drills were circuits of the school's (very extensive) playing fields; they and detentions were carefully timed for Wednesday or Saturday afternoons, after games – the only times when we were allowed into town (Sunday afternoons aside, when all the shops were closed). 'Pages' involved one having to write an essay on what was normally a completely obscure subject of the prefect's choice. In those pre-Google days, the only source was a tatty encyclopaedia in the house library.

Sometimes, one would be offered a whacking with a leather slipper as an alternative to these non-violent but time-consuming punishments. The key factor would be who was going to mete out the whacking. Some prefects were poor in their aim, or held back from inflicting too much pain. Others took obvious and sadistic pleasure in their task – though they were also the ones who tended not to offer any choice of punishment.

If you crossed the line by accumulating too many punishments, there was a further sanction – a caning by the head of house. During our first term, one of the older boys in my dormitory had been told that he would be caned – after lights out, in his pyjamas. It would be 'that week', but he was not told the exact day. The tension was awful. One evening went past; nothing. A second; nothing. On the third, I saw the head of house go into the One Dorm, followed by the other prefects. We heard the sound of beds being moved around (to provide more room for the swing of the cane). The deputy head of house came to our dormitory to fetch him. In a further turn of the screw he was made to stand outside the One Dorm, shivering, for what seemed an age, but was probably only ten minutes.

From my vantage point, I then reported to the rest of the dormitory that he'd been ushered inside. A deathly stillness fell over the whole of the house. One, two, three, four – we counted the strokes of the cane. Then the poor guy emerged, and came back to bed, to a good deal of whispered sympathy. We all knew that he was weeping. Four strokes of a cane, administered by a strong, fit young man, with a good aim, with no intention of holding back, landing in exactly the same place on the backside (as we saw in the morning) hurts like hell.

This particularly uncivilized – and genuinely terrifying – practice fell out of use early on in my time in Otway. Thereafter the cane was used by masters only. But the whacking with slippers continued until, years later, in my final post-A level year at school when I was head of house, I used the arbitrary power with which one was endowed to abolish all corporal punishment by boys altogether.

A second aspect of life in a fifties' boarding school for which Jennings and Darbishire had provided no preparation whatsoever, was sex. I did know about the basics of sexual intercourse, but assumed – as I have mentioned – that this happened once, at the beginning of a marriage. Beyond that, I had no idea. We led very innocent lives. Today, there is little escape for children of any age from sexually charged advertising, media stories and television programmes, and a ready availability of pornography on the internet. There was none of that then.

This made the initiation of the new boys in the Six Dorm into the world of sexual feelings all the more astonishing. On our second evening, the same boy – at twelve, a year older than us – who would later be caned with such brutality opened proceedings by asking each of the four new boys in turn what we knew about 'rubbing up'. Guffaws of laughter came from the older hands, as we made wild guesses that it was presumably something to do with the cleaning of brasses. Our ignorance established, a demonstration about the mechanics of masturbation ensued. This, and associated interests like the length of our penises when turgid, the amount of pubic hair we had – and later, as we went through puberty, who was having an association with whom – provided a staple diet of conversation, and competition.

A third aspect of life at Brentwood for which I'd had no preparation was what to answer when asked the inevitable questions about my family background. In those days, boarders accounted for about a third of the school roll and they tended to come from prosperous homes. Some boarded because their parents were overseas; others because their parents thought they should – and could afford the fees. Although being a direct-grant school meant that there was a significant proportion of pupils who were from backgrounds as modest as mine, they were mostly day boys. The number of boarders like me was small. And the number of scholarship boys whose parents had separated was even smaller.

Divorce equalled shame; and so did living in a council house. From today's perspective, this seems rather curious. Not least since, at the time, some council estates included quite a number of lower-middle-class people – teachers, nurses, police officers. But you did not have to live long in a socially segmented and deeply Conservative town like Loughton to pick up the idea that, for those in power, council tenants were second best, people who relied on the state rather than on their own resources.

Instinctively, I judged that I'd better be very careful indeed about admitting anything about my separated parents, or the council maisonette in which we lived. I had quickly observed how any differences were seized on by the other boys. So, whilst I told the truth, it was by no means the whole truth. My father worked in insurance; my mother was a teacher; we lived in Loughton. That decided, I settled down to my first term at Brentwood, throwing myself into school life and thoroughly enjoying it all. I went home for Christmas 1957 in high spirits.

These did not last.

This was the first Christmas without my father around. The tension between my parents, the violence in the air, was all gone. The circumstances that had led me to believe that the Jennings and Darbishire world of boarding school would be infinitely better than the atmosphere at home had changed. As the new term loomed, the attractions of the better life at home seemed far to outweigh those of Otway House. The first term had been exciting. But I knew the excitement would quickly fade; and that those aspects of life in a fifties' boarding school for which I had been wholly unprepared would be what would preoccupy me once I returned – not least having to embroider where my father was, and where we lived, for fear of being bullied if I told the unvarnished truth.

I went back to school in the Lent Term of 1958 with a deep sense of foreboding about whether I could survive in the alien atmosphere; and, above all, with a longing, a sickness in the pit of my stomach, to be at home, enjoying the new-found tranquillity of family life, as my siblings were. As the days went past, I became more upset. I sought out a little privacy, and wept. I deliberately hung back from my dormitory group for the quarter-mile walk to and from the dining halls, and cried my heart out. I spent time in the house library rather than the common room, and wept again.

Sundays were the worst, especially the evening roll call, and the evening chapel that followed. Dr Brice always played Bach's 'Sheep May Safely Graze' as the opening music to that service. To this day, I cannot hear it without tears coming to my eyes, as I recall sitting in chapel in utter despair on those bleak Sunday evenings, just longing to be transported back to 101 Pyrles Lane, which for all its absence of material comforts was my home.

I began to write to my mother every day, demanding to be allowed to leave Brentwood. With four children at home, including my baby sister, Helen, just a year old, my mother hardly needed the additional burden of a homesick son. But children never think of that – why should they?

My peers at school were incredibly nice to me; so were the senior boys. Dr Brice called me into his study to offer sympathy, to tell me that a lot of boys were homesick in their second term, and that I'd get over things. I just had to hold on.

Three weeks into term there was a 'Long Sunday'. We were allowed out at 8.30 a.m., after breakfast. There was no morning chapel. We had to be back by 5.55 p.m. for roll call and chapel. For my friends, this meant a day out with their parents who arrived in their cars to collect them. For me, by now overwhelmed with self-pity, it meant an hour and three-quarter's journey on two buses. If I was lucky I'd be home by 10.30, and would have to start back by catching the 20A bus at the end of our road by 4 p.m. I spent the last half-hour of the journey fretting about whether I would make it in time. The whole day simply made me more homesick. It was a further graphic reminder of what I was missing – or thought I was missing – at home.

My distress was made worse by a deep frustration that no one appeared to be taking me seriously. Masters and boys alike had been very decent. There'd been no bullying, no calling me a 'crybaby'. But no one was asking me why I felt as I did; nor seeking to offer what in retrospect seems the most obvious of explanations, that given what I'd observed between my parents it was only to be expected that I might feel a degree of turmoil.

One Tuesday in early February, about four weeks after the start of term, I decided to run away. I chose my time carefully. House assembly finished at 7.45. Lights out was 8.45. I had an hour in between before my absence would be noticed. I got my cap (I had no wish to break that school rule) and slipped out. I'd also worked out an unusual if very tedious route, the better to avoid detection. I took a train to Ilford, then caught a 167 bus. The conductor was a little surprised to find an eleven-year-old boy joining his bus for what was going to be the whole of route, but I made up some plausible explanation.

The door of 101 was on the latch. I let myself in. I went upstairs to find my mother emerging from the bathroom, ready for bed. I can still see the look of complete astonishment on her face. She had no telephone (we did not get one until 1964), and our neighbours, the Wythes, the only people in the area who did, were out. So there had been no way for the school to make contact to say that I'd gone missing.

My mother's exasperation with me rather outweighed her sympathy. She went off to the phone box to tell the school I had turned up and arranged for Uncle Norman to drive me back the next morning. On arrival, I was taken to see Dr Brice. He was kind, telling me that no more would be said, but repeated that I had to get on with life at school as I found it. It was the same tune as before.

I decided to run away again that evening. I slipped out as soon as evening prayers were over, and decided to risk taking the bus. About two hours later I walked into 101. This time Dr Brice had got through to the Wythes so my mother – far from pleased – was expecting me. I was given some food, a brief lecture by my elder sister Suzy about what a nuisance I was being, and driven straight back to school, where I was received with a similar *froideur*. To ensure that I did not run away again, all my money was taken from me.

They'd still not got the point.

On Thursday mornings I had to get up early to do a half-hour's piano practice. That Thursday I rose even earlier, and washed and dressed very quickly. The absence of any cash for my fares was not going to deter me from going home. I'd walk, even if it was fifteen miles by the most direct route. I went to my locker to collect a piece of Christmas cake and a wodge of dried banana, the only food I had in my tuck box. I found my raincoat, scarf and cap, and slipped out.

I'd spent much of the night working out the best route. I was a Boy

Scout with a pretty good sense of direction. I reckoned that I should walk about nine miles down the A12 and then strike north-west through to Hainault, Chigwell and Loughton. The day was damp, with occasional drizzle. I made good progress, and was in reasonable spirits for the first half. But eight miles in, the stale cake and the dried banana had both gone. I was hungry, tired and rather wet.

Fifty years ago there was little traffic away from the main roads, especially on a mid-February morning. From the A12 the road went through open fields, with a long drag of a hill to Hainault. As I trudged along, a man on a bicycle pulled up alongside, then dismounted. He was thin-faced, in his twenties, and seemed pleasant enough. He evidently wanted to chat. I was pleased to have someone to talk to, so I told him my story, and explained that I was having to walk home because all my money had been taken from me.

'Oh,' he said, 'I can give you your bus fare.'

'Thank you very much, sir,' I replied. 'I think I'd have to take at least two buses from here, but a shilling should be sufficient.'

'But first,' said the man, 'you see those bushes' – pointing to a copse about a hundred yards across a field – 'you'll have to come into those with me. I want to do something with you.'

I'd come across men like him in the forest, but in relatively safe circumstances, as I always had a chum with me. This was different. The summer before, a boy of about my age had been left in a car whilst his parents had a drink in the Crown on Loughton High Road. He had been abducted, sexually assaulted and then murdered. I knew all too well what could happen. I stared at the man in horror. I said nothing, but took off up the road running as fast as I could, vainly waving at the occasional car that passed. Twice the man rode away from me, only to come back alongside me; but after about a mile of this he finally rode away, never to return. I kept on running for another mile, to make sure.

Five or six hours after I'd crept out of Otway I arrived at 101. Whatever anger the grown-ups felt was over-ridden by evident relief that I was alive and safe. Nonetheless, my mother thought that I should see the family doctor.

In the course of a homily that the road to a successful future for boys like me was bound to be hard, he asked me whether I wanted to be an engine-driver. I liked steam trains. I had a clockwork train set. But I also knew that among the many boards at school celebrating, in gold lettering, 'success' of every description, there was none for engine drivers. To this day, I have no idea whether the answer he was seeking was yes or no.

However, as we talked, and in the conversation I had that evening with my mother, I was at last able to discuss whether I should leave the school, the *cri de coeur* of all the letters that I'd been sending home. The truth was that I really did not know what I wanted, except to be able to stop weeping, and start feeling a little happier. There was an alternative – a day place at the local grammar school, Buckhurst Hill County High. But confronted with this, the grass did not seem so much greener. I also got the impression that the grown-ups had finally realized that I had been making a point and that my unhappiness should be taken seriously.

For the third time in four days, I was driven back to Brentwood. I was taken to the sanatorium, I assume so that the staff could ensure that I was settled. As the only boy in the 'san' that day, I had no opportunity whatever to escape even if I'd felt like it.

The next day, Saturday, I was given my breakfast in the san, and told to return to my classes. I was also told that I was to see the headmaster after chapel.

The head expressed some sympathy with my situation, and said that the school tried to deal kindly with those who ran away once. But good order would break down if boys ran away more than that. If I ran away again, I'd be expelled. For what I'd done so far, he would cane me; three strokes. I bent over. The head was not a sadist. It didn't hurt much.

I cried, but mainly from shock and relief that my month's protest was at an end. As I trudged back to Otway I concluded that feelings were really dangerous. The best way of surviving was not to have them, to be numb, an approach I continued to adopt until my mid-thirties. I had made my point; but they had won.

Over the next seven years, I led a curious yo-yo existence, in which there was remarkably little connection between what happened at school, in term time, and my life during the school holidays. School life was a privileged one of academic work, music, sports and punishments. At home, it was the council flat, pacifism and plumbing.

At school, the years up to O levels passed off normally. In a highly selective school, the classes in the first year were unstreamed. I worked hard. At the end of the year I was one of six pupils in our class to be transferred to the upper stream, who sat their GCE papers after four years, rather than five. This would then give us three years in the sixth form, to allow for Oxbridge entrance examinations, after A levels had been taken.*

In the meantime, I enjoyed cross-country running and rugby. I was very short-sighted even then, and could not wear my spectacles for ball games. Whilst that rendered me hopeless for the finer sports of cricket and football, it was no impediment for house rugby at the crude level at which it was played each Lent Term.

But my favourite extracurricular activity – and the one I was best at – was disputation. Thrown together morning, noon and night, we'd argue. The arguments – about anything and everything – would sometimes continue for days. *The Times* (still with classified advertisements on its front page) and the weekly *Illustrated London News* were our sole source of external news; but we were all surprisingly well informed. In a deeply Conservative environment, respectful of the military, I was the house socialist and pacifist.

---

* In those days Oxbridge exams were taken in the 'seventh term' of sixth form, after A levels. Those staying on for this term could then enjoy two terms off before starting university.

When the third year brought long trousers, detached starched collars and the Cadet Corps, my mother, who was still a pacifist, wrote to the head to ask that I be exempted, and do first aid instead. I went along with this, but I do now regret that I did not have that little taste of service life.

I took eleven O levels in the summer of 1961, a few months before my fifteenth birthday, and I did OK. Maths and physics were among my best subjects; but in those days the arts/science division was rigid. I had been inspired by a truly brilliant history teacher, Peter Watkins, who made the syllabus, which focused on the nineteenth century, come alive and I wanted to study medieval history with him in the sixth form, plus economic history and English. But my marks weren't quite good enough to be allowed to do English, so I was forced to do geography instead. Latin – a requirement for Oxbridge entrance – I failed.

My life in my first four years at school had been superficially sociable, but in truth rather solitary. Brentwood had a large and thriving sixth form and prided itself on having the best academic record in Essex. For me, the change in teaching methods, and in relations with our masters and each other, was dramatic. We boys started to call each other by our Christian names. It was then that my friends began to call me 'Jack', rather than John, and it stuck. It was in the sixth form, too, that I began to make deep friendships – by the end of my three years I was part of a strong and supportive group of friends, every one of them day boys. One, Patrick Carter, became my closest friend at school. Fifty years later, he remains my closest friend; and, wonderfully, for our friendship, he became a member of the House of Lords in 2004.

And it was only in the sixth form that I felt able to tell my friends what I did in the school holidays.

Of my three plumber uncles, the youngest, Norman, was also the most entrepreneurial. He saw that there would be a growing market in domestic central heating, encouraged by higher living standards and technical improvements. In the late fifties he set up his own firm (today, aged eighty, he is still involved) and employed his other two plumber brothers, Derek and Don (the two who had taken out my father's front teeth). I'd always enjoyed using tools and now Uncle Norman said he'd take me on as a plumber's mate in the holidays. For the next three years, my term-time boater and starched collars were swapped for a boiler suit.

Initially I got the filthy, unskilled jobs: crawling in the space under the ground floor, securing and lagging pipes, putting in fibreglass insulation blankets in lofts. I came to no harm, but the prevailing absence of concerns for safety was, by today's standards, extraordinary. We spent a week at a works in Wembley replacing an old coke boiler, which was covered in asbestos. My task was to get inside the soot-encased firebox of the boiler and hold a spanner whilst the bolts were eased. There was soot and asbestos dust everywhere; and not a face mask in sight.

Once, I was working at a house in Buckhurst Hill. The chimney was about three storeys high, with a flue from a boiler poking out of the top. The fitter (not one of my uncles) said 'Right, lad, you're going up the ladder. Take this bucket of cement, pull up the flue lining, and put a fillet round the joint.' I protested that I'd never done this before, and asked why he couldn't go up. 'Because the last time I broke my f***ing leg. Now f***ing get up there. I'll hold the ladder. Don't bloody wobble and you'll be all right.' So I did. My handiwork can still be seen.

Gradually, I developed my skills, and was trusted to cut, bend and solder pipes, and much else. I was intrigued by the physics of central heating too. I've put what I learnt to good use ever since, including for friends.

But the greatest part of the experience was what it taught me about being a workman; what it felt like to be in a perpetually subordinate position. In the main, the people we worked for were decent towards us. But sometimes, we were treated abominably – like the house-proud woman in Wembley who would let us neither wash nor use the lavatory in her house, and who never gave us tea. (I have often wondered since how long it took her to discover that few of the floorboards had been nailed back properly, and that the radiator brackets had too few screws.)

Many years later when the whole family arrived at Chevening, the Foreign Secretary's stately home, for the first of five Christmas celebrations there, my younger brother Will lowered himself into one of the very large sofas in the cavernous drawing room (with paintings by Gainsborough, Reynolds and similar) and said to our mother, 'Here, dear – why the hell didn't you find us a place like this to live when we were kids, rather than that poxy maisonette? If we'd had all this space I'd have never needed to see him [me] or him [our brother Ed], and there'd never have been an argument either.'

But arguments there were, not only within families, but between them. With little or no outdoor privacy, all of us living in the five blocks of maisonettes became extraordinarily territorial. 'Get back up your own block,' was a familiar refrain; and petty arguments between neighbours could turn nasty.

In 1960 bad blood developed between us the Swindell family who lived in the next block. My mother claimed that Mrs Swindell had hit our youngest sister, Helen, a toddler. Mrs Swindell claimed that my mother had hit her son. A male relative of Mrs Swindell's came round to our place, burst in and started shouting all sorts of threats up the staircase. I, a pretty measly thirteen-year-old, grabbed a claw hammer and stood at the top of the stairs (petrified) in case he came up and went for my mother. He left.

Today, the police or the local council would in most cases sort out a situation like this before it escalated. But not then. The police weren't remotely interested in 'domestics' except where the injuries were too bad to be ignored. So my mother went off to Epping Magistrates and issued a private prosecution against Mrs Swindell; she counter-claimed. We all trooped off to court. I gave evidence (and was outraged when the magistrate asked me if I understood what was going on). Mrs Swindell was fined £1, and bound over for a year to keep the peace; her action against my mother was dismissed.

When as Shadow Home Secretary thirty-five years later I was drawing up our policies for government, I explained that my memory of what it felt like to be in such a situation was one of the reasons I was determined to clamp down on antisocial behaviour. The *Daily Mail* found the Swindells, by then living in Hertfordshire. Mrs Swindell described me as 'a little toffee-nosed boy nobody wanted to play with'.[5] But she had added: 'In court, Jack Straw said I pulled [his mother's] hair out. I never did that. I just smacked her face, the same as she did to [my son].'

As I switched back and forth between these two lives, through the socially and economically turbulent sixties, I was working out my politics. It was while I was at school that I first walked the streets leafleting; made the decision to become an MP; made my first political speech; and developed my views on far-left ideologies and totalitarian regimes.

I got really interested in politics in my second year at Brentwood. Apart from an unexpectedly good collection on early British trade unionism (including a history of the Tolpuddle Martyrs), the school library wasn't much help – but the county library was. I took to spending much of my precious Wednesday and Saturday afternoons 'down town' in its reference room. The headmaster was an active member of the United Nations Association, and was so committed to ensuring that all his boys developed an understanding of our political system that he took a weekly civics class. I excelled in this, even winning the Civics Prize in the Trinity Term of 1959 – a fine India-paper volume of the complete works of Shakespeare.

That summer was one of the best of the century. Some bohemian friends of my mother's suggested that I go camping with them to Oxwich on the Gower Peninsula in South Wales. I spent four weeks with them and then took myself back to Loughton to meet up with my sister Suzy for a great adventure we'd planned to the Lake District. Over many months, we'd each saved £5 to cover the costs of the trip. This included five shillings for a bed in a youth hostel, and the cost of the return coach journey, which took about fifteen hours. Once in the Lakes we hitch-hiked. Many of those who picked us up seemed a bit surprised that two children – aged thirteen and fifteen – had been allowed to do this, but we came to no harm.

When we got back, a national political story was unfolding. Harold Macmillan had managed to restore the fortunes of the Conservative Party after the debacle of Suez, which had done for Anthony Eden, his predecessor as prime minister. Riding on a highly successful visit by President Eisenhower in late August, Macmillan called a general election on 7 September 1959.

There had been speculation for months. Earlier in the summer I'd written to each of the main parties to ask them for details of what they were intending to do for the country. I'd had packs of pamphlets back from each, and used to jabber on with my observations as to which party was best for the nation. I had a ready audience in my mother, three of her brothers, and Stan Wythe, who was secretary of the local Labour Party.

I was not due back at school until late September, so in the two weeks after the election was declared I delivered leaflets for the party, tramping round virtually every street on our estate and the surrounding area. One afternoon, sheltering from the rain in a shop doorway, I decided to read one of them. It was the introductory leaflet for Labour's candidate (improbably, a farmer). He described the task of a Member of Parliament, and how he intended to meet it. When the rain eased, I walked home. As I looked up at our block, I decided that being an MP sounded a great deal easier as a way of serving the Labour Party than delivering its leaflets in the rain. I would be an MP too.

The following day, Stan Wythe told me that the local party had been so impressed with all the work I had been doing that they'd decided to ask me to make a short speech at the main election meeting where the candidate was formally to be adopted. I based my speech on my already well-rehearsed – and entirely objective – assessment of which party was best. It worked – not least as the publicity stunt intended. I'd spoken, the chairman told the local paper, 'without a trace of preciousness'.

When I looked up the word in the dictionary, I thought that he had been rather generous to me. I was asked to supply a photograph for the paper. The only one we had was of me in my new straw boater. So there was young Straw, the budding socialist politician, on the front page, wearing one of the strongest symbols of privilege. It was yet another reminder of the two lives I led. I doubt that the irony was lost on the readers of the *West Essex Gazette*.

By election day itself – 8 October – I was back at school. The following morning, I woke early – at six – and went downstairs to see if I could find the 'houseman', who came in each morning to stoke the boilers, so he could tell me the result.

'The Conservatives have won, of course,' he told me. My leafleting had been in vain. Macmillan, the feline Old Etonian, had completely trounced the dry-as-dust Labour leader, Hugh Gaitskell. Not until the abject disaster of 1983 was Labour to run quite such a poor campaign.

The Campaign for Nuclear Disarmament – CND – had been established in February 1958. At its peak in the years 1960–1 it had more members than any pressure group in Britain had had since the Anti-Corn Law League in the 1840s.[6]

Loughton, though overwhelmingly Tory, had a number of left-wing intellectuals including teachers, lawyers and artists, among them the sculptor Jacob Epstein, whose models had scandalized his neighbours. The local branch of CND was large and active, led by a local solicitor and his wife, Edward and Marjory Lewis. They lived in a very large house at Debden Green, in beautiful surroundings on the edge of the forest. Lewis' firm did a lot of trade union work and we happened to know them quite well. In early 1959, Edward and Marjory suggested that I might enjoy spending the four days of the Easter break with them, on the annual march from the Atomic Weapons Research Establishment at Aldermaston in Berkshire, to Trafalgar Square.

Off I went, as I did for the next three years. The marches were organized with military precision by the redoubtable Olive Gibbs, an Oxford city councillor, who I remember as the Joyce Grenfell of the left. The regions of the country were divided by colour, the areas by number. We were 'Magenta 6'. Reading, Slough and Turnham Green were the overnight stops. For a young teenager used to the disciplines of boarding school, it was freedom, and enormous fun.

Though the organization of CND was seamless, its politics were not. There were disputes about tactics, with a breakaway group, the Committee of 100, arguing for 'direct action' – disruptive, if non-violent protests. At the invitation of the Lewises, I went on one of these too – a 'sit-down' in Parliament Square.

By today's standards, it was amazingly orderly. The Loughton contingent sat in the roadway on the west side of the square, facing what is now the UK Supreme Court. The police worked their way around the square, carrying off protesters – who put up no struggle at all – to the waiting Black Marias. I was both excited by the possibility that I might be arrested and apprehensive as to how I would explain this back at school. Then Marjory Lewis saved me from that embarrassment by announcing, in her clipped Home Counties' accent, that it was too bad, we'd have to forget about being arrested that day, we'd miss the coach if we did not leave immediately.

CND was not a simple front of the British Communist Party, as were many other apparently broad-based groups at the time; but the Communist Party was disproportionately influential in the unilateralist movement (as it was in the trade unions) not least because of its discipline and the organizational brilliance of many of its key members. The Labour Party was soon riven by argument over nuclear disarmament; a dispute which culminated in the decisions of the 1960 Scarborough party conference, against the platform, in favour of unilateralist resolutions from the engineers' AUEW union and the T&G. But this conference was also the moment when the shine started to come off CND. Hugh Gaitskell, knowing that he would be defeated, made the speech of his life, one of most eloquent and powerful from any British political leader in the last century. A year later, the decision was overturned at the Blackpool conference. Nuclear talks between the USA and the Soviet Union, and the subsequent Test Ban Treaties, ultimately led to a natural decline in support for CND.

My own Damascene moment about the merits or otherwise of unilateralism came on a rain-sodden tramp on the last Aldermaston march that I attended, over Easter 1962. I had fallen into conversation with a member of the Communist Party.

'Once we've abandoned all our nuclear weapons,' I announced with the absolute confidence of the teenager, 'then the other nuclear states, the USA and the Soviet Union, will follow our example.'

'It won't be quite like that, son' said the comrade. 'The United States should most certainly abandon its nuclear arsenal. But Soviet nuclear weapons are the workers' bombs, and they can't give them up until the threat from the capitalists has been completely eliminated.'

I pondered to myself whether one would feel any better in the moment before being incinerated by a workers' bomb rather than a capitalist bomb, although I did not say this out loud. My fellow marcher was quite beyond reason. But the conversation was invaluable in teaching me at an early age of the attractions, and profound dangers, in extreme positions on the left, whether inspired by the CP, or by the Trotskyists.

CND gave me one set of contacts with the British Communist Party, camping another. A. S. Neill's 'progressive school' movement of the thirties (which was to have such an extraordinary and controversial influence on post-war mainstream teaching) had spawned a number of imitators, including a 'Forest School'. This school had run camps each summer for family and friends. The school itself had folded with the war, but Forest School Camps (FSC) developed into a thriving, utopian, left-wing, non-uniformed version of the Scouts. It was run, inevitably, by an able organizer, and CP member. The camping was hair shirt – wood fires, earth latrines – and creature comforts were frowned upon. For me, these trips were huge fun. There were girls; and the contrast between the rigidities of school and the atmosphere of the camps could not have been greater.

A stunning proportion of those attending FSC camps seemed to live in Hampstead or Highgate, and came from London's intellectual left-wing elite. Happily there were subsidies for children like my siblings and me, which enabled us to attend. My first two camps were in the UK, but the organizers' connections with the CP gave them an easy *entrée* to cheap holidays in Soviet-bloc countries. In the summers of 1962 and 1963, I went on two-week coach trips, camping in what was then Czechoslovakia. These trips were also decisive in establishing an extreme scepticism in my mind about totalitarian regimes. Material conditions for the majority in that country were better than they had ever enjoyed, but what a price – intense shortages of consumer goods (we were all offered ridiculous sums for our jeans), and the fundamental denials of political freedoms symbolized by the border, its high fences, barbed wire and aggressive guards.

These experiences, and my growing political awareness, fed into my studies, especially in history. In addition to the A level syllabus we were put in for an S (i.e. scholarship) level paper, on contemporary issues. This allowed Peter Watkins to range far away from the medieval era, and on to current politics.

Seismic shifts were taking place in Britain. Harold Macmillan, who had so dominated British politics since becoming prime minister in 1957, was on the slide. Hugh Gaitskell, who had failed so dismally at the 1959 election, had at last established himself as a prime minister-in-waiting, trouncing the left on virtually every issue at the 1961 conference. The Liberals, whose parliamentary representation had fallen from twelve seats in 1945 to six in the 1959 election, were gradually becoming a threat to the Conservatives, winning by-elections and turning post-war certainties on their heads.

In October 1962 there was the Cuban missile crisis, the moment that the world came the closest it ever had to a full-scale nuclear war; and then the sudden, apparently mysterious death of Labour leader Hugh

Gaitskell in January 1963, aged 56.[7] In February, after a bitter three-way leadership contest, Harold Wilson became leader.

Suddenly, as spring 1963 gave way to early summer, the Profumo affair burst into life. Even today, a defence minister having a relationship with a woman who was coincidentally sharing her pleasures with a senior Russian intelligence agent would be a good story; and terminal for the minister concerned. Back then, the news was volcanic. The volcano merely rumbled at first, as rumours that John Profumo, MP for Stratford-upon-Avon and Secretary of State for War, was having an affair with Christine Keeler, who simultaneously was servicing a Captain Evgeni Ivanov, a Soviet naval attaché at their embassy in London, and a GRU* agent. The rumblings died down when, in late March, Profumo made a statement to the Commons categorically denying any impropriety.

But the story came back to life very quickly, and with renewed vigour. The rumours were everywhere. *Private Eye* had been established in 1961, and became required reading for everyone transfixed by what seemed to be a collapse on many fronts of the British Establishment. The story erupted on 5 June 1963, when Profumo confessed that he had lied to his prime minister and the House of Commons, and resigned both his ministerial office and his Commons seat.

For this and other reasons, Macmillan's premiership was now in tatters. His health failed and he resigned in early October 1963. Under the wise guidance of Disraeli, the Conservative Party had adroitly embraced the idea of democracy for the common people, but the principle had yet to be established within the party itself – the selection of the leader was in the hands of the grandees in the 'magic circle'. They went through the opaque 'customary processes of consultation' with the various sectors of the party. The result, to much celebration by the Labour

---

* The GRU, or Glavnoye Razvedyvatel'noye Upravleniye, was the Soviet Union's military intelligence agency.

Party, was the appointment as prime minister of the fourteenth Earl of Home, Alec Douglas-Home. I followed it all avidly.

Meanwhile, as Philip Larkin so memorably wrote:

> Sexual intercourse began
> In nineteen sixty-three
> (which was rather late for me) –
> Between the end of the 'Chatterley' ban
> And the Beatles' first LP.

It might have been rather late for Philip Larkin, but for me the timing couldn't have been better. While sex was being invented, I was discovering girls. Brentwood had two girls' grammar schools – the County High School, and the Catholic Ursuline High. My day-boy friends brought me into this mixed circle. We'd meet at the White Hart in Brentwood High Street (close to the Sugar Hut, immortalized in the hit TV series *The Only Way is Essex*), pick up the intelligence as to where the best parties were, and go off either with an Essex girl, or in search of one. On the day that I first heard the Beatles sing the words 'She was just seventeen', I met a High School pupil, Pamela Murphy, who was just seventeen; and went out with her for a year.

I had been away on the second of my camping trips to Czechoslovakia when the A level results were published. I returned some days later. As I went into the back path of our block I bumped into my mother, and asked her what my results were. 'Three Ds. Not very good,' she replied, with scarcely concealed impatience.

I'd been taking extra classes in Latin to enable me to pass my O level, with the hope that I could then try for Oxbridge entrance. But that was off the agenda now. I knew that I'd have to retake at least two of my A levels. I chose a new course – British constitution (now politics) – as one; and for inexplicable reasons, geography, the least inspiring and least well-taught subject of the three I had done previously.

Earlier I'd been made a 'school praepostor' – a senior prefect with authority beyond my house, complete with blue gown. At the beginning of the new school year I was made head of house and deputy head of school. My close friend Patrick Carter became head of school. We were a good team. Out of school, we enjoyed ourselves, but the disappointment of my A level results grated, and I found the restrictions of boarding-school life, even though I was head of house, less and less tolerable. For my very last term, in any event taken up mainly with revision and then the exams themselves, the head agreed that when I was not required in the house I could live at home. I had recently bought a Lambretta scooter for £10 and used this for transport. It had a two-stroke engine, and no battery, with a maximum speed of about 60 mph. (The motorbike driving test in those days was risible. It involved driving round a short circuit of residential streets, using the correct hand signals, and effecting an 'emergency stop' when the examiner – who could be seen a hundred yards away – stepped into the road. I passed with ease – licensed to drive the highest powered bikes.)

With Oxbridge out, I applied to study law at four 'provincial universities', and was accepted by both Leeds and Southampton, provided I got two Cs. But the second set of results were a further disappointment. I got an A in British constitution, but an E in geography (a grade lower than the D I'd got the year before!). I decided to write to the admissions tutor at Leeds to beg him for a place, suggesting that if he averaged my A and E, it would amount to two Cs; and the A did show that I was capable of academic work to a high level.

Fortunately for me, it worked.

THREE

Respected but not Respectable?

I ought to add that we had the impression that Jack Straw, the appropriately named chief troublemaker, was acting with malice aforethought. This impression might be entirely mistaken and I should hate to start a witch-hunt but he seemed deliberately to have brought matters to the point where the British Council had to inter-vene ... All this may, as I say, be quite unfounded but Straw's actions and attitude strongly suggested that the trouble among the party did not happen altogether spontaneously.

ALEXANDER STIRLING, First Secretary at the
British Embassy, Santiago, Chile, 1966[1]

Leeds University was a liberation. For the first time since leaving primary school, I felt socially at ease. I loved the place, learnt some law, and had a great time.

It's easy to be sentimental about the Sixties, but it was an extraordinary time. The axis of the world was shifting; it looked as though the changes to the established economic, political and social order for which my parents and grandparents had fought, might finally happen. On the other hand, our generation had grown up under the shadow of the Bomb, and had been scared stiff during the Cuban missile crisis. We shared a growing sense of anger and frustration at the marginalization of minorities in the 'civilized, democratic world', who had the 'wrong' colour, 'wrong' faith, 'wrong' gender, and 'wrong' sexuality; and at the oppression of majorities almost everywhere – the Soviet bloc, most of Asia, Africa, Latin America, and Europe, west and east. Labour's new leader, Harold Wilson, tried to mould these anxieties into a vision for the future. His 'white heat of technology' speech had been the launch pad. 'Our future lies not in military strength alone, but in the efforts, the sacrifices, and above all the energies which a free people can mobilise for the future greatness of our country,' he had told the 1963 party conference.[2]

The failure of the state's prosecution of *Lady Chatterley's Lover* in 1960 and the Profumo scandal in 1963 were seen as signals of the wider decadence of the Conservative Establishment.* The left in Britain thought it was on a roll. Alec Douglas-Home took his government to the wire, announcing an election at the last possible moment: 15 October 1964, just two weeks after I arrived in Leeds.

I went out to knock on doors, watched Denis Healey reduce a rebarbative Trot to jelly when she accused him of being a class traitor, and heckled the prime minister when he spoke on the steps of Leeds Town Hall. A photograph of this bunch of 'nasty lefties' (me included) appeared on the front page of the *Yorkshire Post*.[†]

But there was more to Douglas-Home than we had anticipated. I watched the election results in the lounge of a women's hall of residence, the only place we could find with a TV (and where the sound system had to compete with the click-click of knitting needles). Our euphoria turned into anxiety as the Tories ran us closer than we'd ever imagined. Our final margin over all other parties was four

---

* *Lady Chatterley's Lover*, D. H. Lawrence's sexually explicit novel, was originally published in Italy and France in 1928 but was subject to a ban in the UK until 10 November 1960. After the ban was lifted, the first print run of 200,000 books was sold out in one day.

† Owned, appropriately, by Yorkshire Conservative Newspapers Ltd.

seats.* The 'thirteen wasted years' had ended, but as two of those four seats were held by Desmond Donnelly and Woodrow Wyatt, already semi-detached from Labour, Wilson would always be vulnerable.†

When Wilson had made his 'white heat of technology' speech, he had also said that the 'challenge is not going to come from the United States ... from West Germany, from France ... The challenge is going to come from Russia.'³ Around the world, Wilson's assumption of power that night as the new British prime minister was trumped by the breaking news that the Soviet leader Nikita Khrushchev, the man who had denounced and replaced Joe Stalin, had himself been ousted and replaced by Leonid Brezhnev.

The Soviet Union not only framed international strategic and economic debate; its Communist ideology and practice also dominated internal British politics. The great divide was not between the main parties, but right through the middle of one of them, the Labour Party. On the one side were the 'Butskellites',‡ the social democrats like Tony Crosland, Labour MP and author of *The Future of Socialism*, who made the case for capitalism with a welfare face; on the other were (in their own eyes, at least) the true socialists, who shared the Marxist–Leninist analysis of capitalism and its ultimate decay, and whose objective was the full implementation of Labour's Clause IV – the public ownership of 'the means of production, distribution and exchange'.

Scientists, engineers and medics made up the majority of the student body at Leeds University; in the main they were on the right, but they

---

* Labour won 317 seats, the Tories 304 and the Liberals 9.

† Desmond Donnelly went on to call for an alliance with the Liberals. He and Woodrow Wyatt voted against nationalization of the steel industry, blocking it for two years. D. Donnelly resigned the party whip in 1968. Wyatt left front-line politics after losing his seat in the 1970 election. He was later appointed a life peer in 1987.

‡ Butskellism was an initially satirical term referring to the political consensus of the fifties. It was based on an amalgam of the names of Rab Butler, leftish Tory grandee, and Hugh Gaitskell, Labour leader from 1955–63.

had full timetables so rarely had the time (or the inclination) to take an active part in student politics. There was a Conservative Association, but student politics at Leeds (principally practised by that sizeable minority studying arts, social science or law) was dominated by the socialist left. Here too, the schisms reflected those of the Soviet Union's history, with the Communist Party and left Labour on the one side, and the Trotskyists on the other.*

I was not a social democrat – that seemed too effete for me – but nor was I ever in the Communist Party. That conversation on a CND Aldermaston march about the 'workers' bomb', with its substitution of blind loyalty for rational argument, deterred me for life from signing up. Nonetheless, the 'CP', as it was always known, was a major influence on the development of my politics. In Leeds, the university CP had some very bright and charismatic leaders – students like Alan Hunt, Jeremy Hawthorn and Mike Gonzalez,† who worked seamlessly with the city's CP, led by Bert Ramelson, a brilliant ideologue and practical strategist, with his own passionate brand of oratory delivered in a heavy eastern European accent. Bert had fought in the Spanish Civil War and

---

* With the collapse of the Soviet Communist Party in the early nineties, and therefore of its satellite parties, including in the UK, the difference between these two traditions on the left may appear arcane. But they were stark in their day, as much psychological as they were doctrinal. The British Communist Party attracted people who were quite conformist in many ways (including collar and tie), and who could point to a working model of a society which 'for all its imperfections' (as the excuse went) was providing a better level of wealth and welfare for the majority than had the western capitalist model. Trotskyism as a movement came out of the 'Fourth International' (1938) in which Trotsky damned the Soviet Communist model (of the Second and Third International) as Stalinist 'state capitalism'. Trotskyists tended to be inherently oppositionist (there has never been a working country-level model); some of its groups took on the characteristics of religious cults, demanding total commitment and loyalty, and having apocalyptic ideas about the developments in our society. Also they tended to be even more authoritarian and less tolerant than the Communists.

† Himself the son of an exiled Spanish Communist.

used to boast that he had shot more Trotskyists in the back than he had Falangists in the front.[4] The CP's relatively small size, locally and nationally, belied its extraordinary influence on British politics. What it lacked in numbers, it more than made up for in dedication and organization. And, when it was not going in for logic-chopping to explain away the Soviet–Nazi pact, Stalin's purges, the vanguard of the proletariat and the invasion of Hungary, it showed subtle understanding of the mood of the British people, and how the sensible left could make some progress. The Labour left at Leeds University worked as part of a broad front with the CP and we spent much of our time fighting the destructive politics of the various active Trotskyist groups.*

It was at the regular, and usually packed, Wednesday afternoon meetings of the Debating Society that the intense political issues of the day were fought out. These meetings were also a forum for some of that era's great political figures. Most memorably, we were addressed by Trevor Huddleston, the legendary anti-apartheid bishop from Johannesburg, who denounced the crimes of the Nationalist apartheid regime in South Africa in a quietly dignified and devastating way to a full house. And rising stars from other universities spoke at our debates – including a young Norman Lamont, then president of the Cambridge Union.

Prior to the main debate there was always 'Private Members' business', when short debates were held on motions moved from the floor. In late January 1965 a motion moved by me gave me a fast learning experience. It was prompted by the news on Sunday 24 January that Winston Churchill had died, aged ninety.

In the unofficial oral biography of Churchill that I had absorbed from my mother, his record as a great wartime leader merited no more than a footnote, and was minor mitigation for a man who stood for

---

* These included the Socialist Labour League, led locally by lecturer Cliff Slaughter, and Tony Cliff of the International Socialists (later the Socialist Workers' Party).

almost everything the left opposed. It was people like my uncles (four of whom had been in uniform) who had won the war. The charge sheet against Churchill was lengthy: he was the Home Secretary who had sent in the troops to quell riots by miners in Tonypandy in 1911; the instigator of Britain's disastrous Gallipoli campaign; the near-racist who had described Mahatma Gandhi as a 'half-naked fakir'; and, most venal of all, the desperate party leader who during the 1945 general election campaign had asserted that, if elected, Labour 'would have to fall back on some form of Gestapo'.*

When, a few days after his death, I moved 'that this House regrets the death of Winston Churchill' there were murmurs of approbation – until I explained that my regret was at the ballyhoo, the ease with which this man's real record had been air-brushed away. There was an embarrassed silence, especially from my friends on the left. I was taken aside by one of the leaders of the Communist Society, and told that, Comrade, I had made a major error, and should re-educate myself. (I did. I learnt to make up my own mind, and not just about Churchill's brilliant contribution to the war.)

I wasn't the only one in our family to have absorbed my mother's view of Churchill. It was shared by my sister Suzy, who was at Keele University. At the end of that week, Keele hosted the live *Morning Service* on the BBC Home Service (now Radio 4), with a special focus on Churchill's passing. A few seconds after the Keele chapel choir had begun to sing the hymn 'Christ is Our Cornerstone', millions of listeners suddenly heard a powerful motorbike revving up – the opening bars of 'Leader of the Pack' by the Shangri-Las, a record banned by the BBC for poor taste. An astonished continuity announcer cut in to take the service off the air and broadcast the solemn music held at the ready for national emergencies like this. A monumental brouhaha, and an investigation, followed. The principal culprit was a man I only ever knew as

---

* 4 June 1945, in an election broadcast.

Yogi Bear, Suzy's then boyfriend. Suzy had been a willing accessory. Yogi was expelled; Suzy, in the third year of her degree, was suspended for the rest of term.

In my first term at Leeds I was allocated to a rooming house on the Burley Road, down in the valley in the heart of industrial Leeds, with a tannery and a vinegar works opposite, and steam trains belching out smoke and smut from a viaduct close by. Eight students were packed into this small terraced house.

The conditions were more spartan even than those of my school boarding house; the landlady took Yorkshire frugality very seriously indeed. Four of our fellow students were engineers with end-of-term exams they had to pass to avoid an ignominious exit from the university. There was much late-night revision at the table in the lounge – with the students clad in sweaters and coats, because the place was so cold. One night at around 11.30 the landlady's husband, who was passing, saw the lights on, came in, and confiscated the fuses for the downstairs lighting circuit, thus plunging the only place we could work into total darkness. The next day we went on a delegation to the University Lodging Office, and had the place closed down.

For two terms I moved into decent, warm digs, with fellow resident Mark Mitchell, after which we moved into a self-catering house.* It was great, but with the freedom came the cold again. Mark was in the basement, dripping with damp; I was in the leaking attic. We became close friends (as we are to this day) and shared accommodation, and much else, for the four years I was at Leeds.

Mark tells me that when he asked me early on what I wanted to do with my life, I replied without deviation or hesitation, 'Labour MP'. I had spoken in the Freshers' Debate against a motion that 'this House believes that politics is a waste of time', which I ended by claiming, 'the

---

* Mark went on to become dean of the Faculty of Social Studies at Portsmouth University.

only reason people believe that politics is a waste of time is because of thirteen years of Tory misrule'. To my surprise, this cliché worked; the motion was lost; not long afterwards I was elected secretary of the Debating Society, my first small step up the ladder of student politics. Later that year I became secretary of the Leeds Students' Union, and its vice president the following year.

The Cold War dominated student politics nationally even more than it did at Leeds.

The International Union of Students (IUS), based in Prague and set up in 1946, had been rapidly taken over by the Soviets as a Communist front organization. A rival western organization, the International Student Conference (ISC), was based in Leiden, in the Netherlands. There were well-founded suspicions – though we didn't know for sure until an exposé in 1967 – that this was, in turn, no more than a CIA-funded front organization.* So the sharp chasm in British politics between the Marxist-influenced left and the social democrats was expressed in an argument about whether the National Union of Students (NUS) should stay part of the ISC, or become 'neutral' and non-aligned. The CP knew that they couldn't possibly muster arguments, or votes, for the NUS to join the IUS, but reckoned that breaking the ISC would still strike a useful blow for socialism, and its trustees in the Soviet Politburo.

The CIA was not the only Western intelligence agency with equities in the ISC, or the NUS. The connection between the NUS leadership and our agencies was a surprisingly ill-kept secret, as alumni of the NUS executive went off to the more opaque departments of the Foreign Office – or to the Fund for International Student Co-operation (FISC), whose officials in turn had remarkable luck in quickly finding careers in the Foreign Office.

---

* The US *Ramparts* magazine published a full exposé in March 1967.

In the summer of 1966 I joined a twenty-strong NUS delegation to Chile, organized by FISC in the UK, and in Chile by the Alliance for Progress (another CIA-backed programme, as later became clear). This was a serious sacrifice. I missed the 1966 World Cup Final.

The elected president of Chile, which prided itself on its relative stability and democracy, was the Christian Democrat Eduardo Frei. The US had poured in aid of all kinds to help buttress Frei's support. When we arrived we found that part of the purpose of our delegation was to give a little help to his student wing. We were to build a youth centre on a hill in a run-down area of Valparaiso, Chile's main sea port.

The project was a shambles. Few of us had any experience of construction sites. Personality clashes erupted. Three of us – John Thompson from Newcastle, Christine Morris (improbably, a former nun) and I – decided to skip work one day to buy ponchos. Relations between us and the trip's leader, Alan Evans, broke down completely. We had certainly behaved badly (I still have a copy of the grovelling letter of apology we wrote), but objected to the leader's punishment – peremptory expulsion from the delegation and an early return home. FISC were brought into the row, so was the British Embassy in Santiago.

It was not until I was Foreign Secretary and I had a rather nervous submission from the Records Branch to tell me that diplomatic telegrams from 1966 were to be released that I realized just how great the embassy's involvement had been, and how absurd was their analysis that this ridiculous saga had been planned by me with 'malice aforethought'.

Back in Yorkshire, in the February of my last year (just before I got down to making up three years' study in three months – I got a 2:2, perhaps unsurprisingly), I was elected to the full-time position of president of Leeds Student Union for the following academic year. I had a great time, and did useful work, introducing a legal aid and advice scheme, and making Leeds the first students' union to affiliate to the National Council for Civil Liberties (now Liberty).

My rise through the ranks of student politics had been fairly rapid, but not as rapid as that of a first-year student taking over as editor of the union's widely read *Union News* – Paul Dacre, now editor of the *Daily Mail*. He shifted the paper's focus on to human interest stories, put attractive female students on the front pages, combined with professional coverage of contemporary issues. From a position of considerable ignorance, I contributed a rather tedious and middle-aged article on drugs. The broad left did enjoy itself; we went partying, drank, talked football. But there was a puritanical streak there too. We wore ties, and the emerging drugs scene seemed to pass us by. I never had to make a judgement about smoking cannabis. It never came my way.

However, within the university, and beyond it, 1967–8, was when the comfortable certainties of a deferential age seemed locked in a losing struggle with disconcerting and sometimes brutal forces that were to become the leitmotif of the following decade. During his first precarious administration, Harold Wilson had, according to *The Times*, 'handled his public relations superbly', and had put the new Tory leader Ted Heath on the back foot.[5] Calling an early election in March 1966, he had then won a landslide with a majority of one hundred. Wilson had kept the United Kingdom out of any direct military involvement in the Vietnam War, but that did not stop the anti-war protests here being directed almost as much against the British government as they were against President Johnson in the US.

I was somewhere, and sometimes uneasily, in the middle of all this. On 2 February 1968, I led the dancing at the University Union Ball with the university's new Chancellor, the Duchess of Kent. The *Daily Telegraph*'s caption to its photograph of us on the dance floor included the line: 'She was greeted by a group of chanting, leaflet-waving, pro-North Vietnam students'.[6]

In the next few weeks the world appeared to erupt, with students in the vanguard. The anti-Vietnam War riots in Grosvenor Square in March were among the most violent in Britain for decades. The assassination of America's civil rights leader Martin Luther King, at the beginning of April, was followed just two weeks later in the UK by the most incendiary speech of the decade, when Enoch Powell, Tory MP for Wolverhampton and Shadow Cabinet member, predicted that if immigration went unchecked, then: 'like the Roman, I seem to see "the River Tiber foaming with much blood".* In May, the streets of Paris exploded as students and workers protested against the government of General de Gaulle, forcing him to call elections for the following month. 'Rome, Paris, and Berlin / We shall fight and we shall win!' went the chant. In June, Robert Kennedy, the US Attorney General and brother of the late president, was himself assassinated, dashing the left's hopes all around the globe of a liberal candidate who might win the Democratic nomination, and the presidency itself. Early August brought a five-day battle on the streets of Chicago surrounding the Democratic National Convention; late August a further reminder of the naked power of the Cold War, when Soviet troops invaded Czechoslovakia to snuff out the beginnings of a popular uprising.

Meanwhile, the British public mood turned from a heady optimism to a sullen sourness. The Labour government, and party, reflecting the deep schism through its heart, was divided over public spending cuts, industrial relations and its leadership. Labour suffered its worst ever results in local government elections in early May (worse even than those forty years later, in 2008). We were swept out of power in every London borough except four: Barking & Dagenham, Newark, Southwark, and Tower Hamlets. In Hackney an all-in wrestler, who'd signed a set of nomination papers in a pub as a favour for a friend, found himself elected a Tory councillor. The haughty detachment from the party of many in Labour's leadership was well illustrated by Social Services Secretary Richard Crossman's reimposition of an increase in NHS prescription charges not long before the local polls, an event in the democratic calendar too lowly for someone of his intellectual calibre to have noticed.

---

* 20 April 1968. Powell was sacked by Tory leader Edward Heath for this speech.

The NUS was not immune from these forces. The centrist leadership was derided for being out of touch, and was savaged by critics like David Widgery* who accused it of engaging in 'Tio Pepe diplomacy',[†] and charged that the NUS 'had all the passion of an ashtray'.

However, the NUS establishment had a secret weapon: the voting system for the election of its executive, unused anywhere else in the world, so it was said, except by a corrupt Australian trade union. This complex system appeared similar to standard systems of proportional representation, but it produced the opposite effect. By redistributing the 'unused' votes of the most, not the least, popular candidates, one strong candidate on a slate could pull up their running mates. (It was this which gave me an early addiction to the interstices of voting systems, for which I have yet to find a cure.)

I had been the fall guy put up by the 'broad left' to try to 'break the slate' by topping the poll, at the NUS biennial conference in November 1967. To everyone's surprise, especially mine, I won – and in doing so knocked a young Tom McNally off the executive.[‡]

The following March, I was the broad left's candidate for president, against the centrist establishment's Trevor Fisk, who won. It's a mark of the seriousness with which the internal politics of the student movement were treated by our elders and betters that this was front-page news in our national papers. 'A group of militants is making an all-out bid to win control of the 360,000-strong National Union of Students,' trumpeted the *Daily Mail*, with the 'militants'' candidate Mr Jack Straw, 21'. It was not as if we were planning violent revolution. Our demands? 'Tougher action to secure higher grants, and a bigger say in the running of student affairs.'[7]

---

* Later a Hackney GP, and author.

† Tio Pepe is a popular brand of sherry. The charge was that the NUS leadership were easily bought off by a glass of sherry with the university authorities.

‡ Now leader of the Liberal Democrats in the Lords, and a justice minister.

In today's higher education market, students are the customers. Their opinion about the quality of what they are purchasing – their education – feeds in to any university's reputation. Not then. Fewer than one in twelve of the age group went on to higher education – and only a tiny handful from estates like mine. The state (or one's parents) paid for almost everything. We were lucky to be there, was the prevailing response when some of us began to question why students could not have a 'bigger say' in the running of the university. Not control, just a say.

However, it was not our rather imprecise demands for 'student participation', but fallout from the Cold War that led to mass student protests across much of Britain in the summer of 1968. In May, there was a disorderly demonstration outside the Leeds Students' Union to protest against the visit of the right-wing Tory MP Patrick Wall, leader of the semi-racist Monday Club, notorious for his support of the white minority regimes in southern Africa. In the aftermath an investigation was conducted which appeared to show that the university had been collecting information on students' political views. They had, of course. The university security officer, a retired Leeds City Police superintendent, a parody of a bone-headed copper, had a large file marked 'Reds'. The information he'd acquired contained few startling revelations – it was almost all public knowledge anyway – but we didn't know that at the time, and suspicions were running high. There were demands for me to lead a sit-in against the university administration in June. I wavered. It was close to the summer vacation. We had a union resolution passed, demanding a public inquiry. My hope was the university would get itself – and us – off the hook. But it refused. So the main Parkinson Building was occupied by several hundred students, led by me. It was a sober affair. My main concern was to identify an exit strategy which would have us 'winning', whatever (as the comrades would say) the objective reality. The university, which could have just sat tight until term ended four days later, happily obliged, and seemingly conceded support for the demands that they had earlier refused. Victory was proclaimed. We cleared up so well that the building had never looked so pristine, and went off for celebratory drinks in the pubs opposite.

I had failed in that first bid to become president of the NUS in March 1968, but I got a consolation prize – full-time deputy, working at the NUS headquarters near Euston station, starting at the end of the summer term. My girlfriend Anthea Weston, whom I had met at a Christmas party in Essex after my first term at Leeds, was just graduating in French from Warwick, and had a place on a teacher-training course in central London.

The Sixties' revolution in social attitudes wasn't quite as complete as is now imagined. As we left university, most of my friends who wanted to live with their partners married them. It was what most parents expected – and landlords too. Anthea and I were no exception. A week before the wedding my best man, Patrick Carter, took me to the pub and presciently asked me whether we were doing the right thing. He knew and liked Anthea; he just wasn't sure we were going to make each other happy. Pat wasn't wrong about this, but by then everything had been arranged. We married on 20 July 1968 at the Anglican Church in Anthea's home town of Harold Wood, Essex; the reception, in the church hall, was teetotal. Armed with our marriage certificate, we found a wonderful two-bedroomed flat in Highbury Place, the fine Georgian terrace overlooking Highbury Fields – all-in for £10 a week.

My first six months at the NUS were uncomfortable. I was an intruder. I had stood against the successful candidate, Trevor Fisk, and was now his deputy. I was given marginal responsibilities, like art colleges, in the hope I'd get bored and go away, but suddenly the art schools erupted. There were long occupations at colleges like Hornsey and Guildford colleges of art. I had something useful to do, and also developed firm friendships with some of those involved, like Kim Howells, later MP for Pontypridd and a fellow Foreign Office minister, and Kate Hoey, later MP for Vauxhall and minister for sport.

I also had my first, unpleasant taste of being on the wrong end of a concerted newspaper campaign. In November 1968 the *News of the World* ran a major 'exposé' about 'The Great Student Plot'. There were ' hundreds – possibly thousands – of little revolutionary groups' straddling Europe 'each linked by a strand to the spider's web of anarchy'. I was a leading light, it alleged, in the Radical Students' Alliance, in charge with Roger Lyons* of 'influence in the National Union of Students'. It was claimed that I had boasted: 'We are bringing the authorities to their knees. The more they clamp down in bewilderment, the more we win.'[8]

The paper's 'team of investigators' seemed not to have noticed the Soviet invasion of Czechoslovakia, since one of their allegations was that we were connected to subversive groups in Prague. This was true, but the British Establishment regarded this as a fine thing (and were assisting this anti-Soviet endeavour). The rest was a complete fabrication, made the more risible by lumping assorted Trots (including Tariq Ali) together with their sworn enemies from the CP-dominated broad left. But it had a serious purpose, not least to damage me. I assumed that my inclusion in this nonsense had been inspired by people in the NUS. This was inadvertently confirmed by Trevor Fisk, who guiltily explained that I should not make any assumptions about his involvement just because one of the 'investigators' lived upstairs from him. With this useful information, I was able to persuade the NUS to meet my legal costs for a libel action against the paper. Before the matter went to trial, the paper conceded an apology and costs. But it took three years, and a huge amount of time.

By the New Year I'd had enough of working in this pernicious environment. I decided to stand again for president, at the April 1969 NUS Conference, against Trevor Fisk, who was seeking the standard second term. My campaign organization was headed by a friend I'd met on the Chile trip, Peter Geldard, improbably (given the fun we'd shared)

* Later general secretary of the MSF trade union – and president of the TUC.

training to be an Anglican priest, and included David Cowling, now the BBC's polling guru. Peter, David and the rest of the team left nothing to chance. Delegates were canvassed, and then, for purposes of quality control, re-canvassed, by people claiming to be from Trevor's team. My team's predictions were just four votes adrift. I won. The news that the NUS had been taken over by a leftie made the front pages of many newspapers – *The Times*, for instance, leading with 'New student leader pledges action'; but the better-informed education reporters had by now spotted that I was no violent revolutionary.[9] My agenda was rather more limited – to make the NUS, in the words of my campaign slogan, 'respected but not respectable' and to transform the organization into one which mattered to its members.

The NUS was then a medium-sized business, with 200 staff, and profitable travel and insurance agencies. What made it so impressive was its research staff, run by highly skilled professionals like Stella Greenall and Margaret Wallis. I learnt from them that a properly researched, well-argued case was worth a thousand vacuous speeches.

Bizarrely the headquarters of the Department of Education, which we occasionally had reason to visit, was on the upper floors of a Mayfair building whose main occupant was the Security Service (MI5). Aside from the careful security at the front entrance, the ministers' doors were always open – including that of the Secretary of State, Ted Short.*

The Labour government and the party itself was by this time deeply unpopular; the party riven by argument over those spending cuts imposed after the forced devaluation of sterling in December 1967, and by *In Place of Strife*, Harold Wilson's and his Employment Secretary Barbara Castle's disastrously handled plan for a major reform of trade union law, intended to rein in the constant unofficial industrial strikes.

---

* Ted served as education minister until 1970, then becoming deputy leader in 1972. He went on to serve as Lord President of the Council and was made a life peer in 1977. He died aged ninety-nine on 4 May 2012.

In Place of Strife had itself been a symptom of the ideological schism in British politics between the social democratic left, and the Marxist–Leninist-inspired left, which so seriously hobbled the Labour Party until the collapse of the Soviet Union and its underpinning ideology in the early nineties. The fact that Harold Wilson, Nye Bevan, Michael Foot, Barbara and others on the 'soft left' sought to straddle this divide, to achieve some kind of dialectical synthesis from it, did not make it any less real. These ideological divisions were also overlaid with personality clashes.

However, by early 1970, Labour's fortunes seemed to be on the mend – and for the first election in British history, students were needed not just as foot soldiers, but in the polling booths: legislation to lower the voting age to eighteen had been passed a year before. For some while it had been uncertain whether students could register to vote from their term-time address. We paid the costs of a test case, which the Court of Appeal decided in students' favour in May 1970.* We were, we fancied, now even more of a force to be reckoned with. Certainly the organizers of the main parties thought so.

As the Labour government's standing had been sliding since the 1966 election, so had membership of student Labour clubs. Many had collapsed. The few of us who had kept our party cards didn't trumpet this fact, but now, with an election looming, we were all faced with a clear choice, which we couldn't dodge. Labour – the devil we knew and, for all its faults and infelicities, on our side – or the Tories. Edward Heath

---

* *The Times*, 15 May 1970, 'Votes for Students' – 'The Court of Appeal has decided that students at university colleges and halls of residence – and students in lodgings – should be qualified for the local electoral roll if they are resident at the university on the qualifying date, October 10, in every year. The decision comes too late to affect an election held this year: but after the next electoral roll comes into force on February 15th, 1971 there is a possibility that students over the age of eighteen will exercise voting power in a number of constituencies, some of which, notably Oxford and Cambridge, are marginal seats.'

is today seen as a left-wing One Nation Tory, the antithesis of his neme-sis Margaret Thatcher. But that wasn't how he appeared then. Wilson had gleefully seized on the conclusions of a Tory Shadow Cabinet con-ference at Selsdon Park (near Croydon) to 'proclaim the existence of "Selsdon Man", an uncouth Neanderthal intent on creating a system of society for the ruthless and the pushing, the uncaring'.[10] This was not complete parody. Norman Tebbit, who first entered the Commons in the 1970 election, observed that the Selsdon Declaration 'marked the Tory Party's first repudiation of the post-war Butskellite consensus'.[11] It certainly made our flesh creep.

'Students for a Labour Victory' was rapidly formed, led by the chair of the Cambridge Union Labour Club, Hugh Anderson, a truly brilliant man who despite being in the terminal stages of testicular cancer, went round the country in pursuit of votes for Labour candidates.* Just before the election I wrote an op-ed piece for the *Observer*, placed alongside one from a young fellow of All Souls and rising star of the Tory Party, Robert Jackson.†

To emphasize the contrast between the modernizing agenda of the Labour Party and those Neanderthal Tory policies, Wilson sought to ride the public appetite for celebrity and youth by organizing a series of 'glittering' parties at Number 10. Anthea and I were invited to one. We were very excited. She bought a new frock. I had my dinner jacket – last used for my dance with the Duchess of Kent – dry-cleaned. I was included, too, in a montage of Britain's bright young things on the front cover of the *Sunday Times* magazine. It was heady stuff.

It made little impression on the voters. Apathy and disillusion were still the prevailing moods of our natural supporters, as I found on the doorstep in Islington, then rock-solid Labour. Ted Heath had none of

---

* Hugh died shortly after the general election.

† Robert Jackson (born 1946), served as Conservative MP for Wantage between 1983 and 2005, before he defected to Labour in 2005.

Wilson's slickness; he was wooden. But his prosaic message about inflation, his warning about a 'three bob [15p] loaf', and his castigation of Labour's 'industrial anarchy' connected. Some polls put Labour ahead by eleven points with just a week to go. They were wrong. Labour's apparent support was fragile and our lead evaporated when poor trade figures were published in the last few days of the campaign. In the event, Heath received over 46 per cent of the votes, with a majority over all the parties of thirty, and a majority over Labour of forty-three.

I'd travelled to Oxford in the late afternoon of polling day to take part in one of those dreary discussions used to fill the gaps on election night until the results come in. My companion on the train back to London the next morning was Gyles Brandreth, later Tory MP for Chester. He was euphoric. I thought the world was about to end. When Heath appointed Margaret Thatcher as Secretary of State for Education I thought it *had* ended.

The Heath government not only had the trade unions in its sights, but students' unions too. We had too much money (from the state), and too much power. The prescription was similar. An official regulator (to be known as a registrar) would be established, to parallel the new regulation of trade unions. With tight public finances, the government was also toying with the idea of student loans in place of grants. The Butskellite consensus which had so comfortably protected the NUS was to go; unless we boxed clever the NUS might go with it.

Inevitably, there were many, especially on the Trot left, who argued that anything less than a confrontation with the Tories would be a treacherous betrayal. My view was that head-on confrontation would simply result in catastrophic defeat. If we put ourselves in the Tory noose, they'd pull it tight.

Heath's ministerial appointments included one piece of wonderfully good fortune. Bill van Straubenzee, Tory MP for Wokingham, was made Margaret Thatcher's junior minister, with specific responsibility for higher and further education. Bill really was a One Nation Tory. He'd been an honorary vice president of the NUS for years, and was a friend of many on the NUS executive. He was no friend of Mrs Thatcher's. He gave us endless, private advice about how we could defeat her plans for the statutory regulation of students' unions, and for student loans. In the end we saw off both – the former by agreeing arrangements with the vice chancellors for better, but non-statutory, supervision of unions' finances; the latter by force of argument, not least by one of several influential submissions written by Stella Greenall.

After considerable effort I finally managed to transfer my party membership to Central Islington Labour Party. This process was an obstacle course in many safe Labour seats, since those controlling the local parties often felt that the way of avoiding internal dissent was, figuratively, to display a 'Full Up' sign on the front door of party headquarters.

Becoming an approved candidate for the London borough elections proved even more hazardous. I was interviewed at some length by the Tammany Hall clique that controlled the list.* Why wasn't I a member of a trade union, I was asked. My answer that I was a full-time president of the NUS cut no ice. The T&G turned me down; finally the GMB took pity on me.

By the summer of 1970 Anthea and I had saved up enough for a deposit on a three-bedroomed house in a Victorian street not far from Arsenal's Highbury ground, at a cost of £7,800.† In the elections the following May, I stood for this ward. Labour won every single seat in the borough – an exact reverse of the results just three years before when we'd lost the lot.

My second term as president of the NUS was coming to an end and I spent some time contemplating what I should do next. There were

---

* Tammany Hall was the powerful Democratic political machine that essentially ran New York City throughout much of the nineteenth and early twentieth centuries, maintaining its power through a mix of charity, patronage, bribery and corruption.

† Houses in this street, Battledean Road, N5, sold in 2012 for over £1 million.

plenty of tempting offers to work in a pressure group, or in the research department of a trade union, but I was worried that these might not last, and that I'd be seeking too much to replicate the excitements of my three years at the NUS. Instead, I decided that I owed it to myself to qualify as a lawyer.

Of the two branches of the legal profession, I had long fancied the idea of becoming a barrister. At the suggestion of the head of the Law Department at Leeds, I'd joined his Inn of Court, Inner Temple; and had started to 'keep term' – i.e. to meet the mandatory requirement to eat at least three dinners a term in hall, for twelve terms. But I knew no one at the Bar, and my first encounter with those who ran the Inn had been far from welcoming.

As an undergraduate, I'd applied for a small scholarship from the Inn. I was interviewed on a languid Saturday afternoon by a panel of 'Benchers', crusty High Court judges who were plainly bored stiff by the prospect of meeting me.

'Where's your sister at university?' I was asked.

'Keele, sir.'

'Isn't that a canal in Germany, Charles?' came the response, as the panel laughed at this condescending joke.* My application had failed.

But I was now older, and a lot wiser about the ways of the British Establishment. Through Patrick Carter (again) I'd developed a firm friendship with Stephen Wegg-Prosser, who had been at Durham University with Pat. After graduating, Stephen had joined his father's well-respected firm of solicitors in West London. He told me that if I did well enough at my Bar Finals, he thought he might be able to find me a tenancy in one of the sets of chambers his firm instructed. With this incentive, I secured a place at the Inns of Court School of Law – and a grant to pay for this from the Inner London Education Authority.

---

* The Kiel Canal is a sixty-one-mile long canal in the German state of Schleswig-Holstein.

My successor as NUS president was Digby Jacks.* He had long been in the CP and was among the best of its members – pragmatic, funny, and alert to the dangers of falling into traps laid by the Tories or the Trots. Digby took on most of my duties some months early, in the summer, so that I could concentrate on my studies, and he would not be left kicking his heels.

My final duty in student politics was to chair the NUS' biennial four-day conference, in mid-November 1971, in a rain-swept Margate.

Eighteen months into Ted Heath's premiership, British politics had become visceral; there was mounting violence in Northern Ireland, terrorism on the mainland, bitter industrial disputes across the country as organized labour fought Heath's plans to rein in the unions. I'd managed till then to insulate the NUS from some of this. I cared about these issues as much as anyone; but if we moved away from our discrete purpose of representing students, and allowed ourselves to become a pawn in the wider forum of politics, we'd be done for. Our work for students would be undermined; we'd be turned into a glorified student debating society; the high probability was that the government would then lose all patience, and pull the plug on our funding.

Some did not, however, share my view. Kate Hoey, from an impeccable Unionist background in Northern Ireland (and niece of the BBC's political editor John Cole) had had a rush of blood to the head, and wanted the executive to support a far-left pro-nationalist position. Faced with such obduracy my usual tactic was to keep the executive in session well into the small hours of the morning, until a sensible consensus was reached. But this time Kate dug in. In the morning she announced her resignation from the executive – six hours before her term of office (and mine) was naturally to end. (I have teased her many times about this since.)

More significantly I had to deal with a wider motion, inspired by the

---

* Digby sadly died on 25 October 2011, aged sixty-six.

Trots, for us to indulge in fantasy politics and commit ourselves to a kamikaze battle with the government.

One of the many reasons for my lifelong contempt for those on the Trotskyite left is that what they do is either 'hobby politics', in Neil Kinnock's memorable phrase, or dangerous cult activity, in which the emotionally unstable are exploited by unpleasant but charismatic leaders. Either way, these groups lack any serious analysis, or any programme that might win popular support – and they've rarely read the texts they quote.

I was to reply to the debate. I scribbled some notes, but most of the speech was ad lib, giving vent to years of frustration that we'd all had to waste so much time on this nonsense when we had much better things to do. 'There are some people in this hall who are guilty of what Lenin once described as an "infantile disorder".'[12] The hall erupted. It was the one and only standing ovation I ever received in the hard school of the NUS. The Trots' motion was defeated. It was a good note on which to leave an organization to which I owed so much, and to which I hoped I'd made a difference. As I did so, *The Times* education correspondent commented that I had said I would make the NUS 'respected but not respectable, and most people, except for blimpish columnists, would acknowledge with gratitude that he has largely succeeded'.[13]

FOUR

Guile and Low Cunning

*I appointed [Professor] Brian [Abel-Smith] for his brains, and
Jack for guile and low cunning.*

BARBARA CASTLE, Secretary of State for Social
Services 1974–6, explaining to an overseas visitor
the qualifications of her two special advisers

A small shard of glass in my backside was all it took to change my view
of the world.

It was 8 March 1973, towards the end of my pupillage. With no briefs
of my own that day, I went off to the Old Bailey with my pupil master,
Michael Goodman, who was representing a man on trial for rape.

At the lunch break I noticed a green Ford Cortina parked just up
from the court's main entrance, but thought no more of it. In the semi-
anarchic seventies, parking restrictions weren't as tight as they are today.

Around 2.40 p.m. an usher came into court to tell us there'd been a
bomb warning. No one was that bothered. There were bomb scares
aplenty in those days. The prisoners were taken down to their cells and
the rest of us ambled downstairs and into the road.

Suddenly the police became very agitated, shouting to everyone to
clear the area. As our group – Michael, the solicitor's clerk, me – got to
the top of the street, there was an enormous explosion. I saw large

sections of the Cortina, airborne; a column of filthy brown smoke. I threw myself on to the pavement, behind a pillar box (and found myself almost cuddling an old tramp). A silence, which seemed to last for ages but which was milliseconds long, was followed by a hailstorm of glass, as the windows of the buildings all around rained down on us. I looked over to the main entrance of the Bailey – thirty yards across the street – and saw that people were badly hurt. I was a jelly, shocked and frightened. We picked ourselves up, checking that none of our group was seriously hurt (happily they were not). Still in shock, we started walking slowly back to chambers.

As we did, throngs of people were coming towards the site of the explosion – not to help, but out of an imperative curiosity. I shouted to a couple that another bomb might go off, but they were as immune to such warnings as moths to a flame.

Back in chambers I discovered that I had a small shard of glass in my backside. A large Elastoplast was all it took to deal with the physical consequences of this bomb, but the emotional and political consequences have lived with me.

In the early days I was frightened, not of another blast, but about how unspeakably angry I felt. I had no idea I had such fury in me. If, in the first week, someone had tried to justify this terrorism to me, I would have flown into an uncontrolled rage, doing to them what the Provisional IRA (PIRA) had tried to do to me – and had done to the poor fellow who'd died from the blast, and the 120 who'd been seriously injured.

I'd long been sympathetic to the Nationalists' cause in Northern Ireland – the Catholic communities there had suffered the most dreadful humiliations ever since partition; they were disenfranchised, the police a partisan force. So why were they doing this to me?

The question was of course absurd. I was collateral damage. Terrorism depends for its political power upon the random nature of its victims. That's how fear is amplified across a whole population. But, in a weird way that the PIRA had never intended, I'm not sorry I had this experience. I found some things out that day, about myself, about violence, about politics, that I would never otherwise have understood. Later, it helped me understand the trauma to the American people of 9/11 (and of 7/7 to the British) – and the huge pressures on government which then follow.

My solicitor friend, Stephen Wegg-Prosser, had been as good as his word. It was his introduction that had led to my pupillage with Michael Goodman in a common law set of chambers. But it all depended on how I did in my Bar Finals. I worked infinitely harder for these than I had at Leeds, and really enjoyed the intellectual challenge of the law, although for a terrible moment, I thought I'd failed.

The results were made known in the most barbaric way. One copy was placed in the middle of a large table in each Inn. There was a scrum as each neurotic candidate worked their way to the front, and searched for their name. I got to the table, and scoured the list from the bottom. I couldn't find my name anywhere amongst the massed ranks of those who'd just passed, got thirds, or 2:2s. I was doomed. Depressed, I retired to a corner of the room.

'Hey Jack, well done. Brilliant. You came very close to the top.'

'You're kidding, of course,' I retorted. But my pal was correct. I'd been placed third in the country. The relief was immense. At long last I'd redeemed myself intellectually, after the personal disappointment of my A levels, and my 2:2 degree.

I had the pupillage, but no money. In those days there was no pay whatever for the first six months – in fact the pupil had to pay his master a hundred guineas (£105). Happily, on the strength of my results, Inner Temple awarded me a scholarship worth £1,000 – around £10,000 at today's prices. Anthea was by then a French teacher at an Islington comprehensive. We'd have enough to get by.

Michael, who shared a room with Nicholas Riddell, a fellow Labour councillor in Islington, was a great teacher, and worked me hard. We became lifelong friends.

After six months I was able to appear in court. My first brief was to prosecute a shoplifter in the Guildford Magistrates' Court. I was so determined to get a conviction that I felt quite sorry for the defendant – a middle-aged woman – when the court found her guilty.

My year's pupillage over, chambers offered me a tenancy, and my practice began to pick up nicely. There was a good mix of criminal prosecution and defence work, landlord and tenant, negligence and contract. The days of highly specialized chambers were yet to come.

When concentration flagged, Nicholas Riddell and I gossiped about the latest shenanigans in Islington's Labour Group. With just five Tory aldermen the borough was effectively a one-party state – an unhealthy and divided one too.*

The Labour leader of the adjoining borough of Hackney, Lou Sherman, had once famously observed that the Labour-controlled London County Council 'had done more bloody damage to Hackney than Hitler'. Though a little hyperbolic, there was a truth here. The bulldozer had been seen as the answer to the development needs of towns and cities across the country. A leaflet for the 1951 Festival of Britain had on its front cover a motorway flashing past a tower block. This was the future – away with the old, up with the new. In London, the LCC had become preoccupied to the point of obsession with comprehensive redevelopment schemes.† (The former market building in Covent Garden, and much of the surrounding area, were earmarked for demolition, to be replaced by concrete 'piazzas', and geraniums in tubs.)

The old guard in Islington shared these obsessions, as did the Greater

---

* Aldermen – senior civic leaders co-opted to councils – were abolished in 1974, under the Local Government Act 1972.

† The LCC was the dominant authority in Inner London until 1964 when London government was reorganized into the thirty-two boroughs of Greater London, with key functions of housing, planning, social services concentrated in the boroughs, and a strategic Greater London Council overall, until its demise in 1986.

London Council (GLC) which had replaced the LCC in 1964. I understood why. These people had lived in London's working-class squalor in the thirties and had been through the Blitz. They wanted to start with a blank page. But neither I nor the other young Turks on the council agreed. In my ward, we had a battle (which we finally won) to persuade the council not to demolish perfectly good late-Victorian housing, but to improve it instead. We were instinctively opposed to 'vanity projects' – a scepticism which has stayed with me, including in respect of ID cards (this went into the LBW – Let the Blighters Wait – file whilst I was Home Secretary) and fox hunting.

Then there was the Angel. The borough had been almost evangelical in its support for a GLC scheme to demolish most of the Angel area, to make way for a huge roundabout. The car was king. Nicholas Riddell and I, with Anne Page, Chair of Islington South Labour Party, fought this internally, but were getting nowhere. Suddenly, we had a brainwave. The three of us set up the Angel Action Group. Anne's phone number ended with the digits '1000', so it looked as if the group was a big organization. We had posters made, with a frightening – but accurate – montage of the roundabout ('twice the size of Highbury Corner' as one of the planners had candidly admitted), and paid a dodgy character to fly-post them everywhere.

Whilst the *Evening Standard* and the local press weren't that interested in what a few rebel councillors had to say, they gave great credence to the Angel Action Group. We were never asked what its strength was and in council committees, to assist our advocacy, we quoted the Angel Action Group. After a lengthy battle, the roundabout plan was dropped, and the council began to tiptoe towards sensible policies favouring public transport. I learnt an important lesson – about the curious cultural antipathy of many journalists towards elected representatives; and their countervailing, lazy readiness to legitimize and highlight the views of pressure groups with a catchy name.

Education in the twelve inner London boroughs was the responsibility of the Inner London Education Authority (ILEA), comprising the

GLC members, and one councillor from each borough. I was chosen to represent Islington. For the first two years I was a backbencher.

In May 1973 I cycled down to County Hall one Saturday afternoon to attend the annual ILEA Labour Group and elect the leadership for the following year. Arriving early, I was asked to see Ashley Bramall, the experienced leader of the Authority, and the chief whip. They explained to me that the behaviour of the cantankerous deputy leader, Ena Chaplin, was now out of hand (I knew this), and they wanted to fire a shot across her bows. Would I stand against her? Reassured that I would lose (I had no ambition whatever for this post), I agreed.

To my surprise, the first ballot was a draw: 22–22.

To my horror, the second ballot was 24–20 in my favour.

I was now, aged twenty-six, the (wholly unprepared) deputy leader of the largest education authority in the country, and chair of its Higher and Further Education Committee. ILEA was, however, very well resourced, with good private offices supporting each chair, so I managed. The NUS had been good preparation for decision-taking.

The position gave me an invaluable insight into the many strengths, and many weaknesses, of ILEA's approach to schooling, dominated as it was by its commitments at secondary level to making all schools comprehensives, and at primary level to 'child-centred' learning (inspired by the progressive school movement of A. S. Neill, and endorsed by the official Plowden Committee in 1967).

These principles didn't worry me. Their practice did. It was striking that many of those with a missionary fervour for comprehensives were part of Labour's grandee tradition, resolute about sending their own children into the private sector. This was a policy for other people's children – and it showed. There was a profound institutional resistance to systematic monitoring of standards; holding teachers to account; providing pupils and parents with a proper idea of progress. Anthea was at the sharp end, working in a difficult ILEA comprehensive. I, and a few others, were so concerned that we got Labour's National Executive Education Committee to agree that we should form a small group to look at standards, a national curriculum, and testing. Our recommendations were treated with scorn – but I was able to resurrect them a dozen years later when I became Shadow Education Secretary.

I still harboured the idea of becoming a Labour MP, but thought I'd better have a trial run first. Through Pat Carter I'd met a couple who were active in the Tonbridge and Malling Labour Party. They asked me to put my name in for the parliamentary candidacy. I did, and was selected. It was a rock-solid Conservative seat but I was at least familiar with this kind of area – Essex had returned Tory MPs since the world had begun. There was still work for Labour to do – and there was a friendly team to do it.

The seventies was quite the most disagreeable decade in Britain's post-war history. The optimism, the excitement, the style of the sixties all went, to be replaced by grunge. This was a raw, scruffy and violent period in British politics, with record inflation; mounting disorder on the streets and at football games; incompetent (and frequently corrupt) police forces; constant struggles with trade unions; ideological and personal rifts in the Labour movement; and posturing by many senior figures who should have known better.

In the sixties Tony Benn had been very much the modernizer. Carefully posed photographs of him and his wife Caroline on a bench in the garden of their Holland Park home were used by the party to reach out to the aspiring middle classes. On Labour's defeat in June 1970, Tony had reinvented himself as the standard-bearer of the left, attributing Labour's declining support to an insufficiency of real socialism.

However, when it came to the squandering of power, it was Ted Heath, and not the Labour Party, who turned out to be world class. Whether one agreed with it at the time or not (I didn't) Heath deserves every credit for his single-minded pursuit of Britain's membership of the European Union. But he was unable to carry his party, still less the country, through one of its most destabilizing chapters, when the world economy was disrupted by the doubling of the oil price, and the Yom Kippur War of October 1973.

The British economy shrank by 1.1 per cent in 1974; the high price of oil gave the miners an immeasurable advantage at a time when most domestic electricity was produced by power stations fired by coal from the nationalized pits.* In late 1973 they sought to press this home, with pay demands which broke the prevailing, centrally imposed pay norms. The National Union of Miners instituted a go-slow, which led to diminishing coal stocks. On New Year's Eve 1973 the Heath government imposed its Three Day Week. Television stations went off air at 10.30 p.m. There were sporadic power cuts. Advice by one minister, Patrick Jenkin, that the public should 'clean their teeth in the dark' was followed in the breach when one national newspaper showed Mr Jenkin's bathroom ablaze with light.[1] Overall, however, it looked as if Heath's tough stance with the unions was gaining him popularity. Should he therefore call an early election, and settle once and for all 'who governs Britain'?

In a drama with strong parallels to Gordon Brown's wavering in 2007, Heath vacillated, and lost the advantage.† Finally, on 7 February 1974, he fired the starting gun, just three and a half years after the last election, and with a working majority.

I managed, just, to juggle my commitments in court with campaigning in Tonbridge and Malling. The first two weeks were hard, with doors slammed in my face and many electors blaming Labour for the industrial anarchy which seemed to be bringing the country to its knees. Then, in the final week, the mood palpably changed. 'Why are we being asked such a daft question; and why are we being dragged out to vote in February?' became a frequent response on the doorstep. The Conservative candidate, John Stanley, became very anxious – not about

---

* ONS, Blue Book 2012, 31 July 2012.

† 'It's your bloody fault' Heath's biographer Philip Ziegler records Heath as complaining to Jim Prior, Leader of the House. 'If you hadn't allowed Central Office to steam this thing up, we would never have got into this position.' 'If you had told us definitely you were against an early election, it wouldn't have been all steamed up,' retorted Prior. Ziegler, *Edward Heath*, p. 425.

me, but about the Liberal Michael Vann. Nationally, the Liberals considered they were in with a chance – their leader, Jeremy Thorpe, even proclaiming as he alighted from a helicopter on to a beach that his party 'should prepare for government'. The local Conservatives' 'Confidential Briefing for Canvassers' had come my way, in which I was described as 'extreme left wing'. Now, in a leaflet pushed through every door, they made a serious effort to demonize Vann, and bolster my vote. If you couldn't vote Tory, vote Labour – for the man (me) who'd been running 'a mature and dignified campaign'. I filed this certificate of political sanity. It came in very handy in the 1979 campaign, by which time John Stanley was Margaret Thatcher's PPS.

My own reckoning was that, despite John Stanley's help, I'd come third. But Vann was convinced he would. At the count we wagered £1 on this. I took the £1, coming third by just eighteen votes.* Despite the cold and wet of this winter poll, the turnout was very high: across the constituency it was 83 per cent, but in some wards nearer 90 per cent.†

Although nationally the Conservatives polled 300,000 more votes than Labour, they won four fewer seats.‡ Negotiations between Heath and the Liberals (who'd won just fourteen seats) proved abortive – so Harold Wilson was invited to form a minority administration. I went back to my work at the Bar. Or so I thought.

Travelling from court on the Tuesday after the election, I vacantly stared from the train window, contemplating my future. That evening, I was phoned by Barbara Castle's husband, Ted. He was a Labour alderman on Islington Council. I knew him pretty well, whilst my total contact with Barbara had been a handshake and two words. Ted asked me to call in for a chat the following evening. I assumed that this was going to be about some local planning issue.

---

* Stanley, Con: 24,809; Vann, Lib: 14,701; Straw, Lab: 14,683.

† Tonbridge Higham West Ward: 88.1 per cent; Higham East Ward 87.1 per cent.

‡ Con 297; Lab 301. The Commons had 635 seats then.

Barbara was there, too. She had just been made Secretary of State for Social Services, responsible for the single sprawling department covering health and social security (DHSS – also known as the 'Department of Stealth and Total Obscurity'). It had been bolted together from two separate (and functioning) ministries for no better purpose than to satisfy the *amour propre* of Richard Crossman.

Barbara told me that Brian Abel-Smith, professor of social administration in the LSE, would be her policy adviser; she would like me to be her 'political adviser'. I replied that flattered though I was, I knew next to nothing about either health or social security; my practice at the Bar was developing well; what guarantee would there be that this new minority government could last past the summer? Would she give me a few days to think about it?

I couldn't decide one way or the other. Michael Goodman, my mentor and former pupil master, told me that I had a great career ahead at the Bar. Anthea wasn't certain, either. Our family finances were only just getting straight. After days of hesitation (causing mounting irritation on Barbara's part) I arranged to see our head of chambers, Edward Gardner, QC, a wise man – and a Conservative Member of Parliament. I put my dilemma to him.

'I've just one question to ask you, Jack. In twenty years, would you rather be a High Court judge, or in a British Cabinet?'

'Cabinet,' I heard myself replying.

'That's your answer, then. You go off and do this. You can keep your seat [in chambers] warm – pay a reduced rent, stay on the board,* return if it doesn't work out.'

He then added with great poignancy, 'I had a similar chance, at a similar age to you. I didn't take it – as a result I've peaked in neither career. I don't want you to make the same mistake.'

It's a nice irony that I owe my Blackburn constituency, and my mem-

---

* The list of a chamber's tenants, in seniority order, displayed outside the main chamber's door.

bership of the British Cabinet, to the avuncular advice of a Conservative MP. I never forgot his kindness.

As well as knowing nothing about the subject matter of the DHSS, I had little idea how the Civil Service worked. I called Barbara's principal private secretary, Graham Hart. 'Don't you remember, Jack?' he said cheerfully. 'I was at Brentwood. Head of school when the Queen came in 1957. Come in. We'll find you a room and a secretary.'

Labour had stumbled into power by accident and we were monumentally unprepared. No one had expected an election before the summer; and few had expected us to win. Posture had become a substitute for policy, as the party had put itself through one of its routine convulsions, the better to weaken ourselves when we were already down. I read through the rather flimsy (and hastily produced) 'Briefs for Incoming Ministers'; digested as many background documents as I could find; and set about establishing a role. The Civil Service method – of detailed and closely argued written submissions – suited me. It wasn't that different from the Bar.

When in early 1975 Margaret Thatcher defeated Ted Heath to become leader of the Conservative Party, Barbara wrote her an effusive private letter of congratulation. She meant it. In character, Barbara, the most prominent Labour female politician of her generation, and Margaret Thatcher, the most successful female British politician of all time, were two peas from the same pod. They were fighters, survivors in a man's world; tougher than most men, obsessed with their outward appearance, loners for whom the idea of active co-operation with their peers was an oxymoron. Some colleagues who had to work closely with them found them a nightmare.

Both could be so headstrong that they secured their own demise by ramming through policies without the consent, or support, of their (male) colleagues, who took their revenge. It was the poll tax for Margaret Thatcher; *In Place of Strife* for Barbara. Their opinions of the men who did for them – Jim Callaghan and Michael Heseltine – were equally incendiary. The difference, however, was that Mrs Thatcher's error came after she had been leader of the Conservative Party for fifteen years and prime minister for eleven years; Barbara's before she had the chance even to bid for the ultimate prize.*

But Barbara, again like Margaret Thatcher, was a dream to work for, provided your loyalty and competence were not in doubt. Both knew how to get the best from the Civil Service, by providing clarity in strategy and policy; by being efficient and courteous; and by not blaming officials for their own shortcomings. As with any group of human beings there was a normal distribution curve of talent. Some officials might have to be moved, and were; that was not, however, a reason for damning the whole service.

The first, almost the only, priority of this new minority Labour Government was to survive, until the time was ripe to call a fresh election and hopefully secure a working majority. Whilst Harold Wilson, Chancellor Denis Healey and Employment Secretary Michael Foot worked on resolving the industrial disputes with the miners and others (which they did, but at a high price), Barbara set about preparing major social security reforms to take pride of place in Labour's offer to the electorate.

One of the major challenges, then as now, was pension provision. On this Barbara was at her best. Focused, forensic, with a gargantuan appetite for work, she and her talented social security minister Brian O'Malley, with a team of dedicated officials, were able to produce in less than six months the plan for a 'State Earnings Related Pension', which received wide acclaim across the spectrum, from the financial press to the trade unions.

---

* In *Fighting All the Way* (Macmillan, London, 1993), p. 449, Barbara recounts the 'gentle Tribunite' Frank Allaun telling her: 'Barbara. I wish you'd never gone to DEP [the Department of Employment and Productivity, from where she produced *In Place of Strife*]. More than one trade unionist used to say to me that you ought to be leader of the party. Of course your bill altered all that.'

After six months in office, Wilson decided that the time was right and called an election for 10 October 1974. Barbara would be spending most of her time going round the country. She asked me to go to Blackburn, to work with her husband Ted, and the local party. In one of the many, extraordinary coincidences through which our lives have intersected, Pat Carter, his wife Julia, and their baby daughter Esther had just moved from Islington to the market town of Clitheroe, near Blackburn. I stayed with them.

The three-week campaign was more leisurely than I'd expected. Ted insisted most days on taking us off for a pub lunch for a good two hours. Barbara was going to win, that was clear. In the end, her majority of 7,652 was the best of the ten elections she had fought since first taking the seat in 1945.*

But nationally, yet again, almost all the opinion polls had overstated Labour's support, and underestimated the Conservatives'. Labour's net gain of eighteen seats gave it a majority of three.

Anthea and I had arranged to stay at the weekend with the Wegg-Prossers, at Stephen's family's place just outside Hereford. Driving back on the M40 on the Sunday, in drizzling rain, one of the tyres blew out. We span round, as the car slid backwards along the central barrier, producing immense sparks. We came to rest in the outside lane, facing the oncoming traffic, which, miraculously managed to avoid us. We scrambled across the road, found a phone box, and called the police. I realized that we were only a couple of miles from Barbara's house in the Chilterns. I called her too. With our car a wreck, we stayed there overnight. I travelled into the office with Barbara – our first day back after the election – whilst Anthea went later, with Ted, who was the world's worst driver. He gave Anthea an even bigger fright when he managed to drive off the Westway the wrong way, down the slip-road *to* the motorway.

*

---

* The seat then had a below-average electorate of 54,200.

The DHSS didn't deal with much that was intrinsically secret, but security was everywhere. The Cold War was at its height. The state had to deal with the enemy without – the Soviet Union – and the enemy within, the Communist and Trotskyist parties, and their fellow travellers. The British Establishment had been shaken to the core by the treachery of MI6 and Foreign Office staff like Burgess, Philby and Maclean, and by the revelation in 1962 that John Vassall, a private secretary at the Admiralty, had been working for the Soviets.* So the internal telephone directory was classified as 'Restricted', the most mundane submission 'Confidential', and the 'Positive Vetting' system, for all staff who had to handle classified material, had been strengthened.

I was asked to fill in a detailed questionnaire about my past. One section demanded details of any family, friends or other contacts who were members or close associates of the Communist Party or various Trotskyist parties, or whose activities might be thought subversive to the state. Where did I start? I'd spent my life with people like that. I set down a list of all the prominent ones I could recall (some of whom were later to join me in Parliament, or write for respectable newspapers like *The Times*).

A man in a mac, with a skin disease which meant that he couldn't shake my hand, and who said he'd come from 'the procurement executive' of the MoD, came to interview me in my DHSS office, for three hours. Then he came back for another three hours. In this second interview he suddenly leant across my desk, looked me in the eye, and asked: 'Mr Straw, do you like men?' The system was obsessed with gays under the bed, since some of those who had been discovered to be spies were gay, unsurprisingly blackmailed into betraying their country rather than facing the ignominy of a criminal conviction for 'sodomy'.

---

* Burgess, Maclean and Philby were part of the 'Cambridge Five': a group of spies (which included Anthony Blunt and John Cairncross) who were recruited by the NKVD (later to become the KGB) during their time studying at Cambridge. John Vassall spied for the Soviet Union in the mid-fifties after being blackmailed by the KGB due to his homosexuality – still a criminal offence in the UK at the time.

'If you mean, am I homosexual, then no, I don't think so,' I replied, staring him back.

Six hours of questioning about all my 'close associates' wasn't enough. The PEFO – the principal establishments and finance officer (and point man for MI5) – stopped me in the corridor, and told me that I'd need to arrange a further interview, this time in 'their' office.

This Kafkaesque encounter took place in an office on Whitehall, all echoing tiles on both floors and walls. I gave my name to the man in the front cubicle. He told me to wait. I spotted an empty bench, and went to sit down. 'Not there,' he shouted, 'there,' pointing to another empty bench which looked exactly the same. A lady in twin set and pearls, with a clipped accent to match (a real life Miss Moneypenny), came and led me down a shadowy corridor into a small office, where I was greeted by a donnish balding man with spectacles.

'I'm an officer of the Security Service,' he greeted me.

'Am I able to know your name?' I asked.

'Terribly sorry, not possible. I have some questions to ask you. Sit down. Now, you've provided very detailed answers to all our questions – and in the course of doing so provided us with some information about some people which we did not know before – so thank you. However, there is a serious inconsistency – or omission – between what you've told us, and what we know about you and your family. You told us that you were close to your elder sister, Suzy, didn't you? Well here's the problem, and the only way I can really explain it to you is by showing you part of the file we hold on you.'

Mr Officer reached for a large manila folder on top of a filing cabinet. It was two inches thick.

'Our records show that your sister was recruited into the Communist Party in 1961. Here, have a look.'

An A5-sized memo on official paper was pushed across the desk. Typed, it said that the writer had been present at an address I instantly recognized as being on the council estate next to ours – where a leading light in CND and the CP, and a few others, had been present when

Suzy, at the instigation of a man called Scott, had agreed to join the CP.

'Is that it?' I asked. 'No, I had no idea that she'd joined the CP, and I doubt that she did either. Suzy's on the left, like we all are, but she's not a joiner of political parties, unless I'm much mistaken. What I can tell you is that Suzy was making a play for this chap Scott; she really fancied him. I suspect she said yes to please him, but I'm sure she did nothing whatever about this "membership" of the CP from the moment she left that house.'

I handed the memo back, but not before I'd noticed another name on it. I knew this man. He now worked for the DHSS but had previously worked for the Ministry of Defence. When the system had been tightened after the Vassall scandal, people like him – too left-wing to get clearance – had often been moved to less sensitive departments, rather than being fired, in return for information. Whilst my vetting had been under way this man had found endless excuses to call into my office, and try to engage me in conversation about the CP front organization he still ran.

Apparently satisfied on this score, Mr Officer then moved on to my time at the NUS. How well did I know Fergus Nicholson, the student national organizer of the CP, he asked.* I replied that I knew him pretty well. I had no illusions about the CP, but they were much more reliable than the multifarious Trot groups we faced, so I did my best to keep them on board, without getting too close to them. I used to see Nicholson occasionally for lunch, in a pub near Covent Garden.

'Oh yes,' said Mr Officer, 'the Sussex Arms. Yes, you saw him on this

---

* Nicholson was a dour Scot, immortalized in my memory as one of a brave band of comrades who stood, with furled umbrella at the ready, as we gathered on the steps of the NUS headquarters to ward off an invasion of Trots for some act of class betrayal. They were led by Tariq Ali, who came leaping up the street shouting 'Occupy, NUS'. Tipped off by the local Special Branch, we had boarded up the building. This, Nicholson's umbrella, and two coachloads of policemen, led Tariq and his band to decide that the revolution would have to wait. They dispersed to the pub.

date, and this date – not so often; and I understand you mainly discussed this . . .' He then spelled out exactly what we had discussed in more detail than I could recall.

Just before my interview ended Mr Officer said to me, 'You're not intending to tell your Secretary of State about this interview, are you? I'm sure there's no need.' I gave him the answer he sought. On the way back to the DHSS I reflected on the fact that the Security Service had begun to put together this file on my family when I was fifteen – and on the scale of the surveillance operation this implied. But oddly it neither surprised nor shocked me. This was the world in which we lived; Britain was still a much freer society than most; and I wasn't keen on moles betraying our national secrets to the Russians.

Twenty-three years later, I found myself Home Secretary, responsible for the Security Service. They were evidently nervous that I might ask to see my file. I told them that I did not wish to do so. I should have no more rights in that regard than any other citizen, which is what I said to Peter Mandelson when he asked to see his file.*

Despite, or perhaps because of, the government's precarious hold on power in the six months between these two 1974 elections, the Wilson government had acted with dexterity. This included Barbara, who had earned herself credit from the way she'd handled her pension reforms, and avoided too many arguments with anyone else.

This apparent tranquillity was not to last. Labour's slim majority was the worst of all worlds. There was no prospect of yet another election to secure a working majority. The government would have to soldier on, in full recognition that by-elections would reduce its majority to zero and below, and that the Conservative opposition, especially once its new leader was in place in early 1975, would use the extensive possibilities then available physically to wear down the government by repeated all-night sittings.

---

* Peter had been a member of the Young Communist League.

But if the parliamentary Conservative and Labour parties understood rather well the limits on the government's freedom of action, the Labour movement did not – or did not want to. Just as Commons' procedures gave the Opposition much more power to disrupt government business than it has now, so did Labour's constitutional arrangements give 'this great movement of ours' ('TGMO') great influence, and considerable power against both a Labour government, and its individual Cabinet members.

The key to this was the National Executive Committee (NEC). Under Labour's 1918 constitution (still in force), the NEC had originally been seen as the 'administrative' arm of the party. It gained a strong policy involvement principally at the behest of Ernest Bevin, who used the NEC's inbuilt majority for the trade unions as a moderate bulwark against what he saw as the adventurism and leftism of key figures like Stafford Cripps in the Parliamentary Labour Party (PLP). In the early thirties Cripps had advocated an 'Enabling Act' to give peremptory powers to a Labour government to do virtually anything it wanted (in the interests of socialism) without further scrutiny.[2]

In the post-war decades, power in the Labour Party continued to be a two-headed hydra – the NEC vs the PLP; though crucially the roles reversed, as control in the trade unions shifted from right to left, whilst the PLP became more mature in its understanding of government and its limits. The pressure on any Labour government from the NEC was considerable; constant effort was required to stack up the requisite votes in the requisite committees, to square trade union leaders, to detoxify some truly potty conference resolutions.

The trade unions controlled 90 per cent of the votes on the floor of Labour conference, and over two-thirds of the membership of the NEC.*

---

* Decisions of each delegation were made in true vanguard fashion by the chosen few delegation members, without having to worry about any bourgeois mandate from a secret ballot of their members.

The remaining seven NEC members were elected by the constituency party delegates, invariably from the PLP – like Michael Foot, Tony Benn, Joan Lestor, Frank Allaun, Eric Heffer and Barbara. Barbara was not alone in having to look over her shoulder all the time, wondering how a particular policy of hers might be used against her in these annual elections. The NEC itself became a battleground, as she knew only too well from the blooding she'd received in 1969 over *In Place of Strife*, courtesy of her Cabinet colleague Jim Callaghan. In retrospect, it's amazing that Labour was ever able to do anything within such an inherently dysfunctional system. (It was I think my efforts to help Barbara navigate through these shark-infested waters that led to her saying she'd appointed me as a special adviser for my 'guile and low cunning'.)

In opposition, the NHS trade unions on the NEC – the National Union of Public Employees and the Confederation of Health Service Employees – had pushed for Labour to commit itself to removing 'pay beds' from the NHS, and a promise to phase them out was duly included in the October 1974 manifesto.

The aim was perfectly laudable – to reduce the opportunity for the better-off to pay to jump the (long) queues for NHS hospital treatment. However, there'd been no 'stress testing' of the policy: either about whether it might achieve the reverse of what was intended – a strengthening of private health care, albeit outside the NHS itself – or about how the very powerful NHS consultants would react. Part of the deal Nye Bevan had struck with hospital doctors in the late forties over the introduction of the NHS was that consultants could continue to maintain a private practice, from the same premises.

The DHSS officials, the Chief Medical Officer and Brian Abel-Smith were all convinced that the policy was fraught with danger, but it was popular with the NEC, the party in the country, many in the PLP; the heavy hitters in Cabinet had other, bigger battles on their hands and were happy to leave Barbara to it. I'd had no clear view of my own about the policy, and anyway I saw my role as helping her.*

For good reasons, and some not so good, Barbara decided to press ahead. She might just have got her policy through intact in calmer times, but she had to fight on too many fronts at once. The country was in crisis. In an effort to control wages, Heath had adopted a national wages' policy which was itself inflationary.† Between the two 1974 elections the new government had conceded further pay rises, and other increases in public spending to calm things down. Now the reckoning was coming – with inflation rising at a rate never before experienced in modern times. By the end of 1975 it would reach over 25 per cent.‡ Inflation at that level is inherently destabilizing of any society, since its effect is never even. All bargaining groups became desperate to maintain their members' living standards, and 'relativities' with other groups. The doctors were no exception.

Barbara found herself in a maelstrom. In April 1975 she managed to get Cabinet to agree the huge pay rise of 34 per cent proposed by the Doctors and Dentists Review Body, but they were still not satisfied. She further infuriated the medical profession (with help from me, I'm afraid) by proposing that the phasing-out of pay beds should be accompanied by direct controls on the private health sector, which the BMA

---

* Barbara's biographer, Anne Perkins, in a comment on my role at this time – 'linksman with the trade unions, with disaffected doctors, with backbenchers, as well as press and policy adviser' – observed: 'This is why Straw was later such an advocate of the relationship between party and government.' She was dead right. Anne Perkins, *Red Queen* (Macmillan, London, 2003), pp. 407ff.

† The so-called 'N + 1' which gave workers 1 per cent above the prevailing level of inflation.

‡ Inflation peaked at 26.9 per cent (RPI) in August and September 1975. It then began to slowly reduce before reaching a further peak of 21.9 per cent (RPI) in May 1980.

said with customary understatement, 'must lead ultimately to the justification for the watchtower, the searchlight and the Berlin Wall'.[3]

But though it enraged the doctors, this red meat of socialism did not calm the party; it merely excited it. The 1975 conference, up in the top ten of mad annual conferences, overrode Barbara's appeals that she was delivering everything they'd asked for, and called instead for a total ban on all private medicine. The spirit of V. I. Lenin was alive and well. The consultants' response was full-frontal opposition. A pay deal with the junior doctors began to unravel; the consultants decided to join with the junior doctors in threatening to provide emergency cover only; ever helpful, the health unions said that they would in retaliation block all pay beds.

Whilst this toxic NHS brew was fomenting, a bigger argument was raging which, five years later, would lead to the fracture of the party and almost its demise – about the Common Market (now the European Union).

The party had not always been split along conventional left/right lines on the issue. In the fifties and early sixties much of the argument against the Common Market had been led from the right, by men like Douglas Jay, Denis Healey, and party leader Hugh Gaitskell, who'd made a powerful speech to the 1962 conference asserting that federal Europe would see 'the end of Britain as an independent nation state . . . the end of a thousand years of history'.[4] Some on the left, like Eric Heffer, had been in favour, but by the time of Heath's successful negotiation of Britain's entry in the early seventies, the issue had broadly settled to provide one key touchstone of what *was* right and left within the party. Heath had only managed to secure a majority in the Commons for his terms when a group of Labour MPs led by Roy Jenkins had voted with the government. Infuriated, the party conference had agreed a call from Tony Benn to renegotiate the terms of entry and put them to a referendum.

Wilson and his Foreign Secretary Jim Callaghan did secure some marginal changes in Heath's terms, enough they felt to recommend to the British people. Wilson's problem, however, was that the divisions inside his Cabinet, and between the Cabinet majority, and the NEC and conference, were so wide that his only course was to institutionalize these splits by allowing the Cabinet ministers who opposed the new terms to campaign against them – from within Cabinet.

There were six such 'dissenting ministers' in Cabinet, of whom Barbara was one.* They formed the nucleus of the No campaign, but with some curious bedfellows from the Tory right – including Enoch Powell, who just a few years before had been treated as a pariah after his 'Rivers of Blood' speech.†

With the political advisers for the other five dissenting ministers, I provided the staff cover for the No campaign. It was hobbled from the start. None of the six – least of all Tony Benn, or Barbara – was willing to concede the campaign's leadership to anyone else. The personal chemistry with the Tory right, Powell included, was if anything easier than within the group of Labour ministers. But the agenda of the Tory right, with its jingoistic echoes of empire, and incipient racism, was complete anathema to them. In contrast, the Yes campaign, coming from the centre ground of British politics, showed a coherent face (even if their analysis was based upon a desperate pessimism about the UK's future, and the terms agreed were not in Britain's interests).

There was supposed to be some equality of arms between the two campaigns, with each allocated a government grant of £125,000, and provided with freepost for delivery of one pamphlet to every voter. But we could raise only a few thousands on top, whilst the Yes campaign raised over £1 million. The Yes campaign leaflet was supplemented by another, 'balanced' leaflet from 'HM Government', which also made the

---

* The others were Tony Benn, Michael Foot, Peter Shore, Judith Hart and John Silkin.

† Powell was now an Ulster Unionist MP (for Down South); he'd refused to stand in the February 1974 election as a Conservative, labelling Heath's decision to call the election as 'fraudulent'.

case for a Yes vote. Above all, in sharp contrast to today, almost all the press – left and right – was aimed against us. Not only were the *Guardian* and the *Financial Times* in the Yes camp, but so were *The Times*, the *Daily Telegraph* and the *Daily Mail*. And, overwhelmingly, the Tory Party backed a Yes vote, Margaret Thatcher included.

When the idea of a referendum had first been proposed in the early seventies, it had seemed to its proponents like a clever wheeze that was bound to result in a No vote. That indeed is what the opinion polls suggested until the campaign got under way. In the event on 5 June 1975 the country voted Yes by a decisive two-to-one majority, and with remarkable homogeneity across the country.*

The patent divisions within the party gravely damaged Labour's standing. The economy was also going from bad to worse. Part of the government's solution was the 'social contract' with the trade unions, in which the latter agreed to pay restraint in return for government measures to create greater equality in our society. This required courageous leadership by trade union leaders like Jack Jones of the T&G. It also provided a focal point against which the self-proclaimed left could define itself.

It is some years since Labour has had the pleasure of Blackpool as its venue for its annual conference. Back then, it was a regular treat; the high point, for posture and vitriol, the *Tribune* rally – in the Spanish Hall of the Winter Gardens, mock baroque, with hillside Spanish villages climbing the walls. All that was missing for the 1975 rally was a depiction of the Spanish Inquisition.

I was an aspiring Tribunite. This was as much tribal as it was ideological. I felt more comfortable with most of those in the Tribune Group, and suspicious of those on the right (some of whom had been active in the NUS, and were later to join the SDP).† For this rally, I had

---

* History repeated itself in May 2011 with the AV referendum.

† Tom McNally, Ian Wrigglesworth, Mike Thomas.

secured a seat close to the front. It was the turn of Ian Mikardo – an unpleasant man with an unpleasant face who was reputed to have been the target of Churchill's remark that he was 'not as nice as he looks'. As Mikardo launched an attack on union leaders for 'selling out' through the social contract, Jack Jones, who had been in the body of the hall, leapt on to the platform, shouting and gesticulating at Mikardo – and (I thought) ready to hit him. It was electrifying; all the unresolved tensions, the impossible-to-reconcile conflicts born of ideological opacity and the dying of the socialist light, there represented in this pub brawl, seen by hundreds in the audience, and millions through their television sets.

Twenty months after my encounter with the shady world of our secret services, it was my turn to engage in some amateur sleuthing – for the prime minister, no less.

As Labour's notional majority of three dissolved to nothing through by-election defeats, it became imperative to keep the Liberals on board. Wilson had a good relationship with their flamboyant leader Jeremy Thorpe, who among other things had been courageous in the stand he had taken against the South African apartheid regime.

In late January 1976 a man named Norman Scott was charged with dishonestly obtaining £14.60 in social security benefits. Scott alleged that he was being hounded for this money because he'd had a homosexual relationship with Thorpe. Thorpe denied this, and claimed that the allegation, and the prosecution, were all a set-up by BOSS, the South African Bureau of State Security. Wilson believed him. He asked Barbara Castle to find out exactly how this prosecution – formally in her name as Secretary of State – had been initiated. Barbara's private secretary, Norman Warner, and I were given this task. The permanent secretary, Sir Lance Errington, a real old-school official who wore the same suede waistcoat, with the same bits of breakfast, every day, was asked to order up Scott's file. He huffed and puffed, muttered that this was quite improper – and obliged.

Norman and I locked ourselves in my room, and went through the voluminous file, which had little sealed pockets in it marked 'Secret – to be opened by Principal and above only'.* We discovered that BOSS were indeed very interested in Thorpe, but that Scott's claim of a long-standing homosexual relationship with Thorpe was well corroborated by the file. Going back eight years, Scott had provided – at dictation speed to a social security clerk – the most detailed and intimate accounts of what had happened between him and Thorpe. It was grotesque that this kind of information should be kept on a benefit file, one more reason to be rid of the scourge of prejudice against gay people.

Norman and I typed up a detailed summary for Harold Wilson of what we'd concluded from the file. Barbara passed it to him the next day.

Wilson backed away from giving Thorpe the unconditional support he had sought. Thorpe resigned as Liberal Party leader in May 1976, unable to withstand the pressure of these (and other) allegations, to be replaced by David Steel. In December 1978 he was committed for trial at the Old Bailey with others for conspiracy and incitement to murder Scott (Scott's dog had been shot). After a sensational trial he was acquitted in 1979.

My walk-on part in this saga would ordinarily have remained under wraps. However, shortly after he had left office as prime minister, Wilson gave a fantastically embroidered account of Barbara's and my role to two journalists, who thought they'd got the scoop of the century, and who alleged that we had tampered with Scott's National Insurance file (completely untrue). It took legal proceedings (paid for by the DHSS) to set the record straight.[5]

*

---

* 'Principal' referred to a position at a particular level in the hierarchy of the Civil Service, later known as Grade 7 and now with no common nomenclature across the Service.

In 1971 Anthea had fallen victim to anorexia. Whether correct or not, I felt partly to blame for the deep unhappiness which lay behind her retreat into the awful darkness of this condition, and, initially, completely unable to help her. After three debilitating years, from which our relationship never really recovered, she did get better. We had wanted to start a family, but this was proving difficult. In 1975 Anthea had a course of fertility treatment, and to our great joy, became pregnant. The baby was born in St Bartholomew's Hospital on 24 February 1976, and was pronounced fit and well. We named our much-wanted baby daughter Rachel. Three days later, little Rachel was not feeding as well as she had been. She – and we – were rushed to the neonatal unit at the Hammersmith Hospital. She was given the best treatment then available, but she became more and more distressed. She died on 1 March 1976, six days old. We buried her in the Islington Cemetery, Finchley, a week later, on a bright spring day with our family and friends grieving with us.

We had loved Rachel more dearly and completely than we had ever loved. Her passing was a terrible blow. I very rarely cry. It made me cry to write this, thirty-six years after this poor, innocent, beautiful little girl's passing.

The early months of 1976 were grim professionally, too. On 16 March Wilson announced that he was quitting as prime minister, as soon as a successor could be elected. The favourite to succeed was Jim Callaghan. Barbara knew she was doomed if he won.

A week later I was sitting in the Officials' Box in the House of Commons for DHSS Questions when I noticed the social security minister, Brian O'Malley, clutch his head and collapse on to the bench. He stumbled from the Chamber and was quickly taken to hospital. He died on 6 April – the day after Jim Callaghan had won the leadership of the party against Michael Foot.* Two days after that, Jim sacked Barbara.

---

* Callaghan 176; Foot 137.

It was a sad end to the ministerial career of a truly remarkable, talented, and occasionally rebarbative woman. Barbara's first duty as a backbencher was to attend Brian's funeral in his home (and constituency) of Rotherham. The whole town was on the streets to pay their respects to him.

Before Barbara had arrived back from being sacked at Number 10, a letter had been delivered to me, telling me that I was sacked too. In other circumstances I might have gone back to the Bar, but I was emotionally flattened by Rachel's death. When Barbara's successor David Ennals asked me to stay on I accepted straightaway.

David was a very nice man, but his method of working alarmed me. He'd go round the room, ask me what I advised, and then say, 'We'll do that.' Cripes, I thought, I'm not the minister. Barbara had relentlessly tested every argument, and come to her own conclusions.

Three days after David had replaced Barbara, my Federal phone rang. (Of all the marks of status in the Civil Service in those days – hat stands, carpets, an easy chair – the big one was a 'Federal' telephone, with a very important bright red handset, and no dial. The Federal exchange connected senior officials, through an amazingly efficient switchboard. It was not a secure system, but often treated as if it were.) Peter Shore, the new Environment Secretary, was on the line. Would I call to see him, he asked; he'd like to offer me a post as his political adviser. I said yes immediately. When I added that I was looking for a parliamentary seat, and would obviously have to leave if I found one, Peter replied that being an MP was the most honourable role he could imagine, and that he would wish me luck.

Peter himself was the most honourable politician I ever met. I had come to know him during the Common Market referendum campaign. He was a man of very powerful convictions, none more so than on the EEC. His own intense patriotism, and internationalism based on the Commonwealth, left no room for what he saw as a Continental construct of little benefit to the UK.

Peter's department covered the waterfront of planning, housing, local government and transport. I knew something about those areas, and was pleased to have some new challenges in a rather calmer environment than Barbara's DHSS. I moved from the Elephant and Castle to the Environment Department's ugly office block on Marsham Street, known as the 'Toast Rack'.*

Though Barbara and Peter were very different characters, both were great teachers. They were never solemn, but they were serious about their politics, and about decision-making. Barbara's judgement was more instinctive than Peter's, but both were careful; they read submissions, understood the importance of detail, were confident in their conclusions, and understood how to get the best from their departments.

The economic and financial crisis which had been brewing from well before Ted Heath called the election in early 1974 was now coming to a head. Sterling was vulnerable. Big public spending cuts were inevitable – and with big cuts, big splits in this great movement of ours.

Peter had spent most of his working life on economic policy. He often remarked to me how few in Cabinet had a grasp of this most crucial subject. He, and a few other heavy hitters in Cabinet, including Tony Benn and Michael Foot, were far from convinced that cuts on the scale anticipated would be necessary. Callaghan, a great party manager, brought them into a small Cabinet Committee known as 'EY' to argue their case with him, and with the Chancellor, Denis Healey. There really was good reason for the very high classification for the papers for these meetings – I had to read them in the Private Office.

Callaghan's approach worked. This group were finally, if reluctantly, convinced that there were few practical alternatives to the strategy which he and his Chancellor set out.

The spending cuts – announced in a mini-budget in December 1976

---

* The site now houses the new Home Office building, the design for which I agreed as Home Secretary.

– were huge, hitting capital investment the hardest.* Peter had to chair a meeting one sunny afternoon when, in one go, £400 million was taken from the (then publicly owned) water authorities' capital – the equivalent of £2.25 billion in today's money.

The mood in the party darkened. 'We've only been put out of power because you f***ers are in power,' a bitter local authority leader exploded at Peter after yet another terrible round of local government elections.

In place of the bust-up between Jack Jones and Ian Mikardo the previous year, the drama at the 1976 conference was provided by Denis Healey. He'd been at Heathrow on the way to Hong Kong for a meeting of Commonwealth finance ministers. Alarmed by the way events were going at the conference, he turned round, got an RAF plane to Blackpool and arrived to speak in the middle of the debate on sterling.

As a special adviser, I was just an observer at conference, but I'd found a seat at the front (Labour's internal indiscipline in those days even extended to the *placement* at conference). I watched as Denis put together some notes, and waved his hand in the air to catch the chairman's eye. However senior a Cabinet minister might be, if they were not a member of the NEC they were treated the same as any other delegate from the floor. Five minutes was all Denis got – and no thanks. He was jeered when he explained (unwisely) that he'd had only a sandwich at lunch, and heckled for the rest of his speech. Such gratuitous humiliations visited on the man on whom the party, and the country, so critically depended, spoke volumes for the party's fundamental ambivalence about whether it really wanted government and power – or whether, in truth, its structure and culture were designed for the impotence of opposition.

Within Peter's department there was none of the fireworks and crises

---

* Capital is always easiest to cut – it hits the private construction industry, not direct public service employment. In economic terms, cuts in investment can also be the most damaging. A lesson we have all yet to learn.

which had so dominated my two years with Barbara. Peter was the ultimate 'safe pair of hands'. But he had a clear idea of what he wanted to do. Post-war planning policy, for good reasons, had led to large-scale moves of people and jobs out of the country's big cities, and into the suburbs and new towns. Thus in my local council ward in Islington, for example, small factories providing stable jobs for local people were progressively eased out. These were 'non-conforming users' – an extraordinary official term meaning that these factories were in the wrong (arbitrary) planning zone. Peter felt that this policy had run its course. Now the priority was the health of the inner cities. He was also seeking to improve the fortunes of the railways, at a time when the prevailing wisdom was that they were in terminal decline.

In September 1976 he set out on an extensive 'inner cities tour'. Around 10 p.m. one evening, when he was already in his pyjamas (black silk), he asked me to call into his hotel bedroom. He'd been told to expect a call from the prime minister. When the call came, Callaghan told him that he was splitting his department. He needed to give 'the transport bit' to Bill Rodgers, whom he had decided to promote to Cabinet. Peter argued with him, suggesting that transferring a 'bit' of a department just to suit a reshuffle wasn't a serious way to run the government. But, as I was later to learn, as long as prime ministers have the power to break up departments on a whim, they will do so, often for the wrong reason, and often at greater cost, and with far fewer benefits, than claimed.

Barbara went in for political posturing from time to time. Peter never did. My time with him and my disgust at the self-indulgence of the 1975 and 1976 conferences saw me gradually shift to a more centrist position in the party, at a time when I was still trying to find a seat to contest.

Ever since the October 1974 election I'd been trailing round parliamentary selection conferences. It was a time-consuming and depressing business – the party was in a foul mood. At one constituency – Hammersmith – I was the subject of a beautifully executed stitch-up by those angling for the local favourite.* I'd told them of my 'reservations' about the government's spending cuts, to which the replies were 'If you were so opposed to these cuts, why didn't you resign as an adviser?' and 'Why did you fail to stop the cuts to Hammersmith Hospital's budget?' On the questions went, until it was time for one last one, the *coup de grâce*. The chairman impartially surveyed the forest of hands – and pointed to a little old lady at the front who had kept hers firmly in her lap. She put on her spectacles, opened her handbag, extracted a note, and ponderously read out: 'Mr Straw. What advice did you give Barbara Castle when she had private medical treatment?'

None, as I told them, since that had happened six years before I'd ever met Barbara. But my answer didn't matter.

Barbara had, by then, announced that she was intending to stand down as MP for Blackburn at the next election. I was luckier there. On 27 June 1977 I was chosen as the prospective parliamentary candidate – thus beginning a thirty-five-year association with the town.

I was able to stay on as Peter's adviser until the NEC formally endorsed me as a candidate a month later. The rules said that I was entitled to three months' severance pay – essential as I had no alternative job lined up. The Cabinet Office objected: I had 'placed myself in a position where I could no longer be employed' so my severance pay was to be nil. It took a personal minute from Peter to Jim Callaghan to overturn this mean-spirited decision.†

I'd kept my place at chambers in the Temple and would have returned to work at the Bar, but for a kindness paid me by one of Jim Callaghan's advisers, David Lipsey.‡ He had told Brian Lapping, editorial director of Granada TV's *World in Action* programme, that I might

---

* Clive Soley, later to become a good friend.

† The official papers about this, including Callaghan's decision, were released by the National Archives a few years ago.

‡ Now Baron Lipsey of Tooting Bec, appointed a Labour life peer in 1999.

be a good bet as a researcher. I saw Brian, and accepted the offer. The job had many advantages – of which immediate cash flow, and fares paid to the north-west (the programme was based in Manchester and London) were two. I spent the next twenty months working with some very bright, imaginative people, seeing investigative journalism from the other side.

The death of a child can sometimes bring the bereaved couple closer together. Sadly, in our case it pulled us apart. Anthea and I had invested so much into the idea of a child, the joy this new person would bring, and maybe the balm they'd apply to some longer-standing fractures in our relationship, that with little Rachel's death our future together fell apart. After the break Anthea and I remained on good terms until her untimely death from cancer on 5 June 2009. But it was I who initiated the separation.

In the early summer of 1974, Norman Warner had come into my room on the ministerial floor of the DHSS to introduce the new private secretary to Brian O'Malley, then the social security minister. She was called Alice Perkins: a twenty-five-year-old 'fast streamer', in a green corduroy suit, looking slightly nervous at meeting someone from this odd breed of 'political adviser'. Alice worked in the next door office to mine. During many conversations I was struck above all by her independence of thought – including over the EU. Membership of the Common Market was taken as an obvious truth in the higher reaches of the Civil Service, never to be gainsaid. Alice, at the time president of the Association of Young European Administrators, spoke fluent French, and was very European. But she took a contrary view, and was quite prepared to argue it.

I got to know her well over the year she was in post, and often speculated to myself how great it would be to get to know her more intimately. But I was spoken for, and so at the time was she. We were, literally, just good friends.

Alice moved to another post in the summer of 1975. We continued to meet occasionally for lunch. Just before Christmas 1976 our friendship turned into something much more. The affection I'd felt for Alice exploded into love for her. Within three months, to her astonishment (and mine) I was talking to her about marriage. I reckoned I'd never be bored, that there'd never be a lull in our conversation – and much more besides. I have often remarked that I'd never marry an MP. It takes a special character generally to put up with the vicissitudes of political life, and in particular with the vicissitudes that are all my own. I wanted to spend the rest of my life with her, and I have.

The break-up of most marriages is a painful, messy business. Mine with Anthea was no exception. We were not making each other happy, and there was by then little prospect that we would. Once the break was final she went on to meet, and to marry, Andrew Watson (first husband of my fellow Islington councillor Margaret Hodge), and to have two children. Andrew provided the contentment that had eluded us, right until Anthea's death in 2009.

Alice and I did not marry until November 1978.* At the time of my final selection conference in June 1977 we were living 'over the brush', as the Lancashire saying goes.† The elders in Blackburn advised that this might not go down too well with the party faithful. Alice had best stay out of town – which she duly did, waiting with friends in nearby Bury for news as to whether my childhood ambition of becoming an MP was now one step closer.

---

* Alice has kept her maiden name of Perkins throughout our marriage.

† The precise origin of the phrase 'over the brush' is much debated but is thought to derive from the common law ritual in which a couple would jump over a broomstick as a form of 'wedding' ceremony.

FIVE

Essex to Acapulco

Some people do indeed regard Blackburn as the
Acapulco of the North

Guardian, 28 January 1976

There had been surprise, followed by hysterical laughter, in the DHSS Private Office when one of Barbara's private secretaries had opened a brown envelope, from the DHSS, to their Secretary of State, telling her by how much her old-age pension had been increased. Barbara had 'advanced' her date of birth by a few years for her first *Who's Who* entry on becoming an MP in 1945. She was in fact born in October 1910 – and so had been a pensioner from 1970. But she looked ten years younger and had the energy to match. Even once I knew her correct age it did not occur to me that she might stand down at the following election, still less that I would have a chance to succeed her in her beloved Blackburn.

By early in 1975 that had begun to change. The Blackburn Labour Party was in a panic over proposals from the Boundary Commission to re-ward the whole borough. To those outside politics, whether the line between St Jude's ward and St Stephen's is on one side of the main road or the other doesn't matter a jot. For those in politics it can be the difference between political life and death.

Two men ran the town. Jim Mason, a courageous wartime pilot who'd been given the sinecure of 'director of photography' in the town hall, but was the nearest I'd ever met to a political commissar;* and Tom Taylor, former leader of the council.† They needed help, they told Barbara, to draw up alternative boundary proposals. Those on the table, they said, would not only make too many council wards marginal, or Tory, they might also lead to the parliamentary constituency being split in two. I was despatched to the town.

A billet had been fixed with the Hindle family. Michael, a local solicitor and party member, was to work with me. His wife, Madge, an actress, was better known than Barbara in those days: she played Renee Bradshaw in *Coronation Street*. They and their two children, Charlotte and Frances, subsequently became close family friends, with Charlotte complaining to this day that at the first meal I had with them I scoffed all the second helpings which had been reserved for her.

Michael and I pored over street maps, electoral registers and population estimates. We drove round every part of the town, and put together our plan, which, as we submitted to the Boundary Commission, better met all the rules than their original, but by happy coincidence (about which we did not burden the commission) would also ensure Labour control of the council.

The commission called a local inquiry, before an experienced barrister. I had a small instinct that I might be stretching the rules restricting the overt party political activities of special advisers. Michael and I therefore agreed that we should swop roles. He, the solicitor, should be the advocate; I, the barrister, should sit behind.

---

* One night on Preston station platform, waiting for the sleeper, a man who'd been deputy director of education in Blackburn, introduced himself. 'Odd place that town of yours,' he said. 'I had to draft the borough's plan for comprehensive schools, and I needed a political steer on it. I was told to go and speak to the bloke who ran the photocopiers – Jim Mason. I got my steer.'

† Created Lord Taylor of Blackburn, a Labour life peer, in 1978.

Michael was brilliant, demolishing all alternatives – especially those of the local Conservatives. With minor changes, the inquiry found in our favour. There was jubilation in the Labour camp, and real anger amongst the local Tories. They sought the intervention of Charles Fletcher-Cooke, the Conservative MP for the adjoining seat of Darwen.

Charles was a rum character. At Cambridge before the war, he'd been a member of the Apostles, the shadowy club to which the double agents Blunt and Burgess had also belonged, and the Communist Party. In 1945 he'd stood as a Labour candidate for East Dorset. He had changed sides a couple of years later, partly, he told me, 'because I thought I'd have a better chance'. His career had almost hit the buffers in 1963 when he was a junior minister in the Home Office. An absconder from an approved school for young offenders had been stopped whilst driving a car (an Austin Princess) which was obviously not his. The explanation he offered – that he had borrowed it from Mr Fletcher-Cooke, with his full permission – turned out to be true, as did the reason why Mr Fletcher-Cooke had been so accommodating. Fletcher-Cooke resigned as a minister, and narrowly survived a local vote of no confidence. Thereafter the waters closed over the matter, and it was never referred to again.

Sixteen years later, his attitude towards his constituents was amazingly insouciant. 'Where are you off to, dear boy, how long will you be staying?' he once asked me in surprise, seeing me on the train from Euston in late 1979.

'Blackburn, Charles, I'm the MP,' I replied. 'I'm up for the whole weekend – it's Remembrance Sunday.'

'You're not doing that, dear boy, surely? Let me give you some advice. I used to do that when I was young. But I couldn't get to every village ceremony – had to explain that I was somewhere else. Now I'm always somewhere else. Cut down on those silly advice surgeries too – otherwise they'll get used to the idea. Be somewhere else.'

Now, in 1975, Charles complained to the prime minister Harold Wilson about what I'd been doing on the Blackburn boundaries.

Barbara, Norman Warner and I had to concoct a plausible draft reply for Wilson which navigated between my presence at the inquiry, and the rules, which on an uncharitable reading suggested that perhaps I should not have been there. This majored on the point that I had been 'on holiday' at the time (and had incurred no costs to public funds). Wilson, a master of ingenious explanations himself, duly signed it. The *Guardian*'s response was an editorial entitled 'Making Hay with Mr Straw', in which they described Blackburn as 'the Acapulco of the North' – which indeed it was and is. And I had started my love affair with the town, which has never waned.

Barbara had wanted to tell her Blackburn party that she would be retiring at the next election shortly after her removal from Cabinet by Jim Callaghan, in April 1976. But the party's regional office thought they'd better conduct a little audit of the Blackburn party first, as it was known to be a law unto itself. Its combined 'Trades and Labour Council' was a creature unknown to the party's constitution; some of its leading lights (Tom Taylor and Jim Mason included) lived in Fletcher-Cooke's constituency, not Barbara's. The 'audit' revealed that the total number of legitimate delegates to the General Management Committee (GMC) – which would be choosing the next MP – was just sixteen. The party was quickly reconstructed in a constitutional manner and Barbara finally announced her retirement a year later, in April 1977.

Barbara had encouraged me to put my name forward for selection, and certainly spoke to activists to recommend me – for which I remain eternally grateful – but the party wasn't going to choose me just because Barbara said so; the relationship had never been like that.

Since Philip Snowden was elected as the first-ever Labour MP for the town in 1906, there have been five Blackburn Labour MPs.* The town has never had a predilection for local heroes and this selection was no

* The others were Thomas Gill, and Mary Hamilton 1929–31; and John Edwards, 1945–50.

different. Local candidates did not make it on to the shortlist. The fact that I was a soft-skinned southerner, from Essex of all places, was not going to be used against me.

The final selection was held in the Victorian splendour of Blackburn's Council Chamber on the last Sunday in June 1977. Tom Taylor took me through my lines in his garden. I drew last in the ballot for speaking order – always good. During a half-time comfort break I bumped into one of the delegates – Mike Madigan – who told me with glee that Mr Miller, one of the other candidates, had come a cropper. Emboldened by this intelligence, my speech – which majored on the town's economic prospects – and questions, went well. After a short wait, the chairman of the party, Cllr Eric Smith, came to tell the five anxious candidates that I had won, on the first ballot. I thanked everyone, signed some forms, and then found myself alone in the completely deserted town centre looking for a call box, to phone Alice. I was mightily relieved.

The audit had brought the Blackburn party into some minimal compliance with the rules. However, I quickly discovered that the underlying organization was in need of repair. The party had not collapsed, as many had in the mid-seventies, but it had rested on its laurels, retreated into the town hall, and then lost control of the council in 1976.

The party's agent and secretary, Cllr Ernest Gorton JP, had been a commando in the war. Thirty years and half a million cigarettes later, he was an Eeyore of a man, who never looked on the bright side of life. Greet Ernie with a cheerful 'How are you?' and he'd reply, on a good day, 'No better'; if you were out of luck, he'd give you graphic detail why. He had his own idiosyncratic bureaucratic ways. He held other offices, besides secretary/agent – including that of secretary for the only fully functioning ward, aptly named after St Jude, the patron saint of desperate cases and lost causes. So he'd type formal letters, from Cllr E. W. Gorton JP, to Cllr E. W. Gorton JP. His manual typewriter's ribbon frequently ran out of ink – so his letters appeared to be in a special form of Braille, just an impression on the page. I discovered why his ward was the only one that functioned. Any new members, wherever they lived, were assigned to it – on the self-fulfilling excuse that it was the only one that functioned. That was if he liked you; if he didn't, you were placed in St Michael's (along with the teachers and others of doubtful repute).

New members were, however, in short supply – and had to run Ernie's gauntlet. From an upstairs room in the party office, I heard a man say to Ernie that he'd called in to join the party. 'Can't you see I'm busy? Come back tomorrow,' barked Ernie. I rushed downstairs, typed up an application form (since none were ever held in stock – that would simply encourage people) and signed him up. The new member, Mike Higginson, later became the treasurer and a great councillor until his untimely death in 1997.

Ernie and I did reach some accommodation, in the end, though it took some monumental rows. And I was not on my own. There was a serious appetite amongst members to get the party better organized. By the time the election was finally called, in the spring of 1979, we had functioning wards across town, and I'd developed friendships with some of the younger members which have lasted a lifetime. One of the many joys of representing this extraordinary town has been the stability of the party. Some of the people with whom I worked then are still active – Sylvia Liddle, Mike Madigan, Bill Taylor, Phil Riley, Andy Kay, Adam Patel, Akhtar Hussain.

In the summer of 1979, just after the election, a group of us young Turks decided to clean up the party office. The back windows in Ernie's office were covered in a thick yellow film – which we'd all assumed was cellophane sheeting, to shield Ernie from the sun. Scrubbing away, Andy discovered it was nicotine.

Helped by my job with Granada, which took me to nearby Manchester very frequently, I was able to build up a better sense of the town too.

Blackburn was wholly a product of the Industrial Revolution. It was a Silicon Valley of the nineteenth century, a boom town whose extraordinary expansion was based on the genius of some local inventors and entrepreneurs – and on the British Empire. Cotton from the slave states of the USA came through Liverpool; it was then spun, woven and finished in towns like Blackburn. Blackburn concentrated on the bottom end of the market. Great mills were solely devoted to the production of cloth for saris. The biggest market of all was India, whose home production was held down by aggressive pricing.

Even as late as 1927, 80 per cent of Blackburn's output was exported, mainly to Asia. The complaint by the *Blackburn Times* (which spoke for the mill owners) that 'as Lancashire feels it', owing to 'war in China and the situation in India, [these] countries have not been doing their duty as consumers of late',[1] was said without any trace of irony, still less of guilt. One key purpose of empire was to provide a protected market for Britain's exports.

Another was Britain's defence. Blackburn is twinned with Peronne, a little town on the Somme in northern France, the site of bloody battles towards the close of the First World War, where many men from East Lancashire lost their lives. They are buried in the Commonwealth War Cemetery just outside the town, with familiar Lancashire names like Ainsworth, Dewhurst, Haworth, Scholes. But more than half of the British soldiers buried there (320 of 577) have names like Ali, Abdullah, Khan and Bhika. These men had never set foot in Britain, but the histories and futures of their families were interwoven with those of their East Lancashire comrades.

From the thirties, in the face of intense international competition – initially led by Japan – the Lancashire cotton industry began a slow decline. In the fifties, other big employers, in engineering and electronics, had moved in. Everyone had a job. In the late fifties there was a sudden upswing in demand for Lancashire textiles. A major shortage of labour was filled by recruiting men from the empire – now India and Pakistan – who knew about weaving and spinning on Lancashire machines in their home countries. Until 1962 these men needed no visa – just a duplicated sheet with their photograph stapled to it. They worked hard, accepted the poor wages and conditions that many white workers had rejected, double-shifted, and hot-bedded, fifteen or more to a single terraced house.

By the time I became a candidate, the Asian community – split pretty evenly between Indian and Pakistani, but almost all Muslim – made up around 14 per cent of Blackburn's population. The textile industry was smaller than it had once been, but still important. Manufacturing dominated.

Today the great-grandchildren and great-great-grandchildren of those who fought for Britain in the Indian Army make up a third of the total population of the town. This is one of the largest proportions of Asian heritage people in the country, and makes Blackburn the youngest town in Britain. It has therefore been in the crucible of the extraordinary demographic change which the nation has experienced in the past thirty years. It's been hard for the white population, who have shown enormous fortitude as the landmarks of their memory are erased and replaced; churches and chapels demolished for mosques and madrasas, different languages on the streets, different dress. Blackburn has been more successful than many towns at accommodating a rapid pace of change. We like to think that it was no accident that we avoided the inter-communal riots which overtook other similar communities in 2001. But segregation is high. As the Christian heritage population has become more secular, so the Asian heritage population has become more religious and there are, in effect, parallel communities.

In the sixties and seventies many of the Asian settlers to the town were not that devout. They drank, they formed relationships with white women. Quite a few settled in white areas. That changed in the eighties. Many more wives and children came to join the men. The Islamic Revolution in Iran, the worldwide proselytization of Islam by the Saudis, led to a new confessional self-confidence amongst the Muslim population here as elsewhere. But Marx was not wrong about the potency of economic forces. Until the early eighties' recession, Asian males in Blackburn were almost as economically active as white men.

With the closure of so many textiles mills, however, a huge gap opened up. White male unemployment increased from 5 per cent in 1980 to 14 per cent in 1984, and then dropped below 10 per cent. In stark contrast, Asian male unemployment rose from 8 per cent in 1980, to 40 per cent in 1983, to 47 per cent in 1985 – and stayed around this level.[2] In other words, nearly half the Asian men, the breadwinners, lost their jobs through no fault whatever of their own. Isolated from the labour market, rejected by the country that had been happy to exploit their cheap, uncomplaining labour, they turned inwards. The focus of their lives became the mosque.

Today, with second and third generations, the communities are becoming more heterogeneous. The great majority of those of Indian and Pakistani heritage living in Blackburn, and in Britain, are responsible citizens, with strong families.

After my divorce from Anthea came through in August 1978, Alice and I fixed our wedding for early November, to ensure that we would be respectably married for the forthcoming election. In the regulations constraining the political activities of civil servants, Alice was in the 'Restricted' category. If I won Blackburn but Labour lost the election, she'd be working for Conservative ministers. So what were the 'do's and don'ts' for her as my spouse?

Alice wrote to her director of establishments, or head of human resources as he would now be known: Brian McGinnis, a bachelor who always read a book in the lift to avoid any risk of conversation, and had a large print of a Salvador Dali crucifixion above his desk. His list of 'don'ts' covered a page – Alice could not do walkabouts or canvass with me, and she could not be 'visibly associated' with my views on anything she might deal with in her own job. If, for example, I proposed the nationalization of GPs, and Alice was 'sitting near [me] with a happy smile, we should certainly have to find you another seat'. She could, however, do a little private entertaining, and those things which were 'entirely consistent with your wifely duties'.[3]

Alice and I took a month off over the Christmas and New Year of 1978/9 for a delayed honeymoon in India. We were lucky that our friends Michael Jay and his wife Sylvia were working in the British High Commission, and we could stay with them at the beginning and end of our trip. We spent Christmas Day with them, David Manning and his wife Catherine, and Michael Wills, at Tughlaqabad Fort, just outside Delhi. David and Michael were also working at the High Commission. It is remarkable how much our lives were later to intertwine. As Foreign Secretary the two senior officials with whom I worked most closely were Michael and David. Michael had served as British ambassador to Paris from 1996 to 2001, and was appointed head of the Diplomatic Service in January 2002. David served as Tony Blair's diplomatic adviser from 2001 until taking up post as our ambassador to Washington. Michael Wills became Labour MP for Swindon North in 1997, and Minister of State in the Ministry of Justice with me from 2007 to 2010.

Alice and I developed an affection for India on this trip, which has deepened through many others since. On our honeymoon, we went right round the country, including a stay in Karmad, in Gujarat State, the home village of Adam Patel. Adam was one of the first Asian settlers in Blackburn, a leading light in the local Labour Party, and is now Lord Patel of Blackburn. We were the first white people to visit the village for ten years. We spotted a Lancashire-registered Ford Cortina in the main square – it was still possible then, before the Soviet invasion of Afghanistan, and the Iranian Revolution, to drive safely from Calais to Calcutta.

Our absence in India meant that we missed much of the 'winter of discontent', the terrible period of industrial conflict, aimed against the Labour government by sections of the Labour movement, which so haunted us for nearly twenty years. But it continued long after our return. Jim Callaghan was hoping to soldier on to October 1979 – the latest possible date for an election. However, on 28 March the government lost a vote of confidence, when the Scottish Nationalists, in an act of rank opportunism, voted with the Conservatives. The election was called for 3 May.

The campaign in Blackburn was straightforward. The Conservative candidate majored on his local ties, and his regular attendance watching Blackburn Rovers at Ewood Park. When he sought to scare floating voters by saying that I was some kind of evil extremist, I produced the certificate of political rectitude so helpfully provided by my Conservative opponent, John Stanley, five years before in Tonbridge and Malling. Barbara came up to help for the last few days, and that made a big difference, too.

On election night the news from across the country was bad (though it could have been much worse). We lost fifty-one seats, the Conservatives gained sixty-two, giving Margaret Thatcher a comfortable working majority.* But I was very pleased with my result. Although my majority was down 2,000 on Barbara's in 1974, I had a respectable majority of 5,490, with the swing against me half the national average.†

Twenty years after I had come back from an afternoon delivering election leaflets in the rain and had looked up at our maisonette, and thought that I fancied being an MP too, my childhood fantasy had come true.

---

* Con 339 seats; Lab 268; Lib 11; others 17. (The SNP's reward for their opportunism was that they lost ten of their fourteen seats.)

† 2.6 per cent to the Conservatives; for England as a whole the swing was 5.8 per cent. *Times* Guide for 1979, pp. 56, 245.

SIX

Drawing the Poison

'Would you tell me where my office is, please?' I asked, on my arrival as a new Member of Parliament in May 1979.

'Office, sir? That will take weeks. But here's a key to your locker, number 166. You'll find it up on the Library Corridor.'

I had thought that number 166 might be next to 165, not far from 170. No – naive. I did find 163, and 177, but none in between. I went up and down the Library Corridor, the Ways and Means Corridor, any corridor with a bank of carefully carved wooden lockers the size of those used in changing rooms. I went and asked again. 'Oh, sorry, sir, didn't we tell you? They all got moved around when Hitler bombed us in the war.* Number 166 must be somewhere, because the previous owner gave us back the key, but we've no idea where it is. You'll just have to keep looking.'

After another week of scouring every locker I could find, I suddenly saw the magic numbers 166. The sequence went 'f', 'g', '103', '166'.

Six weeks later, my luck changed – a bit. I was allocated a grand-sounding room, the Oratory. This had fan vaulting, stained-glass

---

* The Houses of Parliament were damaged on fourteen separate occasions over the course of the Second World War. By far the most damage occurred during a raid on the last day of the Blitz, 10 May 1941, which led to the total destruction of the Commons' Chamber.

windows, plenty of history – and no space. Along with Westminster Hall itself, to which it was adjacent, the Oratory was one of the few parts of the Palace of Westminster which had survived the great 1834 fire.* Charles I's death warrant had been signed by all fifty-nine regicides in this room (though not at the same time). I was later to describe it as an 'elegant Gothic slum'.[1]

There were four of us crammed into this tiny room. Three were Labour. The fourth was mad. This was Neville Sandelson, Member for Hayes and Harlington, embroiled in a long-running battle with his local party who wished to deselect him. I was ambivalent about the whole idea at the time, but almost single-handed he made the case for us all to be put through the wringer of reselection at least once a year.

'Listen to this,' he once shouted to his PA at the top of his voice (the manner in which he conducted all his conversations) and waving a letter. 'Bloody cheek. The secretary of my constituency party has the impertinence to ask me when I'm next going to a GMC [i.e. the General Management Committee, which met monthly]. Outrageous. I was there nine months ago. Take a letter.' His voice rose even louder, so that all twenty poor devils crammed outside in the Cloisters could hear. 'It's to the secretary of my constituency Labour Party, and opens: "Dear Sir or Madam".' He sent the letter in those terms, provoking exactly the reaction he had sought.†

---

* Both Houses, along with most other buildings on the site, were destroyed in the fire of 1834. The fire was caused when the Exchequer needed to dispose of two carts full of wooden counting sticks – which had been used in an archaic accounting system – and the Clerk of Works at Parliament thought it safe to destroy then in the two underfloor stoves in the House of Lords. By the evening of 16 October 1834 the House of Lords was ablaze with the fire then spreading to the rest of the Palace of Westminster.

† Sandelson defected to the SDP in 1981, having (he said) voted for Michael Foot the better to ensure Labour's defeat. He lost his own seat in 1983, endorsed the Conservative candidate in 1987, and rejoined the Labour Party in 1996. He died in 2002.

Unable to stand Sandelson's disruption any more, I hatched a plan, together with one of my room-mates, Allan Roberts, MP for Bootle, and a good friend. I would confide in Neville that Allan was a closet Trotskyist; Allan would tell him that I was a sleeper for the Communist Party. It worked. He fled.

From then on, we were a happy band, though any serious work had to be done in the Commons Library. Still, it was a good place to learn one's trade – just below the Chamber and the Tea Room.

I'd spoken in public often enough by the time I became an MP, but that did nothing to relieve the nerves I felt before my maiden speech. I delivered it in the course of the debate on Geoffrey Howe's first Budget, with Alice and my mother in the Gallery above me. I'd spent a long time in the Reference Room of Blackburn Library, looking at the effects on the town of the thirties' slump. Blackburn had been the unemployment black spot of the north-west. I was very worried (with good reason, as events were to show) that the manufacturing base of the town would be hit hard by the new government's policies. This was the meat of my speech, sandwiched between a fulsome tribute to Barbara, and a reference to one of our predecessors as MP, William Henry Hornby, who'd sat for twenty-three years and never uttered a single word.* (It helped that his family owned more cotton mills than anyone else).

As a special adviser I'd spotted that the most effective MPs were those who concentrated on a few subjects, and sought to master them. I decided I would do the same. In addition to economic policy (tutored by Peter Shore), I majored on housing policy, an obvious choice, and the accountability of the police, an eccentric interest of mine.

I drafted a Ten-Minute Rule bill which proposed much greater

---

* MP from 1887–1910. The Commons Library went to considerable lengths to check Hansard for the whole of this period. They confirmed that he had never spoken.

involvement by local councils in the running of their local police forces, a separate police authority for London, and an independent complaints system.* At the time it was seen as very left-wing. As Home Secretary eighteen years later I was able to implement much of it.

Late nights, sometimes into early mornings were routine. These sessions had one bonus – they enabled us to get to know some of the MPs on the other side. Chris Patten, John Patten, William Waldegrave and Tristram Garel-Jones all became friends first, adversaries second.

In the months after the general election, Alice and I decided that if we were to start a family, we'd need to move to a larger house; and if we were to ever see each other, it would need to be close to the Commons. We found exactly what we wanted in a small square in Kennington, where we have lived ever since, just within the 'Division Bell area'.†

The Division Bell – installed above the kitchen door – gave me eight minutes precisely to drive the one and a half miles from our house, drop the car on the street (impossible now, because of security) and run into the lobby before the doors were locked by the 'Badge Messengers', all very large former NCOs from the military. In the summer of 1981, I'd been in the bath with our baby son Will when, unexpectedly, the bell went off. I dried myself very fast, drove like a maniac and sprinted to the Chamber with forty-five seconds to spare. As I arrived, panting, my way was blocked by a Badge Messenger. 'You've no tie, sir. You can't vote without a tie.'

---

* Ten-Minute Rule bills are Private Members' bills for which MPs ballot for a ten-minute 'prime time' slot to introduce them. They very rarely find their way into law, but are an effective method of raising issues.

† This was the area from which it was possible to get into the Commons' division lobbies in the eight minutes allowed. For an annual fee of £50 an MP could have a repeater bell installed in their home. Ours is still there, above the kitchen door – a relic of the days before pagers and mobile phones.

1 (*right*). My father, and me – aged about six months – in early 1947.

2 (*below*). My brothers, William and Edward, and me, *c*.1955.

3 (*bottom*). My mother hanging out the washing on our 'garden strip' – my boiler suit is on the right – *c*.1961.

4 (*left*). In my Brentwood summer uniform, aged thirteen.

5 (*below*). The 'Pathfinders' group at a Forest School Camp, Norfolk, 1960. My sister Suzy is end right at the rear, I am second right at the front.

6 (*bottom*). My sixth form set, 1963. Patrick Carter is front, second from the left, I am front, end right.

7 (*above*). My sister Suzy and me, *c.*1964.   8 (*below*). Family Christmas, Pyrles Lane, *c.*1975.

9 (*above*). Heckling the Conservative Prime Minister Sir Alec Douglas-Home, October 1964 general election. I am holding the banner.

10 (*below*). Holding the university mace, as the Leeds' Chancellor, the Duchess of Kent, awards degrees, July 1968.

11 (*above*). My first wife, Anthea, 1968.

12 (*below*). As President of the NUS, leading a protest outside the Commons, 1970. Deputy President Tony Klug is on my left.

13 (*right*). Labour candidate for Tonbridge and Malling, February 1974.

14 (*left*). Alice and me, outside St John's Wood Church, NW1, at our wedding, 11 November 1978.

15 (*above*). Barbara Castle, and
my mother, Joan Ormston, at the
count for the May 1979 general
election, when I took over from
Barbara as Blackburn's MP.

16 (*right*). New boy Straw –
November 1979,
Commons' Terrace.

17 (*above*). With son William, silencing Tony Benn, Blackheath, May 1981, on the 600th anniversary of the Peasants' Revolt.

18 (*below*). Presenting a cheque for a new stand at Ewood Park, home of Blackburn Rovers, 1982. The Chairman Billy Fox is on the left.

'But I left my tie at home. I'm very sorry. I didn't have time. I have to vote.'

'You've no tie, sir. You can't vote without a tie.'

I explained again. He refused me again. There were ten seconds to go.

'But I have a tie, sir. Here you are,' he said, producing one from a hook behind him.

I voted, and have never forgotten my tie since.

We moved house just before Christmas 1979, which, as it happened, was a time of considerable sadness. My mother, after years on her own, had met a wonderful man, John Ormston. They had married in July 1979. He had been pronounced fit enough to secure a mortgage – so that aged fifty-eight my mother was able to move from her council maisonette to a home of her own. In early December John had a sudden brain haemorrhage and died a month later. Meanwhile, Barbara's husband Ted Castle, to whom I owed so much, died on Boxing Day.

But alongside the sadness came hope. I received the news of Alice's pregnancy in the New Year, during a late evening committee session on the housing bill. Pausing mid-speech to take an intervention, I opened one of the pink message slips the messengers brought round. It read: '80% certain. Alice.'

Like every previous prime minister who had lost an election, Jim Callaghan dusted himself off and became a dignified and effective Leader of the Opposition. In the first few months, things went as well as they could for a recently defeated party. Margaret Thatcher had none of the dominance and stridency which she was to acquire after the Falklands War.

It was, however, clear that, aged sixty-seven, Jim had no intention of leading the party into another election. We were limbering up for a leadership contest, though no one – apart from Jim – was sure when it would come. That was destabilizing enough. Far worse though, the unresolved

– indeed inherently irresolvable – ideological schism in the party now triggered one of the vilest periods in the party's post-war history.

There were two views. One was that the Labour government had done pretty well in impossibly difficult circumstances – a serious world recession, rising unemployment, widespread industrial strife, and no majority. The other was that it had all been a great betrayal, a failure of will, that we'd been defeated because the Labour government had blocked real socialism. The venom extended to the upper reaches of the party – including the general secretary, Ron Hayward, who asserted, from the platform at the 1979 conference, of his own leader, 'I come not to praise Callaghan, but to bury him [loud applause].'[2]

Leading the charge for real socialism was Tony Benn, who became an even more divisive figure in the eighties than he had been in the seventies. His style verged on demagoguery, and who legitimized some deeply intolerant tendencies among his many supporters.*

Though their purpose was highly political, the left's three key demands were not, on the face of it, ideological at all, but organizational. They had been developed by the Campaign for Labour Party Democracy (CLPD) and were: 1) mandatory reselection of MPs; 2) the NEC having the last word on the manifesto, rather than the NEC and parliamentary leadership jointly; 3) choosing the leader (and deputy) by an 'electoral college' rather than by the PLP alone.

On the first of these, at least, the CLPD had a point. Neville Sandelson's attitude to his constituency party and his constituents was by no means unique. Barbara Castle's memoirs† recount how Home

---

* Tony knew all about the centrists he later reviled. He'd been one: 'In the fifties and sixties while Foot was frequently a rebel and a critic, Benn had been first close to Gaitskell, and then a centrist, pro-Europe, pro-NATO Postmaster General and Minister of Technology under Harold Wilson.' Morgan, Kenneth O. *Michael Foot: A Life* (HarperPress London, 2007), p. 396.

† 'I only have to see you because of your pertinacity on behalf of your constituents.' 5 February 1975, Barbara Castle, *The Castle Diaries 1974–1976* (Weidenfeld & Nicolson, London, 1980), p. 304.

Secretary Roy Jenkins complained to her that she was the only member of the Cabinet who troubled him on immigration cases on behalf of constituents. In too many constituencies, especially safe Labour ones, the sitting MP did little to maintain an active membership base. Many of us recognized that there had to be some change in the rules – though I was worried that unless proper checks were introduced, parties could be taken over by far-left groups and perfectly decent, hard-working MPs despatched to oblivion.

But the other two CLPD demands were pure vanguardism. The one thing that their advocates resisted as bourgeois anathema was that ordinary members of trade unions and local parties – as opposed to largely unaccountable delegates – should have the final say over what went into the manifesto, and whom to elect as party leader.

It would have been better if Callaghan had decided to retire in 1979 before all this came to a head, but he stayed on for another year. As inflation reached 22 per cent and interest rates hit a high of 17 per cent, as sterling's appreciation cut exports and undermined our manufacturing base, as factories in many areas, mine included, were closing by the week, and as the Conservative government became more and more unpopular, we, the Labour movement, chose to turn on ourselves in an orgy of bloodletting. That was the great betrayal, not the absurd claims that all that had held us back from victory in 1979 had been 'more socialism'.

The 1980 conference was, if possible, worse than the 1979 one. I missed it for a very good reason. William, our first child, had been born a week before. I was going nowhere until I was certain that he was healthy.

The internal constitutional battle was not resolved in Blackpool, but at a special conference held in Wembley the following January. This meant that when Jim Callaghan finally announced his resignation as leader on 15 October 1980, the old rules still applied. His successor would be elected by the PLP alone.

*

In the three years since I'd worked for him as his political adviser, Alice and I had developed a close friendship with Peter Shore, and his wife Liz, the Deputy Chief Medical Officer in the DHSS. We'd meet regularly for dinner at their Putney home, with others in his circle such as Bryan Gould,* Bob Sheldon and Robin Cook. To us, Peter seemed the obvious choice as party leader. He had the intellectual weight and the ministerial experience. He cared about the party, nurtured his East London constituency, had none of the baggage of Denis Healey, and seemed more likely to win an election than Michael Foot, considerable though Michael's reputation was at the time. Indeed, in his obituary of Peter, one Conservative journalist observed: 'Between Harold Wilson and Tony Blair, [Shore was] the only possible Labour Party leader of whom a Conservative leader had cause to walk in fear.'³

Peter and Michael Foot were friends. On Friday 17 October 1980, two days after Callaghan had announced his resignation, I was with Peter in his Commons room. Michael came in, and told Peter that on the following Monday he would announce his support for Peter. He didn't want to do it there and then, as he had to give an important lecture on Jonathan Swift in Dublin the following day.

On Monday 20 October I was again in Peter's room. Michael came in, moved his arms and legs around in an inconsequential manner, scratched himself, and then told Peter that he was indeed going to make an announcement about the leadership, but it would say that he would be a candidate. Since this news had been presaged by some well-sourced 'speculation' (i.e. a tip-off from Michael) in the *Observer* the day before, it was not a complete surprise. Michael had been pressed over the weekend by his wife Jill Craigie, and many close friends – like the editor of *Tribune* Dick Clements and Neil Kinnock – as well as by a number of other 'friends', who undermined him from the day he was elected.

---

* Bryan Gould served as MP for Southampton Test from 1974 to 1979 and for Dagenham from 1983 to 1994. Bryan joined the Shadow Cabinet in 1986 and contested the 1992 leadership election.

Peter was as courteous as ever, but mightily aggravated. With Michael's support, he would have beaten Denis Healey. Without it, he'd likely come third.

In retrospect it might seem wholly irrational for any Labour MP with an eye for the future not to have voted for Denis Healey. At the time, however, things looked different. Michael Foot had been an unexpected success as a senior minister in the Wilson/Callaghan administrations, earning plaudits from all sides for his decision-making, and his handling of people. Denis Healey, on the other hand, was regarded by many as having questionable judgement.* He was also brutal with anyone he saw as his intellectual inferior – which covered 99 per cent of the PLP.

The Shadow Cabinet arranged a beauty contest between the two main candidates in the form of a full-day's debate on the economy. Healey opened. Apparently handicapped by a heavy cold, his performance was mediocre.

Foot had the ostensibly more difficult task of winding up the debate. Until the televising of the Commons proceedings, and the alternative attraction of select committees, the wind-ups on major debates were packed, and rowdy, with some members drunk and ready to cause trouble.

I sat listening to Foot, spellbound, thinking, 'This man is the Mozart of oratory.' As the Employment Secretary Jim Prior, who followed him, generously conceded, it was 'brilliant'. It remains the best Commons speech I have ever heard, humorous and carefully prepared, but delivered with scarcely a note.[4] His performance was enough to swing the six votes he needed for victory, and on 10 November he became leader of the party by 139 votes to 129. Peter had recommended all his supporters to vote for Michael. I did so with few reservations.

Peter was rewarded for his loyalty by being made Shadow Chancellor.

---

* In his memoirs, *The Time of my Life*, Healey wrote 'we could have done without the IMF loan . . . if we – and the world – had known the real facts at the time'. Denis Healey, *The Time Of My Life* (Michael Joseph, London, 1989), pp. 432–43.

In turn he brought Bob Sheldon (former Treasury minister), Robin Cook and me into his front-bench team.

We did a lot of careful work on Labour's economic alternative. This culminated, in late 1982, in the publication of *Labour's Programme for Recovery*, which set out how aggregate demand could safely be expanded without the country falling over a cliff, as the followers of Thatcher's 'TINA' ('There Is No Alternative') policies so stridently argued it would. We'd run our numbers through the Treasury economic model, and were pretty sure they stacked up. The aim of this carefully argued document was to gain credibility for our approach, which was being ripped apart by both the Tories and the newly created SDP. To a degree, it succeeded – but at a high price. The *Sunday Times* spotted that, to achieve the growth rate needed, we'd assumed that sterling would have to depreciate by 10 per cent. 'Labour to devalue by 10 per cent' was an irresistible headline – and a damaging one.

A depreciation in the value of sterling was a necessary part of any recovery and this did indeed take place throughout the early 1980s.* Chancellor Nigel Lawson's actual numbers on aggregate demand for 1983–6 were remarkably similar to our projections. Overall, though, we lost more votes than we gained from this exercise. It showed the great dilemma of all major opposition parties: too little policy detail and you'll be accused of lacking a serious alternative; too much and the governing party will pocket your good ideas, whilst finding easy targets to highlight your profligacy or incredibility. The government has all the heavy artillery; they can pound you day after day; all the opposition has is small arms suitable for the occasional skirmish. Ten years later, John Smith, as Shadow Chancellor, made the same error in the run-up to the 1992 election.

Being a member of Labour's Treasury team was great and allowed me to put my anorak tendencies to good use. Bob Sheldon and Robin

---

* In the two years from January 1981 alone the pound depreciated by 22 per cent.

gave me the mind-numbing parts of the finance bills. For example, the dense texts of a new scheme for the taxation of discretionary trusts were discussed in committee in the small hours of the morning, with everyone apart from the chairman, the clerk, the chief secretary to the Treasury, Peter Rees, and me, fast asleep.[5] Peter and I droned on for hours. Even in those halcyon days of the reporting of Parliament, the *Lancashire Telegraph** (and every other paper) omitted to cover this debate. Had my constituents ever discovered what I did at night, they'd have had (more) serious doubts about my mental health.

But I was getting a bit cocky, until Labour's deputy chief whip, Walter Harrison, took me in hand. Walter had been a foreman electrician before becoming MP for Wakefield. He was one of the unsung heroes of the 1974–9 Labour government, helping it to survive with no majority and win vote after vote, until the last fateful division. Stocky, as broad as he was tall, Walter was not a man to pick an argument with. Unwisely, I did.

Walter stopped me in the corridor outside the Opposition Whips Office, and told me that the tactics I was using in my part of the finance bill had to be changed. I thought he was wrong, and explained, in earnest detail, why. He repeated his instruction; I repeated my contrary case, jabbering on. He fixed both eyes upon me and as he did so, I felt a pain between my legs I'd not experienced since the school rugby field. His grip tightened. I rose on tiptoes as he pushed up as well. My mouth came open; only a little screech came out.

'Now, lad. Have you got the point, or do you want some more?'

'Yes,' I whimpered in reply. Walter released his grip. I did as I'd been told.

We all got pretty good at fighting the Tories. The problem was that most of our energies went into fighting each other.

---

* Known as the *Lancashire Evening Telegraph* until July 2006.

The European Union had become the touchstone for a much deeper ideological struggle within the party. Those who, in 1972, had provided Ted Heath with his majority to join, and who'd then been the most evangelical leaders of the Yes campaign in the 1975 referendum, formed the core of a group on the right of the party. They were profoundly disaffected with the direction the party was taking. That was also true for those of us on the 'soft left' half of the Tribune Group. But whilst we thought that we owed it to the party, and our voters, to stay in and fight, the 'Gang of Four' – Roy Jenkins, David Owen, Bill Rodgers and Shirley Williams – decided that the party was beyond redemption and set about destroying it.

The Wembley conference in late January 1981 gave them their excuse. The unions, defying Michael Foot, the man they'd encouraged to stand as leader, voted themselves 40 per cent of the electoral college, with 30 per cent each going to the MPs and the constituency parties. It was a naked assertion of power. The following day, the Gang of Four issued their 'Limehouse Declaration', which swiftly led to the formation of the Social Democratic Party (SDP) itself. Of the four, only Owen and Rodgers were still MPs;* nine other MPs announced their defection from Labour at the same time.

We were then treated to death by a thousand cuts. A programme of phased defections was arranged, the better to damage the party. Twice, I found myself chatting to a Labour colleague in the Tea Room on a Thursday, to wake up on the Monday to the news that he'd defected too. Even thirty years on, it is difficult for those of us who had to endure this treachery not to be bitter.

Mondays in the Tea Room were group therapy, as we discussed the latest assaults from our own constituencies, the SDP, or the far left.

---

* Jenkins had left the Commons when in 1976 he had become president of the European Commission; Williams had lost her Hertford and Stevenage seat at the 1979 election, with a huge (8.1 per cent) swing against her, compared to the average for England of 5.8 per cent.

Happily, there were some old-stagers still around, with memories going back fifty years, who could reassure us that however terrible it was today, it had been worse through the twenties and thirties. Bob Edwards – the MP for Wolverhampton South East – was one. Born in 1906, Bob had fought in the Spanish Civil War. Ten years before that, as part of an Independent Labour Party Guild of Youth Delegation, he'd attended the XVth Conference of the Soviet Communist Party, where he'd met Stalin, Molotov and Trotsky.

'I had that lot at me at my GMC on Friday,' Bob told me one Monday morning, 'and one of them, the age of my grandchildren, started quoting Trotsky. I soon silenced them. I told them: "That wasn't what Trotsky said to me."'

Despite its apparent death wish, the party did surprisingly well in the county council elections in early May 1981. In Blackburn we took seats in areas previously written off as solidly Tory. This gave us the false sense that the public were not noticing our internecine struggles. They were – and if they hadn't been before, Tony Benn's decision to fight Denis Healey for the deputy leadership of the party (under the new rules), would ensure they did now.* At this same time, the existential crisis for the Labour Party was paralleled by an intensely personal crisis of my own. At the end of May, Alice and I took our first break since William had been born seven months earlier. On the plane out to Paris, my right ear felt very blocked. I had a heavy cold and catarrh and assumed that was the cause. Phoning from our hotel room to book a restaurant, I found I couldn't hear at all in my right ear. Instead, I had all sorts of noises – bells, bangs, whistles – making a truly disorientating cacophony.

On our return I went to our GP practice. My usual doctor, a wonderful clinician, was away. Reluctantly I saw his partner. By then the

---

* Benn first announced this in April, but his decision blew up into a major crisis for the party in June when Michael Foot issued a twenty-five-page denunciation of his disloyalty (Shadow Cabinet, 3 June).

catarrh had turned into a serious infection. The GP diagnosed my ear problem as temporary and sent me off to an acupuncturist, on the NHS. The catarrh went, but the infection and the hearing loss persisted. After three weeks of this messing around, I went back and insisted on a hearing test. Shocked that I appeared to have lost all the hearing in one ear, the GP had me at the ENT clinic at St Thomas' Hospital that afternoon. The consultant confirmed what I now feared, that the loss of hearing in my right ear was total and permanent – and there was a high risk that whatever had caused it might lead to the loss of hearing in my left ear too.

Jack Ashley, MP for Stoke on Trent, had lost his hearing in both ears a few years before, through a botched hospital operation. I knew him very well, from the time he'd been Barbara's PPS. He advised me that I should immediately take lip-reading classes, since this was much easier if one still had some hearing left. I did (and very handy it was too at 'reading' the sotto voce comments of Margaret Thatcher and her ministers, from across the front benches in the Commons).

Fortunately for me, the infection did not spread. My left ear still functions. The tinnitus settled to a high-pitched whistle with bells and booms for occasional extra entertainment. There is nothing you can do about tinnitus except learn to live with it. I have, though sometimes it can be very distracting. But I've been lucky; there is plenty else going on in my life. I can easily see how some people become debilitated by it.

Apart from short-sight, I'd always been pretty healthy. The deafness came as a terrible shock. But it also, in a weird way, seemed a metaphor for what was happening around me. As my hearing fell apart, so did my party, and all the aspirations and dreams I'd had about the future.

By now, the virus in the party had spread to Blackburn. A growing group – of Trotskyists in the Militant Tendency, and assorted armchair socialists – were putting me under considerable pressure, testing my ideological purity against a series of impossibilist demands, and quite explicitly threatening me with deselection (the NEC, at Tony Benn's instigation, had just made reselection mandatory).

For all my apparent success, I'd always been prone to 'impostor syndrome' and felt that what I had achieved was bound to be taken away from me. Since that day in early 1958 when the headmaster had beaten me for running away, and I'd decided that feelings were best buried, I had no clear idea how to work through those feelings. Instead, I fell into a serious depression, accompanied by terrible nightmares.

It was Alice's mother who provided me with a route out of this darkness, but it took a long time. Elsa Perkins was a Disraeli Tory, who, on election night 1964, had thrown Alice out of their drawing room when she'd cheered the news that the local Tory MP for Hampstead, Henry Brooke, had been defeated by Labour's Ben Whitaker. Elsa and I had an uneasy relationship, but she had great emotional intelligence, and cared above all about her daughter's welfare. She suggested that it might help if I saw a psychoanalyst. Robert Royston in Islington was recommended to me. Although at first I was highly resistant to the idea of anyone prying into my mind, I began going twice a week. It took me a while to recognize the value of what Robert was trying to do.

Whether professional psychoanalysis is for everyone, I have no idea, but it worked for me. Though the frequency with which I saw Robert tailed off after about ten years, I continue to see him occasionally. I'm in no doubt that but for his help I would have found the challenges of my adult life very much more difficult.*

But therapy was no quick, magic pill. In the summer of 1981 I was in a terrible state; worried about my health, and about my future. I felt under siege. I guess the nasties in the local party could sense this – and applied still more threats. I started to convince myself that, on merit, I should vote for Tony Benn in the deputy leadership ballot at the party's autumn conference. I wrote to Barbara for guidance. Her reply acutely highlights the trap which many of us felt we were in: 'You and I distrust [Tony Benn] because he is a Calvinist and carries with him the

---

* Recently I asked Robert what 'brand' of psychoanalyst he was. 'A Psychoanalytic Psychotherapist', of the 'Middle Group'.

aura of witch-burnings. But when I stop to think about how you should vote (and how I would vote in your place) I am forced to face the alternatives as you are, and when the chips are down, I know which side of the barricades I am on, even if I don't like some of the company. Denis Healey's campaign is a revelation of the fact that at bottom he is a ruthless bully.'

Relieved, I took her advice, and voted for Benn. I should not have done so. My vote was cast not from judgement, but from fear. And it might have made the difference. Healey won by less than 1 per cent.* Shortly afterwards I vowed that I'd rather go down fighting for what I believed than surrender like that again. I also better understood how crude messages, sedulously conveyed with no room for doubt, could command wide appeal, especially at times of hardship and anxiety, and when combined with intimidation of those who dared to hold a contrary view.

Whatever fantasies we'd nurtured that the working classes would emerge from their 'false consciousness' and return us to power dissolved with the Falklands War.

Argentinean forces invaded the Falkland Islands on Friday 2 April 1982. We were summoned back to the Commons the next day for a rare Saturday sitting. Margaret Thatcher was subdued but Michael Foot turned in a vintage performance, giving strong and unambiguous support for a military response.† He remained consistent throughout the war, including over the sinking of the *Belgrano*.[6]

---

* 50.426 per cent to 49.574 per cent. Each MP's vote was worth 0.11 percentage points.

† 'Even though the position and the circumstances of the people who live in the Falkland Islands are uppermost in our minds – it would be outrageous if that were not the case – there is the longer-term interest to ensure that foul and brutal aggression does not succeed in our world. If it does, there will be a danger not merely to the Falkland Islands, but to people all over this dangerous planet.' Hansard, 2 April 2012, col. 641.

If the party had followed his lead, it would still have been Margaret Thatcher and her government who gained most from the British victory, but we would not have haemorrhaged support as we did.

It was not, however, only the hard left who started to wobble. Denis Healey, then Shadow Foreign Secretary, was all over the place. By the time British troops had defeated the Argentineans we had not the least chance of bathing in any reflected sense of patriotism and national pride. Collectively we looked like vacillating apologists for the Argentinean regime. We had a terrible time in the local elections in early May, losing 225 council seats.

The 3 April debate had lasted just three hours, not on a motion to approve the deployment of British armed forces, but merely 'that this House do now adjourn'. I thought it outrageous that no explicit resolution had been required. It was one of the many experiences which made me determined, as Foreign Secretary, that any deployment of British troops into Iraq was made on a substantive motion in the Commons.*

In Blackburn my unequivocal support for Foot's position provided another wearing opportunity to challenge my socialist credentials. The Militant Tendency, and its supporters, were growing stronger by the month. With good friends like Bill Taylor, the agent, and Phil Riley (who had joined the party shortly after the 1979 election and thirty years later is still active), we made one advance – changing the day on which the GMC met from a Friday, when most sensible people wanted to go to the pub or club, to a Monday.† I could go up in the afternoon and be home via the sleeper train by 7 a.m. to help get the children up.‡

In early 1982 we'd embarked on a programme of 'soft canvassing'

---

* I later persuaded Gordon to include a commitment to make this mandatory by law in his major constitutional statement in July 2007.

† Phil spent his working life as a senior executive in the food industry, specializing in IT. On two occasions when I was a minister it was his sage advice which led me to cancel ill-conceived IT projects.

‡ The sleepers continued until May 1992. Today the fastest journey from London to Preston is two hours.

LAST MAN STANDING

and membership recruitment. Traipsing round the Ewood ward in the rain with my pal Andy Kay (also still active), I had enrolled a student, Michael Gregory, into the party. Within a couple of months Andy was berating me for my judgement. 'I thought you could spot a Trot at fifty yards, Jack. You must have had your eyes closed when you signed him up.' The Militant Tendency had an extra recruit.

But not for long. Gregory came to see me in the summer of 1982, and asked if I realized he had joined Militant. 'Hard not to notice, Michael. What can I do for you?'

He explained that he was profoundly disturbed by what he had discovered about the Tendency. It was a 'party within a party', maintained rigid discipline over its members, siphoned off funds collected for good causes like the miners – and was working hard to get rid of me. What could he do to help?

I replied that we had suspected all of this, but lacked hard evidence. The best service he could offer would be to stay inside the organization, say nothing of his doubts, and provide as much proof as he could find. He started to do this. Within a few weeks I realized that he had become psychologically very dependent on me, since no one but his wife and I knew his secret.

After six months of feeding me with much high-grade material, he told me that the strain was too great. I understood, but asked him to swear an affidavit attesting to the truth of all the evidence he'd given me. Michael's report ran to thirty-six closely typed pages.[7]

Nationally the party had begun steps to outlaw Militant, against very strong resistance, led, again, by Tony Benn. Our evidence was the best in the country. We needed to use it to good effect. We decided to seek disciplinary action against those undermining the party. The procedure in those days was incredibly cumbersome. The local executive committee had to bring the 'charges'; the GMC – nearly a hundred strong – had to act as the jury.

The younger members in the Blackburn party were clear about the Militant threat, but the older members had not been so bothered. That

148

changed as soon as it emerged that Militant were targeting people like the party's chairman, Eric Smith, as well. This was a mistake.

Eric was a tough, hard-boiled engineer, never without a cigarette stuck to his lower lip. He had the looks and determination of Arthur Scargill, the far-left miners' leader, but did not share his world view. He used regularly to try to phone me at home at bath time – I was almost always in the Commons – with a peremptory 'Jack in?' This only stopped when Alice, a dripping baby in one arm, replied, 'Jack out.'

Eric had many pals in the movement, principally shop stewards in the engineers' union, the AUEW.* They weren't going to stand for any nonsense. The party was galvanized into action.

Nationally, however, our position was going from bad to worse.

The lowest point was the Bermondsey by-election, on 24 February 1983. It had been triggered when the sitting Labour MP, former chief whip Bob Mellish, had resigned after a dreadful power struggle in his local party between a moribund old guard (which had neglected the party's base in the area), and a group of new members on the far left led by the candidate who had been selected to replace Mellish at the next election, Peter Tatchell. In sharp contrast with his consistency over the Falklands, Foot got himself into an impossible position, first telling the Commons Peter would never be endorsed as a Labour candidate; later, doing exactly that.

Although I never approved of Tatchell's politics, I approved still less of the attacks on him for being gay. Canvassers for the Liberal candidate Simon Hughes were given badges: 'I've been kissed by Peter Tatchell' – not only unforgivable, but completely hypocritical.† Hughes won, however, with a record 44 per cent swing. Labour's vote collapsed.‡

---

* Now part of the union Unite.

† In the 2006 Liberal Democrat leadership election Hughes confirmed that he was gay.

‡ At the 1979 general election the Liberals polled 2,072, in the by-election, 17,017; Labour 19,338 in 1979; 7,698 at the by-election.

This catastrophe led to a flurry of ineffectual discussions about Michael Foot's leadership, some of which I was involved in. These were snuffed out when Foot quickly called another by-election, in Darlington, which we won.

Despite the national position, my local party defied the national trend, winning back control of the council in the municipal elections in early May.

Margaret Thatcher called the general election for 9 June 1983. There'd been a major redrawing of the parliamentary boundaries which had been badly mishandled by Labour. In Blackburn we were hit particularly hard. The constituency I had taken over from Barbara had been too small, 12,000 voters below target. Now the Boundary Commission decided to make it 10,000 above target. 22,000 new voters, in the mainly Conservative west of town, and outlying villages, who had never had a Labour MP before. All the predictions were that we'd lose the new Blackburn seat.

The local party and I had other ideas. Defeat was not on our agenda. The local elections had given us a great base. We'd show them. We did. We worked like people possessed, with Bill Taylor, who had taken over from my first agent Ernie Gorton, directing operations.

The only bright point in this dark period had been the birth of our daughter, Charlotte, in the summer of 1982. During the general election campaign Alice took time off work, and came with the two children to stay with me in a friend's house, in the nearby village of Whalley. As we both later agreed, this turned out to be a bad idea, since I had to leave each morning at seven, not returning until eleven each evening, weekends included.

The Conservatives could read the opinion polls as well as us, and had selected a strong candidate, Graham Mather, then working for the Institute of Directors. He was the most effective opponent I've had in the eight elections I've fought in the borough. He had spotted that if he was to take the seat, he'd need votes from the Asian areas, previously seen by the Tories as not worth the bother. Their problem, however, was that they did not have the granular knowledge of who was who in the Asian parts of town.

The Conservatives had recruited a well-known 'community worker', Ismail Pirbhai, to run their assault on our strongholds amongst the Indian and Pakistani-heritage voters. Pirbhai was energetic, and knew everyone. In the early stages of the campaign he organized well, ensuring that at every street or house meeting there were people ready to criticize me for some act of commission or omission. So pleased were the Tories with Pirbhai's success that they had a photo placed in the *Lancashire Telegraph* of Mather and Pirbhai together.

Bill Taylor decided it was time to strike. He called the Tory agent, Tom Marsden, himself a seasoned campaigner. Blackburn's a big village. Bill and Tom knew each other well.

'What the hell do you want, Bill? We've got an election to win.'

'Yes,' replied Bill (with me listening on an extension), 'there's just something I thought you'd like to know about your chap Ismail Pirbhai.'

'Very good Paki, that Pirbhai, cleaning up votes for us like crazy. So what do you want to tell me?'

'Tom, he's on the wrong side of the law.'

'You're joking.'

'No, Tom. Let me read you this letter from the Police Complaints Board, to Jack Straw: "Mr Pirbhai has a number of criminal convictions, including offences of dishonesty."'[8]

'Just a minute.' We then heard Marsden, with hand over the receiver, shout at Graham Mather: 'You stupid idiot. Didn't I tell you, we could never trust those f***ing Pakis?'

'So Bill, what do you want? You haven't called out of the goodness of your heart, have you?'

'Lay off all the Asian areas – and we'll keep the police letter between us. If not, I'm sure the *Lancashire Telegraph* would be interested.'

The Tories' effort in the Asian areas duly collapsed.

This stroke of luck was not enough by itself, however. We needed, somehow, to find a way to separate me, and the local Labour Party, from what was going on nationally, where our campaign was in melt-down. The manifesto – tagged after the election by Gerald Kaufman as 'the longest suicide note in history' – was a disaster.*

Canvassing (which we were doing every night), poster displays every-where (we've never had more), factory visits, were all fine. A pamphlet I'd drafted, 'Putting Blackburn Back to Work', helped, but none of this was enough.† The answer was the oldest electoral method in the book – the open-air meeting. I'd have to get on a soapbox, and answer every question thrown at me.

I've been doing open-air meetings in the town centre at least once a month ever since – including throughout the Iraq War. They are almost an institution, part of Labour's 'offer' in the borough. I've worked out how to get and keep an audience of shoppers who've plenty else to do on a Saturday morning. Three decades ago they were a daunt-ing prospect. But I did them three or four times a week and they made a real difference.

Across the country, general election night 1983 was terrible. Our popular vote slumped to 27.6 per cent, just a squeak ahead of the SDP/Liberal Alliance. It was worse than 1931, when we gained 30 per cent of the vote (though won only 52 seats). This time, because of the concentration of Labour votes, we lost only 60 seats. But at 209 seats, we were the smallest Parliamentary Labour Party since the war.

In Blackburn, however, we bucked the trend. There was a small swing

---

* It was exceeded in its capacity to alienate voters only by 'Labour's Programme 1982' on which it was based. So in touch with people's aspirations and needs was this holy text, inspired by Tony Benn, that it had paragraphs devoted to the 'licens-ing of horse dealers', the 'responsibility for dealing with stray dogs', as well as an 'amicable and orderly withdrawal' from the European Community and a whole section entitled 'Socialism in One Country'.

† February 1983. Its analysis is very good; its prescription not exactly New Labour.

to Labour; my majority was a respectable 3,009, thanks to the work of scores of people in the Blackburn Labour Party, and no thanks to those who'd drafted our manifesto, nor to those who'd defected to the SDP in the hope of destroying us.

The election over, the disciplinary hearings against the Militant members named by Michael Gregory resumed. For Militant and its fellow travellers nationally, the 'Blackburn Eight' became a cause célèbre. They claimed it was a 'witch-hunt' before a 'Star Chamber'.

The key hearing was set for January 1984. The party officers had wisely decided to keep confidential the list of members of the GMC, who would decide the fate of these eight. Otherwise Militant would seek to nobble as many members as they could.

One Sunday shortly before the key meeting, Eric Smith, the party chairman, was dozing in his chair after lunch, when his doorbell rang. His son Ian answered the door. It was Peter Harris, leader of the Blackburn branch of the Tendency – a large, athletic man (and a good soccer player), wearing Commando boots, demanding to see Eric.

'What do you want, Harris?'

'The list of GMC members.'

'You can't have it. We know what you'll do with the names – go round and frighten people.'

'I'm staying here until I get it,' replied Harris, putting his boot in the door. 'And what are you going to do, Smith? Call the police?'

'No, Harris'. Eric paused. 'Ian, get me the axe.' Ian produced the hand axe the family used for firewood. 'Now, Harris, if you don't get down that path, I'm going to chop your f***ing foot off.'

Harris departed, but the intimidation continued. Eighty-three delegates attended the hearing, held on a Sunday in the Trades Club. The powerful Liverpool branch of Militant sent over busloads of people to picket the meeting. Tony Mulhearn, their leader, stood on top of a phone box ranting into a bull-horn. They barged into the meeting itself and the police had to be called.[9]

Despite everything, the meeting voted by two to one to expel six of the eight 'charged'. It made the national news, since there were few other local parties with the resources, or the officers, to take these insidious people on. They appealed to the NEC. Militant vocally lobbied that meeting too. But on 25 April 1984 – nearly two years after Michael Gregory had first come to see me – the NEC voted fourteen to twelve to confirm the expulsions.[10]

It had been either us or them – quite literally. What a huge diversion of time and effort.

Michael Foot resigned as Labour leader as soon as the results of the 1983 election were in. It was a sad end to the political (though not literary) career of a thoroughly decent, cultured man who fetched up among vulgarians. The verdict of historians has not been kind. Michael did confound the expectations so many of us had about him, which were based not on moonshine, but on the solid ground of his previous ministerial career. Another leader – Denis Healey, Peter Shore – would have done better; but they would not have won in 1983. We were in a civil war for the soul and the future of the party. The divisions, the power struggles, the unions raging at the dying of the light, made this inevitable.

The leadership election was set for the October conference. Peter Shore decided he'd have one last shot; all his friends, me included, gave him active support, but we knew it was hopeless. Peter came fourth, behind Eric Heffer. Neil Kinnock romped home, with over 70 per cent of the total vote, and clear majorities among the constituencies and MPs as well as the unions.

Neil acted decisively to re-establish Labour as one of the two main parties in Great Britain. He brought new and talented staff to work with him, and began a major reform programme, starting with the revolutionary idea that each constituency party member should be allowed a vote on the selection and reselection of MPs ('OMOV').* Neil's efforts

---

* It is a mark of the extraordinary conservatism of many sections of the party at that time, and the triumph of vested interest over principle, that this unanswerable idea was initially defeated when put to conference, in 1984. It was not implemented until the 1993 Party Conference.

were rewarded by significant shifts in our standing in the opinion polls, and in local election results. We were not yet ahead of the Tories, but the SDP/Liberal Alliance fell to a distant third.

Tony Benn had lost his Bristol South East seat in the meltdown of the 1983 general election. His selection as candidate for Chesterfield for a by-election on 1 March 1984 had the potential to reignite the serious splits in the party, which, if some way from being resolved, were now less acute. But a truce broke out. Encouraged by Neil, virtually the whole of the PLP travelled north to canvass for Tony, on the impeccable logic of Gerald Kaufman, that 'we all needed an alibi that we'd been present at the scene of the crime'. The result was exactly what Neil wanted: Benn won, but on a reduced majority.

The date will, however, go down in British political history for a quite different reason. This was the day that the National Coal Board began a series of announcements about pit closures which triggered the year-long miners' strike, the rout of the miners' union, and the swift collapse of deep mining as a major British industry.

Some of this, though it's hard to say how much, could have been avoided if Arthur Scargill had not adopted tactics which played directly into Margaret Thatcher's hands. Scargill, schooled in notions of democratic centralism which made the leadership superior to the people, resisted a secret ballot of his own members, denying them the opportunity to decide for themselves how best to fight for their futures.

It is clear, but only with the benefit of hindsight, that if Neil had from the start vocally called for a ballot, there might have been less collateral damage to the party's election prospects. Neil's biographer says that Neil 'later admitted' that his handling of the miners' ballot 'was the greatest mistake of his period as leader'.[11] I'm not sure he should beat himself up like that. Certainly, it would have been much better if he had given louder voice to what was his consistent opinion. But he could not have foreseen – no more than anyone else could – how events would play out. As the son of a miner, representing a mining area, he was acutely anxious that he might fuel a cataclysmic split in the NUM, and provide Scargill with an alibi for losing the strike. The miners did eventually split, but by then everyone could see that Scargill, not Kinnock, was responsible. Would any other leader have handled this impossible situation better? Differently, maybe, but better? I doubt it. Thatcher and Scargill needed each other; Labour was going to be the victim whatever happened.

And, while this drama was running, Militant was providing a parallel distraction for the Labour Party, and manna from heaven for the Conservatives. I was not involved at all in the detailed decisions over the miners' strike, but I found myself in the thick of the Militant crisis, nationally as well as in Blackburn.

Neil had appointed Jack Cunningham as Shadow Environment Secretary. Jack was very bright, with a doctorate in chemistry and a tough no-nonsense Geordie, the son of a regional trade union leader, steeped in the party. I was made his deputy, covering local government and we became firm friends; I 'honed the bullets, he fired them' (with telling accuracy).

In normal circumstances, this junior post would have been relatively relaxed, the usual opposition mixture of bashing the government and trying to sketch out what we would do in power. But these were not normal circumstances. Whilst Scargill was working so hard to undermine Labour's industrial base (whether he intended it or not), Militant were working like demons to undermine our local government base – crucial to our national recovery. They had taken control of Liverpool City Council; their fellow travellers in London had control of the borough of Lambeth. To control what they claimed as profligacy by 'loony left' councils, the Tories imposed 'rate capping' on recalcitrant councils, through the 1984 Rates Act.

Jack Cunningham and I knew everything there was to know about this blasted Act – we had fought it line by line, night after night into the small hours. But the government had a huge majority in both Houses and it was now law.

One of the fundamental rules of democracy is that a democratic political party cannot pick and choose which laws it says should be obeyed. Sixteen Labour-controlled councils disagreed. They proposed to set no rate at all, in the hope that the government would back down. It was a strategy for the kindergarten, and one the government had thought of. A failure to set a budget would result in the disqualification from office of all the councillors involved, and heavy fines. Pursuing this course would have meant not martyrdom, but oblivion. It wasn't going to happen. It did not, however, stop the issue from becoming the second huge headache for Neil and his leadership.

Instead of spending those years fighting the Conservatives, we spent them locked in combat with our own people, trying to persuade the leaders of these councils to see sense. Most did, after some time-consuming ideological gymnastics. In the end, as quickly as the Duke of York had marched his men back down the hill again, these leaders stared into the abyss, saw the end of their political careers, and surrendered. But not Lambeth, led by Ted Knight, nor Liverpool.

In February 1984 Neil and Jack asked me to go to Liverpool to investigate what the Labour group were up to, and in particular the true state of their finances. There followed a bizarre set of meetings. The leader of the council was John Hamilton, a nice man, not of Militant, but weak. Behind him was the chairman of the finance committee, Tony Byrne, a monkish figure who'd moved from the comfort of Jesuitical certainties to those provided by this Trotskyist sect; and Derek Hatton, the 'Del Boy' deputy leader, and the real power in the place. Eventually, I managed to establish that they needed a 60 per cent rate increase to balance their books.

Liverpool did have a case for claiming that they had been short-changed when central government grants had been allocated. Jack Cunningham and I developed an unusually close working relationship with Patrick Jenkin, the Environment Secretary. In July 1984 he came up with £30 million more in government grants. This prevented the council from going bankrupt, though it had the downside that Hatton was able to claim it as a victory for his tactics, which it wasn't. It simply delayed the inevitable humiliation for Hatton and his Tendency.

I spent the next year going up and down to Liverpool to monitor the situation. In July 1985 Jack and I reported to Neil that the council was likely to run out of money. This time there would be no government bailout. Patrick Jenkin had been replaced by his deputy Kenneth Baker; skilful, highly political, and brilliant with the media.

Neil now seized the chance, which Hatton had delivered him, to finish off the Tendency as a serious force inside the Labour movement. And, by God, with what style did he do this. Neil's speech at the October 1985 Bournemouth conference is *the* leader's speech of the last four decades. There had not been one like it since Hugh Gaitskell took on the unilateralists with his 'fight, fight, and fight again' speech at the 1960 Labour conference.[12]

Unusually, Neil's people did not distribute the whole text of his speech to the journalists. The crucial pages were omitted, to ensure that his ambush was not compromised.

No one who was there will ever forget how he launched into the Tendency with such force and such eloquence:

> I shall tell you again what you know. Because you are from the people, because you are of the people, because you live with the same realities as everybody else lives with, implausible promises don't win victories. You start with far-fetched resolutions. They are pickled into a rigid dogma, a code, and you go through the years sticking to that, outdated, misplaced, irrelevant to the real needs, and you end in the grotesque chaos of a Labour council – a Labour council – hiring taxis to scuttle around a city handing out redundancy notices to its own workers.[13]

Though badly wounded, Militant and its fellow travellers, not least those on the NEC, continued to fight. It took a further year, and exhausting effort by Neil and his staff, to arrange the expulsions of the key members of this organization, and to start to break the insidious influence it had on the party.

Throughout this parliament, it was a case of two steps forward, three back. Relatively good local election results, and a spectacular by-election win by Nick Raynsford* in the inner London marginal seat of Fulham in April 1986, gave us all reason to feel cheerful that after seven bitter, divisive years in the political wilderness, our fortunes were about to change.

On top of this, there was the poll tax – which was to be Margaret Thatcher's undoing four years later. In early 1986, Kenneth Baker, and his deputy William Waldegrave unveiled the government's plans to replace the domestic rates with a 'community charge' (the official euphemism for the poll tax). Under this every resident would in principle pay the same towards local services, regardless of their income.

We could see that once implemented this scheme was going to run foul of a fundamental natural law of politics – that losers are ten times more vocal than winners. In Scotland, where it was implemented in advance of the 1987 election, the poll tax began the destruction of the Scottish Tories as a significant force in Scottish politics. But south of the border, where the legislation was to wait until after the election, it was very different. We produced reams of illustrative data about how badly the tax would hit most voters in most areas. But we hit another natural law of politics – the law of the incomprehensible hypothetical. Until people actually received a demand through their letter box, rather than speculative figures from us which were in turn disputed by the government, they were unmoved by our case. In fact, they were persuaded that the government was at least trying to deal with those dreadful, overspending 'loony left' Labour councils – whose looniness had been confirmed by Labour's leadership itself.

Then in the summer of 1986, our fortunes, not good, changed for

---

* Where Labour achieved a 10.9 per cent swing.

the worse. The triggers were Militant (yet again), reselection – and the MP with the film-star looks, Robert Kilroy-Silk.

Elected in 1974, Robert was an effective junior front-bencher but he had problems in his back yard. His local party, Knowsley North, was trying to deselect him on the usual grounds that he wasn't 'socialist' enough; one of the front-runners to replace him was Tony Mulhearn, the key heavy of the Liverpool Militants.

In late July 1986, Robert announced that he was resigning from his safe Knowsley North seat to take a highly paid post as a TV presenter. George Howarth was chosen to fight the seat for us and Neil sent me to act as his minder. It was the beginning of one of my closest political friendships.

I spent the best part of four weeks in Kirkby. It was a wacky campaign. The council was Labour-controlled, and poor. There were so many housing repair complaints that we had to set up a repair bureau in the campaign headquarters. This led, by pure chance, to ITV interviewing a voter who had had a new front-door delivered and installed by the council; and – as she explained with delight – she had not even had to ask for it. This was, alas, quite correct. A lady down the street had complained to us that her door was falling off its hinges. The council couldn't even get a house number right.

It was however, not repairs, but rats, and cats, which helped turn the election our way.

The Liberal candidate, Rosie Cooper, no shrinking violet, decided that, to illustrate the Labour council's total incompetence, she'd major on the vermin they'd failed to control. With cameras rolling, she dumped a sack full of dead rats on the steps of the council offices – and received the publicity she'd hoped for.

Canvassing that day, I walked up the side of a bungalow in Pitsmead Road, and found the owner painting his down pipe. 'Will you be voting Labour, Sir?' I asked.

'I'm not very impressed with you lot,' he replied. 'But I tell you what. I'm not voting for those bloody Liberals. Filthy bastards, them. You see that building over there?' – pointing over his back garden hedge – 'that's the rear of the Liberal Club. They are forever chucking empty bottles in my garden – and just yesterday, they threw a carrier bag with a dead cat in it. Here, I've got it here.'

Granada TV were filming down the street. I asked this wonderful man if he'd be willing to talk to them about this outrage. 'Only too willing.' I wheeled in the TV crew, whom I knew from my time on *World in Action*. It made a great story, which went national. No one really cared about Rosie's dead rats. But they cared about this poor cat, executed, then denied a decent burial, by the Liberals. It proved what we'd always said about them. No heart, no principles.

Because George was a decent candidate, with ideas which chimed with the electorate, and because we'd kept Militant well away, we got the right result. There was a swing against us of 14 per cent, but he still won by a margin of 6,724.

Despite the overwhelming evidence from across the country that, since the far left were anathema to the electorate, their attempted takeover of the party was fundamentally self-defeating, they carried on trying. Their arrogance was breathtaking, and nowhere more so than in London.

The sitting Labour MP for Greenwich, Guy Barnett, died just before Christmas 1986. Neil had yet to muster the votes in the NEC to take national control of by-election candidates – an imperative, given the national spotlight that was bound to be shone on them. The local party chose Deirdre Wood, a lady of impeccable socialist credentials save for the ability to appeal to voters. Canvassing for her wasn't as bad as canvassing in Bermondsey four years earlier, but it wasn't easy. The SDP's personable candidate, Rosie Barnes, duly won, with a majority of over 6,600. The London far left had just gifted the SDP their first by-election victory over a Labour candidate. It was infuriating; the worst possible launch pad for the imminent general election.

Margaret Thatcher announced the date a few months later: 11 June 1987. With Bryan Gould, Peter Mandelson, Charles Clarke and Patricia

Hewitt directing, the Labour campaign was light years from the terrifying shambles of 1983, but no one in their heart ever believed we could win. What we had to do was survive. We gained just twenty seats, with 30 per cent of the popular vote. The Tories were twelve points ahead; their majority still over a hundred.

The strategic significance of 1987 was the retreat of the SDP/Liberal Alliance. They were pushed back well and truly into third place. Roy Jenkins lost his seat at Glasgow Hillhead.

In Blackburn, there was a respectable 2.3 per cent swing in my favour, giving me a majority of 5,497.* In the nineteenth century Blackburn election campaigns were notorious for their violence and vulgarity. Echoes of this continued. Whilst I was holding an open-air meeting in the market, the local Tories arrived en masse to disrupt it. One of our supporters (and without my knowledge, of course) promptly went into the market, purchased a bucket of fish heads, climbed a spiral staircase and rained them down on our impertinent adversaries.

Early in 1982 Alice and I were asked to Sunday lunch by Alan Howarth, who came from Blackburn and worked for the PLP, and his wife Maggie Rae. Among the other guests were a fresh-faced young man and his wife, both barristers – Tony Blair and Cherie Booth. It was the first time we'd met them. Tony got talking to Alice about my life as a Labour MP, and hers, married to it.

'I'm thinking of becoming a Labour MP myself,' Tony told Alice.

'I wouldn't do that if I were you,' I heard Alice reply. 'That's a really bad idea.' She explained how dreadful the previous two years had been, and how the poison in the party seemed set to continue.

Her advice was well meant. Fortunately for the party, Tony chose to

---

* My vote, over 27,000, was the highest I've ever received. This was the last election in the seat with three candidates only.

ignore it. After a valiant, if hopeless, trial run in Beaconsfield on 27 May 1982, he won Sedgefield at the 1983 general election.

But Alice was not wrong either. The poison did continue. Those who did not live through this period may think that those who did were obsessed with the hard left, the Trots, the Tendency, the factions. We were – beating them was a prerequisite to Labour staying in business. It took heroic effort by Neil Kinnock, for which he has yet to be afforded proper credit, to draw the poison, and put us on the road to power. That consumed eight years; eight wasted years. There would be many more setbacks before we made it.

SEVEN

Other People's Children

What I did meet were intellectual socialists who had a negligible effect on the life of the masses. They were all head. They collected working-class experiences as others might collect stamps or butterflies.

WILLIAM WOODRUFF, Beyond Nab End[1]

Robin Cook was of the brightest and the best; brilliant at what we had to do in opposition – harry the government, plan for power. Yet so quixotic was the system of Shadow Cabinet elections that in 1986 the Parliamentary Labour Party decided to dump him, in favour of someone whose name I've now forgotten and who's left no trace whatever.*

So much for 'the most sophisticated electorate in the world', as the PLP was described in those days, with no irony intended.[2] With the party under continuing assault from the far left, the PLP imposed its own special shackles on Labour's ability to refresh its policies, and appeal to voters, in the form of the annual elections to the Shadow Cabinet.

The particular system used was highly vulnerable to gaming; to

---

* Robin was re-elected to the Shadow Cabinet the following year; and was regularly at or near the top of the poll until we entered government in 1997.

results no one in particular had sought; and – until 1995 and the introduction of secret ballots – to malpractice as well.

I'd been a candidate for the Shadow Cabinet in 1985 and 1986, not with any real hope, but as a marker for the future. After the 1987 election I decided to make a serious effort to win. But first, there was the pre-election-election to the Tribune slate to worry about.

The Tribune Group had been a broad umbrella group for the soft and hard left. In the early eighties, under the strain of arguments over Militant, it had split – with the harder left going into the Campaign Group. Now they, and some in our own group, wanted a joint slate. A number of us – Gordon Brown and me included – thought that was a truly dangerous idea. A battle royal ensued. Gordon and I said we'd rather be on no slate at all than on one where we could be held to ransom by colleagues with whom we profoundly disagreed. In the end, we won that argument. In the ballot proper that followed, I scraped home. I wasn't bothered about that. I was in. Nor did Neil take the least notice of where successful candidates had come in the ballot, since he knew very well how it operated. He gave me a big job – Shadow Education Secretary – and kept me there for the full five years of the parliament.

In a revealing insight into his character, in preparation for the 1987 general election, Neil had resisted the attempts to portray him as presidential on the grounds that it 'just doesn't sit temperamentally with me'. Rather, he saw himself as 'head of team'.[3] He was a very good team leader, as I witnessed. He would have been an effective prime minister, if fate, and the party he did so much to reform, had been kinder to him. If he trusted you – your loyalty, and your judgement – then he returned that loyalty ten times over, even if your conclusions and his were not always in the same place.

On education policy, our starting points were similar. We were both products of the 11-plus; both saw how divisive that rigid system was, how it arbitrarily separated children at the age of eleven, and left many of that 80 per cent who had to 'fail' feeling like failures for the rest of their lives. We both had children in the state system, and were intending that they should stay there.

But in other ways, our experiences differed. In South Wales there'd been a much deeper consensus for comprehensive education than there had been in London and southern England; fewer children went into the private sector, so there was a greater middle-class commitment to the state system, in practice as well as in theory.

In London, particularly in the polyglot inner area, the reality of comprehensive reorganization had been less pretty than many on the left were willing to admit. My first wife, Anthea, had been a good teacher. Islington Green, where she had taught, was by no means the most difficult school in inner London in the seventies. Even so, it had lacked clarity about what it was there for; it had lacked intellectual discipline, and the structure to improve the attainment, and therefore the life chances, of those many children from less advantaged backgrounds.

My experience on the Inner London Education Authority had also influenced me. The Authority had much of which to be proud, but pride can easily slide into complacency. Three things gradually dawned on me.

The first was that ILEA's instinctive measures of success were inputs – the money spent, the resources deployed; they had few explicit measures of outputs – the achievement of pupils as they left – nor of the effectiveness of their staff.

The second was that they had bought into the alibis for under-performance provided by the well-meaning, hugely influential, but intellectually flabby 1967 Plowden Report on primary education. This had declared (using 'our beliefs' as a substitute for data) that most primary education at that time was 'very good'; only 'rarely is it very bad'.[4] This did not accord with my belief, nor my experience.

More fundamental was Plowden's approach to the new schools landscape as comprehensive education was introduced. As the committee pointed out, the 11-plus had set a framework for judging primary schools. 'It set up minimum standards for the abler children, often in our view the wrong ones and distorting in their effects on the curriculum. But at least they were standards. The teachers and parents had some yardstick by which to measure their pupils' work. Now it is going. How are they to know what to expect of children?'[5]

This was – and remains – the most fundamental question to ask of schools. Yet, having recognized that the abolition of the 11-plus would leave a void, Plowden failed to propose anything systematic in its place.

Plowden said that some use should be made of objective tests, but eschewed the idea that parents should be told about them for the most patronizing of reasons: 'The ability of a child as known to its teachers should not in our opinion be written down because his [sic] parents may in the future fail to encourage him'.[6] Plowden proposed much greater 'flexibility in the curriculum' – i.e. leave it to the class teacher – but was stunningly didactic on the question of English grammar: 'Formal study of grammar will have little place in the primary school . . . The theory of grammar that is studied should describe the child's language and not be a theory based on Latin, many of whose categories, inflexions, case systems, tenses and so on do not exist in English.'[7]

Although the committee was blind to what it was saying, to deny the mass of the people access to the formal rules of our language would be to inhibit their future economic progress and their social mobility. I bet they ensured that their own children learnt grammar.

Which led me to my third perception: this was all for 'other people's children'.

Almost all the parents on the Plowden Committee had sent their children into the private sector, or to selective state schools, and would continue to do so. This was true of those in the higher levels of ILEA;* and many in the teaching unions who, whilst lecturing others on the purity of the comprehensive ideal, by chance just happened to live near

---

* The father of one of my first girlfriends was a senior ILEA inspector in French. She attended a private boarding school.

a selective grammar or faith-based school, or did not have children at all.

It was also true of many at a senior level in the Labour Party, who had developed the comprehensive policy in the fifties and early sixties without thinking through what controls on standards should replace the 11-plus. Many of these people were, in William Woodruff's withering phrase, people who 'collected working-class experiences as others collect stamps or butterflies'.

Tony Crosland, the Education Secretary who in 1965 instructed that comprehensives should be brought in throughout the country, did send his stepchildren to a comprehensive. But his comment to his wife Susan that 'If it's the last thing I do, I'm going to destroy every f***ing grammar school in England. And Wales. And Northern Ireland,' highlighted the cavalier approach of so many on the intellectual left.[8]

For me, a supporter of the principle, comprehensive education was never about 'destroying' grammar schools, but rather making their advantages available to that majority of children who failed a particular test at eleven.

It was these concerns which had led in the early seventies to that small group of us on Labour's National Executive Education and Science Committee proposing that a national curriculum and diagnostic testing in schools should be introduced; proposals that, symptomatic of their time, were binned because they failed to satisfy an ideological commitment to an equality of mediocrity.

Kenneth Baker was the rising star of Margaret Thatcher's government. His ruthlessness in facing down 'loony left' Labour councils had led to his promotion to Education Secretary. A major programme of educational reform was a highlight of the Conservative's 1987 manifesto. When Baker put forward his Education Reform Bill, I had to decide how we handled it.

At a personal level, I liked Ken Baker, and admired many of his political skills. But I knew that in combat he'd give no quarter to me or my party. His bill contained some well-prepared elephant traps for Labour. As usual, there were many in the party only too ready to fall into them.

It was easy enough to attack the manner in which Baker's proposals had been brought forward – half-formed, and shambolic – and the substance of some of them, but there was one key set that we couldn't possibly oppose since we'd long supported the idea: to give all schools greater control over their budgets; and then there was the national curriculum, and testing (the taboo issue).

In private, most people in the party who took an interest recognized that after twenty-five years the practice of comprehensive education had become a little detached from the ideal.

My predecessor as Shadow Education Secretary, Giles Radice, certainly saw this. Giles had courageously ensured that our 1987 manifesto committed the party to 'raising standards of performance', through a 'flexible but clear core curriculum agreed at national level, and a new profile of achievement' for all pupils.

But the teaching unions, who had had a bitter industrial dispute with the government the year before, worked themselves into a frenzy against the Baker bill, with hyperbolic claims that it would at best undermine state education, more likely destroy it. The National Union of Teachers (NUT) was the most vocal. It was never affiliated to the Labour Party, but in terms of influence it might as well have been. Its general secretary, Fred Jarvis, was very active in the party, and a long-standing personal friend.* Neil's wife, Glenys, was very involved in the NUT. At a local level, many of our strongest and most energetic supporters were NUT members.

In the early eighties we'd gone in for full-frontal attacks on proposals we half-supported – like the sale of council houses. It had been good sport at the time; we all felt much better after gruelling fights in Standing Committee night after night (which no one noticed); but it

---

* He had been president of the NUS in the early fifties.

had looked very silly at the following election. The net effect had been to add to the sense that we were not a credible party of government.

I was anxious that we should not finish up looking ridiculous at the following election, in 1991, or 1992. My dilemma, however, was to get from where we were, to where I thought we had to be, in one piece.

The party's Education and Science Committee (strongly influenced by the NUT) wanted no truck with a national curriculum and testing for exactly the reasons that I supported them – they would be a test of schools, and of teachers, as well as of pupils. The only way through, I judged, was to call up holy texts. The text wasn't that holy – it was what my little group had written in the early seventies – but it would have to do. I gave a lengthy interview to the *Guardian*'s education correspondent. I was off to Blackburn the next day. I read the interview on the Tube to Euston, and was pleased with my handiwork. The story had come out rather well.[9]

Just before the train left for Preston there was a commotion in my carriage. Two TV cameramen came into the compartment, followed by my leader and entourage. They were making a pre-conference documentary about Neil. In a single movement Neil sat down and opened his *Guardian*. There was a large ring round my story.

'What's this?' he asked. 'It took Glenys and me a bit by surprise at breakfast.' I explained, as best I could. My pitch was not exactly how he would have made the case; but it's a mark of Neil's quality as a leader that he continued to support me on this, as he did on other matters where he may not have been completely comfortable with my position.

Abstaining on the second reading of this bill would have been suicidal, so I led the troops into the opposition lobbies. But some people had spotted my ambiguity about the bill. Disobliging stories began to appear that my performance had been 'lacklustre'. I had to work out a plan for getting back in favour with my colleagues, so that they wouldn't kick me out in the forthcoming Shadow Cabinet elections.

I managed to stay in the Shadow Cabinet for the ten years until we were elected in 1997. But the system was truly awful: a three-month distraction each year as the PLP turned inwards, distorting our ability to think new thoughts, placing a premium on the status quo.

It was also corrupt.

The ballot papers – always yellow – were included in the 'Whip', the weekly set of instructions about how to vote, together with information about party meetings, which came through our mail boxes each Friday. The ballot papers had to be returned the following Wednesday.

I'd heard stories about how the Whips Office collected blank ballot papers from members in return for the favours they dispensed – an overseas trip, a better Commons' room, leniency over late votes – but I'd dismissed these as tittle-tattle.

Two days before the 1989 ballot closed I was joined in the Tea Room by Ray Powell, a senior opposition whip, MP for Ogmore, and don of the South Wales 'Taffia'.

'How's it going, boyo?' he asked me.

I explained that I thought it was going OK, but he knew the PLP as well as I did. Plenty of colleagues made many more promises than they had votes.

'Would you like a vote then, boyo? See here, I've got ten in my pocket.' He opened his jacket, and pulled out a wodge of blank ballot papers. I thanked him kindly, and decided not to ask whether it would be one vote or ten he'd be casting for me. This annual racket was one reason why the results could be so eccentric. Excellent people did get elected, but some very good people had immense difficulty; and for some, their ability to come at or near the top of the polls far outstripped all other known talents.

In 1995, the PLP finally put an end to these practices, by introducing the secret ballot.

And then, with considerable skill, and no casualties, in September 2011 Ed Miliband managed to persuade the Parliamentary Labour Party to abandon for good the system of elections to the Shadow Cabinet, and replace it with appointment by the leader. It's what the

Conservative Party has always done. That's because they are designed for power.

Fortunately for me, a group of serious academics shared my concerns about the education system. The conclusion of their 'Better Schools' research, as it came to be known, challenged the conventional wisdom that schools could do very little to offset the social backgrounds of their pupils. It showed that different schools, with similar pupils, serving similar areas, performed very differently. The key was the quality of the staff, especially the head, and the environment they created in the school. This chimed with everything I thought (and is now regarded as blindingly obvious).

I seized on this research. It was exactly what I needed to navigate safely through my next problem – the publication of league tables of schools' performance.

Regular standardized testing – 'SATs' – was bound to lead to league tables. Such comparisons were always open to misinterpretation. Data showing that a well-financed private school with children from prosperous homes was doing better than a state primary school with half the resources and children from low-income homes would prove little about either school; but data from two similar schools would tell some serious truths about which one was more effective. These researchers were also developing a methodology to rank the 'value-added' of each school, taking account of the attainment of the children on entry.

The teaching unions guessed that a much more rigorous inspection system would inevitably follow the testing, and the league tables – with Education Department powers to put failing schools on probation, or close them down altogether. They opposed it all.

Where I was at one with the teaching unions was over resourcing. The Conservatives' neglect of the fabric of schools, and of proper rewards for good teachers, belied their rhetoric of commitment to the state system. I established annual surveys of 'Britain's Crumbling Schools', and of the acute teacher shortages in many areas.

I don't have any problem with parents who choose the private sector for their children; many of our close friends have done so. Alice and I might have considered this choice had I stayed at the Bar. But I do feel that those who choose the private sector should be careful not to denigrate the state system, nor to claim that additional funding makes no difference. One (of many) reasons why the private sector does well for its children is that they have much more to spend per pupil.*

I was sufficiently wound up about the Tories' 'do as I say, not as I do' approach that I decided to write to each Conservative Cabinet member about whether they sent their children to the state or the private sector, and publish the results. My timing was poor, however; the Tories turned the survey into an own goal against me, over our personal choice of schools.

1991 could scarcely have been a worse year for secondary transfer in inner London. A late addition to Ken Baker's education bill, forced through by an unholy alliance of Norman Tebbit and Michael Heseltine (neither of whom represented inner London seats) had been the abolition of ILEA altogether, with the boroughs taking over its functions. I'd fought this strongly. ILEA wasn't perfect, but breaking it up was going to make things worse. The policy was partisan – and vindictive. The London Labour left hadn't helped, of course. The distinguished ILEA leader, Ashley Bramall, had been ousted when Ken Livingstone had won the Greater London Council in 1983. Ashley's successors were not persuasive advocates against abolition.

One of the good things about ILEA had been the wide parental choice it offered. Secondary schools drew their intake from all over inner London. A significant number of pupils at our children's Lambeth primary school had always gone across the river to Pimlico School, a

---

* The average schools budget per pupil for local authorities in England was £5,042 in 2011–12. (Source: DfE, Benchmarking tables of LA planned expenditure 2011–12.) Average annual fees at ISC schools in 2011/12 for day pupils attending day schools were £10,860. (Source: Independent Schools Council, ISC Census 2012, p. 22.)

large glass and concrete comprehensive a mile and a half away. We looked at a number of schools, and decided upon Pimlico, for its music, and its diversity. But it now came under Westminster's Conservative-led council. I was roundly criticized by Ken Clarke, Education Secretary, who suddenly elevated Pimlico into a 'top people's comprehensive'.[10] The Tory press jumped in, fuelled by a carefully planned question to John Major at Prime Minister's Questions.[11] This was our first experience of having our children exposed in the press. It was not, sadly, to be the last.

Our children's inner-London experience was leavened by regular trips to watch Blackburn Rovers play. The first game to which I took Will was the final of the Full Members' Cup at Wembley against Charlton Athletic, when he was six.* We won, and he was hooked. Once he was old enough to travel by himself Alice would put him on the train at Euston on a Saturday morning in the care of the guard and I'd collect him at Preston. A few years later, Charlotte joined him. They began a regular ritual, travelling up on a Friday evening after school, to stay at our Blackburn home near the town centre, which we had bought in 1985. Before the game I'd feed them fry-ups and other food which good parents try to avoid. We three would have a great time, and Alice got twenty-four hours' peace. Charlotte wrote a wonderfully evocative essay about attending Rovers' games for her GCSE English course work, which gained her high marks. It's on our kitchen wall in Blackburn.

Starting 'big school' is a daunting prospect for any child. About the same time as the disobliging coverage about our choice of Pimlico School, I arranged for Will to be the mascot at Blackburn Rovers, as a treat to look forward to in his first term.

When the great day arrived – 12 October 1991 – everyone in town

* A competition held in English football from 1985 to 1992 for clubs in the top two divisions following the Heysel stadium disaster and England's ban from European competition.

thought that my choice of date was a fix (it wasn't). For this fixture, against Plymouth Argyle, was the very day that Kenny Dalglish took over as manager, appointed by the new owner, local industrialist Jack Walker, the revered saviour of the club. We won, 5–2. The atmosphere in town was electric. After twenty-five years in lower-league football, and three near-misses in the play-offs for Division One (now the Premier League) we were all walking on air. We were into the Premiership the next season, and won it in 1995. For the children this dream come true could not have happened at a better time. (Though, like all dreams, it had to end sometime; and it has, as we dropped from the Premier League in May 2012.*)

Balancing an active political career with parenting is not easy; each family has to sort out what suits them best. In our case, having our main home so close to the Commons made a big difference, as I frequently popped home to see the children in the early evening, before going back to the Commons for late votes. The old Commons hours, with its formal sessions not beginning until 2.30 p.m., turned out to be remarkably 'family friendly' for us. I was able to take the children to school, attend their school assemblies, and when necessary go to the GP with them, whilst Alice who worked normal hours could get off to the office. But for all the help I gave, Alice was the parent of last resort.

There was one other 'normal' ritual for the children – the annual Dads' Camp in the early summer. This had begun when we camped with my brother Ed, and his slightly older children, when Will was five. By the following year, the camp had expanded to include my other brother, Will, and three other dads and their children, plus my sisters and our mum, a hardy camper. It was a wonderful antidote to our usual lives. The camping, over a long weekend, was very basic – wood fires, earth latrines, tiny tents, lots of folk-singing, little washing, and a fair

* Blackburn Rovers were also in the Championship from 1999–2001.

amount of Scotch. I even insisted on going to this camp for the three summers I was Home Secretary, to the surprise of the detectives.

Without the preoccupations of the miners' strike, and Militant, Neil's period as leader after the election in 1987 felt very different from his first. But he still had to battle hard to introduce some common sense into the party's decisions, not least on the choice of candidates at by-elections.

This lesson took a long time for the party to learn. It was obvious to most of us after Bermondsey in 1983, glaring after our loss of Greenwich in 1986, but it took the disaster of Glasgow Govan at the end of 1988 before the leadership were given proper control over by-election candidates.

Glasgow Govan was one of our safest seats in Scotland. We had won two-thirds of the vote at the 1987 general election. Donald Dewar, Shadow Scottish Secretary, asked me to travel to the by-election to explain the horrors of the latest Thatcherite 'reform' – the replacement of student grants with loans (which, pre-devolution, would extend to Scotland).

Labour's candidate was a Mr Bob Gillespie, a man whose obvious qualifications to be an MP I could not discern, who'd been put on the shortlist as a sentimental favour to one of the print unions.

At the early morning press conference, fresh off the sleeper, I began droning on about the complications of this dreadful Tory loans scheme, complete with mind-numbing statistics. I quickly realized that my audience of hard-boiled Scottish journalists were not paying that deferential attention which my presentation deserved. Indeed, they weren't paying any attention to me or my words, at all. Then my eye caught the tattooed legend on the knuckles of Mr Bob Gillespie, sat next to me. 'H-O-N-G K-O-N-G' , the letters spelt out.

The journalists had noticed too. They had their story.

We lost, of course. There was a 33 per cent swing to the SNP.

In Blackburn, too, the madness had not completely dissipated. Eric

Smith, the redoubtable chairman of the party for a decade and a half, had retired, to be replaced by Martin Guinan, previously active in the Communist Party, and a romantic supporter of the Provisional IRA. We did not appreciate each other. I thought he was a lazy fantasist (he had a habit of taking his holidays just before local elections); he thought me, I think, a soft-skinned revisionist from Essex. He decided to lead a campaign to replace me as MP. He had no complaints about the job I was doing for Blackburn; he simply didn't like me. So he put the party and me through the full reselection process, finding an alternative candidate (from Leeds). At the final reselection meeting my opponent received 12 votes to my 120-plus. I emerged stronger from this, but that was scarcely the point. It was such a waste of everyone's time and effort. I was by no means the only Shadow Cabinet member to be put through this mill.

As the eighties came to a close, the landscape, global and local, changed profoundly.* The demolition of the Berlin Wall in November 1989 presaged not only an end to oppression in eastern Europe, but a collapse of the Marxist–Leninist ideology on which it was based. It was not 'the end of history', but the dramas across the decaying Soviet Empire did represent a categorical victory for the liberal, democratic, capitalist ideology of the West, and the intellectual annihilation of the Communist alternative. With that victory came the chance that here in Britain the Labour movement would no longer uneasily have to straddle the theoretical divide which had so hobbled it since its foundation.

For the Conservatives, the events in the East could not have come at a better time. The beginning of a less polarized world coincided with a new more inclusive brand of Conservatism, personified by John Major, who had taken over from Margaret Thatcher in November 1990 after the bloody palace coup against her. He proved his patriotic mettle

---

* Late 1989 also represented a personal change for me – I was Confirmed in the Church of England, by Bishop Jim Thompson, in the Crypt Chapel, at a service attended by Alice and the children.

in the first Gulf War in 1991 and a year later called the general election for 8 April 1992.

In most respects we were far better prepared for this election than we had been for three decades. There was a high level of professionalism in the party's organization; our policy in most domestic areas (albeit not on crime) was light years from where it had been at the catastrophic 1983 election.

Except, that is, on the critical issue of public spending. In education, for example, our manifesto was promising to invest an extra £600 million over the following twenty-two months. It was all, we claimed, very carefully costed, very precise (note twenty-two months, not twenty-four), but these spending pledges were our Achilles heel. Our collective anxiety to show how credible and responsible we were going to be had the opposite effect. The Tories picked us apart; the electorate were told by Conservative Party chairman Chris Patten that they'd suffer a 'double whammy' of extra taxation under Labour. Michael Heseltine stormed 'Taxes to the left of them. Taxes to the right of them. Into the valley of taxes rode Labour.'[12] We were on the back foot.

The Conservatives and their many allies in the press were utterly determined that they should win; in their pursuit of votes and their denigration of Neil, they gave no quarter, abandoned all scruple.

In 1987 we all knew that we couldn't win, but in 1992 most of us had convinced ourselves that we could. We had some evidence on our side. The polls had us either slightly ahead of the Conservatives, or neck and neck. The overwhelming presumption was that at worst it would be a hung parliament, more likely a Labour victory.

This was the first campaign I'd fought from a senior position in the party. I left Blackburn in the expert care of Bill Taylor and Phil Riley, and set off campaigning around the country with a driver, a minder and a bright young researcher from the construction workers' union, Ben Lucas (whom I poached as soon as the election was over).

It wasn't only Neil who was getting it in the neck from the Conservative press. On the morning of Wednesday 1 April 1992, I awoke in Blackburn to find that I was the *Sun*'s main front-page story. 'I'm All Right Jack' went the headline, above a claim in large type that 'Shadow education minister lectures us on the scandal of private education from the luxury of his £300,000 cottage, his £200,000 town house, and his £40,000 flat!' and three photographs of the evidence of my hypocrisy. We did indeed own three homes. Like most MPs with out-of-London constituencies we had to have two; the third Alice inherited when her mother died in 1986. We felt very fortunate, but it didn't seem to me to make me a hypocrite, as they claimed. But explanations like that weren't going to work. I'd simply have to take it on the chin – as I did a few hours later, at an open-air meeting in Blackburn town centre.

That was the same day as Labour's Sheffield rally, which has gone down in mythology as the single event that lost us the 1992 election. The atmosphere at the rally was surreal, unlike any that I've experienced before or since. It had a dreamlike quality to it, a sense of triumph, of celebration, that we'd already won. Each Shadow Cabinet member was introduced in turn as they made the long walk up the aisle to the platform. When I heard 'Jack Straw, the next Secretary of State for Education' I thought that providence was being tempted, and that providence would teach us a lesson. Neil's opening, an imitation of Mick Jagger ('Well, all right'), wasn't quite the image he, or we, wanted in the man we were presenting as the next prime minister; but Sheffield did not lose us the election. If I'd thought harder, it should have been obvious to me that the enthusiasm for a Labour victory was evaporating.

In between being railed at in Blackburn for my three homes, and my walk-on part at the Sheffield rally, I'd visited the Boston Spa depot of the British Library, and had lunch with some of the staff. Mainly women, these were classic swing voters, whose support we desperately needed. My lunch companions were very polite, but as they spoke they were looking over me, to the side of me, never at me. They weren't going to be with us on polling day.

The ladies in Boston Spa were right; the opinion polls were wrong.

John Major won 14.1 million votes – more than any party before or since (including Labour in 1997), on a high 76 per cent turnout. He had 343 seats, an overall majority of 21. In Blackburn my majority edged up just 500 votes, to 6,000.

Nationally, Labour received 2.5 million votes fewer than the Tories. But that figure – of 11.6 million – was over 3 million more than we'd managed eight years before. Neil Kinnock did save the Labour Party from oblivion. He did cure the party of the virus which had made us unelectable – from the venality of the Militant Tendency to the stupidity which had put Robin Cook out of the Shadow Cabinet. But, after four defeats, as the full results came through in the early morning of Friday 9 April 1992, the only question was: could Labour ever win?*

---

* And to cap it all, as we travelled down to London next morning we were told that our cottage had been comprehensively burgled. It hadn't taken much intelligence for local crooks to calculate we'd be in Blackburn, not there, on election night.

EIGHT

Relics and Reality

The student of politics must therefore seek neither universality nor immortality for his ideas . . . His Holy Grail is the living truth, knowing that being alive the truth must change . . . He must be on his guard against the old words, for the words persist when the reality which lay behind them has changed . . . If this is not understood, we become symbol worshippers. For if [a political party is] out of touch with reality, the masses are not.

ANEURIN BEVAN, *In Place of Fear* (Heinemann, London, 1952)

I floated over Westminster Bridge, and into a Commons Committee Room to learn my fate, in a happy haze. On the NHS, and lawfully, I had been given a cocaine-derivative to help an ENT surgeon see better into my sinuses. As he'd heated the white powder over a small spirit flame, and had me sniff it into my nostrils, I had quizzed this young doctor as to whether it was what I thought it was. He mumbled something incomprehensible, adding 'but the dose is too small to have any effect on you'. He wasn't quite correct about that.

It was the end of July 1992, Shadow Cabinet election results day. The three months after our fourth election defeat in a row had been foul. I and my colleagues from the 'class of '79' now faced the distinction –

unique in Labour's history – of serving for eighteen continuous years in opposition, with not a day in government.

Immediately after the election, for the only time in my life, I had thought seriously about packing politics up altogether. The one silver lining of opposition – a big one – was that I'd been able to see my children without the intense pressures of ministerial office. But I was forty-five. I'd be fifty by the next election. There was no guarantee that we'd win then. Labour was world class only in false dawns. Patrick Carter became so worried that I might abandon my political future just as he felt the market was about to move that in mid-May he bundled me into his car, drove me off to our old haunts (various pubs) in mid-Essex, and talked me out of it. I am deeply grateful to him for this act of friendship, one amongst many. The pall from our defeat did not lift until the end of the year, though, and the change of scene from a two-week trip to India and Pakistan.

It wasn't just the defeat, but the atmosphere in the PLP. It felt as if we were going backwards. The jockeying for Shadow Cabinet places was worse, the deals even tackier than usual.

My reaction to the cocaine derivative was not misplaced. I'd just scraped back, but at least I was there.

I'd been one of the many who had nominated John Smith to replace Neil Kinnock as leader. But my relationship with John was nothing like as close nor as fruitful as it had been with Neil. In place of the big Shadow education job, John gave me two-thirds of the Shadow environment post. It was meant as a demotion, and felt that way.

Fortunately it was the right two-thirds for me (local government, housing and planning). I knew the subjects inside out, and the people too. There was no point sulking. I'd make the best fist I could of it, and hope that my colleagues would notice.

The new post did, however, have one big advantage over education – spare time. I put it to good use.

*

John Smith's debut as leader was made all the easier for him by the disaster for the Major government of Black Wednesday – 16 September 1992 – when Britain had had to withdraw from the Exchange Rate Mechanism (ERM), the fixed exchange rate system by which sterling was pegged to a basket of other European currencies. John Major and his Chancellor Norman Lamont handled this so chaotically that support for the Conservatives – which had remained ahead of Labour for the first five months after the 1992 election – slumped badly, and never recovered over the remainder of the parliament. John Smith was terrific at opposition, a brilliant and very witty debater. He exploited the Tories' discomfort with great skill, and did wonders for Labour's morale. There was, however, no misplaced optimism in Blackburn about the enormity of our electoral challenge nationally. There was serious frustration at our predicament.

At the instigation of Phil Riley, its secretary, the local party decided that it wanted much more than a cursory post-mortem. What was it about the party that put people off? Was it the leadership, was it the policies, was it the values? I agreed to draft a series of papers about our predicament, for debate at party members' meetings.

There were plenty of obvious reasons why we'd lost the election, of which our tax-and-spend policies were the most significant. But, I argued, above and beyond those specific policies, people didn't really understand what we stood for, because we weren't certain ourselves. By September 1992 I'd come to a clear conclusion that we could not win without much greater clarity about our ideology. This wasn't some airy, theoretical optional extra, an indulgence for the intellectuals in the party. Party activists are volunteers; they are willing to devote time and energy because they share that party's beliefs. Keynes was right when he commented 'soon or late, it is ideas, not vested interests, which are dangerous for good or evil'.[1]

Still more important than party supporters were the public. They would not trust us unless they trusted what we stood for, and Labour was saying one thing and doing another. It might present a modern face, but its beliefs were tied by its constitution to one of the most explicit statements of Marxist–Leninist values of any left-wing party in western Europe.

We put this 'statement of values', Clause IV of Labour's constitution, on the front of every membership card. Weren't the public entitled to think it was there for a reason? How could they trust that we weren't going to take into state control all the major sectors of the economy if we got the chance, when the text of Clause IV said that was exactly what we should be doing: 'To secure for the workers by hand or by brain the full fruits of their industry and the most equitable distribution thereof that may be possible upon the basis of the common ownership of the means of production, distribution and exchange, and the best obtainable system of popular administration and control of each industry or service.'[2]

It was no good saying that this very clear commitment effectively to nationalize everything we could didn't matter because we didn't mean it. What kind of people did that make us? And even if we didn't think it mattered, our opponents most certainly did. From the right, the accusation was that Clause IV's continued inclusion in our constitution showed that we still wanted its implementation; we had no fundamental commitment to a mixed economy. From the left the accusation was of betrayal – that we lacked the guts to follow through that to which we had all signed up.

My conclusion was that Clause IV had to be fundamentally recast – a view that was shared by some, though by no means all, in my local party. But what about all those ghosts of attempts past where reform had been tried but had failed?

In the early sixties Hugh Gaitskell had sought to change Clause IV, but had been rebuffed by the unions, the conference and colleagues like Harold Wilson, who described Gaitskell's attempt as 'misconceived both tactically and strategically'.[3] This led to the powerful myth that reform would always flounder, and was more trouble than it was worth. I disagreed. As Gaitskell's biographer Philip Williams spells out, Gaitskell did not prepare the ground properly; he and Douglas Jay bounced the party, with predictable results.[4] More significantly, the ideological landscape had changed completely in the thirty intervening years. In the early sixties, plenty of people, including some in the centre of the political spectrum, continued to be much taken with the Soviet Union's alleged economic and scientific progress, and believed in a very strong role for publicly owned industries in the UK. Three decades later, the Soviet Union had collapsed, and support for more public ownership as the salvation of the British economy was confined to the fringes of politics.

I wasn't part of John Smith's Praetorian Guard. Anything I proposed could not, of itself, lead to decisions by the NEC and the conference. But I might be able to kick-start a debate, if I could make a coherent case for change, which I decided to do in a pamphlet.

As Clause IV had become encased in mythology, it had been transmogrified from a prosaic statement of values reflecting the spirit of its time, into a shibboleth – and, for some, it might as well have been graven into tablets of stone. If my project was to get anywhere I had to demystify Clause IV. To do this, I needed to look at its history.

I spent many days in the archives of the party. I learnt that Clause IV's authors were not from the high-priesthood of socialism, but a group led by Labour leader Arthur Henderson, Ramsay MacDonald and the Fabian, Sydney Webb. Representatives from the more left-leaning Independent Labour Party (ILP) were excluded altogether from the drafting.

State control was in the air. The success of Lloyd George's coalition government in the second half of the Great War was widely attributed to what the *Manchester Guardian* had called 'war socialism'. Churchill had said that he wanted the government to 'accept wholeheartedly the path of [the] necessity [of state control]'.[5] There was considerable excitement in Labour circles about the success of the Russian Revolution.

The greatest revelation was that Clause IV was a second-order issue. There were four national conferences of the Labour Party held in 1918 (three whilst the war was still on). In the extensive party record, and the newspaper reports, Clause IV wasn't mentioned once. What dominated proceedings was power – which of the internal organs of the party should have it, and how much.

I sent John Smith the rather prolix first draft of my pamphlet, in mid-September 1992. It was followed by a call on a Sunday afternoon that is still so vivid that I can recall exactly where I was standing when I took it. I had thought that, at worst, John would think there was no harm in having me test the water. He didn't believe a word of Clause IV. He'd told me as much. In his eyes, I was expendable. I knew that too. If my little effort failed, there'd be no backwash on him; if it succeeded, it would open the door for him. But John told me vehemently that I was wrong, from beginning to end. I would stir up a hornet's nest ('look at what had happened to Gaitskell'). I'd damage my own political standing, and very possibly lose my seat on the Shadow Cabinet the following year (a prospect he viewed with equanimity). Asked by me, again, whether he agreed with Clause IV, he replied, 'No, but it should be allowed to wither on the vine.' It was a 'sentimental souvenir, best ignored'.

One reason why John simply didn't see the problem with Clause IV was that his political roots were in the Scottish Labour Party. It was plain from my conversations with him that people in his Monklands constituency, in industrial west Scotland, weren't in the least bothered by the old wording of Clause IV. However, for many people in Lancashire, as well as in my home county of Essex, it was a serious impediment. Unlike many Scots, John seemed unwilling to understand this. I always felt that he had a hauteur towards the English, born of the Auld Alliance.

I told him that I did not agree, and would press on. I was convinced that this, and other key reforms, were essential if we were ever to get back into government.

After four months of further research, and much redrafting, I now turned my ideas into the final draft of a pamphlet, with the arresting title 'Policy and Ideology'. Neil Kinnock gave me considerable assistance, particularly on the wording of a new Clause IV.* Tony Blair gave me much private support, but he was too close to John to break ranks with him publicly, which I wholly understood. I posted the draft to John, and arranged to see him in the Opposition Leader's room in the Commons.

On the evening of Wednesday 11 May 1994, John Smith presided at a Labour Party gala dinner in the banqueting hall of a Park Lane hotel. None of us who were present will ever forget the closing words of his speech that night: 'The opportunity to serve our country. That is all we ask.'

John never got that chance. He died the following morning, after a massive heart attack, aged fifty-eight. The mourning for his loss across the United Kingdom was profound.

John is rightly remembered with very great affection. He showed unbreakable loyalty to his friends. He loved the Labour Party; his affection for Parliament knew no bounds. My own relationship with him had much improved in the last year of his life. My shock at his death, my grief at his passing, was no less deep than that of my colleagues.

I therefore write this next passage with some trepidation. Unfortunately, I saw another side to him. It led me to worry, as it did an increasing number of my colleagues, whether he had the character needed to sustain him as prime minister.

My meeting with John about my pamphlet took place in mid-January 1993. It lasted for over an hour. He was in a dark mood. He railed at me. He repeated the argument he'd made to me on the phone in September that I'd be stirring up a hornet's nest. I responded that the party – and he – had to have the confidence to acknowledge that what was right in October 1917 wasn't necessarily right seventy-five years later. He predicted again, with certainty (and no displeasure in his

---

* My draft and the one finally agreed by the Conference in April 1995 were in substance very similar.

voice) that if I went ahead with my pamphlet I'd lose my seat on the Shadow Cabinet. He demanded that I dropped it. I refused. I told him that if I did lose my Shadow Cabinet seat 'so be it'. I'd had enough of opposition. If we didn't change, we couldn't win.

John then lost his temper. My father used to lose his temper like this. My response then, as now with John, was to close down. I sought to take my leave. 'You can take this with you, too,' he shouted, as he threw the envelope containing the pamphlet at me.

I left. Two months later the Blackburn Labour Party published my pamphlet. As Phil Riley, the secretary, and John Roberts, the chair, made clear in their introduction, the text was mine alone. (We knew it would stir up debate in Blackburn too.) But none of John's predictions (and my fears) that it would be terminal for my career came to pass. In the Shadow Cabinet election later that year my vote went up. The following year I was elected to the Constituency Section of the NEC.

Most of the press gave it a good reception. Predictably, *The Times*, which had been highly critical of John's leadership, wrote an editorial in my support. More significantly, came endorsement from the *Guardian*'s Will Hutton, and from *Tribune*'s political commentator Hugh Macpherson, who wrote that my pamphlet was 'the best contribution that has so far emerged to a necessary debate', and praised me for 'the sheer guts to lay it on the line'. I was extremely relieved. It had been very lonely, preparing the pamphlet in such a hostile atmosphere, with so many colleagues who privately agreed with me keeping their heads below the parapet.

Eighteen months later, Tony Blair had the courage to lead a major recasting of Clause IV as one of his first acts of leadership. It was vital to our regaining the trust of the British people, as election studies subsequently showed.[6]

In his sympathetic biography of John Smith, Mark Stuart quotes Roy Hattersley as saying: 'John Smith hasn't changed his mind on anything since he was seven years old.'[7] For all his wit and charm, John was fearful of new ideas; his loss of control when I sought to persuade him that it might be safe to change something he didn't even want, was alarming. Towards the end of 1993, concern about John's caution surfaced in the Shadow Cabinet, and was filtering out to the press, too.

John was a curious paradox. He had immense inner confidence, but he lacked courage. He appeared almost uninterested in that crucial role of any leader, to see over the horizon, and take people there.

My encounter with a very angry John revealed to me something else about him which would I think have made it difficult for him had he become prime minister.

In *Back from the Brink*, Alistair Darling, an intimate friend of John, gives a clue: 'John Smith was a good man but he lived hard.'[8] Tony Blair, also a close friend, is more explicit: '[John Smith] was . . . a stupendous toper. He could drink in a way that I have never seen before or since. I don't mean he would ever be in drink when he needed to be sober – he was the complete professional – but if there was an Olympic medal for drinking, John would have contended with such superiority that after a few rounds the rest of the field would have simply shaken their heads and banished themselves from the track.'[9]

I observed John's 'Olympic' drinking too. The caveat I'd add to Tony's observation is that it is not possible for someone that dependent on alcohol to determine, in advance, 'when he needed to be sober'.

Whilst I'd moved away from education policy with the 1992 election, I had moved into the sharp end of education practice – as a Governor, and later Chairman of the Governors, of our children's school, Pimlico.

Pimlico was never the 'top people's comprehensive' as Ken Clarke had so extravagantly claimed.* On his third day at the school, William was threatened with a knife. We spent the afternoon at Rochester Row police station. Nonetheless it was a special place; an illustration that

---

* Its GCSE results were around the national average.

ILEA (for all the reservations I'd had about it) was never intent on a 'one-size-fits-all' uniformity.

Pimlico was a specialist school, well ahead of its time. It had a 'special music course' for fifteen pupils in each year, selected for their musical ability and potential. Those pupils benefited greatly (our younger child, Charlotte was on the course), but so did the school as a whole, in two ways. Music permeated the school. More significantly, the course was an incentive for more middle-class parents to commit themselves to the school. A socially wide intake is not an essential requirement for a school to be successful, but it certainly can help.

The school had been well led. The Chairman of the Governors was Ashley Bramall, an old friend from my ILEA days, dedicated to the school. A new head took over as our eldest Will enrolled in September 1991. But she could not cope at the school. Ashley, then 75, retired as chairman; his replacement resigned after a year or so because he said he could not work with the head. I agreed to take over. I then found myself having to manage an increasingly difficult situation, as relations between the head, her staff, and the pupils began to get to danger point. The school's GCSE science results were unsatisfactory.

At the beginning of 1995 all the governors bar one concluded that it would be in the school's best interests if the head were to resign. For legal reasons, the local authority could not agree to us taking this action. I therefore issued a final warning to the head instead. Six months of disruption to the life of the school then followed. In late November 1995 good order and discipline broke down over the head's treatment of a black senior teacher, who was effective in his job and admired by pupils. I had to suspend the head and, over Christmas, write a lengthy statement as to why the governors considered that they had no alternative but to dismiss her. She never returned to work and resigned in the spring of 1996. We then appointed her much-respected deputy, Phil Barnard. Gradually, the school got back on its feet; and then, for a period, began to do really well.

Will gained a place at Oxford to read politics, philosophy, and economics (PPE). Charlotte went to Manchester University's Medical School and is now a medical registrar.

I stayed on as Chairman of the Governors during my first two years as Home Secretary and I've never regretted the time I spent on the Governing Body. It was very hard work. It showed me the critical importance to a school of the quality of its leadership – professional and lay – and that there is never a moment when you can lose your focus on standards.

After my first four years in Parliament, sharing an 'elegant Gothic slum' with three others, I had decided to trade space for convenience. I had taken a room on my own in the former Scotland Yard building for eight years. At the end of 1991 a much better, newly refurbished building had become available, 1 Parliament Street. Half the Shadow Cabinet piled into the second floor. There was Gordon Brown, with so many staff that they had to hot-desk; Mo Mowlam, whose floor was littered with her underwear, and who might, if you were unlucky, suddenly decide in the middle of a conversation, to change some of it; Robin Cook in an eyrie up a little flight of stairs; and Tony Blair, and Donald Dewar opposite. To add to the entertainment, there were occasional sorties to our floor from John Prescott, who occupied a large garret two floors above.

Our proximity gave me a chance to become much better acquainted with many of my key colleagues. The atmosphere was pretty sociable, but it was already possible to discern that behind the close friendship which Tony and Gordon had, there were tensions.

When the two of them had entered the Commons in 1983, it was Tony who was the junior partner. Tony had only just got involved in politics. Gordon had been active for over a decade. It was Gordon who gave Tony assistance with his speeches, not the other way round.

But Tony was at least as ambitious as Gordon (and, as events would show, with greater justification). There was only going to be room for one at the very top of the party. You could see them eyeing each other.

When John Smith died, I was in no doubt that the man to replace him was Tony; Mo felt the same. We both told him, though he needed no persuasion. A few days later, Tony asked me to be his campaign manager, his explanation being that since I was from neither his nor Gordon's camp this broadened his appeal with the party. I readily accepted, and worked very happily with Mo, Anji Hunter and Roz Preston, an old friend who had married one of Alice's first boyfriends. Tony was a star. The campaign was very straightforward. He won over-whelmingly – among MPs, party members, and trade unionists – with an overall vote of 57 per cent.

Tony's election as leader changed my political fortunes completely. I moved from having two-thirds of a second-order job, to having one of the biggest jobs in the Shadow Cabinet, and the one which he'd held from the 1992 election – Shadow Home Secretary.

There now began one of the most intellectually productive periods of my three decades in politics. I assembled a terrific front-bench team: Alun Michael, George Howarth and Kim Howells, and staff who worked together like a dream: Norman Warner, Barbara Castle's principal private secretary, who had moved from the Civil Service, to be social services director in Kent; Ruth Allan, a former probation officer who'd been with Tony's team; Alex Cole (now head of public affairs for Sainsbury's); Ed Owen, former journalist, who was to stay with me for twelve years altogether, on media; and Sue Peters, my wonderfully spiky PA who kept us all together. In Blackburn, my long-serving secretary Anne Higginson capably managed the increasing load of constituency cases.

I covered the waterfront of Home Affairs, from hard crime through to human rights. Tony insisted that all policies were stress-tested, properly thought through. But I was also able to go in for some private enterprise. In the early years of this parliament, I became very worried by a cultural change amongst newspaper editors to downgrade their coverage of Parliament. They blamed this on a shift in readers' attitudes, but they had scant evidence. It was rather a reflection of their institutional arrogance. I asked a young intern, Benjamin Wegg-Prosser, son of one of my closest friends, Stephen, to spend days in the newspaper library at Colindale measuring the shift in coverage over the previous sixty years (literally, with a ruler), and we published the results.[10] I continued to pursue this concern, but without much success.

I made greater progress with another obsession of mine – numbers. Maths was my best subject at O level. I have very few regrets about the way my life has worked out; but given a magic wand, I'd have done maths – and Arabic – at university (and then done a conversion course to enable me to be a lawyer). One of the many great delights of fatherhood was opening the children's imagination to the wonderful world of numbers. I know that I'm an anorak. Engaged on a necessary but tedious task – like swimming forty lengths – I'll calculate prime numbers in my head.

For many, maybe most, numbers are not as friendly as I find them. They are, however, the currency of modern politics. Truthful statistics on which everyone can rely are as fundamental to a properly operating democracy as reliable money. Yet there was real concern, going far beyond the Labour Party, that many of our official statistics could not be trusted. The professional statisticians were trustworthy enough; but the definitions they had to use kept changing, through ministerial fiat, most notoriously with the eighteen changes in unemployment statistics between 1979 and 1997.

I'd got to know the highly qualified statisticians in the Commons Library Research Division very well over the previous fifteen years. With them I developed detailed policies to place our national statistical service on an independent footing. I presented these in a lecture to the Royal Statistical Society (RSS). We made a commitment in our 1997 manifesto. Ten years, and a number of reforms later, we'd done all that we'd promised. Our currency of national statistics is now gold standard. In a lovely touch, the RSS made me an honorary fellow.

It was a heady, exciting period. But in mid-October 1995 I was involved in a self-inflicted train wreck. It was nearly terminal. Everyone else has forgotten it. I never will, but I did learn from it.

Michael Howard was very different from his Conservative predecessors as Home Secretary. From Willie Whitelaw through to Ken Clarke, they had taken the complacent view that there was nothing very much they could do about crime; they bought into the conventional wisdom that sentencing and enforcement were unlikely to make much difference. They had presided over a dreadful reorganization of the prosecution service, and had taken no measures to end the indifferent way in which victims were treated by the system.

As Shadow Home Secretary, Tony took the Tories to the cleaners over crime. His promise to be 'tough on crime, and tough on the causes of crime', his empathetic handling of the public horror at the killing of Jamie Bulger had put the Tories on the back foot. For the first time for decades, we were ahead of them on law and order.

Howard was determined to halt the Tories' slide. He was ambitious too. When he became Home Secretary in May 1993 he began to shake up the Home Office. Among many other changes, he refused to make another internal appointment to head the Prison Service, and instead appointed a complete outsider as Director General, Derek Lewis, who had began his career at Ford Motor Company. He also set out to give the director general much greater autonomy. In future, he as Home Secretary would be 'accountable' only for the service; it would be the director general who would be 'responsible'.

But relations between Howard and Lewis deteriorated. Three Category A inmates (i.e. the most dangerous) escaped from the high security prison, Parkhurst. There was a full-scale inquiry, which was highly critical of the Prison Service's management. Howard decided to sack Derek Lewis. A row blew up over the fate of the governor of Parkhurst, John Marriott. He was dismissed. The question was whether Howard had had any hand in this.

With the passage of years all this sounds complicated, important to those involved, but hardly earth-shattering. At the time it was the major story, dominating the news.

Derek Lewis had, wisely, become a member of the senior civil

servants' union – the First Division Association (FDA). Its general
Secretary, Liz Symons, was well plugged into New Labour. She was
a friend of Jonathan Powell, Tony's chief of staff, and later became a
Labour peer, and an excellent FCO minister when I was Foreign
Secretary. With information fed through Liz, we stirred things up. But
we made one mistake, which I then compounded.

When a minister is in trouble like this, the best thing to do is to let
the issue play out; keep skirmishing, call for inquiries, help the press in
their pursuits of the quarry. The worst thing to do is to try to bring
matters to a head. Almost always the Opposition – which by definition
is not going to be in full command of the facts (or even in possession
of many of them) – will fall flat on its face. This is what had happened
over Westland in 1986.*[11]

Forgetting this, we called a full-scale debate for Thursday 19 October
1995. The motion was prosaic enough – it simply deplored Howard's
'unwillingness to accept responsibility for serious operational failures
of the Prison Service'.[12] But it was regarded by everyone as a censure on
the government, a high-profile occasion.

In the twenty-four hours before the debate I'd been promised by the
FDA all sorts of documentary proof to support our case. This was still
arriving by fax two hours before the start of the debate, and did not live

---

* The Westland affair in 1985–86 concerned the future of the British helicopter
industry. There was a major split in the Thatcher government, with the then
Defence Secretary Michael (now Lord) Heseltine arguing that Westland, Britain's
last remaining helicopter manufacturer, should be integrated with British
Aerospace and the Italian helicopter company Augusta, whilst the Industry
Secretary Leon (now Lord) Brittan argued for a merger with Sikorsky, the leading
US company. The split turned sour when first Heseltine, then Brittan, leaked sensitive internal documents; Margaret Thatcher's poor handling provoked the biggest
crisis in her first seven years as premier. About to face a critical Labour motion,
she predicted that if the debate went badly this would have been her last day as
Prime Minister. She was saved by a less than scintillating performance by opposition leader Neil Kinnock.

up to its promise. If I wasn't going into the Chamber naked, I certainly wasn't fully dressed. The speech I'd drafted was too lawyerly. What I should have done, and fatally did not do, was sufficiently prepare for the hostile interventions from the government side which their whips would have been carefully preparing for me. The Tories were determined from the moment I stood up to unsettle me. They did. The noise levels rose, and so did my tinnitus.

Five minutes into my speech came the missile I should have predicted. Bernard Jenkin (now chairman of the Public Administration Committee) asked me a simple question: did I think that Derek Lewis should have been dismissed? I hesitated. I gave a correct answer – that the issue was not whether Lewis should have been dismissed, but the responsibility of Michael Howard to the House. But it was the wrong answer, and really stupid of me. I should have said, 'No, not on the information we have.' I lost the House. I struggled through the rest of my speech, to mounting uproar.

In reply, Howard turned in a vintage performance. My discomfort was made worse when, unusually, Tony decided to intervene – he was right to do so, but the implication was that my efforts hadn't quite been up to the mark.

The reports of the debate were merciless. I thought that my time on the front bench was at an end. I was in a heap. Alice took me off to our house in Oxfordshire. After a rest, I decided I'd better work out – and quickly – how to rehabilitate myself. Tony called, and saw me at the beginning of the following week. He was wholly supportive, telling me that he had been worked over in a debate against Norman Tebbit; it wasn't pleasant, he got over it, so would I; and he had full confidence in me (a kindness for which I have been eternally grateful). I took sage advice from Peter Riddell of *The Times*, a friend first, journalistic contact second. Dennis Skinner told me that I'd get through it provided my next speech (the following week, on asylum) was a humdinger. I made sure it was, and over the weeks that followed the memory of this dreadful day faded – except for me. Never again, no matter how difficult the subject matter, did I ever have that truly terrifying sense that I was drowning. I made sure I was always on top of my brief. At the suggestion of a constituent of my friend Giles Radice, I also began to take voice lessons with a terrific coach, Yvonne Morley, whose day job was working with actors.

The experience made me a better minister, but the method is not one I'd recommend.

John Major had to run his government right to the buffers of the maximum five years and one month allowed by law for any parliament. In my area, as in many others, we were very well prepared. Most in the party thought that what would win the election for us, alongside Tony's obvious appeal as a leader, was what we were saying on economic and social policy, and on law and order. But there were some who thought that a key to our success would be the fate of the fox.

I have never hunted in my life. I had no natural sympathy for those who did, ever since Alice and I, with an unhappy William, aged six months, in the back of the car, had got caught in a rural traffic jam caused by a hunt. When we asked them to let us through we were met with stupefying arrogance. I hadn't even ridden a horse until I was forty, when, staying at our house in Oxfordshire, we all decided to take up riding, and I got hooked. But well before that I had had an instinct that the idea of banning fox hunting was nonsense, and as a party we should have nothing to do with it. It was something for backbenchers to pursue, not for a serious party of government.

In the run-up to the election there was a pantomime, as I tried to keep any reference to fox hunting out of the manifesto; others to put one in. The result was a barmy compromise, by which the manifesto – all about the future – used the past tense 'We have advocated new measures to promote animal welfare, including a free vote in Parliament on whether hunting with hounds should be banned by legislation.' I spent the following four years as Home Secretary doing my best to ensure that we were not derailed by the issue. This was what Tony had asked me to do, over and over again. Then he appeared for a solo performance on *Question Time*. Asked whether he'd be supporting the Private Members' bill to ban hunting, he replied 'Yes.' I went to see him the next day to ask him why. 'I'm very sorry, Jack, I misspoke.' Somehow, I managed to navigate round this infelicity, and established an official inquiry under the former head of the Treasury, Sir Terry Burns. This bought us time. When I came to make an Oral Statement on the inquiry's report, I could barely get the words out, for giggling at this paragraph: 'There is a lack of firm scientific evidence about the effect on the welfare of a fox of being closely pursued, caught and killed above ground by hounds. We are satisfied, nevertheless, that this experience seriously compromises the welfare of the fox.'[13]

The fox played no serious part in our success in 1997. It was Tony's leadership which did, and his determination to jettison worn-out old policies for ones which would make a difference to people's lives. 'In each area of policy a new and distinctive approach has been mapped out, one that differs from the old left and the Conservative right. This is why new Labour is new', the manifesto proclaimed.

For most, the result of the election seemed a foregone conclusion, But after eighteen years in opposition, I could not believe, that we might win. At 10 p.m. on election night the exit polls had us down for a landslide. Allowing for every possible polling error, we had won. Yet when my brother Ed said 'Well done Johnny, you're going to be Home Secretary,' I turned on him in a fit of extraordinary bad behaviour, refusing to celebrate until the votes were counted.

NINE

Life in the Graveyard

Just remember, Jack, as Home Secretary, there'll be fifty sets of officials working on schemes to undermine your government and destroy your political career; and the worst is, not only will you not know who they are, but neither will they.

RT HON. KENNETH (NOW LORD) BAKER, Home Secretary 1990–2

In politics, every day is filled with numerous opportunities for serious error. Enjoy it.

DONALD RUMSFELD (former White House chief of staff and US Defense Secretary), 'Rumsfeld's Rules'[1]

'I'm making your dad Home Secretary,' Tony Blair told William and Charlotte. It was Friday 2 May 1997. Tony had just won Labour's biggest-ever landslide.

My Labour 'minder', Ed Owen, never short on chutzpah, had spirited the children in through the back door of 10 Downing Street. They were waiting, wide-eyed, in the lobby outside the Cabinet Room.

Within seconds of my appointment, two detectives emerged. The children were whisked home. Ed and I were put into an old armoured Jaguar ('Mrs Thatcher's, sir; seen better days') and taken off to the headquarters of the Home Office, Basil Spence's concrete mausoleum which looked and felt like a Soviet-era Ministry of the Interior.

I was met there by the permanent secretary, Sir Richard Wilson, and Ken Sutton, who had been Michael Howard's principal private secretary until a few hours earlier, and who would be mine for the next two years. Kenneth Baker's gypsy warning was already ricocheting around my brain when Richard invited me to look out of the window of my seventh-floor office.

'What do you see?' he asked.

'A clear blue sky,' I replied.

'Dangerous,' said Richard ominously. 'Just remember – in your job, you can never be sure when an Exocet will come straight out of a clear blue sky and' – pointing at my feet – 'explode right there.'

The Home Office is correctly regarded as a graveyard for ambitious politicians. In the last two decades, Home Secretaries have, on average, lasted just two years. One private secretary, Stephen Harrison, later produced a list of the eighty-five Home Secretaries since the founding of the department in 1782, in order of their length of service. As I came into the office each Monday morning he'd tell me my latest ranking. Getting from eighty-fifth to eighty-fourth was easy – the Earl Temple lasted just four days in late 1793. But I was relieved as I moved further up the order. In politics, the first rule is to survive.

The Civil Service spends the run-up to a general election preparing 'Briefs for Incoming Ministers'. Civil servants were well aware that Labour's tribal suspicion of them had been compounded by our eighteen years in opposition. They also knew that there were going to be very few ministers who had had any executive experience, in any capacity. So the Whitehall machine was well prepared for us.

I was presented with six bespoke ring binders: 'A guide to the Home Office', 'The first fortnight', 'The first three months', 'Constitutional issues', 'Europe' and 'Background briefs'. These had been put together by Clare Sumner, a young press officer. They so impressed me that a couple of months later I appointed Clare as one of my private secretaries, despite the fact that she was 'only' an information officer, and not a member of the high-priesthood of the Civil Service fast-stream. (She has gone on to a stellar career.)

The Home Secretary's office was a rectangular room, covering the whole of one floor, with windows on three sides, and nothing to recommend it apart from the view. It had no desk; just a large oval table at the end furthest from the door. The Home Secretary's chair was the only one with arms. The ministerial lift gave separate access into the room, which had its own private bathroom. Everything had been designed so that the Home Secretary could avoid all unnecessary contact with mere mortals.

We're all different. I'm a fidget. I need to move around and I love talking to people.

Alone in my huge room, I came to something in the briefs which needed clarification. I walked into the Private Office. All fifteen staff stood up. I assumed that this was simply an initial courtesy. Twenty minutes later, I popped into the Private Office for a second time, and they all stood up again. I appreciated the gesture, as I told them, but I also said that they'd never get any work done if they continued like this; the practice was abandoned forthwith.

Michael Howard, whom I have come to know better since we both left the Home Office, is more private than me. His preference had been to remain in his room, summoning private secretaries by phone if he needed them. In the wake of the Derek Lewis affair relations between Michael and his senior officials had become pretty stiff and they were reluctant to disagree with him.

Conscious of this, I now told them all that whilst I would be the one making the decisions, and would expect them loyally to implement what I had decided, I wanted people to speak up, and argue with me, especially if they felt that I was about to fall over the edge of a cliff. If I wanted a room full of people who simply agreed with me, I could easily buy a machine which repeated 'Yes, Home Secretary, you are right.'

Afterwards, brain dead with tiredness, I went home to a little party which Alice had organized with a group of our closest friends. When we then took the children out for a quick meal, the reality of living with protection kicked in. The detectives came too, as they were to do for the next thirteen years.

In the morning, as I headed off for a full day in the office, Alice suggested that I thank the officials for giving up their weekend. I was so spaced out I had no idea it was a Saturday. In between rafts of meetings the members of the Cabinet went to Buckingham Palace to be sworn in as members of the Privy Council and given our seals of office. We were all on a high. Afterwards the Queen remarked that a dog (David Blunkett's) had never attended this ceremony before. Donald Dewar, the new Scottish Secretary, quickly replied 'Ah, ma'am; every dog has its day.'

One of the four Great Offices of State, up there with the prime minister, the Treasury and the Foreign Office, the Home Office's activities originally focused on the internal government of the United Kingdom, especially the maintenance of law and order. As Britain became a more complex, industrialized society in the nineteenth century, its remit expanded; later, various other departments were spun from it.* Despite this, the Home Office was still a mammoth department. Its core business remained maintaining the Queen's Peace. That meant responsibility for the police, prison, probation and fire services, immigration and asylum, sentencing and criminal justice policy, and the Security Service. But the Home Office prided itself on not being a Ministry of the Interior on the Continental model. It had duties on the other side of the equation, of balancing power with freedom, order with liberty, of having consciously to limit

---

* These included responsibilities for control of military forces, colonial business, Scotland, Wales, health, roads, mining, and broadcasting. A separate Northern Ireland Office was not created until 1972. (National Archive records.)

the power of the state which it had to enforce. So it was also responsible for human rights, race and community relations and data protection.

'Tough on crime, tough on the causes of crime' was a critical part of my agenda. But so was securing people's human and civic rights, not least those protecting them from the overweening power of the state. I'd been thinking about how to achieve the proper balance here ever since I'd got Leeds to be the first student union to affiliate to the NCCL, the forerunner of Liberty. The right to a quiet life, to freedom from crime, and prejudice, is fundamental to our ability to exercise our positive freedoms. I wanted to make a difference: to reduce the number of people whose lives were disrupted by crime, but also to do all I could on a socially liberal agenda, to make it much easier for black and Asian people, for gay and lesbian people – and for women – to live their lives to the full.

The Home Office also had an extraordinary, and rather eccentric, range of other functions, among them gambling, horse racing (including the Tote, and National Stud), alcohol licensing and coroners courts. But there were less well-known ones, too, which made up a handy couple of paragraphs to warm up any speech: hypnotism, falling satellites, and at paragraph 19d of the *Distribution of Business Manual* 'across Whitehall, random miscellaneous correspondence which makes no sense whatsoever'.

That first weekend I had two immediate tasks. One was to digest the six volumes of briefs, to ensure that the department was in a position to implement the extensive Home Affairs programme in the manifesto.

The second was to welcome my team of ministers and special advisers. Most came straight from the excellent team I'd built up in opposition. Alun Michael was to be my deputy, covering crime and the police. He'd had huge experience as both a youth worker and a magistrate in Cardiff, and had spearheaded our ideas for local authorities to work in partnership with the police in fighting crime and disorder. Joyce Quin, the very bright, multilingual MP for Gateshead, would cover prisons and probation; my close friend George Howarth* prisons, gambling, drugs, and his own passion, horse racing; and Mike O'Brien, an experienced lawyer who'd won his marginal North Warwickshire seat in 1992, on immigration, nationality, and race and community relations. Gareth Williams, QC (Lord Williams of Mostyn), one of the most brilliant criminal silks of his time, took on constitutional affairs as a parliamentary secretary but a year later, when Joyce moved, was promoted into her post as Minister of State. Gareth was one of the wittiest people I have ever met. During his two short years as Leader of the Lords before his tragic and untimely death from a heart attack in 2003, aged sixty-two, he used to have Cabinet in tears of laughter as he reported on proceedings in the Upper House.

In the two decades since my pioneering days as one of the first ever 'special advisers', Whitehall had got more used to this hybrid breed, and knew better how to embrace them. I brought in Ed Owen to cover media relations and the 'guile and low cunning' aspects of the work, a role once filled, as special adviser to Michael Howard, by David Cameron, and Norman Warner (later Lord Warner) to cover many policy areas on which he had worked in the closing years of opposition.

Beyond that, I didn't have to choose a senior team. In contrast to the American system, in the UK civil servants stay at their desks, transferring their allegiance seamlessly from their old boss to their new one. Unlike some of my colleagues, I never had the least doubt about of the loyalty of the staff I inherited. They were terrific, and I've remained friends with many of them.

Although it was significant, I was well prepared for the overnight change in my working life. I knew all the subject areas intimately, and relished the prospect, after eighteen years in the shadows, of being able

---

* I'd first met George when acting as his minder for the Knowsley North by-election in 1986.

to do the real thing. This change was, however, as nothing compared to the profound change that engulfed my private and family life.

In addition to his warning about officials inadvertently working to undermine me, Kenneth Baker had given me one other piece of excellent advice in the closing months of the Major government. He told me that we would be put under immense pressure to move into the Home Secretary's secure house (in Belgravia). As we had a family, we should resist it at all costs. The security people would advance all kinds of reasons why we had to move; but if we dug in they'd make our own homes secure instead.

He was right. Shortly before the election, eight men, police officers and security experts, came to our home in Kennington and tried to 'persuade' Alice that we would have to move. As a senior civil servant, Alice was used to operating in a man's world but even she found this meeting intimidating. In the end, they gave up, and began to lay in the plans. Our three houses were almost taken to bits, as bullet-proof windows, fire and intruder alarms, and panic buttons for every room were installed. In Blackburn, the police decided that they would occupy the ground floor (which we'd previously let out as a small office), and partition off our living quarters on the two upper floors. At our Oxfordshire house, our neighbours were entertained on the weekend after the election as a huge crane lowered an armoured hut, with a kitchen and loo behind, into the garden. A photograph of this manoeuvre, graphically symbolizing the change of power, appeared in newspapers around the world.*

In London, there was, thankfully, neither space inside for a police room, nor room outside for an armoured hut. Instead, two armed uniformed officers were stationed in our little square. For the next thirteen years, in place of the two cups of tea I'd been programmed to make first

---

* *The Times*, 5 May 1997, 'Merry-go-round as new ministers select their ideal homes from home – the new government.' Valerie Elliott and Richard Ford.

thing, I made four. All over London I still bump into police officers who remember my tea.

It's hard being a teenager in almost any circumstances. My children were inner-London kids, at an inner-London comprehensive. They didn't want to be different. Suddenly, however hard we tried, they were. There were police officers either outside the front door, in the garden, or in the house itself. Not only that, but plain-clothed armed close protection officers from the Special Branch were with their dad whenever he stepped outside the house – in the car, on a train, just walking down the street. These Special Branch officers were professional, discreet, and sensitive to the family's needs. It was nothing like as hard as the intrusion into our private lives from the press, as we were to discover with a vengeance seven months later. But it was still tough, especially on Alice and the children.

For my first post-election weekend in Blackburn, Will and Charlotte came too, to watch the last game of the season against Leicester City. They decided that now my salary had doubled, it was time for me to get rid of all the embarrassing 'naff' clothes I wore, and re-stock my wardrobe. So it was off to Next, a store that I had never frequented before. Charlotte was giving me 'advice' about what trousers to buy when she suddenly turned to me and said, 'Where's he gone, Dad?'

'Who are you talking about? Who's gone?'

'Him, you know, that detective. He was here seconds ago. Now he's gone.'

This particular detective had spent years on surveillance for the Special Branch, sometimes in dangerous circumstances. He was brilliant about being present, but not being noticed. 'I've found him, Dad!' Charlotte announced after a search. 'He's lurking behind the jackets.' I realized that though she found the police an intrusion, she was also anxious about my safety. I was touched, but it's not the sort of burden a fourteen-year-old should have to bear.

*

Before the election, the Civil Service had worked up the detailed policy statements published over the previous eighteen months into submissions and instructions to Parliamentary Counsel on drafting legislation. None of this would be of much consequence unless I could ensure that the Queen's Speech, to be made on the State Opening of the new parliament just two weeks after the election, contained as many Home Office commitments as I could muscle into the programme. Fortunately, their importance to the government's overall programme meant that I had no difficulty doing this.

Pride of place went to the Crime and Disorder Bill, which was much more than just a series of specific legislative changes to the criminal justice system. We were attempting to transform the whole philosophy of thousands of practitioners. All these professionals were ground down by a seemingly relentless rise in crime and social fracture, and by convoluted process. I had to raise their ambitions, get them signed up, and give them the tools to do the job.

The bill laid the foundation for 'tough on crime, tough on the causes of crime' approach, which Labour followed during our thirteen years in government. With a 40 per cent reduction in crime in that period – the first sustained reduction in crime during any post-war administration – it is one of Labour's most positive and enduring legacies.[2]

The bill changed the youth justice system from top to bottom, with a national Youth Justice Board and local youth offending teams bringing police and social services together for the first time, youth intervention panels, and a raft of new orders, including parenting orders. The aim was to combine an effective strategy for dealing with some of the underlying causes of youth crime with a no-nonsense attitude where serious correction of a young offender's behaviour was needed.

There's little comment these days about the youth justice system. The Conservatives tried, but failed, to abolish the Youth Justice Board, but the system has been a success and the reforms worked in large part because of the way they were developed. I set up a task force (led by Hilary Jackson, a very sparky woman who would later become my principal private secretary), involved the professionals from the start, and piloted many of the changes.

Alun Michael's plans to ensure that local authorities and the police had to work with each other to reduce crime and disorder went into the bill. This now sounds pretty prosaic, but it was not seen that way at the time. It brought the police and local councils back together after the quarter of a century in which they had drifted apart; in some areas, as a deliberate act of policy by police chiefs anxious to preserve their autonomy, and wary of partisan interference by local politicians.

For me, the bill presented an opportunity to make a start on what would become a major theme of my time as Home Secretary – measures to attack racism in all its forms. New 'racially aggravated' offences were introduced, with tougher sentences.

There were new orders governing sex offenders and drug treatment and testing. The latter, which drew on US experience, was the first part of a major programme to help that large majority of offenders whose drug addiction drove their criminality to kick both habits.

In opposition I'd done a lot of work looking at how the sentencing practices of the courts could be made more consistent, and predictable. In his 1995 conference speech as Home Secretary, Michael Howard had repeated the old American mantra that 'if you don't want the time, don't do the crime', and had used that as justification for both the introduction of minimum sentences for repeat burglars and drug traffickers, which I kept, and new provisions for 'honesty in sentencing'. Sentencing is complicated. Except for life and certain other sentences where a 'tariff' is set (the tariff being the minimum which has to be served before parole can be considered), the headline term of imprisonment is typically at least twice the actual time that the offender will serve. The holy grail of sentencing policy is to have a system in which victims and the public have confidence, but which also gives prisoners an incentive for good behaviour in prison, and once released, while not leading to an unplanned rise in prison numbers. No prison system can operate without a modicum of consent by the inmates.

Michael Howard's provisions were intended as a trap for us. They were also ludicrously complicated, and in my view would have left the public more confused, not less. I abandoned them. Instead, I wanted to inform the public, practitioners, victims and offenders about the sentences (including non-custodial ones) likely to be handed down for a specific range of offending behaviours. Over the decades, the Court of Appeal had issued many guidelines on sentencing; nonetheless there was too much variation between courts in the sentences they handed down for identical kinds of offending behaviour, and offender. Stealing a milk bottle, or £5 million, are both theft; but plainly warrant completely different sentences.

But I had to tread carefully. The British judiciary is rightly jealous of its independence. In a democracy, it's the responsibility of senior ministers to uphold their rights, however inconvenient or irritating their judgements might sometimes seem. So it was toe-in-the-water time. The bill created a Sentencing Advisory Panel. It did good work. Six years later in 2003, my successor David Blunkett built on this with the establishment of a Sentencing Guidelines Council, placing a duty on the courts to take account of the detailed advice they would lay down. Back in charge of this area, in 2009, as Justice Secretary, I completed the work by merging the two bodies into a single Sentencing Council with clearer, stronger powers, chaired by a senior judge, with distinguished lay members on it, and with a formal role for Parliament, through the Justice Select Committee.[3] I ensured that the Conservatives were on board, since it's pretty hopeless in this kind of area to bash through changes which then fall victim to party politics. The system is now an established part of the criminal justice landscape and a case study about how significant changes can be made if they are introduced a step at a time.

However, if the 1998 Crime and Disorder Act is remembered for one thing alone, it's ASBOs – antisocial behaviour orders. I dreamt these up with the then Blackburn police chief Eddie Walsh in his office in the mid-nineties when we were discussing the inadequacy of existing powers to deal with a dreadful family in Blackburn who had been terrorizing their neighbours. My teenage experience of the powerlessness of being victim to antisocial behaviour when the police simply did not want to know had made me understand better than any research how residents can feel tyrannized by dominant criminals in their area. I was therefore determined to ensure that these orders got on to the statute book in a workable form.

In 1908, the Cambridge philosopher F. M. Cornford wrote a hilarious parody of university politics, which I was first introduced to by a member of NUS staff. I've had a copy with me ever since. In it, Cornford sets out the many tactics used to prevent change – among them the Principles of the Wedge and the Dangerous Precedent – asserting that 'Every public action which is not customary either is wrong, or, if it is right, is a dangerous precedent.' His conclusion is simple. 'It follows that nothing should ever be done for the first time.'[4]

The problem with ASBOs was that I was proposing to do something for the first time. I was seeking to amalgamate a civil order – or injunction – with the procedures of the criminal courts. Some officials in the antisocial behaviour unit did not seem to grasp the importance of what I wanted to do. I assumed that they were one of the reasons why, rather to my surprise, Michael Howard and Ann Widdecombe had been so dismissive of my proposals when we had first published them two years before. I was also up against the very powerful 'not-invented-here' syndrome that pervaded Whitehall.

ASBOs have worked. After I left the Home Office, David Blunkett much improved them, widening their remit to include juvenile offenders as well as adult, and the courts began to grant orders to 'name and shame' people of any age who were giving their neighbours hell.[5] Local newspapers, ever in touch with their readers' concerns, helped greatly in all this. Together, the police, local authorities, youth offending teams and local and regional press established a climate in which both the law-abiding and the law-breaking understood that the right to quiet life is one of the most basic of human rights, and that the law will intervene where this is undermined by the selfish actions of others.

At a national level, though, ASBOs sometimes came under a pincer movement, from the liberal press and lobby groups seeking a different balance of liberties tilted towards the suspect, and from the right-wing press which was anxious to mock the orders and chip away at our otherwise very strong record on law and order. One key criticism was that a high proportion – around half – of the ASBOs made were then breached, with the offender having to be brought back to court on a criminal charge.[6] But 50 per cent success is better than 0 per cent; and those who did breach were often jailed, to the huge relief of their victims. Despite their birth pains, the principle of ASBOs is here to stay. At the time of writing, the Coalition have announced plans to rebrand them and 'simplify' them.[7]

But one aspect of the Crime and Disorder Bill was even more controversial than ASBOs.

Ever since that Monday morning in May 1963, when poor Robertson lay dead in my study because he was 'queer', I have had the most powerful conviction that criminalizing people because of their sexuality is a stain on any civilized society.

The 1967 Sexual Offences Act had decriminalized sex between adult men in private, but much punitive legislation remained on the statute book and public attitudes had changed surprisingly little. 'Queer-bashing' with fists and bottles might be out of order, but 'queer-bashing' with words was not. Never in my time in politics had a political party stooped so low into the cesspit of raw prejudice as when the Conservative government pushed through the notorious Section 28 of the Local Government Act 1988 banning local authorities from 'intentionally promot[ing] homosexuality'. It had no purpose other than to place a stigma on gay people.

To that was added a point-blank refusal to bring the age of consent for gay sex down to sixteen, in line with the age for straight sex. An attempt in 1994 by the Conservative MP Edwina Currie had been defeated in the Commons by a majority of twenty-seven, though a compromise to bring the age down from twenty-one to eighteen had been agreed.

Once in office, I wanted to change the law as soon as possible. I was helped by the European Court of Human Rights, to which a case had been brought alleging that the difference was a breach of human rights. I promised that we would take appropriate action and got the proceedings stayed, but we decided that, since this was an issue of conscience, the proposals should come from a backbencher. In June 1998 an amendment to the Crime and Disorder Bill moved by the Labour MP Ann Keen was passed, on a free vote, with a whopping majority of 207.

But the House of Lords had a different idea. The former Tory minister Baroness Young led the charge: 'I do not myself believe that there is a moral equivalence between heterosexual and homosexual relationships.'[8] Others piled in: 'I regard homosexuality . . . as a sickness.'[9] The Lords defeated the amendment by a majority of 168 – with these unelected peers having the temerity to lecture the Commons about what the public felt about the measure.

Changing the age of consent for gay sex had not been in our manifesto, so we could not rely on the 'Salisbury Convention' to get the measure through. Under the Convention, the Conservatives agree not to use their huge in-built majority in the Upper House to block manifesto commitments. There might sometimes be a little 'ping-pong', as amendments are batted back and forth between the two Houses, but their lordships bow to the democratic will in the end. Not this time. The bigots were digging in; so deep that they were ready to scupper the entire flagship Crime and Disorder Bill (made up almost entirely of manifesto commitments) if the Commons insisted on the age of consent provisions.

Tempted though I was to call their bluff, I could not afford to.

Instead I gained colleagues' agreement to pull Ann's amendments from my bill, and to bring in a separate single-clause bill in the next session. That quickly passed through the Commons, but, in April 1999, was again defeated by the Lords. Eventually, I had to use the Commons' power under the Parliament Acts to override the Lords before it became law in November 2000.

Though sentiment on the Tory benches was shifting (not least as it dawned on some that they could not maintain the pretence that all Tories were straight), the Conservatives' official line was unchanged. When an opportunity arose in the Commons to repeal Section 28, the Tory Leader William Hague issued such a strong instruction for his party to oppose it that he sacked his front-bench London spokesman, Shaun Woodward, for taking a contrary line. (Shaun crossed the floor to join Labour shortly thereafter.) The section was not finally repealed until 2003, because of repeated blocking in the Lords, principally by Conservative peers.

None of the absurd predictions about the erosion of society that would occur if we treated gay and lesbian people equally and with respect have come to pass. Indeed, the reverse is the case. Our society is more at ease with itself. The irony, for the bigots, is that the new openness, including civil partnerships, has by all accounts ensured greater stability, and less promiscuity.

For me, I'm just mightily relieved that today's families do not have to face the appalling and unnecessary loss that the Robertson family did a half century ago, when their talented son committed suicide because he was gay.

The State Opening of parliament on 14 May 1997 was a wonderful event for everyone in the new government, but was especially sweet for those of us who'd spent a generation in opposition. There'd been a little tussle over the style of the Queen's Speech, with Number 10 too anxious for it to contain 'New Labour' language, but the ceremony itself went fine, as did Tony's first Commons speech as prime minister.

The debates on the government's programme then stretched out over five sitting days, with the Home Office's outing on the Monday. My speech was workmanlike, and set out my plans in some detail. The day is not, however, remembered for anything I said, but for Ann Widdecombe's dramatic attack on her former boss Michael Howard.

Never has there been greater evidence of the truth of the proverb that revenge is a dish best served cold. Ever since the sacking of Derek Lewis, the head of the Prison Service, in October 1995, Ann – who had been prisons minister at the time – had been brooding about just exactly where in Michael's body she would insert the blade and how she could cause him the greatest injury.

'There is something of the night about him.' Eight words was all it took to place her victim in a political coma from which it took six years to recover. But the detailed substance of Ann's speech was particularly poignant for me. Hers was the speech I should have made in our censure debate against Michael back in 1995. Ann was charitable as she drew attention to the ways in which I had missed my target, and had failed to exploit the dissembling inconsistencies in Michael's explanations of his actions. Aside from my own failure, it was also apparent that a good deal of the evidence that Ann so skilfully deployed had simply not been available to us in opposition. This emphasized to me yet again one of the hard lessons of opposition: if a minister has suffered a wound, it's best to leave it to fester; going swiftly for the kill rarely, if ever, works.

Meanwhile, I had other preoccupations. The first was keeping the Home Office show on the road; the second was to participate as fully as I could in Cabinet and Cabinet Committee deliberations.

The first issue before Cabinet which caused serious difficulties in the early weeks was whether we should continue with the construction of the Millennium Dome. This had been the brainchild of Michael Heseltine in the closing years of the Major administration, but he had taken active steps to ensure that we were on board. However, by the

1997 election it was well over budget. £100 million had already been spent and there would be significant charges if we were to cancel.[10] Chris Smith, the Culture Secretary, did advise that we should drop it, and go instead for some rather undefined 'virtual' experience. In contrast, I rather fancied the idea of this 'People's Palace', and was much influenced by my childhood recollection of the 1951 Festival of Britain, hugely controversial at the time, but in retrospect seen as symbolizing the moment that the British people released themselves from the pinching austerity of the war years. Gordon was far from keen, but a majority were in favour. So it went ahead.

The building itself is a wonderfully inspired Richard Rogers creation; a dozen years on and counting, it is now being put to good use, but we should have cancelled it that summer. The reputations of all those involved – Peter Mandelson, Charlie Falconer, my great friend Bob Ayling – were quite unfairly dented by sections of the press who rapidly ignored the Tory provenance of the scheme, and used it as a metaphor for the narrative of self-glorification and waste that they wanted to tell about New Labour.

The fundamental failing of our decision-making at that time was ministers' financial and commercial naivety – mine included. We could do politics. Most of us were fully in command of the policies we were executing. But no one round the table had had serious experience of handling multimillion pound projects of this kind. Nor, in the main, had the officials advising us. Plenty of organizations in the private sector invest time and lots of money in projects that fail, sometimes spectacularly. I have never taken the 'four legs good, two legs bad' view of the public/private dichotomy, either way, but the financial disciplines on commercial organizations are much clearer, and therefore the imperatives of having people with the right skills much greater.

The writing-off of sunk costs by aborting a project is not an argument for running up still further excess costs to complete the project; it's usually an argument to quit and move on. Yet I, among others, advanced the reverse of this in respect of the Dome – that as we'd already spent £100 million, and would suffer cancellation costs as well, we were justified in spending another several hundred million pounds to complete this scheme that precious few would ever have started.

Over time, the longer-serving senior members of Cabinet did learn by hard experience how better to judge the metrics of large projects. We also brought in outsiders with the requisite skills. I worked out pretty quickly, but too late to make any difference with the Dome, that the old political adage that 'if you are in a hole, stop digging, and get out' applies equally to investment decisions. Could we have been better prepared for this aspect of decision-taking which confronted us so soon, and so brutally? I think so.

One piece of government-wide business to which we gave less attention than we should have, given its consequences, was devolution.

If England weren't playing in an international sports competition, and Scotland were, I'd be willing Scotland to win. At the NUS, I'd worked hard with my friend Martin O'Neill to merge the Scottish Union of Students with the NUS. I knew Scotland's distinctive history, but naively believed that the generally benign view the English had of the Scots was entirely reciprocated.

That was until the evening of 4 July 1990. Stuck in the Commons for late votes, I was standing next to Martin (by then MP for Clackmannan), with a clutch of other MPs watching the World Cup semi-final between West Germany and England; 1–1 after extra time, it went to a nail-biting penalty shoot-out. As West Germany scored their winning fourth penalty goal, Martin and other Scots started spontaneously cheering. The English had been beaten. I was outraged, ludicrously so in the circumstances. But Martin's reaction taught me an important lesson about how ambivalent even the most apparently Unionist of Scots felt about England.

Our 1997 UK manifesto said that 'a sovereign Westminster Parliament will devolve power to Scotland and Wales. The Union will be strengthened, and the threat of separatism removed.'

Labour had been spooked by the Scottish Nationalists (SNP) ever since their ground-breaking victory in a rock-solid Labour seat in the Hamilton by-election in November 1967. Back then, the Conservatives had been the second party in Scotland, after Labour. Their MPs usually bounced around the high teens or the low twenties (of seventy-two seats in all), with Labour in the low forties. But in the run-up to the 1987 general election, in a panic about Scottish rating revaluation and wanting to attack 'overspending loony-left councils', they imposed the poll tax on Scotland. They lost half their seats and their foundation north of the border became so weak that in the 1997 election they were wiped out altogether. Even today in 2012 they have just one seat.*

The Tories' systemic collapse meant that the SNP were now fast filling the vacuum, and becoming Scotland's second party. Labour's best-ever result in Scotland in 1997 did nothing to assuage the Scottish Labour Party's collective neurosis about the SNP. One of many reasons for this was the derailing of Labour's previous attempt at devolution to Scotland, in the late seventies. In 1978–9 the maverick Labour MP George Cunningham, a Scot representing an inner-London seat, had forced through (with much help from the Tories) an amendment to the referendum legislation, setting a minimum floor of 40 per cent of all eligible voters for devolution to be approved. Despite Scots voting in large numbers in favour of the plans, the floor – designed as sabotage – meant that devolution could not go ahead.†

To avoid this happening again, our 1997 manifesto wisely committed us to bring in devolution with a simple majority. But it also set a breakneck timetable. Referendums in Scotland and Wales were to be held 'not later than the autumn of 1997', with detailed White Papers to

---

* Dumfriesshire, Clydesdale and Tweeddale.

† Turnout was 63.8 per cent. Of those 63.8 per cent, 51.6 per cent voted in favour of devolution and 48.4 per cent against. The 40 per cent rule meant that because fewer than 40 per cent of all eligible voters voted in favour of devolution, it was not approved.

set out the terms of the devolution proposed. It fell to the Cabinet Committee on Devolution to Scotland, Wales, and the Regions – DSWR – to sort all this out.

Committee Room A – also known as the Treasury Room – in the Cabinet Office is the grandest of all its meeting rooms; almost square, high-ceilinged, with windows over Horse Guards Parade, it has a throne at one end, on a little dais. In front of the throne in the midsummer months of 1997 sat the chairman of DSWR, the Lord High Chancellor Lord Irvine of Lairg (Derry to his friends). At the other end of a huge table, directly opposite, sat the Secretary of State for Scotland, Donald Dewar.

In 1972, Donald's wife Alison had left him in the most acrimonious circumstances for Derry – marrying him in 1974. Donald had never got over it. Some said that he and Derry had scarcely spoken a civil word in the intervening twenty-three years. Every other member of DSWR knew this. We had to witness, through meeting after meeting, the smouldering bitterness and contempt that Donald showed Derry, and the toe-curling courtesy that Derry showed Donald. It was excruciating; a gratuitous intrusion into private grief for which none of the rest of us had volunteered.

Aside from the personal pain which both must have felt, this had a serious political effect too. It constricted Derry's ability to be an effective chairman. It was therefore that much harder for the committee to resist Donald's increasing appetite to shift as much power as he could north of the border, without addressing any of the difficult consequences of such a move – particularly those relating to money.

Donald was, and remains, one of my political heroes. His early death in 2000 was a tragedy for his family, a catastrophe for Scottish Labour. No one following him at Holyrood has had anything like his stature, his vision, or his guile. Though completely committed to the Union, it gradually dawned on me that Donald wanted above all to become King of Scotland.

A fundamental part of the difficulty we faced at that time was that the extensive menu for devolution in Scotland had been prepared exclusively in Scotland, by the 'Scottish Convention'. This was a broad-based body of the churches, civic institutions, and the Labour and Liberal Democrat parties. It was worthy and well intentioned, but it looked at devolution entirely from Scotland's eyes, and was wedded to the neurotic assumption that there would be an inverse, almost mathematical relationship between the shift in power to Edinburgh, and the level of support for the SNP. In other words, the stronger the devolution, the fewer the SNP votes.

This approach had two flaws. Tactically, it was wrong. Calibrating what concessions will reduce support for an otherwise irreconcilable position is always tricky. There is plenty of historical evidence that too many concessions are just as likely as too few to feed the beast. Events in Scotland since 1997 have tended to show that.

This tactical error was compounded by the strategic one that the interests of the rest of the Union were treated as second-order. Whether Scotland remains part of the United Kingdom, or becomes wholly separate from it, must be a matter for the Scottish people to decide. But how power is distributed within a Union that is to remain intact must be for all of its parts to decide. That was the heart of Tam Dalyell's 'West Lothian Question'. There is an elegant, if dense, answer to Tam, and one which I have often deployed.* But there's a truth here too, which is that devolution on the scale being envisaged would have consequences throughout the Union, some of them adverse and unintended.

The name chosen for the new devolved Scottish institution encapsulated the problem. Constitutions of federated countries are usually careful in the names used for the legislatures of their component parts, to emphasize their legally subordinate position.† The abortive seventies'

---

* See for example my evidence to the Justice Committee inquiry 'Devolution: a decade on' on 13 May 2008.

† See for example India, the USA, Canada, Germany.

devolution arrangements for Scotland recognized this – there would be a 'Scottish Assembly', not a 'Scottish Parliament'. But in their misguided anxiety to oversell nineties' devolution, the Convention proposed and Labour accepted that this was to be a 'Parliament' – re-establishing what had inevitably been lost through the 1707 Act of Union.

There was another, much bigger error regarding money – how much, and with what strings. The 'Barnett formula' was devised by officials working for Joel Barnett, when he was chief secretary to the Treasury throughout the seventies Labour government. It set out a rough and ready formula for ensuring a fair allocation of monies between the constituent parts of the United Kingdom.

As Joel, now Lord, Barnett – a shrewd businessman – has spelt out on many occasions, it was never remotely intended that the formula should remain unchanged for three decades. But once they had been so badly mauled in Scotland over the poll tax, neither the Thatcher nor Major administrations had the stomach to revisit it. By 1997, close to its twentieth birthday, flaws in the formula, particularly those aspects measuring relative populations, meant that the allocations to Scotland were more generous than they should have been, and therefore less than fair for England and Wales, with Scottish public spending per head running above that elsewhere in Great Britain.[11]

Everyone round the table at the DSWR Cabinet Committee knew this, but there was no collective will to do anything about it. Almost every argument for moderating what we were doing was met with a refrain about the threat from the SNP, or the recital of the holy texts of the Scottish Convention. So we were establishing a devolved administration with a guaranteed income and great power over its distribution, but no balancing responsibility for the revenue raised to pay for this. There was a fig-leaf of a power for the new Scottish Parliament, to raise or lower UK income tax north of the border by up to 3p in the pound, but unsurprisingly it has never been used.

Ever since I had thought about Scottish devolution in a serious way, in the mid-eighties, I had formed the strong belief that Scotland had to have its own legislative powers to deal with a wide range of domestic matters. Scotland is a nation, with a history far more distinctive and separate than even the most self-consciously different parts of England, like Yorkshire, Lancashire or Cornwall. The 1707 Act of Union, whilst it united the Crowns, and the Parliaments, respected Scotland's separate identity, especially its jurisprudence and legal system, its education system, and its relationship between Church and State. My concern about the nature of the 1998 settlement was never with its principle, but about the fact that insufficient attention was paid to its ramifications, with too much conceded to the SNP for the wrong reasons.

Scotland voted in favour of the devolution proposals by an overwhelming majority of three to one.*

We were, in parallel, handling the much more limited programme of devolution to Wales. This was being led by the Welsh Secretary, Ron Davies, who appeared to have learnt his political method from the dons of the Welsh Labour Taffia like Ray Powell.

Whilst the 1979 referendum on devolution to Scotland had produced a small majority in favour, that in Wales had resulted in a resounding No, by a margin of four to one.

Ron was very committed to Welsh devolution, and saw himself as its Assembly's first chief minister. He knew that whilst support for a separate Assembly in Cardiff had increased in the eighteen years since the 1979 referendum, it was touch and go whether his plans would get through.

In those days there was no standing legislation to regulate the fairness of referendum campaigns. With my experience on the No side in

---

* 74.3 per cent voted in favour of the proposition that there should be a Scottish Parliament, with 25.7 per cent voting against on a turnout of 60.4 per cent. (This would have been enough to beat the 1979 40 per cent threshold, had it been in place this time.)

the Common Market referendum in 1975, I was well aware that without such regulation, the government could easily weight any campaign in its favour. Ron certainly stretched what conventions there were. The way I thought he had done so added to my determination, harboured since that stacked 1975 referendum, to ensure that once we had the result of the Nolan Inquiry into election and party funding we should establish a robust regime covering referendums as well.[12]

The result of the Welsh vote was a tiny majority of 7,000 for devolution (50.3 per cent to 49.7 per cent, on a low turnout of 50 per cent). Although the Assembly had a bumpy start, it has settled down – above all because of the inspired leadership shown by Rhodri Morgan, First Minister from February 2000 to December 2009.

'CABINET MINISTER'S SON SELLS DRUGS TO *MIRROR*'[13]

In some ways, juggling my work with the rest of my life became easier once I was Home Secretary than it had been in opposition, because I now had such an extensive life-support system. In others, things became much harder. Alice and I always knew that press interest in our private and family life would intensify the moment I became Home Secretary, but none of us was prepared for the tornado that hit us in December 1997.

Will and Charlotte had come up to Blackburn for the last home game before Christmas. As we were being driven past BAE's huge Samlesbury plant on the way to Preston station I had a call from Piers Morgan, then editor of the *Daily Mirror*. He told me he had a story about Will.

Sensing that this was going to be really serious, I said I'd call him back as soon as we got to the station, where I'd be able to find a quiet corner for a private word. When I did so, Morgan spelt out his 'scoop'. On information received, one of his undercover reporters, Dawn Alford, had chatted to Will in a local pub and he'd sold her £10 of cannabis. Morgan added, presenting himself as a 'friend' (he never was), that he had also learnt that at a party Will was due to attend later that evening, there might be a further 'sting' on him, and advised me to ban him from going (the irony being that it was Ms Alford who had invited him.)

On the train I talked to Will, and then to Charlotte, about what Morgan had told me. The story, sadly, was true. At the end of the evening in the pub, Alford had asked Will if he knew anyone who could supply her with some cannabis. To oblige, he'd gone across the pub, bought the required amount, and given it to her for the same price. As we were later to discover, there was a nasty twist to all this. The meeting with Alford had been arranged by a friend of Will's who was paid £2,000 by a freelance journalist, Peter Trowell, to set it up.

We were in a fix. Although the law was very strict that the names of juvenile offenders or alleged offenders could not be made public, I guessed that the *Mirror* would find some way round this. I told Will he was staying in that night – he'd just have to make some excuse to his friends; and not to tell Alice, who was at a performance of the *Messiah*, until the following morning. There was no point in her being awake all night, worrying.

When you're hit by something like this, paralysis sets in – or certainly did with us. But on the Monday I talked at some length to my private secretary Ken Sutton, Ed, and Mike Granatt, the director of communications. Mike told me that the best thing I could do was to take Will to the local police station immediately, and have him own up. Once the *Mirror* went public we'd have to do that anyway; the longer I left it, the more they'd be able to add to the story by claiming that the man in charge of Britain's criminal justice system was covering up his son's crime. I also talked to Tony, who was as solid as a rock in standing by me.

On the morning of Tuesday 23 December Will received a conditional offer from New College, Oxford, to read PPE. That afternoon I took him to Kennington police station.

Two local detectives were there to meet us, and took Will and me into an interview room. Will told them his story. They then became very formal. They told Will that they were arresting him for the supply of a controlled drug, cautioned him, and reminded us both that though the upper-age limit for the juvenile courts was eighteen, it was seventeen in the custody suites. He'd have to be processed by himself. I'd have to wait. It was all horrible. I felt so sorry for Will. He'd been daft, but no more than I'd been at his age. This had only landed on him because he had the misfortune to have me as his dad.

My protection officers were brilliant, and as always incredibly discreet. I knew that nothing would leak from them; but I knew enough about Britain's police to know that in every police station in the land there were officers or civilian staff who fed the press with stories, in return for money or other favours. It was endemic. The story would come out.

Morgan seemed furious when he learnt that I had taken Will to the police. But what would he have done in our situation? Left himself at the mercy of a tabloid paper? Not likely.

The story of Will's arrest broke on Christmas Eve – but for now, thanks to the law protecting minors, the papers could not name him.

The whole family had gone down to our house in Oxfordshire for a quiet Christmas after the excitements of election year. Instead, we were under siege. News cameras outside the door; TV reports showing a headless Straw out jogging. It didn't take a genius to narrow down to a very short list the Cabinet ministers with teenage children attending a London school.

We did the best we could to enjoy our Christmas but we woke each morning to our story on the news – usually, the top of the news. We had an old fax with a continuous roll of paper, on top of the fridge, which spewed out reams of news reports each morning. I'd made arrangements to see the great Geoffrey Bindman, of the solicitors Bindman & Co., after the holiday. I should have contacted him immediately Morgan had called me. That I had failed to do so is a sign that the whole business had knocked us for six; when I was first told, I simply wasn't thinking straight.

The nightmare continued into the New Year. The press were intent on naming Will, despite the legal ban on doing so. Even an injunction obtained by the Attorney General didn't hold for long. First, his name appeared on the internet (then a minority sport) before newspapers in Scotland – a separate jurisdiction – published. It was hopeless to resist. I called a press conference, at which I explained what had happened, and asked for some understanding. To my surprise the press then treated us with considerable sympathy; and the story began to fade from the papers.

But it was far from the end for us. The police decided, in accordance with standard practice, that Will should be cautioned, not charged.

Then there was his school. They would have to do something, and, as I was chair of the governors I could have no part in it. Will was suspended for a fortnight and sat his mock A levels at his head of year's house. He went on to do well in his A levels and took up his place at Oxford; but the scars from an experience like this, not least the betrayal by a close friend, take many years to heal and it took its toll on the rest of the family too.

Tony had been immensely supportive during the whole of the 'Will Christmas'. Whether because he felt I needed a break (I did), or because he thought I was doing well as Home Secretary, or because a little distance between him and Robin had already opened up, I don't know, but he decided that I should accompany him to Washington DC on his first official government visit to President Clinton. I was over the moon. Nine months before I'd been grinding away in my eighteenth year in opposition. Now this – and my first ride on Concorde as well.

No one knew when the dates for this trip were fixed, however, that the Monica Lewinsky scandal would erupt just as we arrived.

Thanks to Concorde, we touched down before we'd taken off. We had a packed schedule ahead. After the welcoming ceremony, Bill Clinton and Tony had a press conference – a boilerplate item for all such visits. But this was different – it was just a few days since the president, skilfully dancing over the meaning of words, had asserted that he 'did not have sex with that woman' and the press was out for blood. Clinton was assured; Tony very supportive. Afterwards Tony said to me, 'I hope to God Bill's telling the truth about all that.' (As later emerged, only up to a point, Lord Copper.)

On the second day, 6 February, with hell being unleashed all round the most powerful man on earth, a four-hour seminar on the Third Way was held in an upper room of the White House.* Eleven Americans, nine Brits; Bill one side of the table, me next to him; Tony the other side, Hillary next to him. Just before the session began, Bill railed to me about the iniquities of the American press. I'd always thought it better than the British press but was tactful enough not to say so. As we got down to debating the future of the world, an extraordinary calm descended. The Clintons' sangfroid was amazing.

At the end of the session, an official came in to remind Bill of a planned visit that he and Tony had to make to a college, right then. There were expletives from Bill; a 'why didn't you tell me?' refrain. The official patiently explained that they had told the president everything. Bill and Tony went off to the college – it was one of the highlights of the visit.

In the evening there was a grand dinner in the White House, with a terrific jam session from Stevie Wonder and Elton John. As Tony's 'ranking minister' I was paired off with Vice President Al Gore. I didn't in the event spend much time with him – but enough to spot two things. One, that he had a gargantuan appetite for cakes and buns. I can still see

---

* The sessions were 1) The New Economy, 2) One Nation/One America, 3) The Third Way: Defining a New Social Majority.

this large man shovelling them into his mouth from a huge pile at a reception; second, that he could be awkward in the company of strangers, with a rather 'preppy', patrician air that might explain why he was unable to win hands-down against George W. Bush in the 2000 election.

TEN

Stephen Lawrence

My first three months as a senior minister in the first Labour government for a generation had been one of the busiest periods of my life. I'd shown to myself – and I thought to others – that I could handle the raft of decisions that came my way every day. I'd begun to implement the policies we'd spent so much energy preparing in opposition. But, before I could think about a break I had one other important decision to make. The subject had not been mentioned in our manifesto. It was, however, the single decision I took as Home Secretary that has probably had the most long-lasting consequences. It is certainly the one of which I am most proud – the Lawrence Inquiry.

'No blacks, no Irish, no dogs' was a notice which, in the early fifties, I had seen in the windows of East End lodging houses. I was just old enough to remember the 1958 Notting Hill race riots. I had a graphic recall of the disgusting campaign in support of the Conservative candidate, Peter Griffiths, in Smethwick, West Midlands, at the 1964 general election. He did little to dissociate himself from the slogan flying about during the campaign – 'If you want a n***** for a neighbour vote Labour' – to win this traditionally Labour seat.* Harold

---

* His official leaflet read: 'The only SMETHWICK candidate who has ALWAYS called for the STRICTEST CONTROL OF IMMIGRATION is PETER GRIFFITHS. REMEMBER THIS WHEN YOU CAST YOUR VOTE.' Reprinted in Paul Foot, *Immigration and Race in British Politics* (Penguin, London, 1965), Part 4.

Wilson memorably said that for this Griffiths would be treated as 'a par-liamentary leper'.[1]

Many Conservatives were equally appalled by Griffiths' approach. But there had long been an unpleasant racist element in the Tory Party. Before the war this was anti-Semitic, as Michael Foot and others, writing as 'Cato', bring out in their brilliant pamphlet 'The Guilty Men', much of which consists of quotations of toe-curling apologias for 'Mr Hitler', and dismissals of 'the Jew' from Conservative MPs in the late thirties.[2] It is often forgotten that after Hitler's annexation of Austria in March 1938 had unleashed a reign of terror against the Jews, the British government tightened restrictions against Jewish refugees ('The last thing we wanted here was the creation of a Jewish problem,' the Home Secretary, Sir Samuel Hoare, told a delegation in April 1938).[3]

The war over, the right's focus shifted to the new immigrants, first black people (then called 'coloured') from the West Indies, later Asians from India, Pakistan and Bangladesh.

This element had prevented the Conservative Party from taking concrete steps, beyond platitudes, to deal with racist behaviour and language. Their reasons for doing nothing were well aired, not least during the debates on the first Race Relations Bill, in 1965.* The Conservatives left Labour's three anti-racist Acts[4] on the statute book when they resumed power in 1979, but they were never slow to exploit public anxiety about immigration for their own electoral advantage – as they had

---

* Peter Griffiths for example, opened his contribution with this. 'I oppose the Bill as it stands on several grounds. First, in the present situation it is completely unnecessary. Second, it is unlikely that the Bill will achieve the aims it is designed to fulfil. Third, I fear that it is likely to create tension and ill-feeling which does not exist at present. Fourth, I fear . . . that the real intentions behind the Bill have not been fully ventilated.' Ronald Bell MP was opposed to the Bill 'on the three considerations of freedom, expediency, and practicability.' C.M. Woodhouse MP was 'deeply and gloomily convinced that the Bill will be either totally without effect, in which case it is unnecessary, or the first step on the slippery slope of apartheid.' Hansard, 3 May 1965, col. 1008.

in the 1992 general election.* Their protection of the apartheid regime in South Africa had been abject, well illustrated by Margaret Thatcher's dismissal of the ANC as a 'typical terrorist organization'.[5]

I have always sought to be understanding about the emotional and economic insecurity which many people feel when new neighbours, with a different skin colour, culture – and in the case of Asian immigrants, language and religion – move into their area. But seeking to punish the new migrants by discriminating against them would do nothing, and would make a potentially difficult situation much worse.

I vaguely remember hearing a report in April 1993 that a young student, Stephen Lawrence, eighteen, had been knifed to death at a bus stop in South London. Tragically, this was treated as 'just another murder' of a black teenager. The police undertook what we now know to have been a deeply flawed investigation while the media quickly moved on to the next story.

There the matter would have stayed, but for Stephen's parents, Doreen and Neville Lawrence. They knew that their son's murder was a racist killing, and that the police were failing properly to investigate it for one reason alone – the colour of Stephen's skin.

In July 1993, the Crown Prosecution Service (CPS) abandoned before trial charges against five suspects, on grounds of 'insufficient evidence'. A private prosecution, led pro bono by Michael Mansfield QC, also failed. Charges against two of the five suspects were dropped before this trial; the other three were formally acquitted by an Old Bailey jury on the direction of the trial judge, in April 1996.

With the benefit of hindsight, this private prosecution was an error,

---

* Andrew Lansley, as Director of Research at Conservative Central Office in September 1995, was advising ministers to focus on race in the forthcoming election. 'Immigration, an issue which we raised successfully in 1992 and in the 1994 Euro-elections campaign, played particularly well in the tabloids and still has the potential to hurt.' Quoted in the *Independent*, 10 September 1995.

though I understand why in their desperation the Lawrences pursued it. At that time the 'double jeopardy' rule meant that there was no possibility whatever of having the same suspects retried, even if new evidence came to light.

Most bereaved families would have simply given up in the face of such appalling disappointments. Not Stephen's parents. They and their supporters redoubled their campaign for justice and turned their focus on to the need for a full public inquiry into the failures of the police investigations.

There was no obvious support for such an inquiry from the Conservatives in the Commons. The Lawrences' local MP, Peter Bottomley, has always been on the liberal wing of his party, and has not an ounce of racist sentiment in him. Quite the reverse. Yet – to his regret today – he accepted all the assurances given him by the Metropolitan Police Commissioner, Sir Paul Condon, that there had been a thorough police investigation into the murder; and that the failure to secure convictions, though deeply regrettable, was what sometimes happened.[6]

In early 1997 Doreen came to see me to press the case for an inquiry. She was joined by Michael Mansfield, Imran Khan their solicitor and Ros (now Baroness) Howells, a respected local community worker. I listened with great care to their argument, and told them they had made a strong case. But I explained that unless and until I became Home Secretary, I could not make a commitment to establish an inquiry. I needed to hear what the Home Office and the police had to say before making a final decision. I was also anxious not to turn the issue into a political football.

There matters rested until mid-February 1997. On 13 February the inquest into Stephen's death was concluded. All five suspects had refused to give evidence to the inquest on grounds of self-incrimination. The jury returned a verdict of unlawful killing, the result of an unprovoked racist attack. The next day, the *Daily Mail* published its now celebrated headline 'Murderers: The *Mail* accuses these men of killing. If we are wrong, let them sue us', complete with names and photographs of the five suspects.

My long-standing acquaintance with Paul Dacre, editor of the *Daily Mail*, meant that I probably had a better understanding of this complex character than many in the Labour Party, who regarded the *Mail* and all its works as deeply hostile. Paul Dacre was on the right, as he had been when we were at university together, but detestation of injustice is not the monopoly of the left. Paul had a good journalist's healthy scepticism of officialdom, the police included. By pure chance he had also got to know Neville Lawrence when Neville, a painter and decorator, had worked on his house. I knew, too, that Paul was extraordinarily thorough in his journalism. He would never have allowed his paper to run this story unless he had been very confident of the facts.

Once I had become Home Secretary I was determined to establish an inquiry in any event and it is Doreen above all who deserves the credit for pushing me to do so. But there is no doubt that the *Mail's* dramatic intervention – and the suspects' refusal to react to the invitation to sue – profoundly changed public sentiment about this appalling crime. It also gave me much more political 'space' in which to act.

Doreen Lawrence, and key supporters, came in to meet me shortly after the election, as did Paul Dacre. All those involved understood that the questions of any inquiry's terms of reference, power, and chairman, were of vital importance. I was going to have to negotiate a way through the different fears of the police, the Lawrences, and some of my colleagues.

One key individual I had to square, if I could, was Paul Condon. Ministers in one administration are, quite rightly, not permitted access to the papers and records of the previous administration. I therefore did not know exactly what he had told my predecessor Michael Howard, but I assumed that he must have advised strongly against any inquiry.

Condon had become head of the Met just a few months before Stephen's murder and his term of office was due to expire at the end of 1999. He was a competent officer, and I had no doubt of his good faith. He was, understandably, nervous that the whole of his term could become defined not just by the failure of the investigations into Stephen's murder, but also by the much wider shortcomings of the Met under his leadership that any inquiry focused on the murder would reveal. Handling Condon was made that much more sensitive because I was directly his boss.* That meant that those (remarkably few) officials who had day-to-day charge of the Met on behalf of the Home Secretary were also implicated in the previous decisions not to take action.

No government department is a monolith. Many officials could see that there had to be a full and comprehensive inquiry, with the widest powers, but others were more cautious. They recommended that any inquiry should be a general one into race and community relations, and avoid any forensic examination of what had and hadn't happened in this particular case.

Such an inquiry would have satisfied no one; and would rightly have been dismissed as a smokescreen. So I got moving to set up a judicial inquiry with full powers and clear and comprehensive terms of reference. Once the officials knew that was my firm decision, they accepted it and put their energies behind making it happen.

Where a senior judicial figure is needed to head an inquiry, it's the responsibility of the Lord Chancellor, in consultation with the Lord Chief Justice, to identify the best person for the job. Derry Irvine and the Lord Chancellor's Department quickly suggested Sir William Macpherson, a retired High Court judge. I did not know him, but Derry assured me that he would do a thorough job, and I had no reason whatever to doubt his judgement. Moreover, Macpherson came with another

---

* From the Met's foundation in 1829, until the mayor for London and the Greater London Authority began work in July 2000, the people of London had never been trusted with oversight of their police force. The Home Secretary of the day was the Police Authority for London.

important qualification – he was self-evidently a fully paid-up member of the British Establishment (Scottish division). He was twenty-seventh chief of the Macpherson clan, and had had a distinguished military career in the Scots Guards and the SAS. If his inquiry came up with tough and uncomfortable conclusions, as I suspected it might, it would be much harder for anyone to dismiss them than if he had been known as some kind of 'soft liberal'.

The Home Office came up trumps with the rest of the panel, recommending Tom Cook, a recently retired deputy chief constable; Dr Richard Stone, a London GP active in race relations; and John Sentamu, then Area Bishop in Stepney, East London, and much involved with London's black community.

The last task was to settle the terms of reference. By now Tony was taking an interest. He could see that the inquiry could become a huge story, and was anxious that it could destabilize the morale and effectiveness of the police. He asked that I agree the terms of reference with Paul Condon. Various drafts went back and forth across the road between the Home Office and New Scotland Yard. Finally, Condon came up with some minor amendments; whatever his reason for wanting to change the earlier (and to me satisfactory) draft, his new wording was fine. I quickly accepted.

I had been working flat out since the election and had not really had a holiday for two years. Our summer 'break' in 1996 had been punctuated daily by interruptions as we geared up for what we all thought might be an October election. So I was desperate for a proper holiday, but equally determined to announce the inquiry before I left. My public statement went out on my last day in the office, 31 July.

The Home Office had a little television studio in the basement where I did a series of live interviews. I could feel the adrenaline draining from me throughout the afternoon. During the final interview, I suddenly nodded off, and came to as my chin hit my chest. It was so quick that few viewers would have noticed. But I did. It was time for a rest.

*

It takes several months for any full-scale inquiry to get going: premises have to be found, counsel to the inquiry and administrators have to be recruited, and ground rules for the conduct of the inquiry have to be laid down. All this was quietly and efficiently done.

But the inquiry was almost still-born from the start. The attributes that recommended Macpherson to Derry and me were making Doreen and Neville Lawrence's advisers very worried. Sections of the press began a campaign against Macpherson's suitability, and impartiality. The Lawrences were increasingly concerned that the inquiry in which they had placed such faith would be a whitewash. On Monday 16 March 1998, it was both opened and adjourned minutes later following representations from the Lawrences' legal team.

I wasn't the least concerned by the Lawrences' reaction, which I thought was entirely understandable, but I was very irritated with their advisers. I thought that their criticism was completely unfounded, and the way they were expressing it was tantamount to a form of bullying – though I kept all these sentiments to myself. Having got this far, I just wanted to get going. I was not going to be drawn into any negotiation with the advisers, but I was anxious to reassure Neville and Doreen that the inquiry would do what it was intended to do. What I had learnt about Sir William Macpherson assured me that he was both morally courageous and intellectually rigorous. He would relentlessly follow the evidence through to its conclusions. If they did not like what was on offer, there would be no inquiry. No Lord Chancellor, and no Lord Chief Justice, was going to come forward with an alternative nomination in such circumstances.

I met Neville and Doreen the following day and discussed their concerns with them at length. To my great relief they issued a statement that evening to say that, 'Mr Straw has given us assurances and we will be participating [in the inquiry]'.[7]

The inquiry formally reopened on 25 March 1998. From the start, its proceedings were electrifying. The police were the focus of a barrage of criticism, as their failings to conduct proper investigations into

Stephen's death were laid bare. The inquiry heard evidence that senior police officers had initially thought that Stephen's friend, Duwayne Brooks, was a prime suspect for his murder; that there had been hints from a detective that Stephen 'had been a thief'. Just a month into the inquiry, Paul Condon complained – most unwisely – that the line of questioning had been unfair to Scotland Yard. But initial police efforts to brazen out the inquiry quickly collapsed. On 26 May one officer said that he 'regretted' the blunders in this case. The following day the senior detective who had led the murder investigation made the astonishing admission that he did not understand the law on arrests.

'You maintained . . . that not only did you want evidence, you did not have the power to arrest until you had evidence. That was the legal position as you saw it,' asked Michael Mansfield.

'That's perfectly true,' replied the officer.

'Do you not find it rather disturbing that it has taken all this time for you to recognize a fairly basic tenet of criminal law?'

'I think it's regrettable.'[8]

A few days later, an assistant commissioner at the Yard, Ian Johnston, formally apologized to the Lawrence family for the police's failings.

The five suspects were served with a summons in mid-May. Their lawyers repeatedly challenged this, with both the inquiry and in the High Court, but a month later conceded that they would have to appear. They did so over two days. They gave evasive, mainly monosyllabic answers. Violence erupted outside the inquiry premises as they were leaving. Any lingering doubt that anyone might have had about the need for the inquiry was almost certainly removed by the dramatic photographs of these thugs swearing and swinging punches at onlookers.

The evidence sessions concluded on 20 July 1998, almost exactly a year after I had first announced the inquiry. By the normal standards of such investigations, that was fast work. The inquiry team then set about writing their report.

The inquiry was independent. What they put in their findings was entirely for them. As, however, the inquiry was a formally a report to me, it was my responsibility to publish it to Parliament. It was agreed that I would give an Oral Statement to the Commons straight after Prime Minister's Questions on Wednesday 24 February 1999.

I received my copy the week before, on the Monday. The inquiry had done all that had been expected of it, and a lot more. Its publication would represent a landmark in police/community relations, and in the equal treatment of black and Asian people in our society.

Speculation about the report was gathering pace in the press, who were desperate to get hold of it, and spin it one way or the other. I was equally determined to stop them.

I was completely confident that no leak would come from my Department. The Home Office knew how to keep things under wraps. And I was not going to share its content with any other government department.

What about Number 10? The prime minister had a legitimate interest in the report's findings, which would be likely to dominate the news agenda for some time. I was, however, very worried about the culture of leaking and briefing that had developed inside Downing Street. I trusted those immediately around Tony – Jonathan Powell, and Alastair Campbell, in particular – for their integrity, and discretion. Alastair did too much briefing, and this was causing reputational problems for the government as a whole, but he was disciplined, did not go off-piste, *and* I'd had no experience of him blindsiding me. But in my view, some of the other staff in Number 10 were not properly controlled; they were too easily flattered by the attention of lobby journalists and other members of the press.

As a result, when Downing Street originally asked for a copy of the report, 'for the prime minister's weekend box', my initial reaction was to resist. My office and I were then faced with much special pleading, about how it was unfair to allow them only a day to digest the report.

Still leery, I had a bespoke summary of the report, with a few direct quotations, sent over, on the following day, the Tuesday. I should have followed my instinct, dug in and not allowed anyone over there to see the report until the night before publication.

Saturday was a Rovers home game, so this was a constituency weekend. Just four years after our triumph winning the Premiership, we were struggling to avoid relegation. I'd called in to see Rovers' chief executive, the excellent John Williams, on the Friday. He had assured me that winning the next day's game against Sheffield Wednesday would be straightforward. Our 1–4 defeat was the beginning of our inexorable slide. We were awful.

As usual at a weekend, I had two red boxes to do. Charlotte had exams coming up. We settled down on the train to divert our thoughts from Rovers, through the well-tried Protestant remedy of work.

About half an hour into the journey Clare Sumner, my private secretary covering the Lawrence Inquiry, and by happenstance the one on duty that weekend, called me to say that the press office had got wind that the report had leaked to Tom Baldwin, then on the *Sunday Telegraph*. I was apoplectic and had no doubts about the source of the leak.

However inconvenient some leaks may be, there are times when an arguable or even a compelling case can be made that publication, whilst unauthorized, was in the public interest. Indeed, there is now written into law exactly that defence in 'whistle-blowing' cases.[9] But there was no such public interest to justify the *Sunday Telegraph*'s highly selective publication of the leaked Lawrence Report. The whole report, in full, was going to be published by me to Parliament just three days later. Everyone knew that. Indeed, there was a strong public interest against the report's premature, and partial, publication.

I had three linked concerns; the Home Office lawyers identified an important fourth one.

My first concern was about handling Parliament. I had always believed – as I continue to believe – that important announcements should be made to Parliament, not the press. The Major and Thatcher governments had had a pretty patchy record in this regard; we were no better. Too often there was authorized briefing on an issue when Parliament should have been told first. Equally often, such stories leaked out through incontinence by ambitious ministers or their special advisers.

The Opposition were cross, our backbenchers slighted, and Speaker Betty Boothroyd increasingly furious about what they rightly believed was a cavalier approach to Parliament by parts of the new Labour administration. I couldn't argue with this; the leak was both wrong and self-defeating. I also knew that if I did not take action about the *Sunday Telegraph* leak then the assumption would be that it had come from my department, with my authority or connivance.

My second concern was for the Lawrences. They were fully entitled to know what was in the report before it was made public, rather than having to read partial accounts of it in the Sunday press.

My third concern was about Paul Condon, and the morale of the Met. It was patent that the inquiry's proceedings had confirmed his worst fears that it would adversely define the whole of his period as commissioner. His force had had a pasting. Much of this was justified, but there were thousands of Met officers who were very competent, and not remotely racist. As the Met's Police Authority I was very anxious to keep the show on the road. Above all I did not want Condon suddenly to resign, as a protest about the way the report had been handled.

The lawyers' concern was 'privilege'. Statute law gave complete protection – 'absolute privilege' – in respect of the report, but that only ran when it had been published to Parliament. We were potentially at risk of actions for defamation – and not just from the suspects – if we were seen to be complicit in its leaking.

Clare had called me from a shop doorway on Upper Street, Islington, on her way out to an evening with friends. My train wasn't full, but it wasn't empty either; I had to call her back from the train lavatory. I asked her to see whether we could obtain undertakings from the *Sunday Telegraph* not to publish. Unsurprisingly, they refused. We then asked the duty High Court judge to issue a temporary injunction to restrain the paper from publication, which he duly did at 8.35 p.m.

In the course of my sojourn in the train loo I did briefly consider whether to tell Number 10 what I was doing. But since I knew that the leak had to have come from that address, I decided not to, preferring to delay until I could present them with a fait accompli.

Although the *Sunday Telegraph* had earlier told my officials that it did not go to press until 8.30 p.m., a significant number of copies of the first edition, with the Lawrence story, had in fact already left their printers by 8.35 p.m. So the story was out. The next day, the paper went back to the judge and successfully argued for the injunction on the summary report to be lifted. Significantly, they made it clear to my lawyers that they accepted that the restraint on publication should remain in respect of any aspect of the report not by then public, which – thankfully – was still the bulk of it.

Apart from on grounds of national security, government-inspired injunctions to restrain the press from publishing anything are very rare. But these were very unusual circumstances. Nonetheless, a media storm erupted about the gagging of the press. I made an Oral Statement to the House on the Monday, in which I set out why I had obtained the injunction, noting that it was 'no more acceptable to have revealed a premature and incomplete account of the findings of such a full judicial inquiry than it would be for the judgement of a court of law to be disclosed in that way'.[10]

The House split on party lines, though the Liberal Democrat spokesman Robert Maclennan supported me. The Shadow Home Secretary, Norman Fowler, forcefully expressed his party's views. In response I got carried away with my contempt for what I considered to be his synthetic anger, and delivered a below-the-belt reference to the fact that he was the non-executive chairman of a newspaper company. It was a daft, entirely self-inflicted error, for which the Speaker promptly made me apologize.

This whole affair was a damaging distraction from what should have been the story. Thankfully, it is now long forgotten by all but the key players. It is the substance that is remembered.

On the Wednesday, I published the whole report to a packed House of Commons, with Tony sitting alongside to emphasize its importance for the government as a whole. The report needed little gloss from me.

> The conclusions to be drawn from all the evidence in connection with the investigation of Stephen Lawrence's racist murder are clear. There is no doubt that there were fundamental errors. The investigation was marred by a combination of professional incompetence, institutional racism and a failure of leadership by senior officers. A flawed Metropolitan Police review failed to expose these inadequacies. The second investigation could not salvage the faults of the first investigation. The inquiry finds that that first investigation of the murder was 'palpably flawed' and deserves severe criticism. The inquiry concludes: there can be no excuses for such a series of errors, failures and lack of direction and control. A review of the case was conducted in autumn 1993 by Detective Chief Superintendent John Barker. The inquiry has found that this review was factually incorrect and inadequate. The inquiry was concerned that no senior officer at any level tested or analysed the review and that Mr Barker had produced a 'flawed and indefensible' report.[11]

I told the House that Sir Paul Condon accepted the report, including the criticisms it had made of him; and that he would be staying in post for the remaining ten months of his term to begin its implementation.

The report made seventy wide-ranging recommendations. These included a formal definition of 'institutional racism'; a new complaints and discipline system; much strengthened provision for victims within the police and criminal justice system; and a complete overhaul of the Race Relations Act 1976. This, I told the House, would not just be extended to cover the police, as Macpherson recommended, but all public authorities. Critically, the inquiry also recommended that the absolute rule against 'double jeopardy' – that no one could be tried twice for the same crime – should be modified to allow for further trials where new evidence was uncovered.

I concluded by saying: 'I want this report to serve as a watershed in our attitudes to racism. I want it to act as a catalyst for permanent and irrevocable change, not just across our public services but across the whole of our society. The report does not place a responsibility on someone else; it places a responsibility on each of us. We must make racial equality a reality. The report must mark the beginning of that process, not the end.'[12]

The report was well received in the Commons and outside. Most importantly, Doreen and Neville Lawrence were pleased and relieved that its conclusions had been so trenchant. They had been vindicated in their campaign for recognition that the investigation into their son's death had been flawed from the start, because he happened to have the wrong skin colour.

After the alarums at the weekend I was looking forward to a quiet Thursday working in the office, before Alice and I took a long week-end off to stay with our old friends Pat and Julia Carter at their house in France.

It was not to be. Two awful things happened. In the morning, we learnt that the memorial to Stephen at the place in Eltham where he had been murdered had been desecrated. I decided to go down to see it, linking up with Neville and Doreen during the journey. On the way, Clare Sumner, who was with me, was called to be told of a horror story about Appendix 11 of the report. This was in the second volume, which contained all kinds of background documents. I had had no reason to read it, and had not done so.

The inquiry had heard allegations that the main suspects, or their families and associates, had systematically intimidated potential witnesses into silence. The police had a detailed log of all those who had given them information about the murder, in confidence. Appendix 11 was supposed to contain an anonymized summary of this log, with every identifying detail removed. Because of an error within the inquiry administration, every detail had instead been left in the published document – names, addresses, the lot.

I was driven quickly back to the office for a series of hurriedly assembled meetings. The police advised that some of those identified in the appendix could be at very serious risk of reprisal, and that urgent steps would have to be taken to protect them. These measures, which it was estimated would cost at least £1 million, were put in hand immediately. In a few cases, the individuals concerned had to be moved.

Those papers who had close connections with the police, and who had taken a standard right-wing view against any specific anti-racist measures, had found the inquiry's uncompromising conclusions hard to cope with. This debacle was a heaven-sent opportunity, for them and the Tories, to make me the issue, not the report.

Though in those days the Commons routinely sat on Friday, its business was light, and un-whipped.* Alice and I had seats booked on a Friday morning flight to Nice. I called Norman Fowler, and asked if he would mind if the Ministerial Statement which we were bound to make about Appendix 11 was delivered by my deputy, Paul Boateng, in place of me. I told him exactly why. He replied with some relief in his voice that this was fine by him, adding that he had other engagements too, and would rather not be in the House either.

Paul made his statement, very well. Norman's deputy, John Greenway, an urbane man, knew full well that the normal rules of ministerial responsibility could not possibly apply to the report of an independent judicial inquiry. Indeed it would be wholly improper for the sponsoring minister to do anything but publish the report submitted to him. But he responded with uncharacteristic hyperbole,

---

* Un-whipped: no requirement on MPs for their attendance from the party whips.

deploying a blunderbuss rather than a rapier. The charges went wide: to the previous weekend's leak, my gagging of the press, why no official had proofread the report. Paul dealt with these and other manifold criticisms very well.

The Sunday papers, short of any other splash, were however determined to keep the matter going. I'd slunk off to the south of France with someone's wife. Who paid? Whose wife? The answers – we'd paid, for economy seats on easyJet; the wife I was with was the woman to whom I'd been married for twenty years – seemed simply to rile them further. Norman Fowler was in no position to say anything publicly as to why I had not been present to deliver the statement in the Commons, since he had readily agreed to it. But other senior Tories were under no such inhibition. The former Social Security Secretary, Peter Lilley, soon obliged with an omnibus condemnation of J. Straw. The *Mail on Sunday*, and the *Sunday Mirror* outdid themselves with the extravagance of their front-page headlines: 'WANTED . . . JACK STRAW alias THE HOME SECRETARY' from the *Mail on Sunday*, 'FINAL STRAW' from the *Sunday Mirror*. They doorstepped my mother, and extracted some quotes from her; besieged Charlotte, who felt she couldn't safely leave the house; they even criticized us for travelling by easyJet.

What should have been a quiet weekend with friends turned into a nightmare. Outrageously, someone at easyJet had given the press the details of our return flight. We scrapped that, and booked a British Airways flight from Marseilles instead. That wrong-footed the press at the airport, but when we arrived home they were waiting for us. It took great skill by one of the detectives to spirit Alice into the house before they realized who she was. Meanwhile, I went off to the Millbank television studios for a series of interviews.

Of course, it would have been much easier to have handled this if I had not been going away that weekend. But that was hardly improper; nor did I feel that I had been derelict in any way in dealing with the manner in which the Lawrence Report had been made public. But the press wanted their revenge for my injunction, and were determined to have it on any grounds, or none.

In my Oral Statement on the Monday about the injunction, I had announced that there would be a thorough inquiry into the source of the leak. These inquiries often draw a blank, but in this case we knew where to look since the words in the *Sunday Telegraph* story had come from the summary that had been sent to just a few people in Number 10. It took some weeks, but the investigators became convinced as to the source. The evidence was not strong enough for disciplinary proceedings, but I was given the person's name. A little while later I bumped into this person in the corridor between the Cabinet Room and Tony's Private Office. I said 'hello' in a perfectly friendly manner, and then added, nonchalantly, '[Name], just tell me why you leaked that stuff on the Lawrence Inquiry to Tom Baldwin?' They gulped, then burbled, 'But I just showed him the document, I didn't give it to him,' as if that somehow made it all right. I told Richard Wilson (by now promoted to Cabinet Secretary). The individual left a little while later.

Lord Scarman's judicial inquiry into the 1981 Brixton Riots had been as thorough and wide-ranging in its way as the Lawrence Inquiry report. But there had not been the political will to implement his recommendations, and the report simply gathered dust. I was determined that Sir William Macpherson's report should not suffer the same fate. I therefore set up the 'Lawrence Working Party', with Doreen and Neville as members, to agree and monitor an action plan for the report's recommendations. This simple progress-chasing device worked wonders. Sixty-seven of the seventy recommendations had a concrete result, in changes in practice, or law.[13] In April 1999 I announced detailed targets for the recruitment, retention and promotion of black and Asian officers. A new Independent Police Complaints Commission, with powers to appoint its own investigators, and light years ahead of its flawed predecessor, was set up. The prosaically titled Race Relations (Amendment) Act 2000 contained the most far-reaching measures better to secure racial equality, and to sanction racial discrimination, of almost any in the Western world. New provisions for the protection and support of victims were also brought in.

When David Blunkett took over the Home Office in June 2001 he ensured that the momentum on the action plan was not lost. Crucially, he ensured that his 2003 Criminal Justice Act included the changes in the 'double jeopardy' rule recommended by the Macpherson Report. David also kept to my undertaking to Doreen and Neville that the 'Lawrence Working Party' would be operational for as long as they felt it was needed.

But not so David's successor, Charles Clarke, who took over as Home Secretary in December 2004. Charles is a very bright man, whom I have known since our student politics days – Charles had been president of the NUS four years after me. He has many virtues, but he is also a quixotic contrarian. In October 2005 he suddenly announced that he was winding up the Working Party, saying that he was making other arrangements that would suffice. Doreen, her wide band of supporters, and Neville, were justifiably upset by this decision, which was both unnecessary and had no administrative or political merit to it that I could divine.

In early January 2012, nearly nineteen years after Stephen's murder, and thirteen years after the Macpherson Report, two of his killers, Gary Dobson and David Norris, were convicted at the Old Bailey. This could not have happened without Doreen and Neville's persistence in persuading me to establish the inquiry, since this second prosecution had only become possible with the change in the double-jeopardy rule.

Those convictions led to widespread discussion in the media of the Macpherson Report. The consensus was that it had led to a seminal change in the place of black and Asian people in our society. The number of black and Asian police officers has risen markedly – though it will be years before we have broad parity between the composition of each force and the community which it serves.[14] The face of many of our institutions has changed, with the BBC taking a commendable lead.

Among those institutions is the Conservative Party. The first four black or Asian MPs elected post-war to the House of Commons took their seats in 1987; they were all Labour – Bernie Grant, Keith Vaz, Diane Abbott and Paul Boateng. It is to David Cameron's considerable credit that the 2010 Parliamentary Conservative Party has eleven black or Asian MPs among its strength. The party that most wears its civil rights credentials on its sleeve – the Liberal Democratic Party – is now the only major party whose MPs are all white.

Despite this, the British ruling elite is still dominated by white middle-class men. There's a long way to go before black and Asian people themselves consider that their skin colour is no more important than the colour of a person's eyes or hair, in the way they are treated, in the opportunities which come their way. The serious allegations in 2012 about continued racist behaviour by some police officers under-lines why the battle for equal treatment has to continue. But there has been a deep-seated cultural change towards race in Britain. The pervasive, open racism of the fifties and sixties, the pernicious, sniggering racism of the seventies, eighties and nineties is gone. For that we have to thank Doreen and Neville Lawrence, above all others.

Today, every so often, walking down the street or on a bus, someone will stop me, and say 'thank you'. Setting up the Lawrence Inquiry had made a difference to *their* life. These are humbling moments. I was lucky to have the chance to take that decision. If it proves to be the only thing for which I am remembered, it will be enough.

ELEVEN

A Dictator Calls

In October 1998, whilst Sir William Macpherson and his colleagues were busy drafting their report, I took a plane to Marseilles at the invitation of the French minister of justice, Elisabeth Guigou, to give a keynote speech at a conference in Avignon she was organizing on the important but scarcely show-stopping subject of mutual legal cooperation. We'd struck up a good rapport and I thought I'd try to show further respect by making part of my speech in French.

My formal education in the language had ended in 1961 with an O level. My first wife Anthea taught French and spoke it perfectly. Alice was fluent. Their facility had, occasionally, encouraged me to improve my own with various teach-yourself tapes and books. At the Home Office I had readily accepted an offer of a weekly French lesson. This, with homework in between, had raised my French to a passable, operational level.

I had, however, never made a speech in French. Most of the flight from Gatwick to Marseilles was spent rehearsing the first two pages of the speech, in French, while Mara Goldstein, one of my private secretaries, who was a natural linguist, listened patiently and corrected my mistakes. Half an hour before the flight was due to land I decided to leaf through the newspapers for a little light relief.

On page six of the *Guardian* Mara pointed me to a small item saying that General Augusto Pinochet, former dictator and president of Chile, was in London, and that the Spanish anti-terrorist judge, Baltasar Garzón, had asked that Scotland Yard locate him and prevent from leaving the country. Somewhere in my head an alarm bell rang.

'Do you know anything about this?' I asked Mara.

'Not a clue,' she replied.

'As soon as we land, please find out whether there's anything in this,' I told her. 'If there is, it could be tricky.'

Mara began to work the phones the minute we got in the car taking us to the hotel. It was all true. In fact, the Foreign Office had known that there was a strong possibility of an extradition request for at least twenty-four hours, and Home Office officials had been consulted by Spain about the UK's likely reaction to it, but no one had thought it necessary to let me know.

Annoyed, I demanded to see the relevant Foreign Office telegrams. We had no means of secure communication. It was long before the days of laptops and BlackBerries. The only fax machine in our upmarket boutique hotel was in the chef's cubicle next to his steaming kitchen. Now, yards of FCO telegrams and panicky submissions spewed out on to the sawdust-covered floor.

The initial arrest of any 'fugitive', as the subject of an extradition request is known, is nothing to do with the Home Secretary. It is a matter for a judge: in this case, the on-duty magistrate sitting at Bow Street Magistrates' Court, the London court specializing in extradition matters.* The warrant was issued the following day, and by the time I got back that night, Pinochet had been arrested.

Ever since my two months in Chile in the summer of 1966 I'd taken a close interest in the country. I remembered in 1973 the fighter planes strafing President Allende's headquarters, his suicide, and the *coup d'état* which had brought General Pinochet to power for seventeen years.

---

* Bow Street Courts closed in 2006. These matters are now handled by Westminster Magistrates' Court.

The stories of torture and 'disappearance' of hundreds of his oppo-nents had been so frequent and well documented that it was inconceivable for them all to have been fabricated. I felt that there was no point in the United Kingdom leading the campaign for an International Criminal Court and signing up to high-minded inter-national conventions making torture and similar crimes the subject of universal jurisdiction unless we were prepared to act when faced with concrete allegations against an individual. Now, whether we had the courage of our conviction was down to me. I knew what I wanted to do, but I was careful never to share my views with anyone, because Pinochet's lawyers would leave no stone unturned to challenge my integrity, and to have decisions on his case removed from me.

I would also face intense pressure from within government, and Parliament, to cancel the general's extradition as soon as it was put in front of me. Relations with Chile were good. The general him-self was a frail eighty-three-year-old.

There would be countervailing pressure from human rights groups, the left-wing press and other MPs – including, to my surprise, a vehe-ment Peter Mandelson – calling for this 'evil war criminal' to be 'made to face a trial'.

The press devoted many pages of commentary to analysing me, my politics, my personality and my options. Everyone had a strong opin-ion. The Home Office was awash with correspondence. Many claimed this was a career-defining moment for me. Doing a job like Home Secretary, you discover things about yourself. Luckily, I seemed able to take this latest frenzy in my stride.

To ward off the pressures as much as I could I turned myself into something of a Trappist monk. Thousands of people, including fellow members of the government, wrote to me; but I refused to discuss the case with anyone apart from the officials and lawyers directly advising me. Since I had to make every decision in the case on a 'quasi-judicial' basis, I excluded almost everyone – other ministers, my parliamentary private secretary, special advisers, the press office, and, crucially, Tony and Number 10 – from any involvement in the process. I batted off every attempt by colleagues to have a 'private word' with me about the case with the same 'I'm sorry I cannot talk to you about it', and every question when the media were ostensibly interviewing me about something else with the mantra 'I will make my decisions in accordance with the law'. On a visit to Madrid to see my friend Jaime Mayor Oreja, the Spanish interior minister, I had to spend about an hour repeating this again and again as scores of television crews from across Latin America tried to get something more out of me.

Pinochet's lawyers' first move was to ask me to cancel the provisional arrest warrant. I refused. They then sought a judicial review, which was heard by a divisional court, presided over by the Lord Chief Justice, Lord Bingham.

The senior official leading an extradition in the Home Office, Clare Checksfield, was first rate. Juliet Wheldon, the Home Office's senior legal adviser, and a star, quickly recommended that we would need the very best barrister, and briefed Jonathan Sumption. (In 2011 Jonathan became the first person in living memory to be appointed direct from the Bar to the UK's highest court.)

Lord Bingham's judgment followed precedent. Whilst the judicial review against my decision was not upheld, the original issue of the warrant was quashed, because 'sovereign immunity' extended to heads of state even after they had left office.

The Crown Prosecution Service, who were representing Spain, appealed to the Law Lords. The Law Lords' judgment, which came to be known as 'Pinochet 1', was due in the early afternoon of Wednesday 25 November 1998. I'd already prepared a short statement to make if the Law Lords confirmed the earlier decision, since the warrant would then have to be cancelled and Pinochet released from custody. I found that I had an hour with nothing in the diary, so I took myself off to Politicos Bookshop, close by in Artillery Row. But the quiet browse I'd been hoping for proved impossible. Politicos had two televisions permanently tuned to the news. Sky News was on one, BBC News on the other; I was on both. Fellow shoppers were looking at the screens, looking at me, then trying to engage me in conversation. I made a speedy purchase, and went to my room in the Commons to watch the feed from the House of Lords as the judgment was issued.

The Law Lords' decision was landmark and an important advance in the cause of human rights. By three to two the Law Lords upheld Pinochet's extradition on the basis, as Lord Nicholls put it, that 'international law has made plain that certain types of conduct, including torture and hostage-taking, are not acceptable conduct on the part of anyone'. They determined that it would be lawful to extradite Pinochet on thirty-two charges laid by Baltasar Garzón.*

Pinochet's extradition could go ahead. But the process had many stages. This was only the first. I now had to decide whether to issue an 'Authority to Proceed' – then the key decision on what happened to a fugitive. If I refused it, Pinochet would be released. If I granted it, then, subject to what I knew would be interminable challenges in the courts to review my decision, he would be sent to Spain to stand trial.

Shortly after his initial arrest, officials had asked me whether there were any grounds on which my bona fides could be challenged by the highly litigious parties on both sides of the case. I told them about my trip to Chile – four years before Allende had been elected, seven years before Pinochet's coup. I might have met Allende at a reception in

---

* R vs Bow Street Metropolitan Stipendiary Magistrate ex parte Pinochent Ugarte (Amnesty International and others intervening) (No 1) [1998] 4 All ER 897 at 940. The majority cited the Nuremberg Judgment and affirmed the view first elaborated by the Nuremberg Tribunal that: 'Individuals have duties which transcend the national obligations of obedience imposed by the individual State. He who violates the laws of war cannot obtain immunity while acting in pursuance of the authority of the State, if the State in authorizing action moves outside its competence under international law': Judgment of the International Military Tribunal (Nuremberg) 41 AJIL (1947) 172 at 221. See D. Sugarman, 'The Pinochet Case: International Criminal Justice in the Gothic Style?' (2001), Modern Law Review 64, pp. 933–44.

Santiago de Chile, perhaps even shaken his hand, but I'd had no other dealings with him whatever.

I did, however, recall that on my return from Chile I'd written an article for *Tribune*. I'd been very proud of that piece. It was the first I'd ever had published in a national journal. I'd spent hours on it. I managed to find the article in an archive box in our house in Blackburn. To general relief, the article was a worthy, and rather tedious, exposition about agrarian reform under President Eduardo Frei. Not even the Pinochistas were able to claim that it contained any evidence of prejudice against their general.

With that potential hurdle out of the way, the serious task of deciding whether to agree or to reject Pinochet's extradition began. Supporting evidence was obtained from Judge Garzón in Spain, lengthy representations were received from Pinochet's lawyers, and from France, Belgium and Switzerland who, not to be outdone, had now weighed in with their own extradition requests. All of this was assembled in twelve lever-arch files (which had to be wheeled into the office on a trolley), with a day set aside for me to read them and then make a decision, based on certain key tests on which Jonathan Sumption and our lawyers provided further advice.

I read the lot, and formed the view that there was clearly a case for Pinochet to answer, and no other impediment I could see in the way of his being transferred to Spain. I announced my decision to the Commons on 9 December 1998.[1]

Meanwhile, Pinochet's ever-industrious lawyers had made a discovery which they believed might abort the whole process – and very nearly did.

One of the five Law Lords who had heard Pinochet 1 was Lord Hoffmann. He'd been brought up in South Africa when apartheid was at its most oppressive. Like many others from the liberal Jewish community there, he had left South Africa in his twenties and settled in England. He had commendably strong views about unpleasant dictatorial regimes; so did his wife, Gillian. Pinochet's lawyers had unearthed the fact that Gillian worked as an administrative assistant for Amnesty

International and that Leonard Hoffman was himself chair of Amnesty's charity. Amnesty had been granted the right of representation in the case before the Law Lords but Hoffmann had seen fit to declare his position neither to the court, nor to Pinochet's lawyers.

I was dumbfounded that a jurist of such distinction could make such an error, and deliver himself, and the court, into the hands of the Pinochistas. Others who knew him better said that he was so confident that he had all the required judicial qualities, including impartiality, in greater abundance than any of his colleagues, that the idea that he might be perceived as having a potential conflict had simply never occurred to him.

Pinochet's counsel now had a well-primed torpedo to aim at the extradition. They fired it. Deeply embarrassed by the infelicity of one of their colleagues, the Law Lords had (by a decision known as 'Pinochet 2') to 'vacate' their judgment in Pinochet 1, and start again with a differently constituted court.[2]

This second group of Law Lords did in the main confirm Pinochet 1. By Pinochet 3, they found that torture was an international crime over which the parties to the UN Torture Convention (Spain and the UK included) had universal jurisdiction; and a former head of state did not have immunity from prosecution. This was a further landmark in international human rights' law, and its impact went far beyond our shores.[*]

However, for technical reasons, principally to do with the dates of some of Pinochet's alleged crimes, and when the Torture Convention came into force (June 1987) their lordships cut the number of potential charges on which Pinochet could be extradited from the thirty-two found lawful under Pinochet 1, to three. His supporters argued that the

---

[*] In effect the House of Lords vindicated the principle that executive power and sovereignty are subject to the limits imposed by the rule of law.' D. Sugarman, 'The Arrest of Augusto Pinochet: Ten Years On' Open Democracy (29 October 2008), sets out more generally the domestic and international significance of the 'Pinochet precedent'.

cutting of the charges from thirty-two to three implied he should be released.

The lever-arch files, full of new representations, were put back on my desk to help me decide whether to issue an amended Authority to Proceed.

Amongst the representations in my file was a carefully phrased minute from Robin Cook, giving me his very balanced view of the foreign policy implications of any decision I made. Robin told me much later that he had had to rewrite the draft himself, because the weight of opinion inside the Foreign Office was that 'the sooner Straw lets him go, the better'.

That was most certainly the prevailing view across the road from the Foreign Office, in Downing Street. Since I resolutely refused to discuss the implications of the case with anyone – including everyone in Number 10 – I never pinned down why they were so concerned that I might transfer this unpleasant dictator to Spain to stand his trial – something that we had all signed up for. The point they were making was clear enough. I could read the newspapers, which ran almost daily reports about the debt we owed Pinochet and Chile for our victory in the Falklands.

My permanent secretary brought a message into one meeting. 'I've just had a suggestion from Number 10. It's a third way. They think we might use the good offices of the Vatican.' I knew the Vatican had written, and in what terms. But as far as I was concerned this was a matter for determination in this life, not the next. I blew a raspberry and moved on.*
As well as former US president George H. W. Bush, who issued a public statement calling for Pinochet's release, a large group of wealthy and influential supporters now weighed in. Chief among them were the

---

* The newspapers later ran well-sourced stories, claiming that the Vatican had written to the government requesting Pinochet's release (*Sunday Times*, 21 February 1999). The Vatican confirmed it had made representations at the request of the Chilean government.

former Conservative Chancellor of the Exchequer, Norman (by then Lord) Lamont, and Margaret (now Baroness) Thatcher. She wrote to Tony twice. The first letter argued the case – over three pages – for releasing General Pinochet. The second, much pithier, in response to his explanation that this was a decision for his Home Secretary, not for him, more or less questioned Tony's manhood. 'I am dismayed . . . Are you saying that it is proper for the Home Secretary to be guided by the view of private individuals but not to take into account those of the prime minister? Such a proposition is manifestly absurd. In the last resort, you are responsible for all the actions of your government. You will understand that I cannot leave the matter here.'

Tony was by this time twitchy about the whole issue. Every so often after a meeting in the Cabinet Room, he'd call me into his study and suggest, in Delphic terms, that it was time to say goodbye to the general, and then try to engage me in conversation about it. To his mounting frustration I had to tell him that I was sorry but I couldn't discuss the matter with him. If any decision of mine was challenged in court – and in practice, every decision I made would be challenged by someone – and I was asked to testify what representations I had received from him, I would have to say. If he wished, he could of course minute me, as Robin had done, but that too would be disclosable.

Alice said to me one evening, 'Good God, Jack. I go to work to get away from you and the Home Office, but you're outside my window every day. "Jacky Straw out!" from one side, "Jacky Straw in!" from the other. There's no escape.' Every time an important decision loomed, the pro- and anti-Pinochet campaigns renewed their protests, in two police corrals. Alice, by then a director general in the Department of Health, had a large ground-floor room directly adjacent to the demonstrators, and was thus forced to listen to their competing chants, along with fruity comments about my paternity and much else.

Meanwhile, the Pinochistas' efforts to find something that would do for me as Lord Hoffmann's error had done for him were going to ever more extravagant lengths. Gino Peirano, the very nice man whose family had given me digs in in the middle-class suburb of Viña del Mar for three weeks in 1966, had been tracked down. So had an attractive young woman whom I'd taken out a couple of times. Photographs of a group of us sitting on the beach were published in the *Sunday Times* and the *Mail on Sunday* under suggestive headlines.* But to their obvious annoyance, they could never find the smoking gun, since there wasn't one.

I issued the second Authority to Proceed on 14 April 1999.[3] The issue then quietened for some months. The courts had made sensible, bespoke arrangements for Pinochet's remand. He was formally in custody, but in extremely comfortable surroundings in a detached house in Surrey, with an extensive armed guard provided by the Met's Diplomatic Protection Group.

Under the then convoluted extradition procedures, once the Authority had been issued the matter went back to the Chief Metropolitan Magistrate.† Accordingly, at the end of September 1999, almost exactly a year after Pinochet had arrived in the UK, there was a three-day hearing at Bow Street. On 8 October 1999 the Chief Metropolitan Magistrate committed Pinochet on all charges, to await my decision on 'surrender' – i.e. transfer to Spain.

Pinochet's lawyers, having delayed his extradition for nearly twelve months, had few cards left. Spain's case had been examined in the most minute detail by both the highest court in the land, and the senior judge in charge of extradition cases.

But, ever-inventive, they found a trump: the general's health.

---

* 21 March 1999.

† When I announced my decision not to extradite General Pinochet, on 2 March 2000, I also announced that we would be producing a consultation paper on streamlining extradition procedures. This was the beginning of the process of modernizing extradition law.

On 14 October, just six days after the committal decision, the Chilean government, through its embassy, issued a formal request, accompanied by medical reports, claiming that Pinochet was unfit to stand trial. This request led me to suspect that parts of the British government might have been offering 'helpful' advice to the embassy about how best to make their case.

Whatever its provenance, though, I could not simply ignore the detailed assessments of Pinochet's health from experienced medical practitioners. Plenty of people in their eighties do suffer from serious loss of memory and other brain functions. But however distinguished Pinochet's doctors, I was not going to accept their opinion as definitive and, on the advice of my officials, decided that the general should also be examined by our own panel of experts.

On the recommendation of the government's Chief Medical Officer, Professor Liam Donaldson, I appointed four – including a consultant neuropsychologist – all of whom had had extensive forensic experience, on behalf of prosecution authorities, in assessing whether defendants who were pleading incapacity to stand trial had genuine symptoms. I thought they should easily spot whether Pinochet was another Ernest Saunders.*

The medical panel was thorough. Rather to my surprise they unanimously came to a clear view that Pinochet was indeed unfit to stand trial. The Chief Medical Officer concurred.†

---

* Ernest Saunders was convicted in 1990 for offences of share trading fraud. He was originally sentenced to five years. This was reduced on appeal to two and a half years because the court found that he was suffering from the incurable Alzheimer's disease, and he was released having served only ten months. He later recovered from his symptoms.

† He wrote to me on 7 January 2000, 'This authoritative medical report leaves me no reason to doubt the specialists' judgement that the Senator is not fit to stand trial and that his present condition is not one which would be expected to improve. The report also makes clear that the Senator's condition could not be feigned' (HoC Library, Dep 00/446).

My strong instinct was to have all the medical evidence examined in detail before a judge, who would also have been able to hear representations from Spain, France, Belgium, Switzerland and the other interested parties such as Amnesty International, but I was given conclusive legal advice that I had to make the decision. The only way the matter could, at that stage, have gone to court would have been if I had wilfully refused to come to a view. My failure to do so in the face of clear advice to the contrary would, almost certainly, have been declared 'irrational' by the court. That would have been damaging to my reputation, and would have led to such accusations of bias that I might have had to drop my involvement in the case. It would not, in any event, have achieved what I wanted – for the decision on Pinochet's health to be made by a court, rather than by me – since the court, on finding me irrational, would not have taken over from me the discretion that was properly mine, but would simply have directed me to do my duty and decide.

There was, as it were, no 'Get Out of Jail' card for me.

On 11 January 2000 I announced that the weight of evidence led me to conclude that the general was unfit to stand trial, adding that, 'subject to any representations that I may receive, I am minded to take the view that no purpose would be served by continuing the present extradition proceedings'.

Spain and the other parties seeking Pinochet's extradition all smelt a rat. Their suspicions, well placed, about the pressures from the defence and foreign policy establishment of the British government for his release, were compounded by my unwillingness to hand over the medical reports to them. But it is a default rule that all such reports are confidential. Much as I thought it would help my handling of the case if I could make them public, I could see no grounds for doing so. I also believed that any undertakings by the other parties to respect their confidentiality would not last five minutes. Judge Garzón would keep to any promises he might make; so might France, Switzerland and Amnesty; but I was wholly cynical about Belgium's extradition request.

It reeked of posture and opportunism. There was no more chance of them keeping anything under wraps than there was of the Flemish and the Walloons ending their centuries of linguistic conflict.

On 26 January 2000, Belgium and six human rights groups sought a judicial review of my refusal to hand over the medical reports. Three weeks later, on 15 February, the court ruled that the reports should be disclosed 'in confidence'. They were, of course, leaked within hours.

The Home Office medical team had been reviewing their findings in the light of all the representations they had received, but did not materially depart from their original finding that he was unfit to plead.

I'd been up hill and down dale on Pinochet's health. I'd been looking at it for four and a half months. On Thursday 2 March I concluded that I had no alternative but to discharge the extradition request, on the grounds that Pinochet was unfit to stand trial and no significant improvement in his health could be expected.

I prepared a statement to the Commons. I wanted to wait in my room to see his plane take off from UK soil before I made it, in case there was a successful last-minute attempt to obtain a court order to block its departure. The plane seemed to spend an age parked on the runway and it got to the point at which I had to go and sit on the front bench, so I would be there when the Speaker called me. It was only as I was getting to my feet that a private secretary dashed in with a note to say the plane had taken off.

There was much criticism of me from the Tory Opposition, who had taken Pinochet's side all the way through, and great disappointment on my side. In response, I told the House: '[T]his case is unprecedented. Throughout the process, I have sought to exercise my responsibilities in a fair and rational way in accordance with the law. The case has understandably aroused great debate and feeling. Its impact has been felt worldwide. It has established, beyond question, the principles that those who commit human rights abuses in one country cannot assume that they are safe elsewhere. That will be the lasting legacy of this case.'[4]

What I said then has turned out to be true. But when Pinochet landed in Santiago de Chile he gave me a metaphorical 'V sign' by getting out of his wheelchair to wave at the crowds of jubilant supporters I felt double-crossed. True, the medical issues had nothing directly to do with his physical mobility, but the message was clear. He'd tricked the British system, and escaped the trial he had deserved.

The joy at Pinochet's return was by no means universal in Chile. Ricardo Lagos, from the centre-left, had recently won a tightly fought presidential election, and took office just a few days later, on 11 March 2000. He said that the general's 'triumphant arrival' had damaged the image of Chile across the world.

In Chile, a battle then began between those who wanted to see Pinochet brought to trial, and those who were determined to protect him (and no doubt themselves) from censure for the appalling brutality of his regime. Immunities granted by the Chilean Senate were overturned by the courts; prosecutors brought charges against Pinochet, only to have the trials suspended on grounds of his medical incapacity. The immunities were reasserted by the executive and Parliament; again overturned by the courts; new medical evidence of incapacity was brought in. After more than six years of this game of cat and mouse, it looked as if the prosecutors could close in. In November 2006 Pinochet was charged with thirty-six counts of kidnapping and twenty-three of torture. The prosecutor sought his house arrest. The dictator died a few weeks later, on 10 December 2006, aged ninety-one, without any court, in Europe or Latin America, ever having convicted him of any criminal offence.

Judgements about the state of health of prisoners are notoriously difficult. Two cases which arose years later, when I was Justice Secretary, illustrate this well.

In the summer of 2009, whilst on holiday in Italy, I was faced with a 'very urgent' matter which could not wait for my return. The notorious train robber, Ronnie Biggs, was so ill, I was told, that I should immediately release him from prison on compassionate grounds. The medical evidence was that he would die very soon. Sceptical, I examined this carefully, and held a conference call with the head of the Prison Service and other officials. I ordered his release. His health miraculously improved. At the time of writing, Biggs is still alive.

A week later, the Scottish justice minister, Kenny MacAskill, was faced with the much higher-profile decision about whether to release Abdelbaset al-Megrahi, the Lockerbie bomber. I had nothing to do with the decision itself, but I knew a lot about the background of the case. MacAskill was so concerned to ensure that he made the right decision that he even visited al-Megrahi in prison. He was convinced by all the evidence. Al-Megrahi was terminally ill with cancer, and could have only a few weeks to live. He ordered his release on compassionate grounds.

Like Pinochet nine years before, al-Megrahi made a miraculous recovery on the flight home. He too got off his bed and walked, as he arrived to a triumphant welcome from Colonel Gaddafi. He died nearly three years later, in May 2012.

In the Pinochet case, one of the Home Office medical experts was subsequently reported in the *Observer* as commenting that his panel's assessment of Pinochet's capacity to stand trial was not as conclusive as I had made out. Sir John Grimley Evans (professor of clinical gerontology at the John Radcliffe Hospital, Oxford) was asked about the accuracy of my Commons statement that 'the unequivocal and unanimous conclusion of the three medical practitioners and the consultant was that . . . he is at present unfit to stand trial, and that no change to that position can be expected'. His answer was reportedly that he would have to 'hedge' his answer: 'I have no problem with the "unanimous" but the "unequivocal" depends on how unequivocal it was from a lawyer's point of view – that's his judgement . . . All we did was list the medical facts. Whether those medical facts constitute unequivocal grounds for decreeing unfitness for trial is outside our field of competence and outside our responsibilities.'[5] That was not what was said in their report, however. Had there been any serious ambiguity in their conclusions I would have not have discharged the extradition request.*

I greatly regret that I was not able to surrender Pinochet to Judge Garzón. By the time Pinochet's sixteen-month incarceration in England was over, my knowledge of his record was encyclopaedic. It was horrific. Pinochet was one of the worst dictators of the post-war era and it is an enduring source of enormous frustration that I was not able to lead him into the dock.

Some have claimed that, given the ultimate failure of the extradition, it would have been better if I had simply rejected the request the day it had been received.

My answer to that assertion is an emphatic 'No'.

It is vital that we establish clear norms for dealing with alleged crimes against humanity.

Everyone knows that the targets of the conventions to which we have signed up are going to be the leaders, the instigators, of brutal regimes, not the camp followers. If the leaders are skilful they are always likely to have very influential friends and allies – and the money – to exert pressure to avoid sanction. Thus it was with Pinochet. It would have been morally abject for me just to send him away out of convenience, as so many had urged me to do.

There is a second purpose for these conventions – to create a climate where those tempted down the path of repression will think twice, for fear of the consequences. The case changed the law. Under the Torture Convention, immunity for any head of state now ends when they lose office.

---

* Despite conducting a second unhelpful interview with *El Pais* along the same lines as the *Observer* interview, and continuing to insist on the distinction between medical fact and the legal judgment made on the basis of those facts, Professor Grimley Evans wrote to officials on 16 January 2000 to say that the *Observer* article had misrepresented him and that my statement to the House about the report's findings was 'entirely correct and appropriate'. (HoC Library, Dep 00/171).

The Pinochet case was not only a landmark in terms of international law. It changed the face of Chilean politics for ever. The sixteen months Pinochet spent in custody in Britain enabled the Chilean people to come to terms with his legacy in a way they had not been able to do up to that point, and, I suggest, would have found far more difficult but for his detention.[6]

I have never been back to Chile since my 1966 visit. I was on the way there as Foreign Secretary when I had to turn back on the death of the Queen Mother. But I fell in love with the country when I was there, and feel privileged to have played a significant, if wholly unexpected, part in helping to make it a more civilized place.

TWELVE

A Tale of Two Policies

JACK STRAW: *If I do that, I'll lose my reputation.*
CLARE SUMNER, private secretary: *Home Secretary, on Freedom of Information you have no reputation to lose.*

Passed in 1998 to a noisy fanfare by the Labour government, this baleful measure acts like a poison on the national bloodstream, destroying our traditional concept of justice and undermining democracy. While the British public suffers from this lunacy, the only people who benefit are self-serving lawyers and the criminal classes.

Daily Express, 3 October 2011, on the Human Rights Act

The Human Rights Act; the Freedom of Information Act: one damned by the popular press, the other cursed by ministers and officials alike – and I was to blame for both.

They are two major planks of a raft of Labour legislation which has permanently changed our constitutional arrangements. There any similarity ends.

One was crafted with enormous care, and, though now needing some amendment, has great inner coherence and strength. The other is already showing the signs of its wholly inadequate conception and implementation.

The contrasting stories of how these two Acts came on to the statute book is an instructive lesson in what can be done right – and wrong – in the development of policy, in opposition and in government.

The European Convention on Human Rights was agreed by the Council of Europe in 1951 and ratified by the UK government that year. That body – nothing directly to do with the European Union – was the brainchild of the Allies after the Second World War. The Council and its principal instrument, the Convention, were designed to provide standards of behaviour for states in their treatment of their citizens, with the aim of preventing the kind of repression and tyranny that so many had suffered before and during the war.

The United Kingdom took the lead on the Convention. Championed by Winston Churchill, much of its drafting was prepared by David Maxwell-Fyfe QC, a Conservative MP and jurist who had been one of the prosecutors at the Nuremberg trials, later serving as Home Secretary and Lord Chancellor in Conservative governments during the fifties.*

Most other member states of the Council of Europe in due course incorporated the Convention into their own domestic law through one means or another. In the United Kingdom, there was, for over three decades, a bipartisan consensus against incorporation. The argument was that this would be an unnecessary, Continental import; we had these rights anyway.

The first MP to take active steps to break this consensus was a Conservative, Edward Gardner, my former head of chambers whose personal kindness had enabled me to go to work for Barbara Castle.†
Gardner's 1987 Human Rights Bill was a back-bench Private Members'

---

* As Lord Kilmuir.

† See Chapter Four.

measure. Denied support by either front bench it fell at the first hurdle.* I was not in the House that day, but in so far as I'd given the issue any thought, I shared the conventional view that the time was not ripe for Ted's bill.

But his efforts, and parallel ones in the Lords, put the idea on to the political agenda. Gradually, opinion shifted. When John Smith took over as leader of the Labour Party in 1992, he committed the party to incorporate the Convention into UK law as 'the quickest and simplest way' of introducing 'a substantial package of human rights'.† With his death, and Tony's assumption as leader, it fell to me as Shadow Home Secretary to work out how to do this.

The Lib Dems were keen, but the Conservatives' official position had, if anything, hardened, not least because incorporation smacked of 'more Europe'. Michael Howard, then Home Secretary, was resolutely opposed.

The purpose of bringing the Convention into British law was to enable the British people to access their rights in the British courts, rather than having to go to the European Court of Human Rights (ECHR) in Strasbourg. Democracies are characterized not only by the rule of the majority, but by the protection of the rights of minorities and individuals, however unpopular their views may be or unpleasant their behaviour. If incorporation was to be more than a gesture, our courts needed teeth to enforce these rights, otherwise the whole exercise would be risible.

---

* In the key Commons vote, on 6 February 1987, the bill failed by just six votes to get the hundred MPs necessary for a closure motion to force a second reading vote – see Andrew McDonald (ed), *Reinventing Britain: Constitutional Change under New Labour* (University of California Press, Berkeley, 2007).

† In previous decades it had often been leading Conservatives who supported incorporation, most famously Lord Hailsham, who called for a 'bill of rights, embodying and entrenching the European Convention' to address the 'elective dictatorship' of Labour governments in *The Dilemma of Democracy* (Collins, London, 1978).

The key obstacle on which earlier attempts had foundered was that incorporation of the Convention into UK law would give our courts the power to override the sovereignty of Parliament. The tribal sentiment inside the Labour Party at the time inclined us to distrust the judiciary, who were, in this not wholly accurate view, regarded as reactionary elements of the British Establishment.

A profoundly serious issue was exposed here. There is justifiable pride in British institutions, in the sensitivity of our constitutional arrangements. Parliament sits at the apex of these arrangements. Other countries might have superior courts that can strike down 'unconstitutional' legislation, but that has arisen from the terms of their written constitutions. Those texts had almost always been promulgated in the wake of upheaval – revolution, or independence, for example. The absence of a written British constitution is a mark of Britain's stability and resilience. The British people, through their Parliament, are the ultimate source of power, not unelected judges.

But the idea that there was no overriding judicial check on the British state was already being eroded by decisions of the Strasbourg court. British citizens who considered that the UK had denied them their Convention rights were increasingly going straight to Strasbourg. The court's judgments (not just those against the UK), or the anticipation of them, were already modifying the behaviour of UK governments. Legislation on phone tapping (1984), on the Security Service (1989), and on GCHQ and the Secret Intelligence Service (1994) had all been prompted in part by Strasbourg decisions. Individual executive acts of the British government were the subject of adjudication, too. In *McCann* vs *UK* [1995], the Strasbourg court had ruled that the UK had used more force than was necessary when three members of a Provisional IRA active service unit had been shot dead in Gibraltar whilst allegedly about to detonate a bomb. In *Chahal* vs *UK* [1996], Michael Howard had to cancel the deportation of a suspected Sikh terrorist to India after a ruling by Strasbourg that the suspect would have run the risk of torture if he had been returned.

By not incorporating Convention articles into domestic law we were in practice getting the worst of all worlds. We were observing Strasbourg decisions, but we could not benefit from the Strasbourg doctrine of the so-called 'margin of appreciation' – judicial discretion to take account of specific national circumstances – because our courts were denied all opportunity to consider breaches of Convention rights before the cases went to Strasbourg.

Outside politics, there was some serious intellectual endeavour examining how we could find a path which reconciled the benefits of incorporation with the imperative of parliamentary sovereignty. Professor Robert Hazell and his colleagues at University College, London and Professor Francesca Klug of King's College Law School (now at the LSE), in particular, each produced a number of papers which were hugely influential to our detailed consideration of this policy.

The net result was that in December 1996 my front-bench colleague Paul Boateng and I published 'Bringing Rights Home', a comprehensive paper setting out in detail how we intended to legislate, and, crucially, how our courts would not be able to override Parliament.

This paper gave government officials – and their lawyers – a head start on the architecture of the proposed new Act, work which was further refined after the 1997 election.[1] In October 1997 I published both the bill itself and a White Paper, which declared: 'The time has come to enable people to enforce their Convention rights against the state in the British courts . . . In other words to bring the rights home.'[2]

Some of the best brains in Whitehall and beyond had contributed to the structure of the Human Rights Bill. It showed. They had managed with great elegance to square the circle between the enforceability of human rights in the British courts, and the sovereignty of Parliament. Our senior courts were given the power to declare that a particular provision in primary legislation was incompatible with Convention rights. But the same section was explicit that this did not affect the validity or continued operation of any 'incompatible' provision.*

The bill was initially introduced into the House of Lords, where it had an easy passage. On second reading, in the Commons, the House divided on party lines – Labour and the Liberal Democrats on one side, the Conservatives in the No lobby. But the Tories were far from united in their position. One bright new MP, Dominic Grieve (later appointed Attorney General in the 2010 Coalition government), courageously made his maiden speech in favour of the bill. From private discussions with sympathetic Conservative MPs, I picked up that, provided there were some amendments, they might not oppose the bill at the third reading. This was a prize of great value. I am utterly convinced that major constitutional change is best done on a bipartisan basis.

Two particular constituencies wanted changes in the bill: the churches and the press. The churches were worried that their freedoms could be constrained by the Act, but amendments to Section 13 satisfied their concerns.†

Assuaging the press proved more complicated. They had become very used to the absence of any privacy law in the UK, which meant that, provided they were factually accurate, they could intrude into the most sensitive areas of people's lives with complete impunity. By making modest reforms to their own voluntary (and pretty toothless) machinery of the Press Complaints Commission and Code, they had

---

* In this situation, Parliament would decide what to do next. There was a fast-track 'Remedial Order' procedure available under the bill. But government, and Parliament, could decide to make appropriate amendments by primary legislation, or do nothing – and leave the 'incompatible' provisions in force, and, when the inevitable challenge to the Strasbourg court was made, argue there that our courts were incorrect.

† Section 13 of the Human Rights Act says: 'If a court's determination of any question arising under this Act might affect the exercise by a religious organization (itself or its members collectively) of the Convention right to freedom of thought, conscience and religion, it must have particular regard to the importance of that right.'

successfully seen off attempts to introduce a British law of privacy.[3] But they could now see that the incorporation of 'the right to respect for private and family life' would inevitably lead to the courts developing such a law, despite the balancing rights in the bill entitling the press to enjoy 'freedom of expression'. Complex negotiations led to revisions which gave the media significant procedural and substantive safeguards where an injunction was sought on grounds of invasion of privacy.

These changes, to my great relief and delight, were enough to satisfy the bill's critics. On the Commons third reading of the bill, the Conservative's spokesman, Sir Nicholas Lyell, said that in its amended form 'We now wish [the bill] well.'[4] It went through without a vote.

Whilst the Human Rights Act was beginning its tranquil journey through Parliament, something close to mayhem was breaking out within government over Freedom of Information (FoI).

Every Labour manifesto since October 1974 had contained a promise to bring in a Freedom of Information Act, but those few words were about all the serious intellectual consideration that the PLP or the Shadow Cabinet had given to this inherently complex issue.

Others, however, outside Parliament, had been extremely active. None more so than the Campaign for Freedom of Information, a lobby group led by the brilliant and very personable Maurice Frankel. Maurice had provided detailed papers on FoI to the party in the eighteen months before the 1997 election, and had organized an informal seminar on it too.[5] What was lacking, however, were the counter-balancing arguments – which were to hit us when we got into government.

The Campaign was one of a number of lobby groups with a serious interest in constitutional change, whose expectations about what an incoming Labour government would do in this field were very high. Human rights, data protection, party funding, the House of Lords, public appointments, elected mayors, devolution – the list went on. We all became word perfect in the mantra of change.

Including Tony. He devoted his 1996 John Smith Memorial Lecture to this wide canvas. In went a commitment to FoI, along with everything else. 'The first right of a citizen in any mature democracy should be the right to information. It is time to sweep away the cobwebs of secrecy which hang over far too much government activity. If trust in the people means anything then there can be no argument against a Freedom of Information Act which will give people rights to public information.' His pledge was repeated in the 1997 manifesto.

The job of introducing the Act went to David Clark, whom Tony had appointed as Cabinet Office minister.* David had been Shadow Defence Secretary, and was understandably concerned that he had been passed over as actual Defence Secretary by George Robertson.

He knew, I think, that Tony had included him in Cabinet on sufferance, because he felt that he could not completely ignore the PLP rule that all members of the Shadow Cabinet had a right to a seat round the Downing Street table. So David did what many would have done in such difficult circumstances. He went for broke. His major responsibility was for FoI. He became an evangelist for the cause. David appointed as his special adviser James Cornford, a leading social reformer who, as chairman of the Campaign for Freedom of Information, was Maurice Frankel's comrade-in-arms.†

In February 2012, the BBC won a Supreme Court ruling endorsing its right, under the Freedom of Information Act, not to disclose an internal report allegedly admitting bias against Israel in its reporting of the 2005 Israel–Lebanon conflict.[6] In a comment welcoming the judgement the BBC said '[This] will ensure that the BBC is afforded the space to conduct its journalistic activities freely . . . Independent journalism requires honest and open internal debate free from external pressures. This ruling enables us to continue to do that.'[7]

I have long supported the right of the BBC (as with any media

---

* Formally, Chancellor of the Duchy of Lancaster.

† The grandson of F. M. Cornford, author of *Microcosmographia Academica*.

organization) to have the 'space' for such 'honest and open internal debate'. Indeed, the provision in the Act which enabled the BBC to protect the confidentiality of its internal reports was inserted by me.* But what is sauce for the media goose must be sauce for government gander, too. If it is right that the media need 'space' for 'honest and open internal debate', it surely is more important still that government has similar protection for its 'space' to make decisions?

I was very strongly in favour of more openness in government. That was one key motive for my campaign to put the Office of National Statistics on an independent footing. I'd long argued that government had no right to sit on data it collected, nor hold on to factual background papers, for no good reason. But such openness is entirely different from whether or not governments, like any other institution, should have a private space in which those making decisions can be frank with one another – not least because such candour is often a critical factor in the quality of the final decision. This seemed to me to be all the more important given the principle of collective responsibility on which British Cabinet government is founded – the principle that, whatever the internal dissent, ministers have a duty to uphold and explain the decisions for which they are jointly accountable to Parliament.

I therefore thought that there were very strong arguments in favour of properly protecting this space, and all that went with it – papers to Cabinet and Cabinet Committees, their minutes, the shoal of correspondence between ministers by which many second-order decisions have to be agreed; and the officials' work behind all this. So did most of my colleagues, especially all the senior figures in Cabinet.

David was on a mission, however. The Campaign for Freedom of Information no longer needed to lobby government to get its views

---

* Part VI of Schedule 1 of the Act, which made the BBC subject to the Act only 'in respect of information held for purposes other than those of journalism, art or literature'.

across. It had direct access. Like a child in a chocolate factory, James Cornford drafted the White Paper he and Maurice had been dreaming of for years. David endorsed it. It went to 'CRP(FoI)' – soon transmuted into a rather vulgar acronym – the Cabinet committee, chaired by Derry Irvine, responsible for this policy.

Despite the reservations many of us shared, there was little appetite at this stage to stop David in his tracks. We were all consumed with the new experience of running our own departments, protecting our own business, and our budgets. There was a collective naivety, too. In retrospect, our failure to prevent David's proposals from ever seeing the light of day was one of the many mistakes made in the preparation of this policy.

David's White Paper *Your Right to Know* was duly published in December 1997.[8] Its scope was extraordinary. Almost all information held by public authorities was to be eligible for release. The weak exemption provisions had a test of 'substantial harm', and there were no exemptions for categories of documents.

I had, however, managed to protect most of the Home Office's business from David's scheme. CRP(FoI) had agreed to one blanket exclusion from the proposed legislation – for law enforcement activities of any and every kind. This stuck out like a sore thumb, and, as some critics immediately spotted, was wholly inconsistent with the entire scheme of the White Paper.

In contrast to the HRA, where most of the press perceived that they had a vested interest against the introduction of privacy provisions, the FoI White Paper was warmly welcomed by the media. They had most to gain from an FoI regime and dismissed concerns about its impact on the working of government as special pleading. Some expert observers were less sanguine. Robert Hazell, who'd spent a year studying FoI regimes in Australia, New Zealand and Canada, commented wryly that this was 'probably the most generous [FoI regime] yet seen amongst countries that have introduced Freedom of Information. It is almost too good to be true . . . this is an unreal White Paper'.[9]

'Unreal' was one of the more polite descriptions attached to this policy once Cabinet colleagues understood its full implications. There then began a belated campaign to secure its complete reappraisal before any bill was published. We did not want to compound our first error with a second.

This culminated in early July 1998 in an ill-tempered meeting of CRP(FoI) which called a temporary halt to the whole process. I had done some prior organization to ensure the committee came to the correct answer, canvassing my pals. As ever, James Cornford attended the meeting as an 'observer'. Once he realized that his plan was coming off the rails, he wasted no time in ensuring a wider audience for the work of dastardly, reactionary ministers like me.

'The Lord Chancellor, Derry Irvine, and the Chancellor of the Duchy of Lancaster, David Clark, are fighting a rearguard action to save the government's flagship FoI Bill from being mutilated and wrecked by hostile ministers for the second year running,' proclaimed the *Guardian* the following day. 'A Cabinet Committee held on Wednesday night was described as a "bloody battlefield" by a Whitehall source after as many as seventeen ministers clashed over moves to weaken and prevent the bill becoming law next year.'[10]

I was (correctly) fingered as the villain of the piece. 'Who thundered in the *Tribune* newspaper of 29 September 1995 that "Labour wants more openness in government"? None other than Jack Straw in the days before he was a Tory. Last week he attempted to castrate Labour's proposed FoI Act in Cabinet,' wrote Nick Cohen, in the *Observer*.[11] (I was happy that that was all Cohen could quote against me. I remained in favour of more openness but that was entirely different from the gratuitous disruption to Cabinet government implied by David Clark's plan.)

Encouraged by Richard Wilson, the Cabinet Secretary, Tony himself was by now getting extremely worried about the eccentric FoI policy to which his government, in a trance, had seemingly committed itself.

Tony's first reshuffle came at the end of July 1998. He called me to say that I was staying where I was, at the Home Office – but he'd decided to transfer all responsibility for FoI to my department, and me. David would be leaving the government.

My happy task was to abandon the extravagance of David's scheme, and in its place find a scheme that was both plausible, and more modest. (Number 10 proposed that there should be a blanket exemption for them from any of the provisions of FoI. This was more than even I thought the market could bear.)

I had little difficulty in gaining colleagues' agreement to pull back. We'd learnt a lot in fifteen months in government; the Cabinet had been considerably strengthened by Tony's changes to the ministerial team. But there was one huge obstacle – David's White Paper. It became the template against which all subsequent iterations would be measured.

My proposals were published in May 1999 in a consultation paper with a draft bill attached.[12] As well as proposing a more sensible set of exemptions, with a 'prejudice' test rather than the previous 'substantial harm' test, a new Information Commissioner would be there to arbitrate where a request had been refused, but ultimately the decision would remain with ministers. The arrangement would be parallel to that for the ombudsman, whose recommendations can *in extremis* be ignored.

The draft bill went to the Public Administration Select Committee; the Lords weighed in with their own inquiry. Unsurprisingly, given the lobbying all in one direction, and David's White Paper, both made proposals for significant strengthening of the draft. There was then a long interval before we came forward with a revised bill.

Much of the detailed consideration of the bill took place on the floors of both Houses. The debates were free flowing, and of a high quality; good-humoured, without rancour.

Nevertheless, Mike O'Brien, the excellent Home Office minister covering this troubled topic, and I were assailed from all sides. The Conservatives, who in normal circumstances would have been natural allies for a cautious approach to FoI, had abandoned all expectation of returning to government, and simply wanted to cause us difficulties. On our side were all the enthusiasts for FoI-max, ably briefed by the indefatigable Maurice Frankel. There were many occasions when the only two MPs arguing in favour of the government's approach were Mike and me.

As the bill made its slow progress it became clear to me that we were unlikely to get it through at all unless we made some serious concessions. Some had already been made: the Information Commissioner's decisions would, in general, be mandatory, and there would be a judicial tribunal above to hear appeals. But ministers would still be able to exercise a veto to prevent publication if they thought this necessary.

This became the break point. I'd had enough of FoI.

I had never been that bothered by some of the adjectives applied to me for allegedly sabotaging this grand idea. Now, I had half a thought that the best thing might be to bin the whole bill, or kick it into the long grass with a Royal Commission. I saw Tony. He was as exasperated as I was. But he had made that categoric promise in the John Smith Memorial Lecture. There was the manifesto commitment, too. We'd taken immense care over what went into that holy text; we'd dined out on the need for politicians to keep their promises. There was the fact that he, like me, had allowed the David Clark extravaganza to go public. How, credibly, would we explain dropping a bill, with our names on it, which was close to completing its passage through Parliament? Tony concluded our conversation by saying that we'd better let the bill go through provided I kept the veto provisions in. I agreed.

Even that was easier said than done. There was a marathon session on the floor of the House. Mark Fisher, Labour MP for Stoke-on-Trent Central and a consistent advocate for the strongest possible FoI regime, was kind enough to say of this: 'it has been an extraordinary experience for the House to see a Home Secretary reshaping a central part of the bill while on his feet, and doing so with considerable confidence'.[13]

The 'reshaping' concerned the circumstances in which the ministerial veto could be exercised. The wording was tightened and we gave undertakings that veto decisions would be made only after the relevant Secretary of State had properly consulted the full Cabinet.

The result of all this was that whilst we were in office the veto was used on only two occasions – in respect of the Iraq Cabinet minutes, and the papers and minutes of the devolution Cabinet Committee – both times by me.[14]

The Human Rights Act was passed in the summer of 1998, but with a two-year gap before it was to come into force. The delay was to allow public authorities to get used to their new duties and, in particular, for the Judicial Studies Board (JSB) – the judges' training arm – to prepare the judiciary.

These preparations were successful. The JSB did an impressive job. My platform speech at Labour Party conference in 2000 was, by co-incidence, on 2 October, the date the Act commenced as the law of the United Kingdom. There was great satisfaction, within the party and beyond, that we had been able to introduce a sensible, well-planned measure of major reform.

But for one event eleven months later, the early years of the Human Rights Act would have been benign. There would have been some hiccups – there always are with wholly new areas of law. Criminal defence lawyers, and those seeking judicial reviews of government decisions, would have probed the limits of the legislation; some lower courts would have handed down some off-beam interpretations of the Act; but over time the senior judiciary would have developed and interpreted the Act strictly in accordance with Parliament's intentions.

On 11 September 2001, the world changed. One of the many consequences of al-Qaeda's atrocities was to create the toughest possible climate for the infant Human Rights Act to grow.

In an instance, fear became the dominant emotion; and national security not individual rights the dominant imperative on government.

The previous year I had put through Parliament a comprehensive modernization of the UK's anti-terrorism law – the Terrorism Act 2000.

This bipartisan measure, prepared from recommendations by the Law Lord, Tony Lloyd,* was at the time seen just as good housekeeping. The threat from Irish terrorism was gradually winding down as the Good Friday Agreement took effect; and though we knew about al-Qaeda, neither it nor any other international terrorist organization was seen as posing much immediate threat.

With 9/11, the powers of the state to deal with the terrorist threat were pushed to the limit. The delicate balance in a liberal democracy between liberty and order came under attack. Few on either side of the argument acquitted themselves well.

Some senior ministers, upset by what they considered to be indulgent attitudes towards terrorists and other law-breakers, began openly to criticize the courts. In November 2001, David Blunkett warned judges, 'The law will be made by those who are held to account for both making it and changing it.'[15] In February 2003, he said, 'Frankly, I'm fed up with having to deal with the situation where Parliament debates issues and the judges overturn them.'[16]

Bashing judges is counterproductive. The British judiciary have spent centuries building up, and then protecting, their independence from the executive. Their immunity from political interference is enshrined not just in our constitutional conventions, but in their terms of employment. Once appointed, senior judges are in practice irremovable; they are generally in post for longer than even the most durable of Cabinet ministers.

Pushed into a corner, the judges were bound to react, and they did. The backlash came in December 2004 in the Law Lords' judgment in the Belmarsh case.[17] This declared that provisions to detain without trial foreign national suspects who could neither successfully be prosecuted here, nor deported, was contrary to the Human Rights Act. I tried to be more restrained than David, but I criticized the judgment,

---

* Lord Lloyd of Berwick.

saying that the Law Lords were 'simply wrong'.[18] It was a silly thing for me to do. It is central to the operation of the rule of law that courts are able to make judgments that are inconvenient, or worse, to the executive; and are accorded proper respect for this distinctive task.

That said, some of the language used by their lordships in the Belmarsh case was, in truth, as intemperate as their political critics had been. Lord Hoffmann said, 'The real threat to the life of the nation, in the sense of a people living in accordance with its traditional laws and political values, comes not from terrorism but from laws such as these.'[19]

Charles Clarke, by then Home Secretary, quickly made changes to the law to accommodate the judgment; in place of detention, a system of house arrest was introduced, known as 'control orders'. But this and other controversial judgments by the courts gave added fuel to those in the press and Parliament who had never liked the Human Rights Act. It was a 'villains' charter', the 'criminals' friend', went the cry.* The Conservatives committed themselves to repeal the Act and replace it with an ill-defined 'British Bill of Rights'.

Gradually, however, it has been dawning on the critics that the Act has brought many benefits for the law-abiding, as well as ensuring that even the most horrible law-breakers are treated in a humane way. In 2009, the Director of Public Prosecutions, Keir Starmer, pointed out that the Act had done far more to advance the rights of victims than it had those of criminal suspects.[20] Some of the Act's strongest critics themselves availed themselves of its protections. The owners of the *Daily Telegraph*, the redoubtable Barclay brothers, made extensive use of the Act to advance their dispute with the government of Guernsey, even as their newspaper was opposing it.[21]

For many, the penny finally dropped with the question of whether

---

* See, for example, the *Express* on 3 October 2005 commenting on Ian Huntley's sentence.

serving prisoners should have the right to vote. It was over this issue that the crucial distinction between the Human Rights Act and the Strasbourg court became clear.

In a case brought by the convicted killer John Hirst, the High Court declared that the long-standing ban in British law prohibiting convicted prisoners from voting whilst in jail *was* compatible with Convention rights under the Act.[22]

Strasbourg, however, took the contrary view.[23]

What this brought home was that the problem with the Convention arises not from the interpretation of the Human Rights Act by the British courts, but from the Strasbourg court.

In most of the high-profile cases, the senior courts here – the Court of Appeal, and the UK Supreme Court – have endorsed Parliament's original intentions.

If we had repealed the Act, and stayed subject to the Convention – the Conservatives' position before the 2010 election – the situation would have become worse, not better. We would have lost all the benefit of the UK courts applying their own interpretations of Convention case law and would still have been subject to the vagaries of the Strasbourg court.

There are some changes to the Act that I think would improve it – notably regarding the way British courts digest Strasbourg case law. But despite this, and despite the pressure it has come under, the Human Rights Act has survived so far. In my view it will continue to be a key and beneficial part of our constitution for decades, if not centuries, to come.

The Human Rights Act is relatively short – twenty-two operative sections, thirty-two pages – and well constructed.

The contrast with the Freedom of Information Act is stark. It's long – eighty-eight operative sections and 109 further paragraphs in the Schedules – and contorted in its construction. Insufficient attention is given to its administration. Its drafting failed properly to take into account the extraordinary explosion of the internet which was just beginning as the measure became law.

The Act does have explicit provisions for charges to be made for each request. That was the original intention. But, before it was brought into force in 2005, it was decided that no charges should be levied. This was an error. It has added to the administrative cost and has created the anomaly that whilst individuals may be charged under the Data Protection Act for information about themselves, information about other people is free.

That error was not mine; but the fact that once the Act came into force its provisions would be retrospective was. I should have spotted it. It is one thing for information to be subject to the Act when it has been prepared and held in the knowledge of the Act's provisions. It is quite another – and inherently wrong – that the records of those who could have had no knowledge of the Act should be subject to it.

The big problem, however, concerns the space that – to re-quote the BBC – government 'requires [for] honest and open internal debate free from external pressures'. There are provisions to protect the internal working of government in Sections 35 and 36. In practice they have not done so. A series of decisions by the Information Commissioner, and the Information Tribunal above him, have whittled away the safeguards we thought the Act provided, and made almost any internal record of any discussion vulnerable to disclosure. Some of the rulings have been eccentric – for example, one arguing that the provisions in Section 35 about the preparation of policy did not apply once the policy had been settled.*

It is hard to say with any precision how far the Act, and the way it has been interpreted, has had a 'chilling effect' on discussions, and the records of those discussions, but there is much anecdotal evidence that

---

* This was the argument over the DSWR Cabinet Committee papers. See Information Commissioner's report to Parliament (HC218), 5 January 2010.

it has. The fact that the Information Commissioner had to issue a warning about the use of personal email accounts suggests concerns by him that ministers and officials have altered their behaviour to circumvent the Act.[24]

The paradox of FoI is that in meeting the insatiable demands of its enthusiasts it has effectively made good decision-making more difficult, and degrading of the historical record more likely. Nor has FoI increased trust in government, as its proponents promised. Recent evidence by the Ministry of Justice to a Commons select committee suggests the reverse.[25]

In his memoirs, Tony Blair describes FoI as 'utterly undermining of sensible government . . . There is really no description of stupidity, no matter how vivid, that is adequate.'[26]

My own view is that we could have had a more modest, and durable, Act if we had given it the kind of careful thought, in opposition, that we devoted to the Human Rights Act, and if we had properly taken account of overseas experience. That more modest Act would not have suppressed, for example, information about MPs' expenses, but would have supported, not hindered, the operation of good government.

THIRTEEN

Calamity Jack

It is now a commonplace that Mr Straw has risen in the pecking order that prevailed when Labour came to power. Talk of the 'big four' (Blair, Brown, Prescott and Robin Cook) has waned. Ambition has damaged Mr Brown and events have halted Mr Cook . . . On his present form . . . you can no longer rule out a Prime Minister Straw.

BAGEHOT, *The Economist*, 30 January 1999

Jack Straw has gone from one embarrassment to the next . . . Just look at some of Jack Straw's gaffes from the past few months . . . He allowed enormous queues to build up outside passport offices. And he allowed enormous queues to build up outside immigration offices. He published a Freedom of Information Bill that makes some things more secret. He forgot to renew key parts of the Prevention of Terrorism Act and didn't tell Parliament. He got his facts wrong on asylum and issued a retraction blaming his officials . . . We had a spy scandal a day and he didn't tell Tony Blair, never mind Parliament . . . 'Calamity Jack'.

ANN WIDDECOMBE, Shadow Home Secretary,
Conservative Party conference, October 1999

There's never been a huge demand in Blackburn for *The Economist*, great journal though it is. Rather than send someone out to scour the town's newsagents, Ed Owen, my political adviser, faxed me the 'Bagehot' article, with a scribbled note of congratulation at the bottom.

I was rather proud; it felt like a serious recognition for my work in the shadows, as well as in the light. But I was wary too. Proverbs 16:18 – 'Pride goeth before destruction, and an haughty spirit before a fall' – had been the text of many sermons I'd slumbered through. I told Ed that, gratifying though the comment was, this was a dangerous moment. It would be appreciated neither by my peers, nor by the gods. Bubbles always burst.

It wasn't just shares in Straw that were above their natural asset value. There was a bull market in Tony and the whole of his administration. For around the first two years of any incoming government there is a ready-made alibi – 'it wasn't us, it was you lot'. We benefited from that, and from the extraordinary spell that Tony, our star, had cast over Britain's media. It couldn't last, least of all in the Home Office.

It didn't.

Cock-ups, crises and fiascos piled up so swiftly that the senior statistician in the office, Paul Wiles, knowing of my anorak interest in his subject, introduced me to the 'Poisson distribution', a mathematical theorem which shows how independent events that occur with a known average rate will sometimes bunch together.* As the *Sunday Times* reported, 'Jack Straw has his own algebraic formula and for him it could mean the difference between survival and an early political death'.[1]

The crises were in two groups. First, there were the 'known unknowns',

---

* The Poisson distribution gives the probability of x number of events taking place in a given time interval as $e(-m)$ multiplied by $m(x)$ divided by x, where e is 2.72 and m is the mean number of events per time period. The assumption is that all events are equally likely and are independent of each other. As well as explaining a bad week at the Home Office, it helps to explain why you wait for ages for a bus and then three come along at once.

where I knew that chronic difficulties could erupt into full-blown near-catastrophes, but I didn't know when, nor how the eruption would happen – or (much worse) I did know, but couldn't do much about it. Then there were the 'unknown unknowns', acute dramas which, like one of Richard Wilson's Exocets, came straight through my seventh-floor window and landed, fizzing, and lethal if handled in the wrong way.

Top of the first group were immigration and asylum, with prisons running a close second. In the second group came the passports fiasco (though this one should have been anticipated), the dangerous terrorist I had to release, the British spy I'd 'let off', the Afghan hijack, the petrol crisis – and others too numerous to name.

Immigration (with asylum) is one of the single most difficult domestic policy issues for any government, though it's more sensitive for Labour governments because we represent more constituencies with significant black or Asian communities, because it is alleged that we are 'softer' on the issue, and because it's the Conservative-leaning press that takes the greatest interest.

Go through parliamentary and press reports of the last sixty years, and the constant charge against the Home Office is incompetence – a sentiment well captured in the ill-judged comment by John Reid, Home Secretary 2006–7, that the Home Office was not 'fit for purpose'.[2]

I could not have survived unscathed for four years as Home Secretary if I had not been relentless in my pursuit of greater competence and efficiency in the department. But if the fundamental difficulty over immigration and asylum had ever been simply one of competence, the ascent to the sunlit uplands would have been easy. At root it isn't about competence. It's about purpose – albeit in a way that John Reid failed to comprehend.

The central problem is that there is not one clear aim or purpose that everyone – Parliament, press, public, officials – is pursuing with resolute single-mindedness, but two. They are diametrically opposed and sometimes the same people flip between them. One is to 'let them in', the other is to 'kick them out'. Drawing the line in individual cases whilst operating a fair system can be horrendously complicated.

In general, people want the tightest possible controls to stop unlawful immigration into the country, and to ensure that only well-founded asylum-seekers are allowed to remain in the UK. But in any particular case, the very same people may seek precisely the opposite. I can think of many occasions where the same MPs who in public were calling for tougher action in general, would then write to me (or even meet me) to argue that justice, or mercy, required that an exception should be made in a particular constituency case. Like any immigration minister I always looked at these cases with great care. But, as I often had to explain, an exception for one had to be an exception for all in the same circumstances, otherwise decision-making would become arbitrary and capricious.

This fundamental conflict was well illustrated by the cause célèbre of Nigerian-born Ben James, whom I had decided to deport when it emerged that he had overstayed his student visa by fourteen years. The *Daily Express* took up his case and launched a 'Save Ben' campaign, attracting 30,000 signatures. It helped that, although he was indeed an illegal immigrant, he had entered the country as a child, and was now a successful businessman. He wasn't the usual tabloid press caricature of an illegal immigrant. He was one, nevertheless, but in the end, following a huge media campaign and a fresh ruling in his favour by the independent adjudicator, I revoked the deportation order and allowed him to remain in the UK. Did I give in to media pressure? Maybe.

Asylum itself presents even greater inherent conflicts than immigration. We were proud signatories to the Geneva Convention on Refugees, which requires states to give refuge to people with 'a well-founded fear of being persecuted for reasons of race, religion, nationality, membership of a particular social group or political opinion'.[3] The Convention was originally limited to protecting European refugees displaced by the war, but in 1967 it was extended to cover the globe.[4]

When the Berlin Wall came down, effective border controls across much of Europe and beyond collapsed. There was conflict in the Middle East. The Balkans went up in flames. At the same time, international air travel became much easier. Passports became a form of illicit currency. There was a dramatic, unanticipated increase in the numbers claiming asylum in the UK and most other prosperous countries. In 1986 there were 4,000. Ten years later that had risen to 30,000.[5]

Countries in which there is serious political persecution are typically countries where there is also great poverty. 'Economic migrants' have an incentive to obscure their real purpose with stories of tyranny. For both groups – genuine refugees, and those simply wanting a better life – there are networks of criminal 'facilitators', parasites who make a good living from other people's desperation by arranging travel, providing forged papers, and inventing stories to fit the rules – for a large fee. Sorting who should stay and who must go is hard. Handling this administrative complexity, with its contradictory 'let the right ones in, kick the wrong ones out' objectives, requires hugely detailed regulations, skilled staff, and a judicial superstructure to decide appeals.

Navigating safely through the politics requires all that, and more. We live in a democracy. Anybody can see their local MP. There are four times as many lawyers as there were forty years ago; voluntary groups, and activists on both sides of the argument. It would be tricky at the best of times – but most times were far from that.

The many front-line staff who I met in the Immigration and Nationality Directorate (IND) of the Home Office, now known as UK Borders, were, with few exceptions, dedicated and skilled. There was a problem, though, in how they were organized and led.

'I was once exiled in Croydon [IND's headquarters] for three years,' a senior official airily told me one day.

This single sentence spoke volumes not just about this individual, but more generally about the attitudes of the most talented officials to working in immigration and asylum operations. Policy – thinking about what to do – was Whitehall, close to ministers and high status. Implementation – doing it – was the suburbs, and lower status. The separate 'Classes' (as they were called) of the Civil Service – clerical, executive and administrative – had formally been abolished years ago,[6] but their spirit lived on. The clerical grades were the private soldiers; the executive grades, the senior NCOs who ran the regiments day-to-day; the administrative grades, the officer class.

IND was run by clerical and executive grade officers, with a smattering of the officer class, often reluctantly posted for 'career development', eager to depart quickly for better things. As a result there was less of an instinctive grasp of the complexities and challenges facing IND at the top of the Home Office than there should have been. Alongside this, there was a systemic Whitehall problem (yet to be resolved) with the management of large-scale IT schemes. This mix was to prove near-catastrophic for IND, and for me.

In one of the four 'Briefs for Incoming Ministers' there was a line telling me that a new IT system for the computerization of the immigration and asylum caseload would come on stream by November 1998. This, I was informed, would lead to savings of 1,200 jobs, and 40 per cent of the annual cost. The contract with Siemens had been signed by Michael Howard in April 1996 and its terms, as I was to discover, were virtually unbreakable.

The Home Office was immensely proud of this new kit. I was shown the 'model office' at IND HQ in Croydon, where case papers were being scanned into the system so that the whole process could be 'paperless'. But this brave new world started to unravel within the year. In June 1998 we had to admit that the 'change programme' had slipped 'by about six months'. In July, Siemens, as main contractor, parted company from Perot, the principal subcontractor. Discontented IND staff began to leak. In September, the *Daily Express* reported that the plan looked like 'being derailed for a year'.[7] The National Audit Office began to take a close interest. Their report in March 1999 was withering.[8] Their recommendation was that the Home Office should consider whether the project 'might be too ambitious to be attempted in one go'.[9] The system was indeed seizing up.

The backlog of asylum cases alone reached 76,000 in June (up from 52,000 the year before), and hit 90,000 by November. The total backlog, including immigration cases, was even worse – rising from 151,000 in March 1999 to 219,000 in June. In an interview with the *Guardian*, I commented that 'Murphy's Law is operating. Everything that could go wrong has gone wrong.'[10] My permanent secretary, David Omand, described the IT system as a 'Doomsday machine'.[11] David was one of the best senior appointments I ever made. He did know about management, and IT (he had just come from running GCHQ). He was fundamental to getting IND back on its feet.

David and I spent days in Croydon, talking to staff, and working through a recovery programme. Gradually performance did begin to improve. But by early 2001 it was clear that the only sensible decision was to abandon the whole wretched programme – as I announced that February.[12]

As the chairman of the Public Accounts Committee, David Davis, aptly summarized, there had, on this scheme and so many others in Whitehall, been a 'horrible interface' between civil servants 'who understand all there is to know about, for example, the National Insurance system but know little of how a computer works, and the technicians who know just the reverse. They don't spend enough time at the start of a project explaining where they are both coming from.'[13]

Whilst IND and all its cases were falling into a black hole, Mike O'Brien and I were trying to get through a major bill to streamline the immigration and asylum process, and restrict financial support for those in the queue. Under the previous arrangements, housing asylum-seekers was the responsibility of the local authorities where they landed, or made their claim. This was putting unsustainable pressure on Kent County Council and some London boroughs and had already fuelled serious public resentments. I feared – and so did many Kent MPs – that violence and disorder might follow. So I proposed a policy of 'dispersal', by which asylum-seekers became the responsibility of a new National Asylum Support Service (NASS), which would allocate them to areas mainly outside London and the south-east where there was much less pressure on housing. This didn't make me particularly popular, but I believed it was necessary. Nor did my proposal that claimants be given vouchers for food and other necessities, rather than cash, which we knew was leading to abuse. The opposition to the voucher scheme was intense.

There were some tender reforms in the bill – including the reintroduction of an appeal right for family visitors – but most of it was tough. Pre-Iraq, it became the major item on the far left's charge sheet against New Labour, so much so that the Trotskyists in the Students Union at Leeds University won a ballot to ban me for life.*

The Trots were, however, the least of my problems. The voters, especially the bulk of lower-middle-class and working-class Labour supporters, were in a completely different place. They felt insecure. They wanted to know that our borders were controlled, that the system was in safe hands. Tony was, quite rightly, concerned about how the issue might hit us at the election.

Though Ann Widdecombe, as Shadow Home Secretary, did her best to exploit the IND chaos, it never quite got to danger point for me. Partly this was because the Siemens contract had been signed on her and Michael Howard's watch. More significantly, though, the 'customers' of IND who were being inconvenienced (and worse) by all the delays were immigrants and asylum-seekers, and not in the main British voters.

But it was precisely those voters who were the victims of the passport crisis that erupted in the spring and early summer of 1999; the single most career-threatening issue I ever handled.

The Passports Service was an 'executive agency'. These were established from the late eighties as part of Mrs Thatcher's new approach to

---

* The ban was lifted in November 2007.

the provision of services delivered by central government. The theory was that if these services were hived off to semi-autonomous bodies, their management would have greater freedom to get on with the job. There was some merit in this, but nothing like as much as the enthusiasts thought. Even from Opposition I had profound concerns that the way they operated was leading to a lack of accountability and ministerial grip.

This was never more true than of the Passports Agency, as I – and half a million people desperate for passports – was to discover.

At first sight, transferring passport administration to an agency made perfect sense. There was no politics, no inherent controversy. The business of issuing passports accurately, promptly and efficiently could safely be left to those who knew the business best.

That though, was the problem. It was out of sight, out of mind for the Home Office. Targets were set. They were met. Virtually no one in the Home Office had any idea what the agency was actually up to, still less was there any routine supervision of their work. They did not feature at all on my radar – until disaster struck, and I discovered a catalogue of elementary management errors that still bring me out in a sweat.

In summer 1996 the agency decided to digitize passports to cut down on fraud; replace its existing computer system; and, through 'outsourcing' or a private finance initiative (PFI), improve its efficiency and effectiveness. They signed the contracts to do all this (with Siemens, again) within two months of the 1997 election – our watch – and, as with IND, they tried to change too much, too quickly. This operational error was then compounded by the policy decision that children would henceforth need their own passports.

We were in for a perfect storm; and we got it.

By May 1999, there were more children's passport applications than anticipated. The pressure on the system increased and delays lengthened. As they did, people began applying much earlier than normal and the backlog built up even more, reaching unheard-of levels. Soon, free two-year extensions were offered to those queuing at passport offices, but even this wasn't enough. The telephone enquiry service in the Liverpool office virtually shut down, but the applications could not be transferred to the other offices, because they were all overwhelmed too.

The storm broke in mid-June, with a thunder clap and a deluge. A story that had been on the inside pages was suddenly the main headline. The normal backlog for the time of year had already more than doubled to 488,000, with a thirty-four-day wait instead of the promised ten; in the space of two weeks it shot up to peak at 550,000, with a wait of seven weeks.

It was the equivalent of a run on the bank, with similar, and disastrously photogenic, results. It was rational for people desperate not to miss a holiday or a business trip to try to get themselves as far up the queue as possible. In Glasgow some started queueing at midnight; in London at 4.30 in the morning.

One of the London passport offices was just down the street from the Home Office, the queues a constant reproach to a monumental balls-up with me in charge. The then owner of Harrods, Mohamed Al Fayed, who was furious with me for rejecting his application for British citizenship, joined in the fun. He sent one of his quaint Harrods' coffee carts to dispense free refreshments to his fellow victims of Straw's incompetence.

Returning from the Commons on the Monday afternoon of 28 June as the storm raged, I decided, on an instinct, to dump whatever office meetings I had and go and work the queue. It was the most important decision I made in the whole crisis.

I was appalled by what I found. Mothers with babes in arms were being given no special facilities. Two I spoke with had been waiting three hours in the pouring rain. With the informal agreement of those higher up the queue I got a fast track going for them. We dished out thousands of free umbrellas. I did everything I could to support and thank the staff, who were bearing the brunt of the public's anger, but who weren't remotely responsible for the chaos.

But when I inadvertently gave out the Private Office's 'internal' phone number to a reporter masquerading as a holidaymaker in distress, I made the crisis much worse. The number was published alongside the headline 'Got a problem with your passport? Just ring this number and Jack Straw will sort it out.' Havoc ensued. My Private Office was swamped with calls. We quickly changed the number and set up a functioning call centre with Home Office volunteers, using the number I'd blurted out.[14]

As the crisis unfolded it became clear to David Omand and me that the Passports Agency had simply frozen in the headlights. Its chief executive was a decent man, but I felt he had been lulled into a false sense of security because the agency had repeatedly met all its targets.

One or two of his colleagues, though, revealed themselves as being able to cope brilliantly under fire. Liberated, they quickly came up with sensible ideas to resolve the crisis. A deal with the Post Office was agreed, so that they were able to extend the validity of passports for two years, relieving the pressure on the Passport Offices. More staff were brought in.

We got it all sorted out in the end, but not before I had endured one of the more uncomfortable weeks of my ministerial career. The day after I'd worked the queues, Mike O'Brien was asked the 'panic' question on the *Today* programme and fell into a classic journalist's trap. His answer was, at one level, accurate: 'The difficulty is that millions of people are phoning up because of the panic that is going on, partly as a result of the reporting of this.'[15] Inevitably, the Corporal Jones headlines followed: '"Don't panic" says minister'. As in *Dad's Army*, of course, everyone did – and Mike and I got it in the neck for appearing to blame the public, not ourselves.

My luck had run out in another way as well. My first two opponents as Shadow Home Secretary – Norman Fowler, then Brian Mawhinney – did not have their hearts in the job, and it showed. Both had been in Cabinet. Both knew they would retire before there was another Conservative government. Neither had the energy left for the grinding task of being knocked back day after day, the lot of any opposition party flat on its back after a catastrophic defeat.

But Ann Widdecombe did. It was an inspired appointment by William Hague. His timing was spot on, too. Appointed in early June, just as the passport storm was gathering, she embraced her new challenge like a woman possessed. She was everywhere; a terrier with my ankles in her jaw, refusing to let go.

The day of Mike's *Today* interview, Ann had called a debate to condemn 'the government's handling' of the passport crisis. He had provided her with a perfect text. Mike was an excellent minister, and a loyal friend. I was determined to stick close to him, as he always had to me. In my response to Ann I made a full apology ('abject', according to the press[16]) for all the inconvenience to those whose trips abroad had been disrupted by our failure to provide an efficient service.

It was an uncomfortable six hours, but we won the vote, as we were bound to do. Gradually, the recovery programme worked. By early September, the ten-day target was being met and calm had returned. I then used the next three months to sort out a longer-term strategy for the Agency, and put its finances into proper order.

But this was not the only fiasco to be presented on a plate to Ann Widdecombe. Poisson's distribution theorem was being proved in real time. In the space of a week, I had to go to the House three times. Jack Straw, said Ann on the third occasion, 'smiles engagingly; then apologizes humbly; and he then shrugs helplessly'.[17] I'm not sure about the 'helpless' bit, but on all three occasions there was nothing for it but to 'apologize humbly'. However difficult it might have been, any attempt to avoid taking it on the chin would have been even worse. The House rightly expects ministers to take responsibility, not to body-swerve, nor seek to blame others.

(In Opposition I'd had plenty of time to observe which ministers understood this and handled the House properly, and who resorted to evasion and circumlocution, which always backfired. In April 1995, I was sitting idly on the Opposition front bench waiting to make a point of order. Paddy Mayhew, the Northern Ireland Secretary, was on his feet making a statement on the official inquiry into a fire in the Northern Ireland Parliament building which had destroyed much of the Commons Chamber there. The report was a catalogue of utter incompetence. Everyone knew that whatever else Paddy's daily tasks, these did not extend to checking the wiring of the Stormont building. But when asked who was responsible, he replied simply that he was. 'That is not to underestimate the criticisms that have been made. As the Secretary of State, I of course take responsibility for that.'[18] I heard myself shouting from a sedentary position, 'Unlike Michael Howard.'

By pure chance I found myself that evening sat next to Paddy at an official dinner. I congratulated him on how he had dealt with what could easily have become a very grumpy House. 'Dear boy,' he said, 'let me give you some advice. Whenever you find yourself in the detritus – and you will – just put your f***ing paws up. Don't argue. Apologize.' It was very good advice.)

The week's second debacle arrived by fax. In late May, as the passport storm was brewing, an article in the *Criminal Law Journal* was faxed to the Law Officers. It claimed that the annual continuation order renewing the provisions of the counter-terrorist laws had omitted a 'Part IVA'. The consequence of this, claimed the author, was that the serious criminal offences of the possession of an article for suspected terrorist purposes and the collection of information likely to be useful for terrorist purposes did not exist. A foreign terror suspect who had spent several months in custody, and was now on bail subject to conditions, was awaiting trial for this non-existent terrorism offence.

When I saw this little time bomb, I asked for legal advice. After some weeks the categoric answer came back that the author of the article was correct. At the time of the suspect's conviction, the offence had not been on the statute book. The suspect would walk free, and I could expect a claim for compensation.

It was one of the many moments in the Home Office when I had to gasp for breath. But there was no other option. So it was down to the

House to explain myself. Before I did, I told my Private Office that I did not want to know who had made the omission. No purpose would be served. I was quite sure that he or she was beating themselves up enough without me adding to their distress.

My statement was received with the incredulity it deserved. In response to Tam Dalyell's astonishment about the saga, I replied that the 'United Kingdom's greatest legal minds – and ministerial minds, great or otherwise – missed' the defect in the continuation order. This, amazingly, included all the defence lawyers in the suspect's case. Alan Beith asked what I had said to people in the Home Office when I had learnt about the omission. 'I have now become a fully paid-up member of the Home Secretary club,' was my reply.[19]

Despite the huge and serious legislative programme we were pursuing, 'events', as Harold Macmillan famously observed, continued to drive many of the Home Office headlines.

On a Sunday morning in mid-May 1999 I had been running circuits of Battersea Park with one of my detectives. For me, keeping fit wasn't just a matter of enjoyment or waistline, but of mental health. Whatever pressures were piling in, I had to have my two or three shots of serious exercise a week, otherwise I felt I'd go potty (or more than I already was).

As we approached the last half-mile, we both sped up and raced to the finish. It was a dead heat. Fifteen years older than my running companion, I was delighted he hadn't beaten me. It was, however, a really stupid thing to do. The price I paid for my vanity was a badly damaged right knee.

Two months of physiotherapy failed to restore the knee to working order, so the orthopaedic surgeons decided that an operation was necessary. The surgery was fixed for the second week in September, when Parliament wasn't sitting and all was expected to be quiet.

I had the operation on the Tuesday and, despite Alice's entreaties (not for the first, or last, time), went off to Blackburn for normal constituency appointments on the Friday. That was daft, too. I was on crutches, and still very groggy from the general anaesthetic. My Blackburn PA Anne Higginson took me in hand, sent me back to our Blackburn home and cancelled all appointments on the Saturday.

I was woken around 9 a.m. by the incessant ringing of the phone. It was the Downing Street switchboard, with Stephen Lander, director general of the Security Service, on the line. I had regular 'bilaterals' (a Whitehall term for meetings involving two people) with Stephen, but for urgent operational matters, like emergency intercept warrants, Home Office staff, not anyone from the Service, called me. I guessed something was up.

'Have you seen the front page of *The Times*?' he asked. I explained that I was hoping not to see any pages of any newspaper that day. Stephen then told me that *The Times*' story was about Melita Norwood, 'the most important British female agent ever recruited by the KGB. Jack Straw has ruled out charges. She lives freely in the Home Counties.'

Far from ruling out charges against this woman, I did not know the first thing about her. Dozy though I was, my memory was still functioning, and I could not recall ever seeing a single piece of paper about her. In any event, even had I wanted to decide, as *The Times* alleged, that she 'should not be prosecuted', I had absolutely no role whatever in the prosecutorial system, which was in the hands of the Attorney General and Director of Public Prosecutions, who jealously guarded their independence from political influence.

An embarrassed Stephen told me that the Norwood story had come from the 'Mitrokhin' archives, thousands of secret Soviet intelligence documents which the defector and former KGB officer Vasili Nikitich Mitrokhin had handed over to Britain's Secret Intelligence Service. I had apparently seen a brief note about this archive some months before, but it had certainly not alerted me to Mrs Norwood's existence, nor to the fact that the prosecution authorities had decided in 1992 not to prosecute her, wanting to keep the material secret so that leads on more recent espionage could be followed up.

The Times was not going to allow a few inconvenient facts to get in the way of a good story; nor were the rest of the press. I knew that I'd soon be in the middle of a media frenzy. When it erupted, it was one of many recess events when I dearly wished that Parliament had been in session. I could have gone straight to the House, and knocked it on the head. As it was, I had to make do with issuing a detailed statement setting the record straight (*The Times* did not, of course, run that on their front page). The whole affair added a useful line to Ann Widdecombe's witty 'Calamity Jack' speech to her party conference four weeks later.

Along with all the security measures the Home Office had installed in our homes, there came a special ISDN phone line. This was partly for the secure, encrypted telephones, but also for an ISDN box that enabled me to give studio-quality radio interviews from my study.

I normally enjoyed doing *Today* interviews, and even when I didn't I thought that I should not avoid them, unless there was a good reason, like pre-empting a statement to the House.

Once the first twenty halcyon months as Home Secretary had come to their abrupt end – almost the day after the *Economist* article appeared – the interviews I gave *Today* followed a predictable pattern. My radio alarm would go off at 6.30 a.m., just as the presenters were setting up the agenda for the rest of the programme. I'd lie there, half-comatose, thinking 'That's a Home Office issue; so's that – and that – and I only know anything about the first. Oh God, I'm on at 8.10.' Panicky phone calls would follow to the duty private secretary and press officer. In these days before email, we had an industrial-size fax in my study which would be wheezing out briefs almost until the interview began. Ed Owen would call; we'd discuss how best I should navigate my way round John Humphrys' aggression or, worse, Jim Naughtie's seduction.

If the gods were really unhappy with me then at 7.50 precisely the Downing Street switchboard would call, and Tony would come on the line, offering me 'helpful' advice about how I should handle myself. It was always well meant, and often useful, but it wasn't quite what I needed as

I prepared to get my brain straight for a fifteen-minute live grilling on the latest local difficulty the Home Office and I had encountered.

Very early on the morning of Monday 7 February 2000 I was woken not by the radio, but by a call from a bleary duty private secretary. A hijacked plane had landed at Stansted Airport.

Since becoming Home Secretary I'd taken part in various emergency and counter-terrorist exercises. The first had involved a terrorist takeover of an oil rig in the North Sea and I hadn't been all that keen on taking part – not least because the exercises took place over the weekend. But I learnt their value. They speedily took on a reality of their own; and one developed useful experience of the chains of commands, and rhythm of a crisis. By chance, the exercise due to take place the following week was to be a hijack. Now we had a real one.

The plane had come from Mazar-e-Sharif, in the north-west of Afghanistan. It had landed three times – in Uzbekistan, Kazakhstan and Moscow. Each time a few passengers had been allowed off; but each time the authorities had allowed it to refuel and take off again, no doubt relieved that it would become someone else's problem.

I asked who had allowed it to land in the UK. It's for the Foreign Office whilst it's in the air, the Home Office only when it has landed, I was told. Robin Cook couldn't be raised, so David Manning, at that time an FCO director general, had made the decision in his stead. David had been a friend of ours for twenty-five years since we'd met him in Delhi with the Jays on our honeymoon. I trusted him in every way, and guessed that if there had been any practical alternative to having the plane on UK soil he would have found it.

There were 156 passengers and ten crew on board. Essex Police and the other agencies were well prepared. The Cabinet Office Briefing Room – COBRA, the government national security crisis management centre – was opened. Four crew and a few passengers managed to escape. Negotiators made contact with the hijack leaders. In the early morning of Thursday 10 February, five days after the plane had left Afghanistan, the crisis ended with the release of all 151 passengers then on board, and the surrender of the hijackers. One acute problem was solved; a chronic one, much more intractable, was going to replace it.

It quickly became clear that this was not a normal hijack. About half the passengers were complicit in the conspiracy. They and the hijackers now wanted to claim asylum in the UK. Whatever sympathy one had for the asylum-seekers, desperate to flee the medieval brutality of the Taliban regime, we couldn't allow such a blatant breach of international law to be rewarded.

Tony was very jumpy about the potential fallout if we mishandled this. William Hague and Ann Widdecombe lost no time in seeking to exploit the issue, with William asserting the need 'not to allow this country to reinforce its growing image as a soft touch for asylum-seekers'.[20] They both knew well that the hijack could just as easily have taken place under the Conservatives, and that the rise in asylum applications went back to the collapse of the Berlin Wall, not the election of a Labour government; but they also knew, as did we, that the public was always likely to side with the Tories' demand for ever-tougher controls on immigration and asylum – except of course for all those individual cases where they took the opposite stance.

The dilemma was, how tough could I be without being in breach of our clear obligations under the Refugee Convention? After taking advice from senior lawyers, including Charlie Falconer (who had been Solicitor General and would become Lord Chancellor) and the Attorney General Lord Williams, my statement in the House that afternoon included a carefully constructed sentence: 'Subject to compliance with all legal requirements I would wish to see removed from this country all those on the plane as soon as reasonably practicable.'*

---

* Hansard, 10 February 200, cols. 417ff. There is provision in the Refugee Convention (under Article 1F) permitting refusal of refugee status for those convicted or suspected of involvement in certain criminal acts. But to my frustration these provisions proved inadequate in this case, and many others, to prevent successful asylum claims. These provisions need to be revised.

We pushed the envelope as far as we could. William Hague had to acknowledge that I was bound by our international treaty obligations, which the Conservatives had never proposed we abrogate, and conceded that 'all asylum applications must be looked at on their merits'.[21] But the issue was still toxic for us, and constantly used as a potent symbol of how 'soft' we were on immigration.

About half the passengers did return to Afghanistan in the end. I quickly decided that three of the asylum-seekers, plus their five children, should be allowed to stay, but rejected claims from twenty-seven others and their families. Their appeals wound their way through the tribunals and the courts. The key hijackers were convicted of hijacking and other offences but quashed on appeal. Though the danger of persecution from the Taliban was removed, when the regime collapsed after the invasion in late 2001, most of those who did not return to Afghanistan immediately after the hijack are still in the UK.

The frequency of 'calamities' abated during the first six months of 2000, but one weekend in mid-June saw Exocets coming out of a clear blue sky again.

The weather was good on Saturday 17 June. Alice and I were at the cottage and decided to go off for a bike ride. These rides were always under supervision, with the detectives trailing us, but they were still very enjoyable. We stopped at the Swan pub, in Swinbrook. As we were enjoying beers by the bridge over the River Windrush, one of the detectives came up to me, phone in hand. 'There's a problem, boss,' he said. 'English fans have been rioting in Charleroi, Belgium – and the office wants you to sort it out.' Dressed in T-shirt and cycling shorts, I began to work the phones. The Belgian police had arrested hundreds of our supporters at a Euro 2000 game. They wanted them deported back to the UK, and wanted us to lay on the transport. The Ministry of Defence were as helpful as they could be, offering transport planes. The much bigger difficulty was the safety of their crews – many of the 'fans' would be aggressive, drunk, or both.

The bike ride was abandoned. The rest of the weekend was spent organizing the return of these hooligans, and working out what to say to the Commons on the Monday. We had already strengthened the law against football disorder, with a 'handout' bill sponsored by a back-bench Conservative MP, Simon Burns, with our full support. But some key parts had been watered down under pressure from the lawyers' lobby. New proposals had been announced a couple of weeks earlier. The silver lining of the Charleroi disturbances meant that I'd now have the space to push through the tough and necessary measures we had wanted all along. Since their implementation they have been critical to the marked reduction in football violence at home and abroad.*

That might have been enough for one weekend, but Poisson's now familiar theorem was being demonstrated yet again. As I was shaving on the Monday morning I was called to be told that fifty-eight illegal migrants had been found dead, suffocated on a lorry coming off the Zeebrugge ferry at Dover. It was an utterly appalling tragedy. Later that day I therefore had to make two Oral Statements, back to back.

With so much business in the Commons – and my red boxes – I had decided to ration any overseas travel to the minimum – mainly EU meetings, and roughly annual visits to the US. I made one exception, however, and in early September 2000 I embarked on a week-long trip to India and Bangladesh. There was a lot of business, but the trip was also a lot of fun.

I'd avoided alcohol for most of the trip. When we boarded the BA flight back to London at Dacca we were offered some rather good

---

* Home office figures show that football-related arrests in England and Wales fell to a new record low in the 2010–11 season.

champagne. The trip had been successful, but tiring. We quaffed one bottle, then another. The rest of the journey was spent in a happy, hazy sleep.

I'd been kept in touch with the news from the UK, but whenever I was abroad it was difficult to measure the importance of a story. Whilst in Dacca, I'd seen the odd piece about public protests against rising fuel prices, but nothing more. Driving back from Heathrow in the early morning of Monday 11 September, the story ran in more detail on the radio news, but it still didn't feel that we were about to be engulfed by the most serious crisis to hit Tony's first administration.

I got home about 7 a.m. and went to bed to catch up on some sleep. I left our daughter Charlotte a note to ask her not to wake me before noon.

At 8.30 there was knock on the bedroom door. Charlotte appeared, a mug of tea in hand. 'I'm very sorry, Dad,' she said. 'I've told them to go away, and call back this afternoon, but they've phoned again. They say he's got to talk to you, now.'

'Who's "they", who's "he"?' I asked in a semi-conscious daze.

'Number 10 Switchboard; Tony. It's about the fuel crisis,' she replied.

It was a rude awakening. Tony explained the scale of the problem, and told me (without exaggeration, as events were to show) that there was a danger we could run out of fuel. The consequences if we did were stark. He wanted me to take charge of handling the crisis, and getting the tankers moving again. Of all the myriad responsibilities of the Home Office I'd never seen anything to suggest that these included the supply of petrol, which I'd rather thought was a matter for the Department of Transport. On the other hand, the Home Office had had centuries of experience managing crises. I discovered that as Home Secretary I was chair of a moribund Cabinet Committee that had been active during the dock strikes of the seventies, called the Civil Contingencies Committee, with my permanent secretary as the deputy chair. I dressed quickly, asked the detectives to collect me as soon as they could, and got to the office.

By today's standards, fuel prices weren't too bad. They were around 81p per litre for both petrol and diesel – substantially lower in real terms than they are today.[22] But they had risen significantly since the beginning of the year, by about 6p a litre for petrol and 4p a litre for diesel, off the back of an increase in the price of crude to $30 a barrel (it's rarely below $100 today). Some farmers and other small business-men said that the increases were forcing them towards insolvency. Taxation on petrol and diesel typically accounts for around 75 per cent of the retail price. The protesters' focus was on us. We were to blame.

Most public protests come and go without seriously threatening social stability, but even in the UK with our freedoms, and our func-tioning democracy, the line between order and chaos is a fine one. The natural restraint that normally holds people back can dissolve in a trice. It is almost impossible to predict when that critical point will be reached. We saw this with the riots in the summer of 2011. However, whilst the public had no sympathy with the 2011 rioters, they were, in the main, on the same side as the 2000 fuel protesters, even if they did not necessarily approve of their tactics. This was a protest of the 'little people', against an over-mighty government with an impregnable majority. As the press quickly spotted.

We were all taken by surprise at the speed with which the protests accelerated. We had not anticipated the way the twenty-four-hour TV news channels, Sky News, and BBC News24, which had only recently started to build up significant audiences, would so amplify the effect of a protest in one area that the protests rapidly appeared to be nation-wide; in consequence, they were nationwide.

The protests had begun on the previous Friday, 8 September, at the Stanlow Shell Oil refinery near Ellesmere Port, Cheshire. They were led by a local farmer, David Handley, running a loose grouping called Farmers for Action. Handley was a classic Poujadist. Like Pierre Poujade, whose agitation was directed against the French Fourth Republic, Handley saw himself as standing for the rights of the common man against the political elites.

He and his colleagues had organized a blockade of Stanlow, to 'persuade' the tanker drivers not to deliver to the petrol stations.

Footage of the Stanlow blockade had been shown again and again on the news channels. Blockades sprang up at almost all the other refineries in the country. The managers of the refineries were being very cautious, with good reason. A tanker carrying 33,000 litres of fuel was a very dangerous proposition.

The Civil Contingencies Committee assembled in an ornate meeting room in the Cabinet Office with the portraits of past grandees looking down. Ministers painfully compared notes about what they thought was happening in their constituencies. No one had a plan. There was little sense of urgency. Action would await the elegant drafting by the Cabinet Office Secretariat of the minutes, telling us what they thought we ought to have decided. David Omand, who was as ever brilliant, whispered in my ear, 'Why don't we run this crisis the way we would run the response to a terrorist incident: use COBRA.' He pulled together a team from around Whitehall – from the Ministry of Defence, the police, the security agencies, the Transport Department – and set up camp in COBRA, which still had maps of Sierra Leone on the walls. It seemed strange at first to adopt the 'battle rhythm' of crisis management for a purely civil contingency, and it took ministers and officials some time to get used to a more decisive style.

What was terrifying was that there had been no contingency planning whatsoever for a crisis of this nature. We were well schooled in terrorist outrages, hijacks, public health epidemics. But for a petrol crisis, nothing. There was not even a readily available map of all the oil refineries in the country and where the pipelines went. We didn't know the metrics of the daily demands on production. Nor did we have any reliable way of communicating quickly with all local authorities. The Cold War civil defence arrangements had been run down but not replaced by a modern equivalent.

I thought I remembered that, like other EU countries, we had to keep a strategic reserve of fuel – 67.5 days' worth, for some reason. I asked where this was. 'Sold off' was the answer, by order of the Treasury. Photographs were produced of the tank farm where part of the reserve had been stored; but the tanks were empty, and the farm was being dismantled. Some clever clogs in the Treasury, in a classic penny-wise, pound-foolish wheeze, had worked out that the pipelines going round the country contained more than 67.5 days consumption, so we could score their content against our obligation to have a reserve. The only problem, as I discovered, is that oil products go round the pipeline in order of their density, starting with the heaviest oil first, finishing with the lightest; the system was then cleaned and the process started again. There was nothing like 67.5 days' worth of useable petrol and oil in the pipelines. Had there been a proper reserve, in tanks, we could have made supplies available in military or requisitioned tankers for essential users like hospitals, and alleviated some of the panic.

The military had been activated, but the oil companies were asking for effective country-wide protection of their drivers if they were to restart product deliveries and the police were having to make it up as they went along with no national doctrine to guide them. The chief constable of the Cheshire force – which covered the huge Stanlow refinery where the crisis had started – sometimes appeared to me more concerned to assert his autonomy from the Home Office than he did actively to assist with the crisis, to my great frustration and that of the local MP Andrew Miller.

Despite well-documented threats to the tanker drivers, there appeared to be tacit sympathy from many people whose sense of the natural order of things had been put out of joint by such a successful and dominant Labour government. Many would have enjoyed watching Tony get a bloody nose. The press enjoyed our discomfort; William Hague and Ann Widdecombe sought to exploit it.

But we also had plenty of vocal support. The trade unions were magnificent. All the unions were worried about the disruption to the economy. It was, in the main, members of the T&G who were caught in the front line of the dispute. As I later told the Commons, the oil companies had logged 180 separate incidents of intimidation by the protesters against their drivers. If just eighteen such incidents could have been laid at the door of the trade unions, the press would have had a field day.[23]

Skilful though Farmers for Action had been at the beginning of the dispute, their error was in not knowing when to stop. Over the next forty-eight hours the crisis spread to the NHS, with some NHS Trusts having to cancel all but essential operations. The National Blood Service was having difficulty in moving supplies around the country. Alan Milburn, the Health Secretary, one of the sharpest minds in the Cabinet, helped facilitate strong statements of protests by nurses and other NHS staff against the blockade.

By the Tuesday the nation was about to run out of fuel. Panic buying meant that some petrol stations already had none. And worse, the full impact of the 'just in time' philosophy of a modern economy became apparent, with few organizations any longer maintaining their own stocks, whether of fuel or of commodities, so that any hitches in the supply chain would quickly lead to production-line closures. A priority rationing system would have to be put together very quickly from scratch.*

Tony called David Omand and me to see him in his study early that evening. It was good to escape from the basement bunker of COBRA into the air.

The sun was streaming through the Downing Street windows. Tony was dressed in a loose T-shirt and gym shorts, having been on his exercise bike. He told David and me that he wanted the nine o'clock

---

* We debated for example in COBRA whether taxis were priority vehicles and concluded not. A decision that was swiftly reversed when it became clear that hospitals had contracted with taxi firms to bring essential staff to work. Later, David Omand was to discover from the Official Cabinet Office History of the Second World War that our predecessors had debated the same issue in the forties and made the same mistake. Such is the absence of collective memory.

main BBC TV news to be able to announce that the tankers were moving freely from the blockaded terminals. I looked at him with some incredulity; muttered something about pushing water uphill; and explained that whilst I understood the seriousness of the situation if the blockade were to continue, I could conceive of no way we could end it in under three hours. Tony had already told a press conference earlier that day that within twenty-four hours we would 'have the situation on the way back to normal', which wasn't particularly helpful either. But I understood why he was so anxious, and why he felt that he had to be out there leading from the front. Better that, than paralysed.

Tony called a meeting for the next morning, with the oil majors, the police, and others. Meanwhile, he phoned the most senior people we could find in the oil companies to get them to appreciate the scale of the disaster we were facing. In fact, in parallel, we'd already organized for representatives of the oil companies to be brought together in a room in the COBRA bunker. Each had a laptop connected back to their logistic systems, which enabled them to prioritize deliveries to key users such as major hospitals. This bought time for the high-level strategy to bite. We'd also been joined in COBRA by Malcolm Brindred, a senior executive at Shell, who was incredibly helpful. He and I have been firm friends ever since.

It all came back to the police. The drivers would move, and the companies would tell them to move, if the police could guarantee safe passage.

We'd already been looking at the emergency powers available. 'DORA', the Defence of the Realm Act 1914, had been subsumed into the 1920 Emergency Powers Act, which was still on the statute book. This gave the government, by Royal Proclamation, the facility to activate all the diverse, and draconian, powers in the Act. Ted Heath had issued five such proclamations to deal with the severe industrial disorder that had peppered his early seventies' premiership. The Act's provisions might have been effective; but Parliament had to be summoned within five days to endorse any proclamation. There was a fine judgement to be made: if we moved too early on this we could exacerbate the protests, and appear to be even less in control of events than in truth we were. The last thing any of us wanted was to have Tony's leadership compared to Heath's.

There were more limited but useful powers under the 1976 Energy Act, under which we had already obtained an Order in Council to help ensure delivery of fuel to essential services.

The crisis got worse before it got better. On the Wednesday, just 20 per cent of normal fuel deliveries were made. The supermarkets said that some stores might soon run out of food.*

By the evening the police had started to get better organized – even in Cheshire – as they realized that they had to abandon their soft treatment of the protesters to stop the life of the nation grinding to a halt. Of a total of 13,000 petrol stations, 2,000 around the country now received supplies. Staff from local authorities were deployed on to forecourts helping ensure priority users got what little fuel there was. Military tankers were deployed. Much more significantly, the oil companies' tankers started moving again, with police escorts.

On the Thursday, the protests – and the crisis – began to abate. The protesters had started to get the message that lives really were likely to be lost as a result of their actions in shutting hospitals and dislocating society. Finally deciding to 'adjourn' their blockades, they imperiously gave the government sixty days to act on their grievances or face further protests.

It had, in the familiar (if misquoted) words of the Duke of Wellington about his victory at Waterloo, been 'a damn close run

---

* The industry, police and Home Office finalized plans for prioritising deliveries to emergency services and other essential customers – but the actual logistics of simultaneously refuelling such vehicles, whilst trying to block other customers from garage forecourts across the country, looked daunting.

thing'.* I'd been involved in plenty of calamities, but these had been confined to the Home Office. This was different. It was existential for the government, and for Tony. It hit our public support, with the polls giving the Conservatives a significant couple of percentage points lead for the only period in that parliament. Fortunately the lead dissolved pretty quickly, but we couldn't predict that at the time.

The sixty-day ultimatum from David Handley and his fellow protesters gave us a breathing space to prepare for a next time. We were determined never to be caught on the back foot again. Tony had me chair an ad hoc Cabinet Committee, I toured the major oil refineries, talking to the managers, and especially the drivers. The police were stiffened, and so were their contingency plans. In the event, the deadline came and went without a whimper.

After a ten-month period in quarantine following his first resignation in December 1998, Peter Mandelson had returned to government in October 1999, as Northern Ireland Secretary. He quickly earned a high reputation for his work. By early 2001 he was in line for post-election promotion. Peter and I were political allies, rather than close personal friends. We occasionally saw each other for a gossipy private lunch.

Shortly before Christmas 2000, Barbara Roche, the Home Office minister who covered immigration and nationality, and Mike O'Brien, who had held this brief before Barbara, referred up to me a Written Parliamentary Question from Norman Baker, the Liberal Democrat MP for Lewes. The question asked what 'representations' had been received from Keith Vaz – then the Europe minister in the Foreign Office – or from Peter about citizenship applications from G. P. and S. P. Hinduja, two of four brothers from a family of successful Indian businessmen.

Baker was known to have good contacts in the British press, and

* The duke's actual words were: 'It has been a damn nice thing – the nearest run thing you ever saw . . .', using 'nice' in its archaic sense, to mean 'close'.

almost certainly had been asked to put down the PQ as part of a fishing expedition. The issue was sensitive for the party, and particularly for Peter, because S. P. Hinduja had financially underwritten the 'Faith Zone' in the Millennium Dome, and was a Labour donor too.*

I had some iron rules about PQs: 1) answer that question, not one you'd prefer to answer. Dodging is defensive; 2) provide as much information as possible, up front – far better that, than have details dragged out of you later; 3) get the answer back quickly. Delay breeds suspicion.

Before the break I agreed a draft answer, and had this faxed to Peter's and Keith's offices for their comment – my usual practice with PQs that affected a fellow minister.

Keith and Peter had each made enquiries to Home Office ministers about the citizenship applications of the two brothers. Although not germane to this PQ itself, Peter had raised direct with me (after a lunch in May 2000) the application of a third brother, Prakash, and had passed me a detailed letter about this.

Both Keith and Peter were initially sensitive to the idea that their 'enquiries' on behalf of the Hindujas could be classed as 'representations'. My view was clear. If these 'enquiries' were not 'representations', what were they? I would be dancing on the head of a pin to make the distinction. There was nothing wrong with taking up someone's case – MPs did it every day; the wrongdoing would arise if special favours had been shown. There was never the least suggestion that Keith or Peter had ever sought favours for these men.

By the time the Commons returned after its Christmas break, the PQ was well overdue. It had to be answered. Keith quickly accepted the draft. Peter continued to be nervous about it.

Mike O'Brien had the clearest possible recollection that in 1998 Peter had spoken to him about the 'general circumstances surrounding the

---

* Sir Anthony Hammond QC's report, 'Review of the Circumstances Surrounding an Application for Naturalisation by Mr S. P. Hinduja in 1998', cleared the Hindujas of any wrongdoing.

refusal' of S. P. Hinduja's application for citizenship.[24] By early 2001 Peter had no recollection of this. I believed both of them. If Peter was anything like me, then as a busy senior minister, it was often difficult to remember things that had happened two weeks before, let alone two years. But I had no reason whatever to doubt Mike, either. He was of the highest integrity. In the circumstances he was much more likely to remember the conversation with Peter, than the other way round. The PQ answer would have to reflect this conversation.

The matter still unresolved, I spoke to Peter on the phone on 16 January 2001, with a private secretary on the line. I went through my draft answer with Peter, raising with him the 1998 conversation between him and Mike. The draft was amended, again; sent over to Peter's and Keith's offices. A good month after it had been tabled, Mr Baker received his answer on the Thursday, 18 January.

Then a quirk of fate intervened.

Alice and I were staying in the Chilterns for the weekend in a cottage borrowed from Michael and Sylvia Jay. It snowed heavily overnight and on the Sunday, Alice and I went for a lengthy walk over hills. It was magical. In the late afternoon I dealt with one box. In the car on the way back to London, I dealt with the other. The Sunday papers, which hadn't been delivered earlier, because of the snow, were in the car, too. I skimmed the front of the *Observer*. It had a report headlined 'Mandelson helped Dome backer's passport bid', but the opening paragraphs seemed inoffensive.

I missed entirely, until the next day, a key sentence 'I [i.e. Peter Mandelson] was always sensitive to the proprieties. The matter was dealt with by my private secretary. At no time did I support or endorse this application for citizenship.'[25]

If I'd read that on the Sunday, and my brain had been in gear, I would have called Peter; reminded him that it wasn't the whole story; and suggested that he put out a correction. But events spiralled out of control. Rather than clarifying the matter, Peter dug the hole deeper, by claiming on *Channel 4 News* on the Tuesday that he hadn't changed his story.

On Tuesday evening Alice and I went off to the Whitbread Book Awards. Most of my evening was spent in a stairwell, on two long calls to Tony as he tried to piece together what had happened. Next day he decided to ask Peter for his resignation. This was announced, but did not take effect until after Peter had handled Oral Northern Ireland Questions, which he did with great dignity, and had then sat next to Tony for the following half-hour's Prime Minister's Questions.

Peter took exception to my saying in an interview that evening that he had 'told an untruth'. I'm not sure how else I should have described it – maybe 'misremembered' – but our relationship never fully recovered.* I had gone to great lengths to square the PQ answer with him, not only because he was a fellow minister, but also a good colleague for whom I had (and have) a high regard. I had no reason whatever to disadvantage him.

Six years before, at the pre-broadcast dinner for *Any Questions*, I'd found myself sat next to Michael Portillo, a fellow panellist. This was shortly after Michael had got himself embroiled in an extraordinary controversy by roundly criticizing the quality of public examinations in other European countries.† Out of the blue, Michael said to me that he 'attempted political suicide' about once every three months. I was often struck that both he and Peter appeared to be unnecessary risk-takers – flying too close to the sun. Peter was always brilliant in the advice he

---

* In his memoir *The Third Man* (HarperPress, London, 2010), Peter refers to the statement drafted by Tony Blair in which it was said that he (Peter) accepted 'that when my office spoke to a Sunday newspaper at the weekend, I should have been clear that it was me personally, not my official, who spoke to the Home Office Minister' and 'regretted that as a result, information that was "incorrect" had been given to the media by the prime minister's spokesman' (p. 313). Peter also commented that the series of interviews he had given 'turned out to be a huge mistake' (p. 311).

† 'If any of you have got an A level, it is because you have worked for it. Go to any other country, and when you have got an A level, you have bought it.' Speech to Southampton University students, 1994.

gave to others (me included); it was a great shame, for the party and for him, that he was less good in the advice he gave to himself.

Tony was driving public sector reform across Whitehall. One of his teams, led by Michael Barber, whom I'd known since he'd been a researcher at the National Union of Teachers, was very helpful. Michael ran a kind of in-house management consultancy first for DfES and then for Number 10. He understood how to get organizations on side for change. His proposals led directly to improvements especially in IND, and the way it processed its thousands of cases.

Whilst Michael Barber had an instinctive understanding of how government worked, the same could not be said for the former director general of the BBC, John Birt, who somehow inveigled himself into Downing Street in advance of the 2001 general election, and got others there to believe that he would be able to find the holy grail of crime-reduction policies. Unleashed by Number 10, he began to interfere in the Home Office's work, for no good reason, so far as I could see, and even less understanding.

This made for a difficult last few months at the Home Office, compounded by David Blunkett, who coveted my job, and ran a brazen and very public campaign for it with help from papers like the *Sun*. I asked David to desist. I wanted a move anyway – what was the point of trying to undermine me? (More recently he has apologized for his approach.) And there was Charles Clarke, whom I had brought into the Home Office and who was so impatient for advancement that he spent some time trying to persuade Number 10 that he could do a better job, forming an alliance with John.

There was mutual irritation with Number 10. The centre thought that I'd been captured by the department. I thought they'd been captured by the fairies.

Manoeuverings for Cabinet appointments always increase prior to elections, especially if you are expected to win a second term. Planned for our fourth anniversary in early May 2001, the election had to be delayed for a month because of the foot-and-mouth crisis. In the absence of doubt about the result, the contest became one between New Labour and the press. (Intelligent, articulate, witty, sometimes devastatingly effective against Tony, if life were fair William Hague should have been running us closer in the 2001 election.)

Across the country, I met apathy on the doorstep, as voter after voter told me that they would have a rest from the polling station – 'we'd win anyway'. My argument that we could only win if people put their crosses on sufficient ballot papers was met with condescension.

For me, the four weeks of the election would have been unmemorable, but for Wednesday 16 May, my 'Thank God for John Prescott' day.

It was the launch of the manifesto. To generate interest, we'd all been despatched to Birmingham, where with much razzmatazz, and various Cabinet ministers (me included) as spear-carriers, Tony spelt out the further future which New Labour had to offer. Like my Cabinet colleagues, I had no serious work to do there, except fix my smile ('Your naff look again, Dad,' was always Charlotte's verdict). My mind was on other things – the Police Federation's Annual Conference in Blackpool.

British police have, in general, a justified reputation for calm and restraint under the most intense provocation on the streets. They make up for this at 'Fed' meetings, notorious for being the most raucous in the calendar. The 'Met Fed' was the bolshiest of all. I'd made a point of addressing them regularly at their mass meetings in Central Hall, Westminster. Between the heckles and catcalls I'd often reflected that it was as well I'd been trained in the hard school of politics, the NUS, the Militant period, and endless soapbox sessions in Blackburn.

To help establish an atmosphere of decorum at the national Fed meeting, the Home Secretary of the day was normally accompanied by a full platform of very senior officers weighed down with gold braid –

and, crucially, the 'Address' took place first thing in the morning, before the bars opened.

But, thanks to foot and mouth, my long-planned address was now to take place in the middle of the election campaign. To avoid any suggestion of partiality, no senior officers could accompany me. No gold braid, no restraints, almost naked I went into the conference chamber. Worse still, I'd had to delay my arrival until the afternoon because of the manifesto launch.

I'd deliberately drafted a pro-police, tough-on-crime speech; but for all the difference it made I could just as well have read out the telephone book, or launched an attack on the 'all coppers are bastards' theme.

Gentle heckles turned into catcalls, then slow handclaps. I ploughed on grimly, and left quickly. On the train back to London, I told Ed there was only one thing to do – buy a large bottle of red wine, and drink it. Around Crewe, Ed took a phone call from Justin Russell back in party HQ, and began giggling. 'Tony's upstaged you in the disaster stakes,' he said. 'He got monstered on a visit to a Birmingham hospital.'

An hour later, around Rugby, and well into the second bottle, Justin rang again. Ed started laughing, hysterically. 'It's all OK, Jack. There is a God after all, and he likes you. John Prescott's lamped a voter. It's the top story everywhere. Tony's the second. You'll be lucky to make page seventeen.'

When the results of the election came through, our share of the vote had dipped, but was still close to 41 per cent, with the Tories 9 points behind on 32 per cent. We lost just 5 seats, and had 413 to the Tories' 166 – a remarkable result for a second term, and a triumph for Tony.

Nationally, the turnout dropped to 60 per cent, the lowest since 1918. In Blackburn, my local party spent most of their time in much more marginal adjoining seats, whilst I was campaigning across the country. Our turnout slumped to 55 per cent. My share of the vote – at 54 per cent – scarcely moved.

When I left the Home Office, they held a valedictory party for me. It was a lovely occasion. The detectives gave me a large steel kitchen knife with 'Special Branch 1997–2001' on the blade. The jokers in the Private Office presented me with a self-inking rubber stamp saying 'WALOB' (short for 'what a load of bollocks'). Best of all was a fine Waterman fountain pen, with the inscription 'Jack Straw – 21st Longest-Serving Home Secretary'. Phew.

FOURTEEN

Life in the Air

Zimbabwe, and Gibraltar.

My answer to a close friend who'd asked in July 2001 what
were the biggest issues facing me as the new Foreign Secretary

I had told Tony Blair some months before the election that I'd like a
move from the Home Office. I'd enjoyed my time as Home Secretary,
but I was running out of road. Others, champing at the bit, could see
whether (as they had been so assiduously briefing the press) they could
do a better job.

My preference, which I thought Tony had agreed, was to take over
John Prescott's huge department covering transport, planning, local
government and the regions. JP was keen on the idea as well and called
me on election day to agree the choreography for a friendly handover.

Number 10 had instructed senior ministers to be back in London by
11 a.m. on the day after the election. We were, but the hours went past
without a word, so I checked in with the Downing Street duty clerk.
'Don't call us, we'll call you.' I didn't think that my ministerial career
was about to end, but I guessed that there was some other drama being
played out. (There was – Tony was involved in a monumental three-way
row with Cherie and Anji Hunter; Cherie felt Anji's future lay outside
Number 10.)

At 5 p.m. I'd had enough of sitting around, so I called my detectives and said that I was going to fetch up at Downing Street, and wait there.

Reshuffles are the moment of supreme power for any prime minister, and for his staff too. They were rather surprised to see me. I was secreted into a small room off the Cabinet Room lobby. I spent the time re-reading a detailed minute I'd sent to Tony the week before, confirming our conversation about how I'd run JP's department, and refreshing my memory on what the manifesto had to say in this area. Around 6 p.m. I was called in to Tony's room.

'I'm not giving you JP's job,' he said. 'I'm making you Foreign Secretary.'

'F*** me,' I said, and almost fell off my chair.

'Don't you want the job, Jack?'

'I do want it, thank you very much. I simply was never expecting it. I thought Robin [Cook] was staying.'

Robin was not exactly 'clubbable', but we were friends, and we trusted each other. I was certain that he would know that I had never coveted his job. His accurate diary record of the conversation we had later that day said, 'If I was surprised to be moved from my job . . . [Jack] sounded even more surprised to get it.'[1] He was also relieved that Alice and I had no interest in taking over the Foreign Secretary's official residence on the upper floors of 1 Carlton Gardens (I would use the lower floors, for meetings and functions), though we did take over Chevening, the wonderful country house (better than Chequers) near Sevenoaks that was allocated to the Foreign Secretary.

'There's just one thing we do need to get clear if you are going to be Foreign Secretary,' Tony added, once he'd established that I did want the job. 'The euro. If Cabinet recommends that we go in, I have to know that you'll be onside.'

'The man's not daft,' I thought to myself. Close though we were, Tony knew that we came at the issues of the EU, and the euro, from different positions. I saw myself as a 'practical European', not an enthusiast. I'd long believed that the euro was fundamentally flawed. Gordon's famous 'five tests'* for us to join had been a great relief to me. I'd written them into my red pocketbook (they are still there). I'd never asked Gordon outright; I didn't need to. It was obvious that since he'd not only set the exam paper but would be sitting it and marking it too, this was the one test of his life he'd be determined to fail. I judged that there was in practice no risk that Gordon would ever bring Cabinet a proposal to join. I nodded assent to Tony, shook his hands and went out, very happy, to begin another extraordinary chapter of my life.

My daughter Charlotte was on a gap-year project in remote eastern Uganda. There was no way of contacting her quickly. She found out about my appointment from a Ugandan friend whose addiction was listening to the BBC World Service. Will had, for the second time, been spirited into Downing Street by Ed Owen. I met him in the lobby. He gave me the hug of his life.

The detectives led me – still fazed – across Downing Street, and down the steps to the Ambassador's Entrance of the FCO. I was met by my new permanent secretary, the brilliantly wily John Kerr – or the 'posh Scot', as I used to tease him – and Sherard Cowper-Cowles, the principal private secretary, later famous within the Diplomatic Service for lavishing overblown praise on his masters in his telegrams.

They took me up the stairs to the Foreign Secretary's magnificent office overlooking the Downing Street garden, Horse Guards Parade and St James's Park. I was so tired that once I'd picked up a box full of the inevitable 'Briefs for Incoming Ministers', I went home, where Alice had, as four years previously, assembled the same small group of close friends to celebrate.

Sherard Cowper-Coles was in his last week as private secretary. Robin had appointed a successor, Simon McDonald, an Arabist who'd

---

* Hansard, 27 October 1997, col. 584. They were 1. Sustainable convergence, 2. Sufficient flexibility to cope with economic change, 3. Effect of investment, 4. Impact on financial services, 5. Whether it is good for employment.

been serving in Saudi Arabia. He came in to see me on the Saturday, as white as a sheet. He was followed by an equally pale Michael Williams, a distinguished international diplomat with much UN experience, who'd been Robin's policy adviser. Both nervously asked me if I would be keeping them on. I told them both that I had no reason to doubt Robin's judgement – and I never did.

I'd always taken an interest in foreign policy, but in my twenty-three years in the House I'd never had a foreign policy brief. The FCO was going to be a very different challenge from the Home Office, whose subject matter I had known inside out.

At the Home Office I had got actively stuck into EU diplomacy on the vast Justice and Home Affairs agenda. I had discovered that I enjoyed the process of negotiation, and wasn't bad at it either. Politics in most other EU nations is much more personal than it is in the UK. Our institutions are more powerful, and stable. And, since so many EU governments are elected by proportional systems, coalitions are the order of the day; for European politicians, doing deals behind closed doors is a way of life. Personal relations of course matter here, but they matter much more in Europe. I had quickly developed strong and trusting friendships with a lot of my fellow justice and interior ministers, worked out where they were coming from and sought to use these relationships to advance and defend the UK's interests.

All that had been on a familiar field. This was different. I'd always admired Douglas Hurd (Conservative Foreign Secretary 1989–95) and I now sought his avuncular advice, which was immensely helpful. He gave me a reading list, though to my relief I found that I'd already read at least half the books. I wasn't as unprepared as I had thought. I've always enjoyed political biographies and histories of all kinds. Alice had taken history at Oxford and had a lifelong interest in the subject. When I'd been on *Desert Island Discs* in 1998 my chosen book had been *The Franco-Prussian War* by (the other) Michael Howard, which had told me more about the causes of the two twentieth-century world wars than even A. J. P. Taylor.[2] I was further reassured when I read Henry Kissinger's *Diplomacy* at the top of Douglas's list. What any good foreign minister needs, said Kissinger, as well as stamina, application and an ability to negotiate, is an appreciation of history. I had long subscribed to the old saw that, 'a nation without a history is like a man without a memory'. This job was living history.

The Foreign Office, like the Home Office, was founded in 1782. There the similarity ended.

The Home Office is housed in an austere sixties' concrete mausoleum; the Foreign Office in its 1860s palace, the most glorious and ornamented of all Whitehall buildings, designed by George Gilbert Scott on a brief from that most belligerent of prime ministers, Lord Palmerston, to celebrate Britain's imperial power, and to intimidate foreigners.

The methods of the two departments are very different. The Home Office uses executive decision (by the thousands) and legislation (volumes of it) to secure social control and tranquillity at home. Where the Home Office works by diktat the Foreign Office has to work by persuasion – though (as Palmerston famously showed) that persuasion might need to be backed by the threat or use of force.*

The people are different, too. There are some very bright people in the Home Office, but their number is greater in the Foreign Office. The officials in the Diplomatic Service are instinctively much more comfortable with politics than some Home civil servants. When serving in posts abroad, they are the public face of British interests and of the

---

* Palmerston's use of gunboat diplomacy even extended to consular support for our citizens. Don Pacifico was a Portuguese Jew living in Athens but he had been born in Gibraltar and therefore had British citizenship. His home in Athens had been burnt down in 1847 in a riot. Pacifico sought compensation from the Greek government. When the latter refused, he appealed to the British government. In 1850 Palmerston sent gunboats to blockade Piraeus. The Greeks paid up, but this incident led to Palmerston having to make a three-hour defence in the House of Commons, in which he made his famous 'Civus Brittanicus Sum' speech.

British government, and are, in many ways, autonomous. However, that could sometimes lead to a disdain for mere politicians, amongst some of the very senior people at least. When I became Foreign Secretary, there was a group that described themselves as the 'Senators' and scarcely concealed the reservations they had about me. Thankfully, by the time I left this approach had all but disappeared.

My first week was a whirlwind.

On the Monday it was off to the EU Foreign Ministers' Council. I spent much of my time on the phone, to Tony and others, discussing junior ministers for my team. Just before lunch John Williams, my press secretary (another great appointment inherited from Robin), told me I was to do a 'grab' with the media. I went out; the lights went on. 'I'm delighted to be here for my first meeting as Britain's new Foreign Secretary, in Brussels.'

'Luxembourg,' came Ed Owen's stage whisper, loud enough to be caught on camera.

Tony announced his junior ministers later that day. Joining me in the Foreign Office were Liz (Baroness) Symons, Peter Hain, Ben Bradshaw, Denis MacShane and Valerie (Baroness) Amos.

Tuesday saw a state banquet at Windsor Castle for President Mbeki of South Africa; Wednesday a NATO Council in Brussels, and the farewell party for the staff of the Home Office; Thursday a European Council – an EU 'summit' of both heads of government and foreign ministers.*

Despite this hectic start, there was one other big difference from the Home Office – the amount of work. I had assumed, and so had Alice, that if anything there would be an even heavier load. Initially, at least, the reverse was the case. There was much more travelling, of course. But I had half the box work I'd had in the Home Office, no legislation to speak of, and once home I was disturbed far less.

---

* Under the 2009 Lisbon Treaty, membership of the European Council is now restricted to heads of government only.

I put the time to good use.

First, developing a sense of what I wanted to achieve as Foreign Secretary. Since I knew that I would be judged by results and nothing else, I decided to avoid labels. Robin's 'ethical foreign policy' had been used, albeit unfairly, to trip him up. It wasn't that anyone wanted to be 'unethical' but the label was unhelpful.

Second, I wanted to build relations with key foreign ministers. Joschka Fischer was leader of the Greens in Germany, and Vice Chancellor in Gerhard Schroeder's coalition government. His life had been so extraordinary, he could probably not have risen to the top in any other nation than liberal, forgiving, post-war Germany.

He had first visited the UK in the mid-sixties when he had eloped with his eighteen-year-old fiancée to marry at Gretna Green. The worst of this impecunious existence, he claimed, had been the execrable food at the Carlisle Woolworths' café – for which he would frequently, and quite publicly, blame me. (I retaliated.) In the seventies, as I was being (more or less) well behaved as a British student leader, Joschka was leading more physical street protests, in the Putzgruppe (literally 'cleaning squad') in Frankfurt.

Despite his political past, and a colourful private life, Joschka was for many years Germany's most popular politician. He was a brilliant orator in English as well as German; he had great judgement, and was a load of fun.

I first met the Russian foreign minister Igor Ivanov at the G8 Foreign Ministers' Conference in early July. Boisterous and entertaining, he once gave me a full-size vodka-filled glass Kalashnikov. (I gave it to Charlotte for her twenty-first – she still has it, un-drunk.)

Four weeks after the election, in early July, saw me in Washington, to meet Colin Powell, George Bush's first Secretary of State, and Condoleezza Rice, then National Security Adviser, later Colin's successor. Alice and I were to become firm friends with them both.

At the State Department, in the aptly named Foggy Bottom, Colin's deputy, Rich Armitage, came to greet me. Rich is a huge man; the same age as me, with muscles bulging out of his suit in every direction. He was a navy man and Colin army; they were the closest of friends, from their days working for Caspar 'Cap' Weinberger at the beginning of the Reagan administration in 1981. Rich was famous for his pithy epithets. Almost the first thing he said to me was, 'Mr Secretary, you know the problem with some of the guys in this administration? They ain't never smelt f***ing cordite.' He, and Colin, knew from experience that war was more full of horror than ever it was of glory.

Of many other acquaintances I made in those first few weeks, one of the most important was Prince Saud al-Faisal of Saudi Arabia. The prince had been appointed in 1975, the year his father, King Faisal, was assassinated by his cousin. He is now the longest-serving foreign minister in the world by some margin. Wise, shrewd and compassionate, he was a source of great counsel to me over the years.

The first three months of the job were quiet. I made some minor decisions about troop deployments (measured in hundreds) in the Balkans, and about independence for Macedonia.* There were unproductive wrangles with other P5 nations (UN Security Council permanent members) about 'roll-over' resolutions on Iraq sanctions.†

And there was Zimbabwe.

One of the greatest foreign policy achievements of Margaret Thatcher's first administration – thanks to the heroic efforts of the then Foreign Secretary, Peter Carrington, not his boss – was a settlement of the seemingly intractable issue of Zimbabwe.

---

* To this day, Macedonia has officially to be called 'FYROM' – the Former Yugoslav Republic of Macedonia – due to Greek sensibilities over the historic territory of Macedonia.

† A 'roll-over' resolution is where an existing resolution has been continued in force for a limited period, typically six months.

Resolution had defied successive British governments ever since the white supremacists' leader Ian Smith had made his Unilateral Declaration of Independence from the UK, in November 1965.

In a classic piece of old-style diplomacy, the Lancaster House talks that Lord Carrington chaired in December 1979 agreed a constitution for a rapid and peaceful transition to black majority rule, under the presidency of Robert Mugabe.* The British government rallied donors to support the new Zimbabwe, and £630 million of aid (£1.9 billion at today's prices) was pledged. The first phase of land reform, in the eighties, partially funded by the UK, resettled 70,000 landless people.

By the nineties, the Mugabe government's mismanagement had led to mounting civil unrest, which was met by an increasingly autocratic and illiberal response.

The fundamental problem, however, remained land.

Fifteen years after independence, despite majority rule and a 'willing-buyer-willing-seller' land reform programme, whites made up less than 1 per cent of the population but still held about 70 per cent of the land. Unsurprisingly, Mugabe decided he would have to take decisive action and in 1997 issued a demand to the British government for more assistance with land purchases.

The response of Clare Short, International Development Secretary in Tony's first Cabinet, was so ill-conceived that it soured relations between the two countries, and was later described by the long-serving president of neighbouring Zambia, Kenneth Kaunda, as 'criminal'.[3]

In her letter of 5 November 1997 Clare wrote to Zimbabwe's agricultural minister:

> I should make it clear that we do not accept that Britain has a special responsibility to meet the costs of land purchase in Zimbabwe. We are a new government from diverse backgrounds without links to former colonial interests. My own origins are Irish and as you

---

* Lancaster House Agreement, 21 December 1979.

know we were colonized, not colonizers . . . We do, however, recognize the very real issues you face over land reform. We believe that land reform could be an important component of a Zimbabwean programme designed to eliminate poverty. We would be prepared to support a programme of land reform that was part of a poverty eradication strategy but not on any other basis.[4]

The letter was incendiary. Mugabe and his government were beside themselves about it. It was absurd of Clare to suggest that there was some kind of moral equivalence between the abject, and very recent, subjugation of the black majority in Zimbabwe, and someone like her. In any event Clare was a Secretary of State in the government of the United Kingdom, the former 'colonizer' of the country. The Thatcher government had, correctly, accepted that we did have a 'special responsibility' towards meeting the costs of land purchases in Zimbabwe.

Robin told me at the time that he was almost apoplectic about it, but he and Clare were barely on speaking terms anyway. Michael Williams quipped that offered a choice between a walk across St James's Park to see Clare, and a trip to Ulan Bator in the hold of a cargo plane, Robin would always have opted for the latter. Tony had his own (and growing) problems with Clare, including her close association with Gordon, and may simply have decided not to fight her on this issue.

Three years later, in 2000, when Mugabe began a compulsory land redistribution programme, Robin made efforts within the Commonwealth structure to reach a settlement with the Mugabe government, and put the intense embarrassment of Clare's intervention behind us. President Obasanjo of Nigeria agreed to broker the talks, which were held in Nigeria's capital, Abuja, in the first week of September 2001. With the inestimable Valerie Amos at my side, I joined the foreign minister from Nigeria, Don McKinnon, Commonwealth Secretary General, and other Commonwealth ministers.

(I later got to know the Nigerian foreign minister, Sule Lamido, pretty well. On a walk across St James's Park to the Commonwealth HQ one day I idly asked him how many children he had.

'Just a second, Jack,' he replied, 'I'll work it out.' He started count-ing, then recounting, on his fingers. 'Twenty-five,' was his conclusion. 'But I have more than one wife,' he added with a twinkle.)

The Zimbabwe delegation was led by their foreign minister, Stan Mudenge. He greeted me like a long-lost friend – reminding me that he'd been a student activist at neighbouring York University when I'd been at Leeds. As soon as the meeting opened, and Stan began, I had instant recall. He was the guy with bottomless lungs whose stock in trade was to talk and talk until his adversaries were begging for mercy. Our shared experiences proved very helpful, however.

Half-way through the day, the negotiations stalled. Stan was digging in. Unexpectedly, the Nigerian President Obasanjo arrived – and just sat there, glowering at Stan, asking the occasional very pointed question of him. It worked. Thanks to him, and then to Valerie's efforts, we reached provisional agreement.

The text of the deal had to be endorsed by President Obasanjo. Calls were made; the president was unavailable. Sule was sent off to find him; an hour went past; two hours. Then Sule confided in me that the pres-ident liked 'a little recreation' in the late afternoon. We'd simply have to wait. He finally turned up, signed the communiqué, a press confer-ence was held, and we all got on our planes home – with some hope that our labours might have made a difference. But for the cataclysm that engulfed us a few days later, they might have.

In the Home Office the challenge had been to keep out of the news; in these early weeks in the Foreign Office, it was the opposite. Though I had enjoyed the relative peace, I was beginning to get a bit twitchy, in need of a fix of good coverage.

On the morning of Monday 10 September 2001 I went off to Manchester to make a 'keynote' speech about the importance of Brit-ish foreign policy. It sank. The newspapers on the morning of 11 September ignored it. I took solace, with Alice, in a breakfast viewing of the Vermeer exhibition at the National Gallery.

In the early afternoon of 11 September I was holding a meeting to discuss troop deployments in the Balkans with Defence Secretary Geoff Hoon and the Chief of the Defence Staff Michael Boyce. One of the private secretaries, Mark Sedwill, came in.

Mark had an air of urgency about him. He switched on the television, and said: 'You need to see this. Something really serious going on.'

Geoff and Michael, as stunned as I was, left swiftly for the MoD. My first observation was the hardly original 'This changes everything.' But everything did change that day. 9/11 defined our foreign policy (and much of our home policy) for years after that, and in many ways still does. For the United States, which hadn't, on its own mainland, suffered such casualties at the hands of a foreign enemy since the 1812 War, or losses at all on that scale since the Civil War in the 1860s, the experience of 9/11 is as indelible on their national psyche as Dunkirk is on ours.

Tony was in Brighton, about to give one of the more difficult speeches in any Labour prime minister's calendar, to the Trades Union Congress. It is a mark of his statesmanship, and his remarkable qualities as a leader on the world stage, that he was able to find exactly the right words, in the right tone, to match the sense of shared dread and apprehension that was spreading rapidly across the globe. He said, 'This mass terrorism is the new evil in our world today. It is perpetrated by fanatics who are utterly indifferent to the sanctity of human life and we, the democracies of this world, are going to have to come together to fight it together and eradicate this evil completely from our world.'[5] This speech, as he later recorded, was given a better reception than any he had enjoyed before (or after) at the TUC. He and his office ensured that emergency procedures were being put in place by the Ministry of Defence and the Home Office. Flights over London were suspended.

Tony got back on his train to London for meetings with ministers and officials. Meanwhile the FCO was putting together arrangements to support the families of British citizens killed or injured in the atrocities, but it was long days and weeks before many families knew what had happened to their loved ones.

My concern at this stage, though it may seem odd from this distance, was, as I told Alastair Campbell, that we (i.e. Tony) should not get too far ahead of the US in terms of what we said.

Tony easily fitted the proverb 'Cometh the hour, cometh the man', but there was less certainty that the US president George Bush would. The clips of him when he had received the news of the attacks had not been especially reassuring – though who knows how Tony (or I) would have looked if the attacks had been on a London office tower, on Whitehall, and the Palace of Westminster.

Not only were we wholly unprepared for the fact of 9/11, but we were unprepared for the phenomenon behind it, of a hatred justified by a perverted view of the holy texts and canon of Islam.

We knew about religious bigotry. We had had it in our backyard – in Northern Ireland. In previous centuries different views of the Christian truth had been the excuse, and the occasion, for the most appalling brutality. We knew about martyrdom – my school song celebrated the memory of a Protestant martyr at the hand of a Catholic tyrant. And, from Europe's twentieth-century history, during which more people had been killed in conflict than in any other century or continent, we knew all about the depths to which fellow members of the human race could stoop in pursuit of power and ideology.

We knew, too, about an international terrorist organization called al-Qaeda claiming to act in the name of Islam. During the many difficult and fractious arguments later, especially over the mounting civilian casualties from terrorism in Iraq, there was often an implicit assumption, sometimes an explicit assertion, that the international Islamist terrorism behind the atrocities of 9/11 and so much else had been caused by our intervention in Afghanistan and Iraq, not the other way round. More than once I had to remind my audience that 9/11 happened before our invasion of Afghanistan, and was its cause, eighteen months before the Iraq War began; and that there was already a long list of the innocent victims of al-Qaeda well before 9/11 – including the

224 killed and nearly 5,000 injured in the bombings of the US embassies in Kenya and Tanzania in August 1998,[6] the seventeen killed and thirty-nine injured in the bombing of the USS *Cole* in Aden in 2000, and those killed and maimed by the previous attempt in February 1993 to blow up the World Trade Center by planting a truck bomb in the underground car park. But before 9/11, we didn't begin to comprehend the contemporary power of Islamic fundamentalism.

I had had a tiny personal foretaste of this phenomenon, in Blackburn, when protest against the publication of Salman Rushdie's *Satanic Verses* was at its height. In 1989 at a meeting in a community centre, about forty men were sat in a large circle around the room; all Muslim, apart from a couple of councillors and town hall officials, a police inspector, and me. The meeting had begun well enough. Then, as the police inspector and I tried calmly to explain that in the United Kingdom there was no legal power to ban books because their contents were deemed offensive, some of those present became possessed by a fury I'd never witnessed before, in any context. The offending volume was kicked across the room, and back again. Impossible demands were made of me, as the senior politician present, to have the booked banned forthwith. Attempts to provide balm through reason only inflamed the fury. More worrying, the others in the meeting, most of whom I knew as decent moderate people, seemed intimidated into silence by the sheer emotional force of those with the most extreme views. It was almost a spell; a spell that continued to work for some days thereafter, and had a farcical consequence. Local elections were imminent. We lost this rock-solid Labour council seat to the Conservative candidate, whose only message was the slogan 'Vote Bikha, Vote Tory, Ban the Book'.*

I'd long taken a layman's interest in comparative religion, including Islam. An understanding of the history of our continent is impossible

---

* May 1989 – Lancashire County Council elections, Bank Top and Brookhouse Ward.

without it. Prompted by this experience, I'd sought to learn more about Islam, but I was still only at the foothills.

There had been very little about this issue, which was to dominate our lives from 11 September, in my incoming briefs. But Peter Westmacott, then deputy undersecretary and now British ambassador to Washington, showed real prescience in coming to see me early on to talk specifically about his concerns about developments in the Muslim world. He told me how much he had learnt from the writings of the theologian Karen Armstrong. He recommended two of her works – *Islam, A Short History* and *The Battle for God – Fundamentalism in Judaism, Christianity and Islam*. I read them, and have been a fan of her writing ever since.

Nor had Afghanistan featured much in the briefs. Diplomatic relations with the country had been suspended in 1989 when the Taliban had taken power. Our embassy building in Kabul was being looked after on a care-and-maintenance basis by a locally engaged skeleton staff.

As a pawn in the 'Great Game' with Russia, Afghanistan had featured large in Britain's imperial past. Our experience in the nineteenth century had taught us the costly lesson that, however violently disputatious the Afghans might be between themselves, they were pretty united in their dislike of foreign intervention. But to protect India, the jewel in the empire's crown, we had continued to exert control and influence. It was 1919 before we granted Afghanistan autonomy over its own foreign policy.

In the latter half of the twentieth century, the Great Game had shifted. It was between the Soviet Union and the USA. Growing military aid from the US to Pakistan was seen as a means of offsetting Soviet influence in India. It was also to a degree the Soviet leadership's excuse for their 100,000-strong invasion of Afghanistan in 1979, one of the most disastrous of all twentieth-century military adventures.

The Soviet invasion led to decisions by the United States from which they, and the rest of the world, continue to reap a whirlwind. Afghanistan became the theatre for a major proxy war between the two superpowers. Aid and materiel from the US, and from Saudi Arabia, was poured into Pakistan to enable them to train and equip the Mujahideen, the guerrilla forces fighting the Soviet Army and their local allies. Pakistan's Inter-Services Intelligence Directorate (ISI) was used by the US to run the networks in Afghanistan.

Over a million Afghans, mainly civilians, died during this ten-year conflict. When the Soviets retreated, beaten, in 1989, civil war filled the vacuum. Pakistan sent thousands of troops and much other assistance in support of the Taliban, who eventually took control of the central and southern parts of the country in 1996, and established their Islamic Emirate of Afghanistan.

This profound humiliation hastened the collapse of the Soviet system itself just two years later. Some, like Zbigniew Brzezinski, Jimmy Carter's National Security Adviser between 1977 and 1981, might argue that the United States had little real choice but to aid Pakistan – and its allies in Afghanistan – since a Soviet Union wholly dominant in the region could have caused the most serious disruption in Pakistan to the east, and helped further entrench the Iranian regime to the west.*

Whatever the justifications for America's strategy at the time, it led to a series of unintended consequences against their interests, including a vicious, fanatical regime in Afghanistan which was quite content to provide a safe haven for the most dangerous terrorist organization the world has ever seen: al-Qaeda.

From that moment on the second Tuesday of September 2001, foreign and defence policy dominated Tony's premiership. For all of us involved, the pace and focus of our lives changed completely.

Tony set that pace. Within a week he had visited New York and Washington. It was 9/11 that put the relationship between Tony and

---

* He calls arming the Mujahideen a 'historic decision' and he is 'pleased to say we supported them [Pakistan] very actively'. National Security Archives interview with Dr Zbigniew Brezinski, 13/6/97.

George Bush on an entirely different plane. He had meant 'shoulder to shoulder' when he said it, not just as a metaphor, but literally.

For once, Europe (Russia included) and America really were united. In sharp contrast to what was to come over Iraq, there were no dramas at the United Nations, either. An initial, condemnatory UN Security Council resolution (UNSCR) on 12 September[7] was followed two weeks later by one authorizing military action in unambiguous terms. The legality of our military involvement, then or later, has never been an issue.

Three other Security Council resolutions were passed before the year was out.[8] These included UNSCR 1386 which approved 'the establishment *for six months* [my emphasis] of an International Security Assistance Force to assist the Afghan Interim Authority in the maintenance of security in Kabul and its surrounding areas'.[9]

The Taliban were given an ultimatum: to hand over the leadership of al-Qaeda and to dismantle its network or face invasion. No one was holding their breath for a positive response. None was forthcoming. Operation Enduring Freedom began on 7 October 2001, with British involvement in the preliminary bombing campaign. This was followed by troops on the ground, including a battle group of British forces.

In late October I went back to Washington to talk to Colin Powell, the Deputy US Defense Secretary Paul Wolfowitz and Vice President Dick Cheney, about the strategy for Afghanistan. I was concerned about how long we could hold the coalition together.[10]

I had met Dick Cheney once before, and was to meet him many times thereafter. He was ever courteous, but I never warmed to him, nor he to me. He was cautious, if not suspicious, about who I was, what I stood for. Once during a routine meeting in his study in the White House, he suddenly said to me, 'This is confidential,' with the implication that but for this caveat I might go and brief the press about his inner thoughts.

Paul Wolfowitz was a very different character. This was my first meeting with him, but our close family friend Richard Danzig, a

Democrat who had served in Bill Clinton's administration as Secretary of the Navy and knew Wolfowitz well, had spoken of him in positive terms. His politics were not mine (nor Richard's). Post-9/11 he became evangelical in his pursuit of the 'war on terror', and his fixation with Saddam Hussein verged on zealotry. Yet he was a true polymath, with an engaging personality; always worth listening to, not least for an intelligent, authentic view of that Praetorian Guard of the Bush White House, the 'neocons'.

Eleven years since the invasion of Afghanistan, the inadequacy of the overall political strategy becomes clearer by the week. But the approach in the early months certainly worked.

Kabul was liberated just five weeks after military action had begun, on 13 November 2001, with considerable help from the Northern Alliance, the main Afghan opposition force to the Taliban. Its former leader Ahmad Shah Massoud had been assassinated by the Taliban just two days before 9/11.

One of Massoud's closest associates was a young eye surgeon, Dr Abdullah Abdullah, half Tajik, half Pashtun, who had run much of the medical support for the Northern Alliance in the internal conflict against the Taliban in the late nineties. He, like so many of his country's elite, spoke perfect English. He was thoughtful, and well read, but what I remember most is his sad eyes. I first met Dr Abdullah on one of my early visits to Tehran. The Iranians had long been allies of the Northern Alliance.

The ground for a new, democratic constitution for Afghanistan was laid at the December 2001 Bonn Conference held under the auspices of the United Nations. However, as Sherard Cowper-Coles later noted in his book on the subject, 'I came to see that the Taliban had never been defeated in 2001–2; that the Bonn settlement that had followed had been a victors' peace, from which the vanquished had been excluded; and that the constitution resulting from that settlement could last only as long as the West was prepared to stay in Afghanistan to prop up the present situation'.[11]

342

At the time, though, exercising authority from Kabul was seen as essential if the Taliban were to be stripped of their power, and the safe haven they provided for al-Qaeda removed.

I made my first visit of many to Afghanistan in mid-February 2002, travelling there via meetings in Turkey, Israel and the Occupied Territories. I had invited both Michael Ancram (now Lord Lothian), the Shadow Foreign Secretary, and the Liberal Democrats' foreign affairs spokesman, Ming Campbell. Michael could not come, but Ming joined me for the trip. My institutional hostility towards his party had never undermined my personal friendships. I liked and trusted him. Since the Lib Dems had been unambiguous in their support for our position on Afghanistan (as had the Conservatives), I thought I owed him the opportunity to judge for himself the conditions on the ground.

The last leg of the journey, in the dead of night, was in an RAF Hercules transport plane. We all had to don the heavy bullet-proof jackets and helmets with which I was to become very familiar. The passengers sat on webbing seats. The loo was a bucket. Because there were women on the flight, the RAF had rigged a sheet of plastic around it for modesty; usually they didn't bother.

I was invited to sit in the cockpit. This was one of the older 'Hercs', with a four-man crew – two pilots, an engineer and a navigator. Once over Afghan airspace, two other crew – 'loadmasters' – came up from the back of the plane and began to scour the skies with night-vision goggles, looking for any signs of ground-to-air rockets that might impede our journey. The US had given the Pakistanis at least 2,000 Stinger missiles for use by the Mujahideen against the Soviets, and there was no way of knowing whether some of these were still available to the Taliban.

We'd had the news that most of the runway lights at Kabul Airport had been knocked out by an earlier plane; and that President Karzai's civil aviation and tourism minister, Abdul Rahman, had that day been assassinated by a mob of hajjis – pilgrims – at the airport, angry that they had been kept waiting for a plane to Mecca.* There was therefore a little nervousness as we came in for final approach.

'One hundred feet, eighty, sixty, fifty, forty,' went the navigator.

'F*** and s***; what the hell is that?' cut in the pilot, swerving as we touched down.

The pilot, with good reason, thought that a man he had spotted in the middle of the runway had a rifle in his hand. It was in fact a broom. The man had been sent out to sweep the runway, and simply hadn't noticed our arrival. Fortunately he was safe, and so were we.

'Oh, hello Mr Straw, I last met you in Macedonia,' said a British squaddie in a strong East Lancashire accent as we were processed through a small office on the side of the runway. 'I'm from Blackburn.' We had a brief conversation about which street he lived in, how his mum was, and Blackburn Rovers, just back in the Premiership. All politics *is* local.

We then headed for the reopened British Embassy, which, whilst the Taliban had been in control, had been looked after with loving care by the Afghan staff. The silver sparkled; the linen was crisp; the lawns trimmed. I presented an honorary MBE to the principal caretaker and his colleague in a touching ceremony in the garden.

But this was now less an embassy, more an operational forward base. The compound was packed with diplomats, intelligence and signals experts, special forces. The bed I was given took me straight back to school – a heavy metal frame, sinking wire springs, and slightly damp blankets. But since I can almost sleep standing up if I need to, I still got a good rest. Ming had to share a room with Ed Owen, which was certainly a sacrifice. Everyone else slept on camp beds in the drawing room and received a warm tumbler of water with which to perform all ablutions.

---

* Later reports suggested that this had in fact been a political assassination.

Next morning, 15 February 2002, saw meetings with both Hamid Karzai and Dr Abdullah Abdullah.

Karzai truly is one of Afghanistan's aristocrats; his family were loyal supporters of the last king, Zahir Shah. A brilliant linguist, he speaks English like an American.

Karzai is also the great survivor of world politics. In the West even those of us who have had close protection haven't had to worry over much as to whether an assassin's bullet will bring an abrupt end to our careers. In Afghanistan this was a constant preoccupation. The Taliban would dearly have liked to dispatch Karzai then, and still hold this ambition today.

Bullets aside, he has shown immense skill and patience simply in remaining as the head of state for more than a decade. His fault, as I was to discover, is being too willing to tell his listeners what they want to hear. In the end, to take one example, I got very tired of his claims that his government's counter-narcotics strategy was a success, claims all the more difficult to swallow since we knew, and he knew, that people close to him were still heavily involved in this immensely profitable trade.

It was not, however, my official meetings that made the greatest impression on me during that first trip, but a visit to a girls' high school on the edge of the city.

The school had been two storeys high, but the upper storey had been seriously damaged by shelling during the late-nineties civil war. It had been unoccupied whilst the Taliban controlled the country, since they had the prehistoric notion that girls should not be educated. Now a group of teachers and parents were putting the school back together.

A knot of women came over to talk to me. One of them was both a teacher and a parent of one of the girls at the school. I shall never forget this lady's face. It told me that she was, in the words of the prophet Isaiah, a woman of sorrows, acquainted with grief. She was youngish – in her thirties; she'd obviously been very attractive, but she was worn down. Like so many of her compatriots she had witnessed more death and suffering than most of us in the West could ever imagine.

This lady produced from her gown a single sheet of photocopied paper. It was a record of a Kabul criminal court, reciting her conviction for educating her daughter.

This encounter told me more about the monstrous nature of the Taliban regime than any number of books, diplomatic telegrams, or meetings with senior Afghan politicians.

The international community has now been in Afghanistan not for the six months of that early Security Council resolution, but for eleven years – longer than the two world wars put together. Our involvement has become increasingly problematic. In March 2012 the reputation of the United States forces in that country reached its lowest ebb, in the aftermath of the wanton slaughter of innocent men, women and children, killed in their beds by a rogue US soldier.

But there is, however, one undeniable achievement. We have begun the emancipation of Afghan women. There are now 2.7 million girls in school compared to a few thousand under the Taliban, and sixty-nine female MPs in the Afghan parliament. ActionAid recently conducted a poll of 1,000 women from different tribes, regions and social backgrounds and found that 72 per cent believe their lives are better now than ten years ago. It is their future that is most at risk from any resurgence of the Taliban as foreign forces prepare to leave by 2014. Of the women polled by ActionAid, 86 per cent feared a return to Taliban rule, with many of them citing their daughters' education as their primary concern.

FIFTEEN

The War That Nearly Was

If Pakistan is preoccupied with its neighbour to the west – Afghanistan – it is obsessed by its neighbour to the south and east – India. Its politics, its military spending, even its *raison d'être* have been defined by and distorted by the single issue of its territorial dispute with India over Kashmir.

The early months of 2002 were, for me, dominated not so much by Afghanistan (nor by Iraq) but by Kashmir. India and Pakistan had already been involved in four bloody wars over Kashmir.* In 2002 there was almost a fifth. In public, we deliberately played down the risk so as not to create panic – one reason why so little is recalled of this potential nuclear conflagration today. However, the situation was very dangerous. We came very close to war. Had it happened, the casualties and the destruction would have overshadowed all other conflicts of the previous sixty years.

Kashmir had been a 'princely state' within the Raj. Its maharaja and most of its elite had been Hindu, but over three-quarters of its population were Muslim. The speed of the British withdrawal from India led to turmoil in many parts of the country, terrible inter-communal

---

* In 1947/48, 1965, 1971 and 1999. There was also a war between India and China over that part of historic Kashmir that China was occupying (and still does).

conflict between Muslims, Sikhs and Hindus, and population transfers across the new borders. Thousands were killed or wounded. The bloodshed was particularly acute in the Punjab, just to the south of Kashmir.

So hasty and poorly executed was the end of British rule in India that some critical questions were left unresolved before midnight on 14/15 August 1947, when the two separate and independent states of India and Pakistan were born. One of these was Kashmir.

Muhammad Ali Jinnah and the leaders of his Muslim League expected that Kashmir would, in its entirety, become part of Pakistan. With a vacuum in place of order, and inflamed by the massacres of their Muslim brothers and sisters in the Punjab to the south, an insurgency in Kashmir quickly developed. The Hindu maharaja sought the assistance of the new government of India. Their price was an end to the maharaja's prevarication over the terms of the treaty of annexation of Kashmir by India. The maharajah signed this treaty on 25 October 1947. Two days later, Indian troops moved in. Pakistan responded with a large force of irregulars. The stage was set for the first Kashmir war.

At the end of 1948, with United Nations involvement, this first war was brought to an end with a de facto 'Line of Control' (LOC) splitting Kashmir into 'Indian-administered Kashmir' and 'Pakistan-administered Kashmir'. India calls these areas 'Jammu and Kashmir' and 'Pakistan-occupied Kashmir'; Pakistan calls them 'Indian-occupied Kashmir' and 'Azad [Free] Kashmir'. The LOC is still there today.

The UN Security Council passed four resolutions to help end the conflict.[1] The key one – UNSCR 47 – committed both countries, and the UN itself, to the holding of a plebiscite 'as soon as possible' by which the peoples of Kashmir could decide their future for themselves. The Indian government was required to reduce its troops to the 'minimum strength'. In contrast, Pakistan was required to secure the withdrawal 'from the State of Jammu and Kashmir of tribesmen and Pakistani nationals not normally resident therein who have entered the State for the purpose of fighting'. There was no recognition in this or subsequent resolutions of any right by Pakistan to station its own troops in the area.

The plebiscite has never taken place.

Pakistan, and those in the semi-autonomous province of 'Azad Kashmir' blame India for this. They further claim that India has consistently flouted the authority of the UN Security Council. India counters by claiming that Pakistan has never implemented its obligations under the resolutions, particularly the withdrawal of all 'fighters', who remain in Kashmir, many funded and organized by the ISI.

There is also the inconvenient fact that all these resolutions were passed under Chapter VI of the UN Charter, not Chapter VII. This is a critical distinction. Chapter VI is for the 'Pacific Settlement of Disputes'; its language is of 'recommendations' and 'calls' by the Security Council. Resolutions under this Chapter are therefore advisory in nature. It is Chapter VII that gives the Security Council mandatory powers (including the use of military force). No Chapter VII resolution about Kashmir has ever been passed.

Myths have a life of their own. They may contain truths, or untruths, or some of each. What matters is that they are believed. A plebiscite on Kashmir has become the totem for all those who want to see India out of Kashmir; and a moral justification for the military incursions by 'freedom fighters', or 'terrorists', according to one's point of view, across the LOC. The campaigns of this Kashmiri movement have been given added power over the years by their claims of the heavy-handed, in some cases brutal way in which they say Indian forces have suppressed disorder amongst the Muslim communities in 'Jammu and Kashmir'; India would, however, counter this by claiming that the insurgency has been led by terrorists from across the LOC and that a firm response is the necessary reaction of any state in these circumstances.

Britain was partly responsible, by its actions in the run-up to Partition, for the continuing Kashmir imbroglio; and Kashmir has since become a potent issue in some areas of Britain itself.

More than half a million of those of Pakistani heritage now settled in Britain came from Kashmir. These Kashmiris have a strong culture and their own language, and they are well organized. Many towns have

Kashmiri Associations. They have used their influence here to lobby our political parties to back policies favouring the Pakistani view of Kashmir's future.

Blackburn has its own Kashmiri Association and many of its members also belong to the local Labour Party. In the eighties a resolution supporting a 'free Kashmir', and condemnatory of India, was put to our party meeting. There was a presumption in the room that all the Muslims would support it and that the rest of us, knowing much less about it, would let it go through. Then Adam Patel was called to speak. Adam is a highly respected figure who has lived in Blackburn since the early sixties. 'I'm a Muslim too,' he said, 'but you don't speak for me. I'm Indian. There are two sides to this issue, not one.' Blackburn's Muslim community is – unusually – split fifty/fifty between those of Pakistani and Indian heritage and Adam found ready support. The resolution was modified, and it's never been a live local issue since.

But elsewhere in the UK it has – so much so that a pro-Pakistani Kashmir motion was put through the party conference in 1995 and became known as the 'Brighton Declaration'.[2] A diplomatic storm with India was triggered when Robin Cook made some Pakistani-leaning remarks in the margins of the royal visit to the two countries in October 1997.

The mini-debate in my own constituency party meeting fired my interest in the subject. After a little background reading I quickly understood that perceptions about the conflict were as polarized as those about, say, Ireland or Cyprus.

Having a large Indian and Pakistani population in my constituency certainly helped me to understand the conflict, but so too did my 1992 trip to south Asia. The visit to India had been organized by the Commonwealth Parliamentary Association, but immediately afterwards I went by myself to Pakistan, as a 'guest of the government'. I visited Muzaffarabad, the capital of Pakistan-administered Kashmir and from there we went to a 'refugee camp', not too far from the LOC. The residents of the camp intrigued me. The LOC is heavily patrolled, and much of it is in a hostile physical environment. I couldn't work out how so many apparent 'refugees' could have crossed the border, why so many of them were fit young men, and why there were obvious signs of military training around. I started asking all sorts of questions. After a while, to my great surprise, I was offered straightforward answers. Some were genuine refugees, but most were 'freedom fighters' who in time would be sent across the LOC to provide 'assistance' to their Muslim brothers and sisters under Indian occupation. All with the full knowledge and consent of the local and national governments, if not their active involvement.

I'd also learnt now about how violent these terrorist organizations could be when, in 1995, a constituent of mine, Paul Wells, on a walking holiday in Jammu and Kashmir, was abducted by the Islamic militant group Harkat ul-Ansar. His remains have never been found.

In May 1999 large-scale infiltration of Pakistani forces and Kashmiri fighters into the Kargil area across the LOC led to a three-month war between India and Pakistan. India eventually regained the territory. The chief of the Pakistani army, said to be the author behind the infiltration, was Pervez Musharraf, who, in October that year, following a *coup d'état*, became head of a military government, and later the country's president.

On 13 December 2001, a Pakistani-terrorist squad got into Parliament House in New Delhi.[3] Twelve people died. Though no minister or MP was killed or injured, the attack at the very heart of India's democratic system was a trauma that no government could ignore.

With echoes of the nonsensical claims by some that 9/11 had been organized by the CIA, the Pakistani military spokesman Major General Rashid Qureshi claimed that the attack was a 'drama staged by Indian intelligence agencies to defame the freedom struggle' in occupied Kashmir, and further warned that India would pay 'heavily if they engage in any misadventure'.[4]

India and Pakistan had both become nuclear states well before the Kargil conflict in 1999, but, that war, though bloody, had been confined to the disputed territory of Kashmir.

This was different. The Indians, led by the right-leaning government of Prime Minister Atal Bihari Vajpayee and Home Minister L. K. Advani, believed, with good reason, that the attack on their parliament had occurred with the knowledge, and probably the consent, of at least part of the Pakistani military. The dissembling of Major General Qureshi did nothing to undermine that belief. In the weeks immediately after, both sides mobilized thousands of troops. The scene was set for a major confrontation.

It was with this brewing that a major piece about my first few months as Foreign Secretary appeared in the *Guardian* in early January 2002. 'The sure-footed Home Secretary of New Labour's first term looks hesitant, struggles to command the House of Commons and – probably worst of all – allowed Jeremy Paxman to make mincemeat of him on *Newsnight* last month.'* *The Times* followed. However thick-skinned one thinks one is, these things are never pleasant. At Alice's suggestion, I held a series of brain-storming sessions in Carlton Gardens with key commentators and experts. There was nothing I could do but try to prove over time that such judgements were misplaced. It was my handling of the Kashmir crisis that really shifted the notion that I might not be up to the best job in the Cabinet.

One of the hazards was that Pakistan wanted Kashmir made an international issue before the UN, whilst India wanted to avoid that like the plague. I stuck like a limpet to my formulation: 'Kashmir is a bilateral dispute with international implications.'

It was this crisis too that turned my professional relationship with Colin Powell into a lasting friendship. Led by Colin, the US and the UK agreed that, as the tension increased, and the build-up of forces escalated, we would need intensive hands-on diplomacy with both the

---

* 4 January 2002. This posthumous praise from the *Guardian* made me smile. When I had been Home Secretary they had tried to bury me alive.

Indian and Pakistani governments. In the period that followed scarcely a week went by without at least one of us – Colin, Rich Armitage, Condi, her opposite number David Manning and I – visiting the region.*

At the beginning of 2002, in response to intensive diplomatic pressure, including a visit by Tony Blair, President Musharraf delivered a speech in which he pledged, 'No organization will be allowed to indulge in terrorism in the name of Kashmir.'[5]

There was, however, the all-too-predictable chasm between the words uttered in Islamabad and the reality on the ground, orchestrated from Islamabad. By early May, when the heavy winter snows began to melt, there was an increase in terrorist activity, including an attack on a passenger bus and residential quarters of the Indian army base at Kaluchak, killing thirty-four people, mainly women and children. A week later, the prominent moderate Kashmiri politician Abdul Ghani Lone was assassinated.

A million men under arms were now massed on the LOC. There was a high risk that a minor skirmish, a patrol in the wrong place, could trigger the major war we all feared. Blood was up amongst the populations on both sides.

On 22 May, the Indian prime minister Vajpayee warned his troops to prepare for a 'decisive battle.' On 24 May, and lasting for several days, Pakistan began a series of missile tests which included nuclear-capable weapons.[†]

During the Cold War, the key nuclear-weapon states had invested great intellectual and strategic effort to articulate their 'doctrine' for the use of nuclear weapons, and had developed great expertise about the

---

* Our two ambassadors there, Rob Young and Hilary Synnott, did untiring work, as did Bob Blackwill, the US ambassador in India, who had been trained at the Rich Armitage School of Diplomacy.

† There had been missile launches by both India and Pakistan throughout 2002.

'collateral damage' that could be caused by their deployment. But here, neither side appeared to have anything approaching a sophisticated idea of what would happen if they did start exploding nuclear materiel. They were sleep-walking towards Armageddon.

Sir Rob Young, the astute British High Commissioner, hosted a dinner on 28 May. The food – curried fish – was lovely; the conversation, terrifying. It turned on our expectations for war. A map showing the Indian troops massed just across the border from Lahore, Pakistan's second city, was displayed. India apparently believed that it could take Lahore without triggering a Pakistani nuclear response. We didn't share that comfortable analysis. Our overall sense was that there was a high probability of war breaking out in the following two weeks – indeed that had been the clear message to me from Indian ministers I had been talking to.

The whole world was now very worried. Russia's President Putin, and the Chinese president Jiang Zemin were both exerting strong pressure, especially on India and Pakistan, their respective long-term allies. President Bush and Tony were working the phones to the two heads of government.

At the end of May I had a key meeting with President Musharraf. He was, as always, impeccably polite; but beneath his military bearing lay the Pakistani nationalist whose life had been devoted to the struggle against India; and underneath that was a vulnerable human being. In democracies, false moves can lead to a humiliating loss of office. In countries like Pakistan, they can lead to death.

I then went to India, where I had talks with the prime minister. Security around President Musharraf was very tight, but nothing compared to that around Vajpayee's compound. It had been less than twenty years since then prime minister Indira Gandhi had been assassinated by one of her own bodyguards. My detectives were held at the perimeter and my party was taken in a buggy down a long drive.

Vajpayee must rank as one of the most unlikely political leaders in history. 'Conversation' with him was extraordinary, unnerving. I'd say something, expecting a response. Nothing. Just silence that sometimes went on for five minutes or longer. I was often convinced that I must have sent him to sleep. His eyes were closed. He was immobile. Suddenly he'd spark. There'd be a completely coherent response – then a lapse back into his apparently catatonic state. But underneath all this he was as sharp as mustard, and somehow managed to hold his government together for five years.

If I'd been Indian, my natural political home would have been the Congress Party, not Vajpayee's BJP, which was too sectarian for my liking. I'd seen the violence that followed the sacking of the Babri Mosque at Ayodhya in late 1992 by supporters of the VHP, BJP and Shiv Sena party. But many senior people in Vajpayee's Cabinet were really interesting, and attractive figures, among them Jaswant Singh, the foreign minister, almost the perfect English gentleman from a princely family in Rajasthan; L. K. Advani, the home minister, an upright, cultured Sindhi, then aged seventy-four but still active as chairman of the BJP Parliamentary Board; and George Fernandes, the defence minister.

Fernandes, the only Christian in Vajpayee's government, could not have had a more different background from his high-caste Hindu colleagues. Initially training to be a priest, he left in protest against the seniors' better food and conditions. He went to Calcutta, slept rough on the streets, became a trade union agitator, and was arrested during the emergency in 1976 on charges of smuggling dynamite to blow up government offices. A committed socialist, he got elected in the poor state of Bihar. By the time I met him in 2002, he was in charge of India's huge defence forces. Meetings with him were punctuated not by silence, but by the barking of his dogs.

But whoever I was talking to – and whether they were Indian or Pakistani – I continuously reflected on the dignity and forbearance these justifiably proud people from cultures far older than ours showed to us Brits, the successors to a country whose Raj ruled their huge subcontinent for nearly two centuries. I wonder how quickly we would have forgiven the humiliation, had the imperial relationship been reversed.

Still, neither side was getting the point. We produced detailed assessments showing the likely destination and effect of nuclear strikes in major cities in both countries. A Pakistani strike on New Delhi was very likely to kill a lot of Muslims, both back in Pakistan, and hundreds of miles away in Bangladesh; whilst an Indian strike on Islamabad would kill plenty of Hindus, Sikhs, Jains and Christians, as well as Indian Muslims. The Americans reinforced all this by publishing a Defense Intelligence Agency report that suggested a worst-case scenario: 8–12 million people would be killed in the initial nuclear exchange, with millions more certain to be killed in the resulting spread of radiation.[6]

At the bottom of the Grand Staircase of the Foreign Office, there is a memorial for all those in the Diplomatic Service killed in the service of their country. Every year, in the week leading up to Remembrance Sunday, there's a touching ceremony there. Service abroad is generally safe, but sometimes it can be deadly and every Foreign Secretary has to worry about the security of the staff. I decided in late May that we would reduce staffing at our posts in India and Pakistan, and send most of the spouses and children home. I outlined most this at a meeting of all the staff in Delhi, and sought to provide as much reassurance as I could. But there was no disguising that the situation was very frightening indeed. As Yogendra Narain, India's most senior defence official, stated on 2 June, 'We . . . must be prepared for mutual destruction on both sides.'[7]

One of the senior ministers commented to me during this visit, 'We can't attack each other while you are here.'

'That's why one of us always is,' I replied.

But what pulled both sides back from the brink was, of all things, a co-ordinated US and UK travel advisory notice. On 31 May Colin Powell and I announced a significant strengthening of our advice, warning our citizens not to travel to India or Pakistan, and, if there, to leave immediately. This shocked the Indian elite, who suddenly realized that the astonishing progress in their lifestyles and in India's position as an emerging world economy would be seriously damaged if war broke out. As I said in response to a complaint about the effect on the Indian economy of our travel advice, 'If India wants to be a world-class economy, you can't mess around with nuclear weapons.'

Even so, the belligerent stance of the Pakistanis still had to be corrected. Colin Powell sent in his own, not-so-secret weapon – Rich Armitage. With his huge military experience, and the fact that he represented the world's most powerful nation, Rich could talk to President Musharraf in a way that I certainly could not. He was by all accounts brutally direct.*

By mid-June this pressure started to work. The Indian government accepted Musharraf's pledge to end militant infiltration into India. On 10 June, air restrictions over India were ended and Indian warships removed from Pakistan's coast. Even so, the situation remained tense, with Musharraf saying that Pakistan would give no undertakings not to be the first to use nuclear weapons.

I returned to India and Pakistan in July. One thing that had worried me about the international community's dealings with Pakistan was that in public we rather pulled our punches on our suspicions that it was up to its neck in sponsoring 'cross-border terrorism' against India. I decided that I would spell out our concerns. In Delhi, my message was, unsurprisingly, received well. I then flew to Islamabad. Angered by what I had said, President Musharraf was 'just too busy to see [me]'.[8] A source at the Pakistani foreign ministry briefed the press that 'We have no regrets if Jack Straw takes Musharraf's refusal for a meeting as a discourteous act. He used Indian jargon while discussing the sensitive issue of Kashmir.'[†] I had to make do with a meeting with the

---

* Though reports that he told Musharraf he would 'bomb Pakistan back to the Stone Age' are pure myth.

† The FT had also reported that I had called Musharraf a 'congenital liar'. I assured the Pakistanis that I had never used such language about the president, 'even when talking to myself'.

Pakistani Minister of State, Inam ul-Haq, after which there was the usual bear-garden of a press conference. I repeated what I had said in Delhi. The questions were aggressive, especially from two men sitting at the front of the hall. I can still see them now. Afterwards one of our staff told me that they were well known as part-time journalists, but full-time members of the ISI.

It was then the flight back to Delhi, where Jaswant Singh hosted a dinner in Hyderabad House, which included Brajesh Mishra, National Security Adviser to Prime Minister Vajpayee, David Manning's opposite number. Brajesh was one of the Indian officials who played a critical role throughout the crisis. As well as being incredibly shrewd and experienced, Brajesh was one of the funniest raconteurs I have ever heard.

Intensive work, not least by David Manning, Condi Rice and Brajesh, led to India and Pakistan agreeing a 'Composite Dialogue' on issues including Kashmir, with Pakistan downgrading its unattainable demand for a plebiscite.*

This Dialogue has stuttered along ever since, with progress punctuated by some cross-border terrorism, and disturbances in Jammu and Kashmir against the abuse of human rights of the majority Muslim population. But the level of violence is significantly down. Since 2010 peace talks between India and Pakistan have resumed and there have already been signs of progress through the agreement of confidence-building measures and Pakistan's reciprocal 'in principle' offer to India of 'Most Favoured Nation' trading status.† Critically, the establishment by the Union government in India of a panel of three interlocutors to assess the situation in Jammu and Kashmir has seen the number of protests decline and tensions ease.

---

* A relief to them, if truth be told; because many of the Kashmiris wanted a third question on any ballot paper – 'independent Kashmir' – in addition to the straight choice between India and Pakistan envisaged by the Security Council back in 1947.

† Pakistan has yet to make good on this promise.

A lasting peace depends not on redefining the fixed de facto international border of the LOC, but on progressive steps to make the border all but irrelevant to the conduct of normal lives on either side. That has been the genius of the settlement in Northern Ireland. It would be of huge help to Pakistan, allowing that country at last to define itself by its own great potential, not against its neighbour.

But it could be a long wait.

On 15 August 1947 the territory taken over by what was then West Pakistan was amongst the most prosperous of the whole of British India, with the great port of Karachi in the south, and the breadbasket of the western Punjab to the north. This new nation could have done at least as well as independent India.

However, in the decades that followed it fell further and further behind. Its GDP per head is $2,800, compared with $3,700 in India. Pakistan's own data suggests its growth has averaged around 3 per cent in recent years.[9] This compares with 8 per cent for India. Its democracy, its society, is deeply fractured. The army, not the people, is sovereign. Intra-communal violence, much exacerbated by extremist Islamist groups, is a cancer debilitating the nation.

Pakistan's tragedy impacts directly on the United Kingdom, as families desperately seek ways for their children to emigrate here, pressuring young people in the UK into marriages that all too often end in failure and unhappiness.

A plebiscite on Kashmir's future has never seemed a more distant prospect. Life for all on both sides of the Line of Control can improve markedly when that reality is digested, but only then.

SIXTEEN

Iraq: The War of Choice

The question in my mind is how many additional casualties is Saddam worth? And the answer is not very damned many. So I think we got it right, both when we decided to expel him from Kuwait, but also when the president made the decision that we'd achieved our objectives and we were not going to go get bogged down in the problem of trying to take over and govern Iraq.

DICK CHENEY in August 1992, US Defense Secretary during the First Gulf War 1991, Vice President 2001–9[1]

We have learnt that sensitive diplomacy must be backed by the threat of military force if it is to succeed.

KOFI ANNAN, UN Secretary General[2]

I could have prevented the United Kingdom's involvement in the Iraq War. I did not do so. I chose to support the war. Here's why.

When war broke out in 1980 between Iraq and Iran, the West backed Saddam Hussein against the theocratic regime of Ayatollah Khomeini. But it was complicated. The Soviet Union was Iraq's biggest arms supplier (closely followed by France). Elements of the US administration

361

covertly provided arms to Iran. There is also evidence that Israel supplied arms and materiel to Iran, with the aim of prolonging the conflict and weakening both nations.

The Iran–Iraq War ended in 1988 in stalemate; around 1.5 million people had perished for no territorial gain. Three years later Saddam invaded Kuwait, triggering the 1991 Gulf War. This ended in his defeat and a determination by the international community to disarm him of his chemical and biological weapons, missile system, and nuclear capability. Key Security Council resolutions were passed in 1991 after the war had ended making it mandatory that Iraq should do all this. Sanctions were imposed until there had been full compliance.

In the UN, and the UK, the strong sentiment was for Iraq to be isolated as long as the Saddam regime posed any danger. Here the arms-to-Iraq scandal,* and the increasing effectiveness of the Kurdish lobby, reinforced that view. Russia and China, however, were in favour of a swift normalization of relations with Iraq, with their huge trade in oil products one way, armaments and machinery the other. Ever mercantilist, France, too, saw getting back to business as usual as an important priority. America's great ally in the region, Saudi Arabia, did not appreciate the secularism of Saddam's Ba'athists, but did appreciate their marginalization of Iraq's majority Shi'a population, and the country's role as a counterbalance to the apostate Iran.

Within Iraq, Saddam remained as powerful as ever; uprisings imme-

---

* A year later, arms to Iraq began to dominate British politics, becoming increasingly toxic for John Major and his fading government. A British machine-tool company, Matrix Churchill, with the complicity of the British government, had covertly supplied the regime with high-grade components and machine parts for some very powerful weapons. It became clear that Matrix Churchill's products may have helped Saddam to prosecute the 1991 Gulf War, in which the United Kingdom had been a key adversary. A judicial inquiry was established under Sir Richard Scott. Its publication, in February 1996, was the occasion for Robin Cook's brilliant demolition of the Conservative's position (Hansard, 15 February 1996, col. 1144/5), which ranks with Michael Foot's 1980 speech as among the best oratories I have heard.

diately after the war among the Kurds in the north, and the Shi'a in the south, in part encouraged by insinuations of US support (which was never forthcoming), were ruthlessly crushed.

Through the 1990s, Saddam was confident, with good reason. He judged that he had more to gain than to lose by refusing full co-operation with the inspectors. But for 9/11, and the war which followed, he would have been right.

By August 1998, the conditions in which the weapons inspectors (UNSCOM) were working became so intolerable that they withdrew. There has been dispute ever since as to whether this withdrawal was voluntary, as Iraq claimed, or a 'constructive expulsion' as the inspectors claimed. Under pressure from the US and UK, Iraq readmitted the inspectors later in the year. Their final withdrawal in December was quickly followed by Operation Desert Fox, the US/UK-led airstrikes on Iraqi military installations. It appears that these had limited effect. The Iraqi ambassador to the UN commented, 'If we had known that was all you [the US] would do, we would have ended the inspections long ago.'*

Desert Fox did, however, damage further the already fragile international consensus lined up against Saddam. Russia, France and China called for the lifting of the eight-year embargo on Iraq's oil exports, and a recasting of UNSCOM.† By the close of 1999 the Security Council finally agreed a new weapons inspectors' agency (UNMOVIC), along with the offer to suspend the faltering sanctions regime should Saddam comply fully with the inspections process – but of course he never did.

*

---

* In conversation with Charles Duelfer, later chairman of the US-led Iraq Survey Group. Charles Duelfer, 'In Iraq, done in by the Clinton–Lewinsky affair', *Washington Post*, reprinted in the *Japan Times*, 29 February 2012.

† As Hans Blix, the head of the UN weapons' inspectors agency, UNMOVIC, was to say in early 2003, if 'Iraq had provided the necessary cooperation in 1991, the phase of disarmament [under UNSCR 687] could have been short-lived and a decade of sanctions could have been avoided'. See Cm (2003) 5769, p. 83.

In the run-up to the Iraq War, many claimed that the alternative approach – of containment – had never been given a chance. It had.

Saddam's manipulation of the oil for food programme, the illicit oil trade, and the almost endemic smuggling eroded the sanctions' effectiveness – as did the exit of the inspectors in 1998. As the Iraq Survey Group noted, 'By 2000–2001, Saddam had managed to mitigate many of the effects of sanctions and undermine their international support.'[3]

In 2001 and 2002 the US and the UK sought to rescue, and strengthen, the collapsing sanctions regime, but Russia and China wanted the sanctions lifted, not strengthened.* We could not get agreement to the full package of so-called 'smart sanctions' we wanted – in particular, a tightening of the proscribed trade between Iraq and its neighbours. The resulting UN Resolution 1409 was inadequate and stood no chance of plugging the gaping holes in the sanctions framework. This failure to get comprehensive and robust 'smart sanctions' effectively marked the failure of the 'containment' policy, especially for those who viewed Iraq as a significant threat.

One of the many ways in which 9/11 changed everything was the change in the United States' willingness to tolerate dangerous, rogue regimes. There was never the least evidence of any link between Saddam and al-Qaeda – despite the best efforts of Vice President Dick Cheney and his staff to prove otherwise. But Saddam's slow-motion escape from the shackles of sanctions was causing immense frustration in Washington. I think this was partly due to President George W. Bush's sense that his father should have followed through the military victory

---

* My statement to Iraq Inquiry (4 May 2011): The *Daily Telegraph*, for instance, quoted a Russian diplomat in May 2001 (after the first failed attempt to get the full 'smart sanctions' package) as saying that Russia 'will not accept this idea of smart sanctions. This is not about easing the sanctions but about strengthening them. We believe the sanctions should be lifted.'

in 1991 by removing Saddam from power. That view was, I am sure, felt more personally by Vice President Cheney who, in 1992, had been so vocal in asserting that Saddam's removal was worth 'not very damned many' US casualties. But renewed concern about Iraq was also based on the serious threat that Iraq, once freed of international sanctions, would reassert itself as a dangerous and unpredictable regional power. After all, there was only one nation that had launched missile attacks on five of its neighbours, invaded two of them, and used chemical weapons to massacre thousands of its own population. Post-9/11, the United States became infinitely more cautious about what risks to its security, direct and indirect, it was willing to entertain.

Few things stay secret in Washington for long. By the end of November 2001, the American press was widely reporting on the fact that the US Defense Department was examining the military options against Iraq.

In the third week of January 2002 I went on a long-planned joint visit to central Africa, with Hubert Védrine, then French foreign minister. The trip was notable in three respects. One was in establishing a common approach to otherwise conflicting post-colonial interests in the region. The second was that we covered four of the countries in that vast continent in a single day – breakfast with President Kabila in Kinshasa; lunch with President Kagame in Kigali; afternoon tea with President Buyoya in Bujumbura; and dinner with President Museveni in Kampala.

The third was that I was able to talk at some length on the plane journey with Hubert about France's strategy in the post-9/11 world. Though Hubert was to lose his post a few months later, the time wasn't wasted. He was an authentic voice of the French Establishment, with its high suspicion of the United States and its distrust of the UK. Hubert's description of the US as the world's 'hyper-power' got little traction in Britain, but a great deal in France.

The following week saw me back in the hyper-power's capital, for one of my regular rounds of meetings with Colin Powell, Condi Rice, Vice President Cheney and CIA director George Tenet.

President Bush had made his 'axis of evil' State of the Union speech the day before. There were the inevitable questions from the British press pack: did I agree that Iran, Iraq and North Korea did form an 'axis of evil'? If so, why had I not said so before? If not, wasn't I insulting our closest ally? It was the usual 'have you stopped beating your wife?' stuff.

The truth was I thought that it was a terrible conception.* What point was the president trying to make? Was this an exclusive list? Was there some connection between the three countries that we'd all missed? Had the diplomatic consequences, especially on the relatively moderate Khatami government in Iran, been thought through? Now that he had suggested a link, at least in terms of threat, between the three, how was he going to explain it if he took action against only one? But I wanted neither to praise the speech, nor to damn it. It was time for some unbearably boring quotes. Thank God for the compound sentence; the subordinate clause. I was Mogadon, free, without prescription. Even so I generated headlines, with the *Daily Telegraph* headlining 'Straw mocks Bush speech' – an indicator of the feverish atmosphere of the time.

In April 2002 Tony went to see President Bush at his ranch in Crawford, Texas. The trip has subsequently gone down as the moment at which Tony pledged UK support for a US war against Iraq, support that would be given 'in blood'. I was hundreds of miles away at the time on a visit to the Caribbean, so I couldn't have heard him say that. Strangely, the man who claimed he had said it, Christopher Meyer, the British ambassador to Washington, wasn't there either. It was David

---

* An internal MoD memo from 27 February 2002, discussing the 'axis of evil' speech and how it should be handled, called the phrase Bush had used 'unclear and ... unfortunate'.

Manning and Jonathan Powell who attended those meetings at Crawford which were not *à deux*.

Tony did, however, make a public speech during his Crawford visit. That, and his statement to the Commons a week later on 10 April, set the scene for the central drama of his premiership, and the most burdensome decision that any of us would ever take. In his Commons statement he said:

> For the moment, let me say this: Saddam Hussein's regime is despicable, he is developing weapons of mass destruction, and we cannot leave him doing so unchecked. He is a threat to his own people and to the region and, if allowed to develop these weapons, a threat to us also.
>
> Doing nothing is not an option. As I said in my speech in Texas, what the international community should do through the UN is challenge Saddam to let the inspectors back in without restriction – anyone, any place, any time. If he really has nothing to hide, let him prove it.
>
> I repeat, however, that no decisions on action have been taken. Our way of proceeding should be and will be measured, calm and thought through. When judgements are made, I shall ensure that the House has a full opportunity to debate them.[4]

'Jack. You've got to say how you *felt,* especially when it comes to Iraq,' was a much-repeated injunction as I discussed the content of this book with family and friends. They know only too well that I have a tendency first to get into the numbers and the facts of any issue.

Like almost everyone else, I felt that Saddam was a terrible man, with the blood of thousands on his hands. But these emotions could not add up to a policy. So I did immerse myself in the facts, and in Iraq's history. The 200 pages of UNSCOM's final report (December 1998) provided me with a critical baseline about what biological and chemical weapons Saddam had possessed at the end of the Gulf War, which of them had been destroyed, what was left, and where they might be. The International Atomic Energy Agency (IAEA) reports provided similar background on Saddam's nuclear programme. I talked to as many experts as I could find – my private secretary, Mark Sedwill, who had been an UNSCOM inspector in Iraq from 1996–7; Michael Williams, the special adviser I'd inherited from Robin; and the many officials in the Foreign Office who'd specialized in the Middle East. Tony and his office also laid on a series of useful seminars with outside experts.

The issue was not what we felt about Saddam but what we did about the threat he posed. What were the limits of the coercion with which we should back our diplomacy; and, if that diplomacy failed, deploy? That in turn depended in part on the threat the world faced, in our judgement, if we did nothing.

If I was asked which single individual most influenced my view that Saddam did pose a serious threat to international peace and security, my answer would be unambiguous: Dr David Kelly, who tragically died in July 2003.

Dr Kelly was a microbiologist who started his career at the UK's Biological Weapons Establishment at Porton Down, and later became a weapons inspector. As a member of UNSCOM's staff, he made thirty-seven trips to Iraq during the nineties. I met him just once, in September 2002, when he accompanied me to give evidence to the Commons Foreign Affairs Select Committee. At the hour long 'pre-brief' I was struck both by Dr Kelly's depth of knowledge and understanding, and by the clarity of his belief that, if diplomacy failed, then military action would have to follow.*

*

---

* This was confirmed publicly in the Hutton Report, which quotes from a letter Dr Kelly wrote on 30 June 2003: 'I was personally sympathetic to the war because I recognized from a decade's work [as a weapons inspector] the menace of Iraq's ability to further develop its non-conventional weapons programmes' (Hutton, p. 26).

On the face of it, executive decision-making in the United States should be simple. All authority is invested in one person: the president.

In practice, the US system is anything but simple. It's also alien from the British system. When John Maynard Keynes was negotiating crucial financial support for the UK with the USA during the last war, he found the processes by which the administration reached a position both baffling and maddening:

> There is no clear hierarchy of authority . . . There is perpetual internecine warfare between prominent personalities. Individuals rise and fall in general esteem with bewildering rapidity. New groupings of administrative power and influence spring up every day. Members of the so-called Cabinet make public speeches containing urgent proposals which are not agreed as part of the government policy. In the higher ranges of government no work ever seems to be done on paper; no decisions are recorded on paper; no one seems to read a document and no one ever answers a communication in writing. Nothing is ever settled in principle. There is just endless debate and sitting around . . . Suddenly some drastic clear-cut decision is reached, by what process one cannot understand, and all the talk seems to have gone for nothing, being the fifth wheel to the coach.[5]

Keynes' comments are just as accurate today. If you are going to influence decisions in Washington, you have to get into their 'interagency' system. The Bush administration was divided, by ideology and personalities. The whole time I was Foreign Secretary, I worried about Vice President Cheney's instincts, and his preoccupation with atoning for his 1991 failure. Don Rumsfeld was a more fully paid-up member of the human race, and his 'Rumsfeld's Rules' – a collection of observations about how to be an effective leader – are replete with good sense and self-criticism. But he had some scary neocons around him who were obsessive about America's exceptionalism (its difference from and superiority to all other countries), hostile to anything or anyone who got in the way of America's freedom of action. With Dick Cheney, he bears the greatest responsibility for the catastrophic failure properly to prepare and execute a plan for post-invasion Iraq.

On the other side was Condi Rice, the president's National Security Adviser, and his Secretary of State, Colin Powell.

Condi was always incredibly loyal to the president. She was very guarded indeed about her views of the 'principals' on the National Security Council (NSC), such as Dick Cheney and Don Rumsfeld, and their even more partisan deputies and assistants. That said, her recent memoirs highlight her intense frustration with their approach.

At first sight, Colin Powell and I might be regarded as unlikely friends. He, a military officer, and Republican; me, an elected socialist politician from a pacifist family.

The military are often parodied as a bunch of Rambo figures: brainless, gun-toting, gung-ho. My experience on both sides of the Atlantic taught me that this personality profile is more common amongst politicians (and journalists) than in the Armed Forces. Those who, in Rich Armitage's words, have 'smelt cordite' are less keen to put others in harm's way than those who have never had to face battle.

This didn't make Colin Powell a pacifist; not remotely. But it did help to make him one of the sanest men I have ever met, and one of the most compassionate, with an astonishing capacity for work, a soldier's lexicon, and a rip-roaring sense of humour. We came to trust each other completely. We were constantly in touch. On Iraq and indeed most issues we became closer to each other's positions than to those of our bosses.

As the Iraq drama intensified so the calls between us multiplied. On a Sunday I always spoke to Colin when I got back from church, when he'd just got up. During the week, his favourite time was when he was winding down after a day at the office, having a quick break before evening engagements. Sometimes when State Ops or Downing Street switchboard called asking me to hook up with Colin's encrypted phone, I'd already gone to bed. I'd go upstairs to my study, where the calls often went on for forty-five minutes, sometimes an hour. And afterwards I'd make a note of any action points whilst they were fresh in my mind. It was the frequency, timing and duration of these calls that led Alice to quip that 'Colin Powell is the other man in my life' (and, anyway, she had taken quite a shine to him).

The United States easily had the military capacity to invade Iraq and take Saddam down on its own, without assistance from any other nation. But President Bush was rightly anxious that if the US acted unilaterally it could find itself seriously isolated; and that partners for a military coalition could be of great assistance in making the peace, once Saddam had been removed.

The spectre of Suez had been by far the most potent influence over successive British governments' engagement with the US since the fifties. It continues to rank as the greatest debacle by far of any British post-war foreign policy and marks the moment when the United Kingdom had to abandon any idea that it was a Great Power. President Eisenhower's humiliation of Britain then had been total. Ever since, British governments have taken the view that the best way of influencing the US system is to 'stay close' to them in public, and debate with them from the inside.

Early on, Jonathan Powell had said to me that we had to 'get right up the arse of the Americans'. The vulgar riposte from my office was 'Yes, but we don't need to clean their teeth from the inside.'

I was worried about the course on which we were embarked, and inherently more sceptical than Tony of some of the arguments being advanced in Washington. I was concerned that our approach – public support and private pressure – would lead the US to take our support for granted, rather than holding them back.

I understood why Tony had adopted this approach, not least because it was what I was doing with Tony. I felt a powerful sense of loyalty to him, and obligation as the country's Foreign Secretary. Whilst publicly I was always supportive, I made my own view very clear in private – when my messages to Tony were unambiguous and often in writing.

However, when telling people things they didn't want to hear, Tony frequently used ambiguous, elliptical language. I continually worried that Bush heard Tony's nuanced phraseology as offering unconditional support. Time and again, on Iraq and the Middle East especially, Colin told me that this was exactly what he was picking up inside the US administration. 'The Bush team took TB's comments as full support, and pocketed them,' is Colin's subsequent comment to me.

Notwithstanding all of this, I did share Tony's view that if we stood back from the US we would have no traction with them at all – and military action, without any prior UN diplomatic process, would go ahead anyway. If we engaged with them, and got them to return to the Security Council, there was a chance, maybe a good one, of ensuring full compliance by Saddam without resorting to war.

Regime change was never my objective, nor was it lawful for the UK. But I certainly believed that Saddam posed a serious threat and that if he were left unchecked he would resume his active aggression.

It required great effort to persuade the US to go down the UN route. To understand why, you have to understand how the US viewed the UN. The Americans were key architects of the international institutions established after the carnage of the Second World War. The UN had been designed to overcome some of the major defects of its predecessor, the League of Nations (which the US had boycotted). The veto rights of the permanent members of the Security Council therefore ensured that they could not be committed against their will to actions they considered against their interests; and the US had been physically bound into the new system by placing the headquarters in New York, rather than in distant, sanitized Geneva.

But the proximity of the UN, and the fact that the US is by far its biggest funder, has had its disadvantages too.* Inefficiencies, its

---

* The US provides 22 per cent of the UN's main budget and 26 per cent of its peacekeeping budget.

apparent weakness in the face of atrocities, and the annual grand-standing of egregious dictators attending the General Assembly, feed their way into American domestic politics to a degree unknown on this side of the Atlantic. One wing of the Republican Party – including John Bolton, Colin's Undersecretary in State – had always been openly hostile to the UN, seeing it as an unnecessary drag on America's freedom of action.

On 23 July 2002, as the Kashmir crisis was calming down, Tony called a ministerial meeting for a major discussion on Iraq. I ran through the four countries that posed a potential threat to world peace because of their unauthorized and highly dangerous weapon systems – North Korea, Iran, Libya and Iraq. I thought it important to raise the issue as to whether we should contemplate not joining the US in any American military effort against Iraq. I was concerned that the case against Iraq (why did it merit the most severe action? what differentiated it from the other three?) had not at that stage been made; and also about the potential consequences for Tony's leadership, and the survival of his government.

I was also worried that the UN route was still not in the bag. I suggested to Colin Powell that I should meet him privately in mid-August. I was due to go off for a family holiday ahead of this meeting and, before I left, I sent Tony a lengthy, handwritten letter, setting out the hazards ahead if our handling of Iraq went wrong. It ended: 'And you know where some (not so loyal) are on all this – licking their lips at the possibility of regime change nearer to home.'

Colin and his wife Alma were staying with friends in the Hamptons. With Concorde still flying, a day trip was easy. I had just my private secretary, Simon McDonald, and a detective with me. We took a helicopter from JFK Airport, and were with Colin well before lunch.

The three of us – me, Colin, and Simon as note-taker – sat on the deck, with an unbroken view to the Atlantic across a reed-covered lagoon, and discussed how we could secure the chance of a peaceful conclusion to the growing crisis over Iraq. Not for the first time, and certainly not for the last, Colin opened up to me about his intense frustration with parts of the administration; in particular Dick Cheney and Don Rumsfeld. Colin had known both for decades,* but he said to me more than once that something had changed about both of them, and it had not been for the good. I talked frankly to Colin about Tony and other key personalities in his administration. I left the Hamptons pleased that Colin and I were in agreement and hopeful that although it was going to take great effort, we might be able to get the Bush administration to go to the UN.

Although the Washington infighting continued and Dick Cheney made a very public attempt to have the US bypass the UN, President Bush finally seemed to have agreed. The plan was that he would announce this in his speech to the General Assembly on 12 September, the day after the first anniversary of 9/11.

The United Kingdom sits next to the United States in the UN, not because we are close allies but simply because of the alphabet. I'd been slipped an advance copy of the president's speech. Like Colin and Condi in the next set of desks, Jeremy Greenstock, our permanent representative to the UN, and I had both spotted that the crucial line, on working with the Security Council 'for the necessary resolution', had been omitted altogether. I immediately assumed dirty work at the crossroads. But simple human error, not venality, was to blame. Fortunately the president spotted the omission and ad-libbed, though he made the key line plural not singular – 'We will work with the UN Security Council for the necessary resolutions.'

Meanwhile, back in Whitehall, an 'Iraq dossier' was being prepared,

---

* Colin had been Ronald Reagan's National Security Adviser when Cheney had been a senior member of Congress; and chairman of the Joint Chiefs of Staff when Cheney was Defense Secretary, during the Gulf War. Rumsfeld had been Defense Secretary for Gerald Ford in the seventies, and had ever after straddled Washington politics and business.

which later acquired great notoriety because some of the intelligence on which it was based turned out to be defective.

Parliament was recalled on 24 September 2002 for its first major debate on Iraq and Tony presented the dossier to the Commons. But the debate was significant for another reason. It opened with Tam Dalyell making a point of order that war against Iraq could only be supported if authorized both by the UN Security Council and by the House. War is an act of state. Through the twentieth century there had been no practice or requirement that the elected House of Commons had to give prior approval for any major deployment of British military forces, and there had been much resistance, from the military and from prime ministers, to the idea that they should. Ever since the Falklands War I had thought this preposterous. So I strongly agreed with Tam that any decision to go to war needed to be endorsed by the Commons but I couldn't say so at the time. Over the following weeks, and in concert with Robin Cook, Leader of the House, I persuaded Tony that it was essential.*

Earlier in the summer there had been a mounting and understandable clamour for more and more explanation about why we and the US were now taking the threat from Iraq so much more seriously than we had before 9/11. People assumed that we must know much more than we were letting on. Through the CIA, SIS and the other agencies, we did, of course, have access to what we believed to be reliable intelligence about Saddam's continuing intentions in respect of his banned

---

* For this to happen we had to break the strong convention that war was an executive decision and not for Parliament. The key debate to go to war over the Falklands had lasted just three hours, on a Saturday morning, on a motion 'that this House do now adjourn' (see Chapter Six, page 147). At the start of the Gulf War the prime minister made a statement and a government debate took place the following week. But like many conventions and traditions, this one was of relatively recent provenance. During the Napoleonic Wars the Commons had made substantive military decisions. It had to do so again.

weapons. The mistake we made – on both sides of the Atlantic – was to believe that the best way to respond to this clamour was to include a declassified summary of some of the intelligence in the dossier.

After the invasion, Andrew Gilligan's 'exposé' on the *Today* programme about the 'forty-five-minute' claim in the dossier, using information apparently gleaned from David Kelly, came to be used to support the allegations that we had gone to war not just on a false prospectus, but on one we knew to be false. That was not the case. The dossier got less coverage than we had anticipated. The forty-five-minute claim was covered on the London *Evening Standard*'s front page, and in some of the morning papers the next day. It then fell away. I had completely forgotten about it until the Gilligan story. In all the speeches I made on Iraq outside the House I think I included it once. It was scarcely ever mentioned in the Commons; not by me; not by anyone during the final critical debate on 18 March 2003 as to whether we should go to war.

And whatever the defects of this September dossier (they were many) there was something of a process behind its production. Not even this could be said of the further (February) dossier which was drafted at very short notice, and given to six journalists during a flight to Washington with the prime minister. Later dubbed the 'dodgy dossier', it sought to give further information on Iraq's security apparatus, its repressive regime, and its concealment of WMD. Much of its 'intelligence base' was a plagiarized doctoral thesis. I was incandescent about this. It had never been seen by the Foreign Office, still less by me. In evidence to the Foreign Affairs Committee I later said that this 'dossier has been an embarrassment to the government and lessons have been learnt'. I described the saga as a 'complete Horlicks', which led to much debate on talk radio shows, and happiness by the manufacturers of this famous bedtime drink at the free publicity, who sent me two jars in appreciation.[6] When they arrived, my principal private secretary Geoffrey Adams, who had taken over from Simon McDonald in the summer of 2003, joked, 'Next time, Foreign Secretary, perhaps you could say that it was a complete Bollinger.'

The irony is that the substance of the case for war was all to be found in incontrovertible, open sources; in the successive UN Security Council resolutions, in the reports of the weapons inspectors; and in the documented behaviour of Saddam and his regime in concealing the continued development of its banned weapons programmes under the noses of the inspectors, and the intelligence agencies as well.* In truth, it is more than an irony. It was a fundamental flaw. The case would have been much stronger if we had relied on the UN resolutions and what lay behind them and had never offered up any nuggets of intelligence.

To bring this out, and partly provoked by my fury over the February dossier, I decided to publish my own dossier. Simply entitled 'Iraq', it contained all the key public documents – the main Security Council resolutions from 1991, UNSCOM and UNMOVIC reports, EU and NATO statements on Iraq, and, for good measure, my speeches to the Security Council. This, and another published in March, were far more persuasive than the earlier dossiers in making the case – which the Security Council had accepted in 1441 – that it was time for the Iraqis to comply.

It was one thing to have President Bush declare in favour of going to the UN. Turning his twelve words about 'necessary resolutions' into a text that would command a majority in the Security Council, and had teeth, was quite another.

---

* In relation to concealing weapons programmes, and the suspicion with which we needed to treat any undertakings in this regard, I found one set of facts particularly persuasive. Four years after the Gulf War, Iraq had been running an extensive biological weapons programme including anthrax bacillus, smallpox virus, and VX nerve agent. It was only the lucky break of the defection of Saddam Hussein's son-in-law, Hussein Kamel Hassan al-Majid, which led to the details of this programme becoming public. The year after his defection, Kamel was lured back to Iraq, where he was brutally murdered.

The first task was to pin down an acceptable draft. Inevitably parts of the US government weren't bothered about securing a consensus in the Security Council. If the other members of the Council supported it, fine; if they vetoed it, fine too. In October President Bush was given Congress approval for military action. The US could go ahead anyway, with or without the UN. We did have common ground, though, in wanting to secure a resolution which authorized military action without any need for a second resolution if Saddam did not comply.

The early drafts from the US were unacceptable to us. To resolve this, we organized a six-way conference call (on a very poor line), with Colin, Condi and John Negroponte, their ambassador to the UN, on the US side, and David Manning, Jeremy Greenstock and me on our side. We made good progress, but there were still some outstanding issues, which could only be resolved by Tony talking to the president.

It was by then a few days before Labour's annual conference in Blackpool and it was arranged that Tony would call from the main conference hotel.

Apart from a duty private secretary, no civil servants are allowed to attend party conferences. If the call had taken place in Downing Street there would have been time to brief Tony, and I could have listened to the call from David Manning's office. But no such comforts were available in Blackpool. A hot, airless side room had been taken over as the secure communications centre. As the call was hooked up, I parked myself there, sweating. Tony had his mind on the conference and simply didn't make the key points. I told him that, however embarrassing, he'd have to make the call again. It was fixed for later that evening.

Tony and I share a clean-shoe fetish.* When I went to brief him on

---

* This fetish has a good Labour pedigree. I came across the following in Alan Bullock's biography of Ernie Bevin (p. 370): 'Churchill was outraged to learn that Bevin [then wartime minister of labour] cleaned his own shoes . . . He instructed one of his aides to see at once that a Royal Marine was sent to act as his batman. Bevin was embarrassed: "I wouldn't like you to do that Prime Minister . . . I get such splendid ideas when I'm cleaning my boots."' Neil Kinnock also shares this fetish.

his second call he was sitting on the very large double bed in his room, with the most extensive shoe-cleaning kit I'd ever seen, carefully spit-and-polishing his toecaps. 'Say hello to Cherie,' he said.

'Where is she?'

'In the bathroom.'

Politely declining, I got on with reciting what we wanted him to say. Thankfully, he absorbed it and the call went well. We had a text to broker with the other members of the Security Council.

There then followed an extraordinary five-week period in which not just every phrase, but every word, and even the punctuation, was the subject of the closest debate and argument. I often spent hours each day in telephone calls with Colin, Dominique de Villepin and Igor Ivanov, as well as with the Chinese foreign minister Tang Jiaxuan and the foreign ministers of the non-permanent members of the Security Council. Dominique had taken over as French foreign minister from Hubert Védrine in May 2002. He spoke perfect English and was immensely cultured, writing poetry to relieve the tedium of EU meetings. The key to understanding this proud man was that his heroes were Napoleon Bonaparte and General de Gaulle.

None of the other P5 foreign ministers held elective office. They each operated within a presidential system. But I had my other day job to do: representing the people of Blackburn. My fortnightly visits to the constituency were sacrosanct. My diary secretary in the Foreign Office and my office in Blackburn worked brilliantly together to fit my life in the air with my life on the ground. Despite everything, I only missed scheduled advice surgeries two or three times during my five years as Foreign Secretary. But my Blackburn visits led to some bizarre mental juggling. Frequently I'd have to excuse myself in the middle of an interview with a constituent to take an urgent call from a fellow foreign minister, in a back office of whichever community centre we were in; scrub around and find the briefing if I was lucky, busk if I was not.

In the autumn of 2002 there was a council by-election in a Labour ward. The BNP had put up a plausible candidate. Canvassing every single voter was imperative.

On a damp Friday evening I was door-knocking in a street of terraced houses built by nineteenth-century mill owners. Three times I was pulled back to talk to other foreign ministers. On the third occasion it was Igor Ivanov, wanting to discuss twenty words in the draft resolution. 'Where are you speaking from?' he asked in his deep, resonant Russian-accented English.

'From a police van on Shorrock Lane, Blackburn, Igor. I'm going from door to door asking people to vote for our by-election candidate.'

'Ah Jack. In Russia we do not have that problem.'

At that moment, I wished that I didn't have 'that problem' either. Despite our efforts, the BNP won the seat, by eighteen votes.

It may sound weird, but I enjoyed the intensity of negotiating Resolution 1441. It played to my strengths. As a lawyer you are taught the critical importance of words; the detail matters. I have a very retentive memory. By the end of the process I could recite whole sections of the resolution. I still can.

It was a great team effort by Jeremy Greenstock, David Manning, Peter Ricketts (the FCO's political director), and me – as well as some brilliant Foreign Office lawyers and officials in London and New York; and, of course, Colin and Condi and their teams. We argued so intensely over every last detail because everyone knew what was riding on it.

The resolution was finally passed on 8 November 2002. At first, fourteen of the Council's fifteen members were in favour. Then Syria, a non-permanent member, reluctantly decided to come in with the rest. The Syrian foreign minister, Farouk al-Sharaa, one of the more difficult people I have ever had to deal with, called me when my car was in Regent Street, and engaged me in the most contorted explanation as to why his country had taken so long to make up its mind.

I felt a great sense of relief and achievement that we had come this far. The resolution was comprehensive; it was mandatory, based on Chapter VII of the UN Charter; crucially it recognized 'the threat Iraq's noncompliance with Council resolutions and proliferation of weapons of mass destruction and long-range missiles poses to international peace and security'. The resolution closed: 'the Council has repeatedly warned Iraq that it will face serious consequences as a result of its continued violations of its obligations'.[7]

Everyone who had been involved in the negotiation knew what 'serious consequences' meant: military force. That's why we had spent so many hours and days arguing over the text; and it was why I was later to become exasperated by those who claimed that the words did not mean what they said. They did. That's why those words were there. The French in particular had agreed them in return for a key change (to trade an 'or' for an 'and' elsewhere in the resolution, with the effect that Iraq would only be in further material breach if it failed two tests rather than only one).[8] I had been happy to agree this trade, not least because, like Dominique, I wanted the bar on further material breach to be a high one.

The resolution provided the best hope there was of resolving the crisis through peaceful means. The obligations it imposed on the Iraqi government were easy to meet. Iraq had to make a full declaration of all its WMD programmes, and allow the IAEA and UNMOVIC inspectors unrestricted access. I often said that 'we would take "yes" for an answer'. There would have been no possibility whatever of war if the inspectors had reported in unequivocal terms that Iraq was complying with 1441. Resolution 1441 was the means of enabling Saddam to say 'yes'. But we could only resolve this peacefully with the threat of military action. That this approach might be successful had been demonstrated when the Iraqis had dug in against letting the inspectors back – until President Bush announced that he was going to go through the UN. It was strong evidence to me that the UN route could work.

In 1991 Saddam had been too slow to grasp what could happen if he failed to withdraw from Kuwait. He was known to be stubborn. Even so I thought – naively as events turned out – that with tens of thousands of US, UK and other troops massing on his borders, he might get the point, and realize that if he complied he would be able to stay in power. Regime change had been a formal US policy since 1998.* But it was not, and could never have been, the UK's objective; nor the Security Council's.

On 7 December 2002 Iraq submitted its 12,000-page declaration. Hans Blix, the executive chairman of UNMOVIC, described this document as mostly 'a reprint of earlier documents, which does not seem to contain any new evidence that would eliminate the questions or reduce their number'. He also complained that Iraq had to take 'seriously' all the disarmament issues left unresolved when UNSCOM had left Iraq in 1998, 'rather than brush[ing these] aside as the evil machinations of UNSCOM'.[9]

However, as we entered the New Year I was optimistic about a peaceful resolution. Walking through Portcullis House, the new parliamentary building across from Big Ben, after a session in the Commons gym, I bumped into Trevor Kavanagh from the *Sun* and Phil Webster from *The Times*, both of whom I had known for ever. They asked me what I thought the odds were of avoiding war. I replied, 'Sixty/forty.' Although the exchange had been on lobby terms, it found its way into the papers the next day.[10] I wasn't sorry. I wanted to pull back on the idea of a 'rush to war' and in particular to avoid Hans Blix's next report, due on 27 January, being the decisive moment.

Colin called me early that month to say that Dominique de Villepin

---

* When Bill Clinton signed an Act of Congress, the Iraq Liberation Act, to that effect.

had proposed that France, which had the rotating monthly presidency of the Security Council, wanted to hold a special Security Council meeting to discuss 'counter-terrorism'. I smelt a rat, and told Colin as much.* Colin called me back to say that Dominique had promised that it was not a set-up, and he thought it would be unhelpful if he stood in his way. OK, I said.

In fact it was not OK and it set off an extraordinary series of events. Over a seven-week period, four ministerial-level Security Council meetings were held. They were among the most serious and dramatic meetings in which I have ever been involved.

The 'counter-terrorism' meeting itself, on 20 January, passed off without incident. We all then trooped off for lunch at the French Legation; except our host, Dominique, who was nowhere. He arrived thirty minutes late. He had called a separate press conference, at which he had effectively denounced the US. 'Unilateral military intervention,' he said, 'must be perceived as a victory for the maxim "might is right",' an attack against the primacy of the law and international morality.'[11] It soured relations, especially with Colin, which was daft of the French since he was far more sensitive to their position than anyone else in the US government.

Anyone of my generation remembers how frightening it was to live through the 1962 Cuban Missile crisis, when the two superpowers came close to unleashing a nuclear war. That had partly been defused by a dramatic presentation to the Security Council by the US ambassador

---

* Though France had co-operated pretty well over 1441, relations between them and the 'Anglo-Saxons' had started to go downhill from the autumn. I had witnessed President Chirac pick a fight with Tony as we all left a European Council meeting in the October. Tony always had impeccable manners. Chirac quite gratuitously insulted him, over an aspect of the Common Agricultural Policy. Lord Palmerston famously observed that 'Nations have no permanent friends or allies, they only have permanent interests.' But how those interests are advanced does depend significantly on the personal chemistry between leaders.

to the UN, Adlai Stevenson. Having demanded to know from the Soviet representative whether his country was installing missiles in Cuba, Stevenson had then showed photographs that proved the existence of such missiles, just after the Soviet ambassador had implied they did not exist.

The NSC in Washington thought that it was time for a repeat of this 'Adlai Stevenson' moment, with Colin laying out the charge sheet against Saddam. I could tell that Colin had the deepest reservations about this idea. Those turned into alarm when the vice president's office wrote him a script rehashing all the earlier nonsense about a connection between Saddam and al-Qaeda. So concerned was he that he spent days at Langley, the CIA's headquarters, painstakingly working through intelligence.

After Colin had made his presentation against the Iraqi regime at the Security Council meeting on 5 February 2003, I said that I thought he had set out a 'powerful and authoritative case'. Most others thought so too. Later it emerged that some of the intelligence was defective, part based on forgery. In an interview with Barbara Walters two years later, Colin described it as a 'blot' on his record: 'It was painful. It's painful now.'[12]

The intelligence failure over Iraq has, to say the least, been painful to all of us involved in it, me included. But I know how carefully Colin had examined the evidence before he used it. And the disagreement in the Security Council was not about the evidence against Saddam. The French, the Germans and the Russians all had very effective intelligence agencies of their own. Far from disputing the veracity of what we said, they supported it. The disagreement was about whether military action was appropriate.

As February progressed, the divisions in the international community widened. A third meeting of the Security Council was called for Valentine's Day. The atmosphere was anything but affectionate and made much worse by Don Rumsfeld's ill-judged remark about France and Germany being 'old Europe'.

Dominique was in his element. He made a powerful, flamboyant case against military intervention, to much applause. As I went over the draft of my speech, I had to do something to lighten the leaden atmosphere. I tried out an opening line – 'I speak on behalf of a very old country, invaded in 1066 by the French' – and showed it to Jeremy Greenstock. He pulled a face. I then had a little inspiration. Swap 'invaded' for 'founded'. Even the French might laugh. They did; thankfully, so did everyone else.

The fourth and last ministerial meeting of the Security Council was to take place three weeks later, on 7 March. It was in the intervening period that the visceral divisions within the international community became set in concrete.

One of Dominique's refrains was that there could be 'no automaticity' about military action. I agreed with him. That was the whole point of 1441. There was nothing 'automatic' about it. It was only if Saddam remained in 'further material breach' that the 'serious consequences' – military action – would follow.

The legal adviser to the Foreign Office, Sir Michael Wood, had taken exception when he read a summary of a conversation I had had with Vice President Cheney, in which I had said that I believed that we did not legally require a further resolution after 1441 to authorize military action. That was my view. It was also the view of Jeremy Greenstock's counsel in New York – and, critically, became that of Peter Goldsmith, the Attorney General.[13] But we believed that a second resolution would help greatly in Parliament, if we concluded that military action was necessary and sought parliamentary approval for it.

We didn't need the second resolution in order to go to war. If Saddam was in further material breach, that was already authorized by 1441. A second resolution was needed to prevent war. One with a clear timeline to an ultimatum, and clear steps for Saddam to take, would make it much less likely that force would be needed, since even he might realize that the game was up, and comply. The draft of this second resolution therefore contained six benchmarks on full co-operation, the destruction of the unauthorized Al-Samoud missiles which the inspectors had discovered, and the making available of thirty scientists for interview outside Iraq. None of these would have posed any practical difficulty to the Iraqi regime.

We can never know why, with hundreds of thousands of troops ready to invade Iraq, Saddam made the gamble that he did, and chose to tough it out. One reason was, I think, Iran. He couldn't contemplate his sworn enemy discovering how weak he was. Another key reason in my view was the increasingly mixed messages he was receiving, especially from France, Germany and Russia. They had all signed up to 1441. Now they appeared to be backing away from its natural consequences. They knew that giving Saddam more time, with no certainty of any action even then, would simply degrade the whole effort to get him to comply, and with that the authority of the United Nations. Saddam's strategy up to 9/11 had worked. Sanctions had been falling apart. I think he believed that he could secure this outcome again, and that the international community would then leave him alone – to rebuild his weapons systems, and re-establish himself as a key power in the region.

Diplomacy would only work with a credible use of force behind it – as everyone on the Security Council well knew.

The day before I left for this last Security Council meeting I called in to see Tony after Prime Minister's Questions. I told him that if he were to put British troops into Iraq, with the Americans, the following week, and without a second resolution, 'the only regime change that will be taking place will be in this room'. It was not about what I would do. I'd support him. But I felt in my bones that we would not muster the numbers when it came to the vote in the Commons.

I had decided to get to New York with a day in hand.

Just before I left London I was given a copy of a draft UNMOVIC Working Document.[14] Running to 167 pages, it was by far the most detailed and up-to-date assessment by the inspectors of 'unresolved disarmament issues'. It made an indelible impression on me. It confirmed my view that Iraq's non-compliance with Security Council require-ments going back to 1991 was profound, and that the international community now had to take action to deal with the threat it posed. That evening in New York I met Dr Blix. I told him I'd read every word of the document. 'That's more than I've done,' he replied. I was aston-ished. It was his report; the most comprehensive UNMOVIC had yet produced. But he hadn't read it. I became even more worried when he went vague about when it would be published. I assumed that he would make it available in advance of this crucial meeting. In fact, he left it until after it was over. Until then, I had a good opinion of Dr Blix, but my confidence in him was shaken by this.*

I'd drafted and redrafted my speech to the Council, but it still wasn't right. I'm generally a good sleeper, but I was wide awake at 3 a.m. New York time and rewrote it all.

I've never been a natural orator, but on a good day I can hold my audience. You can't survive in the bear pit of British politics unless you can think on your feet, and not get trapped by your written text.

There's a large coffee bar just outside the Security Council Chamber. Known as the Quiet Room, it's normally very noisy, as officials and security men keep one ear for the television feed, the other for their own conversations. One of my detectives told me later that after the first minute of my speech the whole place went quiet. So did the Chamber itself. I had their attention; and I went for it, picking up on what 'my good friend Dominique' had just said.

'Dominique . . . said that the choice before us was disarmament by peace or disarmament by war. Dominique, that is a false choice.' In his speech he had referred to a lot of diplomatic pressure on Iraq from the

---

* Dr Blix has since said that, 'My gut feeling, which I kept to myself, suggested that Iraq still engaged in prohibited activities and retained prohibited items, and that it had documents to prove it' (Hans Blix, *Disarming Iraq*, (Pantheon, New York, 2004), p. 112).

Non-Aligned Movement, the Arab League and the EU, adding, disingenuously, that the US and UK forces had 'lent support' to that pressure. I picked this apart. We had to back our diplomacy with a credible threat of force. 'I wished we lived in a different world where this was not necessary, but sadly we live in this world and the choice, Dominique, is not ours as to how this disarmament takes place, the choice is Saddam's.'

I continued, saying that Saddam has shown this week 'that he can act with astonishing speed when he needs to . . . It takes time to fabricate falsehoods, but the truth takes only seconds to tell.'[15]

There was not a word in my speech about intelligence. It was the indisputable facts of Saddam's behaviour that convinced me we had to act. Most telling of all, I asserted, was his response to the demand in 1441 that Iraq gave 'immediate, unimpeded, unrestricted and private access to all officials and persons whom UNMOVIC or the IAEA wish to interview' in locations of their choice.[16]

There were 3,500 such people on UNSCOM's lists. Just twelve private interviews had been allowed – with the rooms bugged by the Iraqi Security Forces. 'The restrictions placed on [these] interviews is itself the most incriminating evidence that Saddam has something to hide.' It was was one of the best speeches I have ever made, but it was not a moment for self-congratulation.

I was now convinced that unless there was a last-minute change of attitude by Saddam, for which I hoped and prayed, war was inevitable. Whether the UK would be part of the invasion was still unclear though. In a note to Tony on 11 March I outlined how it was still far from certain that we could win a vote on war in the Commons.

Tony got the Americans to agree to a week's delay for the start of military action, which was just as well. Efforts were made to garner the minimum nine votes for our second resolution. The wonderful Valerie Amos went round Africa to get Angola, Cameroon and Guinea on board.

But as this was going on, President Chirac released his wrecking ball. In a live television interview on Monday 10 March he declared '*Ma position c'est que quelles que soient les circonstances, la France votera "non".** We might – just – have got those nine votes, with the Africans, and Chile and Mexico. But their leaders would not put their heads above the parapet knowing that France would veto 'whatever the circumstances'. The second resolution was dying.

The irony was that President Chirac's intervention, although it weakened our negotiating position abroad, strengthened the potential support for military action in the Commons.

The efforts to secure a consensus on the resolution continued. A summit was held on Sunday 16 March in the Azores, between President Bush, Tony, the Spanish prime minister José María Aznar, and the Portuguese prime minister José Manuel Barroso. Despite the most intense diplomatic efforts, the resolution was in a coma. The next day I sent instructions to Jeremy Greenstock formally to withdraw it.

When the Cabinet met at 4 p.m. on Monday 17 March, and agreed that we should go to war, Robin Cook, the Leader of the House, decided to resign from the government. Robin and I remained good friends; and though we ended on different sides of this, the most serious of any decision we had taken in government, we had earlier worked together to insist that the Commons had to have the last word on military action.

The Commons' normal business was interrupted at 8.40 p.m. for me to make a statement setting out the Cabinet's decision. That was followed by Robin's Personal Statement explaining his resignation. He was forensic, eloquent and generous, and received an unprecedented standing ovation.

Straight after, I met up with my key officials in my Commons room. There was one face around the table that I did not recognize. This was nothing unusual. Ministry of Defence officials, or those from the agencies, sometimes popped up at meetings like this. And this chap could

---

* President Chirac interview with TF1 and France2 television on 10 March 2003: 'My position is that whatever the circumstances, France will vote "no".'

easily have been an official – earnest, balding, bespectacled. I started the meeting; then instinct took over.

'Would you like to introduce yourself?'

'Oh,' he said, in perfect English, 'I'm a journalist, from Belgium. I'd come down the wrong staircase; then saw you all, and thought it must be a press briefing.' Good try. He was quickly ushered out.

Tony opened the main debate the next day, and made one of the best speeches of his life. I had told my Foreign Office ministers, 'If we lose tonight, we can't send in the troops, and the government has to resign.' My task was to wind up the debate.

Alice, Will and Charlotte were up in the Gallery, to hear my speech. None of them shared my view. Each of them, if they had been free agents, would have been on the march against the war in mid-February. Will was president of the Oxford University Student Union and his failure to go caused him some difficulty. The test of loyalty is to give support even when you fundamentally disagree. By God, they passed that test.

In closing I said:

> I impugn the motives of no one in the House. The different positions that we have taken all come from the best, not the worst, of intentions. But as elected Members of Parliament, we all know that we will be judged not only on our intentions, but on the results, the consequences of our decisions. The consequences of the amendment would be neither the containment nor the disarmament of Saddam's regime, but an undermining of the authority of the United Nations, the rearmament of Iraq, a worsening of the regime's tyranny, an end to the hopes of millions in Iraq, and a message to tyrants elsewhere that defiance pays.
>
> Yes, of course there will be consequences if the House approves the government's motion. Our forces will almost certainly be involved in military action. Some may be killed; so, too, will inno-

cent Iraqi civilians, but far fewer Iraqis in the future will be maimed, tortured or killed by the Saddam regime. The Iraqi people will begin to enjoy the freedom and prosperity that should be theirs. The world will become a safer place, and, above all, the essential authority of the United Nations will have been upheld. I urge the House to vote with the government tonight.[17]

149 MPs voted against the motion; 412 in its favour. We were at war.

SEVENTEEN

The Aftermath: The Wrong Choices

At the time the president was listening to those who were supposed to be providing him with military advice . . . They were anticipating a different kind of immediate aftermath of the fall of Baghdad. It turned out to be not exactly as they had anticipated.

COLIN POWELL, 30 April 2006[1]

'You are going to be the proud owner of 25 million people,' he [Colin Powell] told the president. 'You will own all their hopes, aspirations, and problems. You'll own it all.' Privately, Powell and Deputy Secretary of State Richard Armitage called this the 'Pottery Barn rule'. You break it, you own it.

BOB WOODWARD, *Plan of Attack* (Simon & Schuster, 2004)

The invasion began on 20 March 2003, two days after our vote for war. Less than a month later, on 12 April, the Iraqi Army collapsed, and Baghdad fell to coalition troops.

This high-intensity military action had been well planned, and executed. The aftermath was anything but.

British officials had been involved for months, with their American counterparts, in planning for the day after Saddam fell. Our effort had not been helped by Clare Short's reluctance to have her Department for International Development (DfID) fully engaged. This was a handicap but not an overwhelming impediment.

There are arguments both ways about whether development aid should come under a separate ministry, or be directly attached to the foreign ministry. International practice varies, but the indelible reality, either way, is that development aid *is* foreign policy. However it is presented to the public, whatever the aid department's staff believe they are there for, the aid policies pursued by any government have clear foreign policy consequences. Clare certainly understood the wider uses of aid: she used it to pursue a parallel foreign policy wherever she could. The difficulty in co-ordinating what DfID and the FCO were doing was not at root a problem of personalities, but of governance, through the absence of any clear legal framework regulating the way in which the prime minister, the Chancellor and the Cabinet made decisions. The irony is that had there been such a structure, it would have been Clare, not Tony, who would have been constrained.

Colin had told me the previous summer that he had warned the president that the war would involve him becoming 'the governor of 25 million people, in eighteen provinces'. Colin understood the enormity of the task only too well, and set his Department of State to work, but he was the first to recognize that the lead would have to be taken by the military.

At a Security Council lunch after the second meeting in February 2003, Colin had told the ministers round the table that the US had had considerable experience in 'nation building' after the Second World War, establishing effective governance from the chaos of defeat in Germany and Japan. They would do so again. The challenge of introducing governance by the rule of law was always going to be far greater than it had been in post-war Germany. Germany's confessional divisions had long dissipated, Iraq's were still intense. Germany had a memory of some strong institutions, and an experience of democracy. Iraq had neither.

But the vibes from Washington even then were reassuring. Defense was in the lead; State in support; the NSC knitting it together. What only emerged later was, in Condi's words, the 'high-handed, dismissive way' the Pentagon froze out the rest of the administration, with disastrous consequences.[2]

I got wind of this on a visit to the region, six days after the fall of Baghdad. The US-led Office for Reconstruction and Humanitarian Assistance (ORHA) had established a temporary HQ in a hall at the back of a Kuwait hotel. I could not believe the shambles before my eyes. There were around forty people in the room, who, somehow or other, were going to be the nucleus of the government of this large, disputatious and traumatized nation. ORHA was being led by General Jay Garner, who had overseen humanitarian relief in the Kurdish area after the 1991 Gulf War. A nice man but to me patently out of his depth. 'The Garner mission collapsed almost on arrival and could barely manage itself, let alone the country', was Condi Rice's verdict. She also says the failure to ensure the security of post-Saddam Iraq was an extraordinary dereliction of duty on the part of Don Rumsfeld's Defense Department, and Vice President Cheney;[3] for his reluctance to take effective charge, I would add President Bush.

By the time I made the first (of many) visits to Iraq, on 2 July 2003, ORHA had been replaced by the Coalition Provisional Authority (CPA), under the headstrong Paul Bremer. Thankfully, he'd been joined by John Sawers, former ambassador to Egypt, and later Sir Jeremy Greenstock.* On the back foot, the CPA were trying to get a grip of the situation. Even so, there was relative calm on the streets of Baghdad.

It did not last. On 19 August a large terrorist bomb ripped through the UN building in Baghdad, killing the wonderful Sérgio Vieira de Mello, the head of this mission, and twenty-one others, including Fiona Watson, a British citizen who had previously worked in the Commons

---

* John Sawers became my political director and is now Chief of SIS.

Library. This was a diplomatic as well as a personal tragedy, and a huge setback for the rebuilding of Iraq.

The situation went from bad to worse. On 29 August Ayatollah Hakim, one of the senior Shi'a clerics, was assassinated in the holy city of Najaf, along with a hundred other worshippers.

Al-Qaeda-organized or inspired terrorists were behind most of this carnage, but they were aided by one of Paul Bremer's many capricious decisions, made after only the most cursory consultation with Washington, and none with us. In pursuit of the de-Ba'athification of Iraq, he had ordered the complete disbandment of all of Iraq's security forces. Before the invasion the US had been set on a sensible course, to remove the top 1–2 per cent of Saddam's party apparatus, not the entire 1.5 million who worked for it, and for whom Ba'ath membership was simply a way to earn a living in a dictatorship. Similar restraint had been shown in Germany after the war and it had worked.

Colin was furious when this emerged; so was Condi; so were we. It was crazy. Every former member of Saddam's vast army and police force was now jobless, with a grievance against the occupiers; and access to weapons, since the arms dumps had not been secured.

Unsurprisingly, the Shi'a community sought to retaliate. They were aided in this by Iran, which was also unsurprising, given that Iran had provided refuge and support to the Shi'a community during their decades of suppression by Saddam. Later, Iran, either directly or through Hezbollah, supplied the roadside IEDs (improvised explosive devices) that caused so many casualties among British and other troops, which was unforgivable. I am not in the least naive about Iran, nor the intentions of some of the Shi'a militia in Iraq, but it must be the case that, had it not been for the intense provocation from al-Qaeda and its associates, and the security vacuum left by Bremer's dreadful decision, there would have been both less occasion, and less excuse, for Shi'a retaliation.

We also had to deal with Dick Cheney and Don Rumsfeld's resistance to the UN's full involvement in the rebuilding of Iraq. As Condi has commented, 'our problem wouldn't be too much UN involvement, but too little'. She added, 'The hubris did not end there, however. As we were looking to the first proposals for rebuilding Iraq, we made what turned out to be a terrible and ultimately unenforceable decision. The Pentagon wanted the contracts to go to the countries which had supported the war . . . in practice it made the United States look petty. Eventually we would want help from everyone – *a lot* of help – to rebuild Iraq.'[4]

I liked President Bush. In private he was least like the external image of any leader I have ever met. In contrast to his public image, in private discussion he was bright, thoughtful, focused. His politics aren't mine, but that's hardly the point. However, what emerges, both from our experiences at the time and all the records now available, including his own memoirs, is that he presided over an heroically dysfunctional administration, the inadequacies of which were disguised by the nation's economic and military might.*

Maintaining a collective front with the US was hard going. How could we explain away the consequences of decisions – of which the incontinent de-Ba'athification was only one – in which neither we, nor the sensible people in the administration, had been involved? Then there were the entirely unauthorized failures, like the complete breakdown in military discipline and common humanity that led to the horrors of Abu Ghraib. Facing twenty-minute live interrogations on the *Today* programme – as I did frequently – was not a task to which I looked forward, but it had to be done. We'd got the country into this. We had to explain.

Though Abu Ghraib was the single most egregious example of the US administration's failure to live by its founding principles of the rule of law, it was not the only one.

---

* The United States has the world's largest economy. Its annual military spend is equal to the combined spend of the next seventeen countries.

Countries at war, feeling they face an existential threat, invariably put their survival above all else. We did in the Second World War. But, as we'd learnt from the early years of the Northern Ireland troubles, taking short cuts with human rights is not only wrong, but self-defeating.

Having somewhere to house al-Qaeda terrorist suspects picked up in Afghanistan and elsewhere was necessary. Treating them in a grotesquely humiliating way, as those photographs of Guantanamo Bay graphically showed, was not. Worse still was the use of 'black prisons', of interrogation techniques like water boarding; and the refusal to give these suspects a trial process worthy of the name. Dick Cheney and George Bush justify these methods on the grounds that they helped keep the United States safe.[5] I doubt that's true. There have to be limits if civilized societies are not to fall to the level of the terrorist. Even if the matter is to be reduced to a utilitarian calculus, for every life saved from intelligence provided under torture, how many are lost from the additional terrorist recruits such methods invariably provoke (another lesson from Northern Ireland)?

The British government did not approve of any of this. Nor was it ever our policy to be involved in the unlawful removal of suspects from one jurisdiction to another. I spent hours, days, negotiating with Colin, and later Condi, for the release of British suspects in Guantanamo Bay. They were, as ever, helpful. Ultimately the British suspects were all released, by January 2005.

As the terrorism in Iraq increased in intensity, some resorted to kidnap. For me, handling these cases was amongst the most difficult of the many difficult consequences of the Iraq War – not difficult in terms of the decisions I had to make, but in terms of the emotional impact on me. These individual cases brought me face to face with the responsibility I had for this war.

Among the easiest targets – for these terrorist groups – were foreign civilians, including two British citizens, Ken Bigley and Margaret

Hassan. Whenever this happened, enormous effort was made by the British Embassy in Baghdad and our security forces to secure their release, sometimes with success. But on occasion these efforts came to nought, with desperate consequences for the individuals and their families.

Ken Bigley, a British civil engineer working in Iraq, was kidnapped in September 2004 with two Americans. News of their murder by their captors came through whilst I was in New York for the September 2004 UN General Assembly.

For very good reasons, the British government had long followed a policy of never paying ransoms to kidnappers. That had not, however, stopped us from seeking to negotiate with the captors, to see whether there was anything short of a ransom (or its equivalent) which might facilitate release. Our expert teams had tried everything. The captors had decided to up the stakes by posting footage of Ken on the internet and giving information to Al Jazeera. The negotiations had dragged on; all the while we were becoming more anxious about Ken's welfare. Finally, whilst I was on a trip to the Middle East and Turkey, news came through that he had been killed. I was able to cut short the trip, and be back before this became public. I went up to Ken's home in Liverpool that evening to see his family. They were extraordinarily dignified in their grief, and understanding for what we had sought, but failed, to achieve.

Margaret Hassan's circumstances were very different from Ken Bigley's – she was married to an Iraqi and was a long-term resident there; but like Ken she had the misfortune to hold a British passport. Margaret was kidnapped on 19 October 2004. Again, we did everything that we could, but again tragically to no avail. She was murdered by her captors in November 2004 and her remains have never been found.

Different families react in different ways to the unbearable pressure of a kidnap. There's no 'should' about it. You simply have to treat all families the same, put in the same effort, and hope and pray. Margaret's family were intensely opposed to our military involvement in Iraq in any event. They saw me, as a senior member of the government, as in part responsible for her predicament, and then for her death. Some of the meetings I held with the family were difficult. I did my best in these. The truth was that if there hadn't been a war, Margaret would not have been captured or killed.

Gradually, and after much unnecessary loss of life, some security was restored. The first democratic elections in Iraq for fifty years, on 30 January 2005, led to a high turnout in Shi'a areas, a low one in Sunni areas, and relatively few casualties.

Britain's general election – and Tony's third victory – was on 5 May 2005. It was the most difficult election since 1983, and the nastiest and most personal I had ever fought. From the moment I had crossed my personal Rubicon and actively supported the war in Iraq I had known it was bound to be thus. Tony was impregnable in his Sedgefield redoubt. My seat was inherently less safe than his, and also less safe than my majority implied. With nearly one in three voters of Muslim Asian heritage (and plenty of the white electors not keen on Iraq either) I was an obvious target. Every one of the six other candidates was anti-war – including the Conservative, an articulate Asian lawyer from Dewsbury.

The candidate who attracted the most media attention was Craig Murray, the former British ambassador to Uzbekistan, who had taken early retirement from the FCO, and, it was said, had used part of his lump-sum payment to finance his campaign, which was well organized and high-profile. His campaign bus was an old Green Goddess military fire engine. I've no idea what possessed him to believe that Blackburn voters would be more likely to vote for him if he drove around in this vehicle, but it was one of many reasons why his campaign foundered.

In the previous four general elections I'd spent most of my time campaigning in marginal seats, rather than in Blackburn itself. This time, Blackburn demanded my constant attention.

Thank God for the Blackburn Labour Party. Without the teams of loyal members, and the efficient organization we'd built up over a quarter of a century, I'd have been done for. My agent, Bill Taylor, the party secretary, Phil Riley, and the most respected figure in the Asian community, Adam Patel, had been with me throughout that time. Many others had been active in the party for decades.

My opponents could label me a 'war criminal', but they couldn't touch me when it came to work for the town. Throughout this intense period as Foreign Secretary, as well as keeping to my schedule of five walk-in advice surgeries a month, with just a handful of cancellations, I'd also remained committed to the regular open-air question times in the town centre throughout the Iraq crisis. These were not comfortable occasions, attracting a large and often hostile audience; many people did say, however, that I deserved some credit for being willing to face the heat.

Then there were the regular residents' meetings, an idea we'd stumbled on by accident. The Mill Hill ward won by the BNP during the negotiations over UN 1441 is adjacent to the equally white Ewood ward. This had been the BNP's next target. Much of the housing was in poor condition, drug dealing was rife – and they had found a great issue. The Blackburn Royal Infirmary in the ward had been moved to a brand-new hospital complex a mile away. According to an urban myth spreading like wildfire, the now empty building was to become 'the largest Islamic college in Europe'.

In late January 2003, whilst the Iraq drama was being played out in the Security Council, I had been in town for the usual weekend engagements. We had arrived early at the advice surgery – bang next door to the Ivy pub, where I always go before Rovers games. I suggested that we popped in for a quick drink. I was pounced on by the regulars, demanding to know why 'they' – the council, the government, me – were not listening to their concerns about their area. I told them that I did not have time then – my advice surgery was due to start – but I'd call a public meeting in the community centre as soon as I could.

On 28 February, the place was packed. About 250 residents turned up, including many BNP supporters. Bill Taylor, who was leader of the council as well as my agent, was on the platform with me, as were the chief executive and the local police chief. The atmosphere was threatening, and distrustful. Improvising in an attempt to calm the meeting, I said that it was going to be part of a process, not a one-off; a careful note would be made of everything said; we'd write to everyone who signed the attendance sheet; and there would be a follow-up meeting nine months later.

Few of those present really believed that any of this would happen. But it did. The old hospital site was quickly zoned for housing and funds were found for a major improvement programme for the existing housing in the area.

We'd alighted on a successful (and obvious) formula for effective, if informal, local democracy. So we quickly established a schedule of similar meetings in each ward of the town, on a six- to nine-monthly rota. Attendance has always been good. They have made a tangible difference to both the quality of life in local communities and, as important, to people's sense of control over their lives.

It wasn't part of some well-planned strategy, just an idea I'd hit on in order to extract myself from the awkward situation in the pub. But it had an important impact on the level of underlying support for me in the 2005 general election.

The critical factor, though, was the loyalty and commitment of Asian Labour members. Across town, people like Mohammed Khan, Ibby Master, Akhtar Hussain, Salim Mulla, Shaukat Hussain, Abdul Patel, and countless others were put through the fire by my opponents, who piled activists into the constituency, and then set about a campaign of psychological, religious and sometimes physical intimidation. The short message was that no proper Muslim could possibly vote for the infidel Straw. They projected a hostile video on to the gable end of Akhtar's shop, and much else besides. But my loyal supporters were undeterred. Virtually none of them had supported my position on Iraq; but I think they thought 'Jack might be a bastard, but he's our bastard.'

On one of my visits to Iraq, Barham Salih, then deputy prime minister, and a great Anglophile, had asked me in a desultory way whether there was anything he might do for me when the election was called. 'Yes,' I had said, 'please come to Blackburn, and campaign.' He did – addressing a meeting of key Asian leaders. A Sunni Muslim like them, Barham spelt out why he, and those he represented, supported the war and why I wasn't an infidel. It was a turning point in the campaign.

Nine months later, when Tony made a barbed comment to me about my 'Muslim constituents' – implying that I jumped to their tune – I was cross. It was an insult to those constituents, especially those in the party closest to me. They worked their socks off for the party, for me (and for Tony), out of belief in our values, and personal loyalty and respect, when they were fundamentally opposed to what I'd done. How dare anyone suggest that I was in their pocket, or they in mine.

Despite all the hard work campaigning, eight days before polling day I was almost a gonner.

After my one Foreign Secretary trip abroad during the whole campaign – to Luxembourg – I went to Reading. I combined a visit to see my brother-in-law in hospital (he'd been injured in a cycling accident) with some campaigning in the two marginal Reading seats.

The late afternoon train journey back to Blackburn was going to take about four hours. Great, I thought, I can have some peace. I was offered a drink, but luckily instinct told me not to have one. An hour into the journey the phone rang. Tony was on the line. 'Peter Goldsmith's legal advice on the war has leaked – all thirteen pages of it. I want you to do all the media.'

'But it's Peter's advice, not mine,' I replied. 'Hadn't he better do it?'

'No, that wouldn't be fair on Peter. You know all the issues, you know the resolutions off by heart.'

In the time it took for the train to get from Leamington Spa to Preston, Bill Taylor and Ed Owen booked a hotel just outside Blackburn, and arranged for five satellite trucks from five broadcasters to do five live interrogations of me. I rushed home, changed my shirt, collected reams of briefing from the fax, and from 10 p.m. till around midnight I was on the air. It was serious high-wire stuff. David Hill was generous enough to say I'd done OK, and I think I had. Even so, the selected quotations from Peter Goldsmith's advice made for very damaging stories all over the next day's papers. After the election Bill told me he had thought the leak would be terminal for me.

To mocking from family, and party workers, I never stop working on polling day until 9.55 p.m. – five minutes before the polls close. Charlotte came out with me that evening. We managed to persuade an elderly man in his dressing gown to accept a lift to the polling station. And there was a portent of the result, when we spotted Craig Murray's Green Goddess. It had broken down.

At the count, national and international media, hoping for a scalp, were out in force. They were disappointed. To my relief, and utter astonishment, my majority had just dipped, from 9,249 in 2001 to 8,009, with a swing of 1.9 per cent (well below the national swing of 3.1 per cent). Because I had so many opponents, my majority obscured the drop in my vote (from 54 per cent to 42 per cent), which was not good. But no one noticed that – and there was a further delight for the now ecstatic Labour supporters when Craig Murray polled fewer votes than the BNP.

In November 2004 Colin Powell resigned as Secretary of State on President Bush's second election, and was replaced by Condi Rice. I'd got to know her pretty well, but her prime contact in the UK had been with the prime minister's diplomatic adviser – first David Manning and then Nigel Sheinwald when David went to Washington to take over as UK ambassador from Christopher Meyer (to great relief on both sides of the Atlantic) in September 2003.

Once she was Secretary of State, I'd be working with her as closely as I had worked with Colin. Condi made her first overseas trip to London in February 2005. We were very pleased, and wanted it to go well. After meetings with Tony and with me, there was a press conference at the Foreign Office, packed with journalists from across the globe. Condi remembers it best for the questions we had on Iran, suggesting that there was 'a chasm' opening between the US and Europe on how we approached Tehran's nuclear ambitions. There was something of a difference of emphasis here, but we played it down.

I recall the occasion for a different reason. We were being asked about the allegedly slow progress towards democratic government in Iraq. I recited a well-rehearsed, formulaic answer; so did Condi. Then the tone and the register of her voice changed.

'Democracy can take a long while. When the Founding Fathers spoke of "We, the people" in the Declaration of Independence, they didn't mean people like me.'

'Wow,' I thought. 'She meant that.' This brilliantly professional and famously restrained public servant had suddenly opened a window on what it felt like to be black.

I'd been writing a weekly column for the world's most important newspaper (it is to me), the *Lancashire Telegraph*, ever since the Iraq War (I still do). I devoted my next column to what she had said, and sent it to her. I'm not sure if that triggered the idea, but she invited Alice and me to her home town of Birmingham, Alabama.

We went in October 2005, with the Mannings. It was a most memorable trip. I was old enough to recall reports of the civil rights' marches, the intense racism of the Deep South, the disenfranchisement of black voters, and the colour bars. But it's one thing to learn about these things thousands of miles away. Quite another to be there; to talk to those who'd experienced the lash of Police Chief Bull Connor's cops; suffered the night terror of the Ku Klux Klan. In 1963, four little black girls, one of them a friend of Condi's, had been killed by a racist bomb at the 16th Street Baptist church. We went to a service to dedicate a memorial to these innocent victims, then walked to the Kelly Ingram Park, holding the hands of four little girls dressed in pink and white for the occasion.

Condi's parents had been teachers; she had grown up in a modest but respectable neighbourhood. She told me she'd had virtually no serious contact with any white people until her family had moved to Denver, Colorado when she was thirteen. Outside her old house, she said, 'You see the end of this street; and that one? My father and his neighbours had to take their rifles, and build barricades, to keep out the Ku Klux Klan thugs who'd already burnt one house in the street. Without their right to bear arms, who knows what would have happened.'

Earlier in the year I'd been trying to persuade Condi to support a UK initiative for a Small Arms Treaty, to no avail. I now saw why.

The trip ended with my one and only visit to watch an American football game, a grudge match between Alabama and Tennessee, in Tuscaloosa. Condi is as fanatical about American football as I am about Blackburn Rovers, but much more expert. So expert, that she was tipped to head up the National Football League when she left government. We went out of the tunnel to huge cheers; not something that's likely to happen at Ewood Park. They weren't for me, but for Condi – her home state is very proud of her. I waved nonetheless. It would have been impolite not to. And potential Blackburn voters are everywhere.

The quality of these personal relationships really makes a difference. I take one example of many. Shortly after Condi had taken over as Secretary of State, genocide in Darfur in eastern Sudan went before the Security Council. At issue was whether the Council would refer Sudan to the International Criminal Court (ICC). We had been great advocates of the ICC; Robin Cook had played a major part in its establishment. The US had long taken a different view, refusing for their own good reasons to ratify the treaty (they thought it challenged their sovereignty). For us, there could be no argument but that we'd support Sudan's reference to the ICC. Condi and I talked through how this should be handled. A story that we had sided with the French (as we were) with the US vetoing the resolution would not be a good idea. I knew that Condi herself wanted something done about the Sudanese government's behaviour but she faced intense opposition from within the US administration. It is greatly to her credit that in the end the US simply abstained on this resolution and we got it through.

I invited Condi to make a return visit to Blackburn and the northwest. Security had not been a problem in Alabama but it was in Lancashire. Despite my good result at the 2005 election, anti-war feeling had run high. It was strong among many in the white community, and intense in part of the Muslim community. When the visit took place in late March 2006 there were the inevitable protests including a large one outside Blackburn's town hall. But there were as many who turned up in support of Condi, and the town as a whole was delighted that she'd taken the trouble to visit.

Some of the councillors and Muslim leaders had decided to boycott the visit, which was daft. They missed an extraordinary, private session which Condi held in the Council Chamber with a large group of Asian men and women. The men, as ever, tried to dominate proceedings, with questions about Iraq, Palestine and Afghanistan. Then one of the women invited the men to stop hogging the questions. The session took on a magical quality, as a serious discussion broke out about how women from minorities could break through, and the audience suddenly realized that they had much more in common with this black woman who had been brought up in a racist state than they had ever imagined. Alice and I have often said how sorry we are that the session had not been taped. Had it been, though, it would not have been the same.

I had intended that Condi should come with me to that weekend's Rovers game. Mr Murdoch put paid to that. Sky moved the game to the Monday. I asked the club how easy it would be to put it back to the Saturday. Fine, they thought, if I could find £250,000. Instead, we visited the ground, where Condi met her fellow American, our great goalkeeper Brad Friedel.*

The last part of the visit took place in Liverpool, whose early riches had come from the slave trade, and where Condi visited the Slavery Museum. After a concert and a dinner, there were fond farewells in front of the cameras.

Away from the media, I then bid Alice goodbye. I slipped into the hotel's service lift, got into an unmarked vehicle and was driven to John Lennon Airport, where I boarded Condi's plane, unnoticed. We were going to Baghdad.

I was completely knackered, and looked it. Condi very kindly offered me the bed in her cabin, and said she had somewhere else to sleep. I accepted with gratitude. I should have listened more carefully; 'somewhere else' was the floor; it led to some interesting press stories about what a cad I'd been in taking Condi's bed.

Our key objective was to persuade Dr Ibrahim al-Jaafari to step down as acting prime minister. We were only the messengers. A proud and stubborn man, he couldn't garner enough votes to secure his position. The other Iraqi leaders didn't want him. But they wanted us to do the deed.

We played a 'good cop/bad cop' routine, and finally got through to him. In April 2006 Nouri al-Maliki, a Shi'a leader from the Islamic Dawa Party, was elected prime minister – a position he still holds at the time of writing, six years later.

*

* His gloves and a signed ball still sit in the State Department viewing gallery.

It was not until after the midterm US elections in November 2006 that Don Rumsfeld was replaced as Defense Secretary by the respected Bob Gates. Early in the New Year Gates then put in place the 'surge' of over 20,000 additional troops under the leadership of the talented General David Petraeus.

UK combat troops withdrew from Iraq in April 2008; US combat troops in December 2011. 179 men and women from the UK forces died in Iraq; 4,486 from the US and 139 from other forces.[6] The best estimates of civilian casualties is around 100,000.[7]

Was I right, not just in supporting the war, but in actively prosecuting military action against Iraq?

It's the most difficult and momentous decision I've ever made, or ever will make. Tony thanked me immediately after the vote, adding, 'I couldn't have done it without you.' This was gracious of him, as I told him, but it made my sense of responsibility all the greater because if I had argued publicly against the war, the UK would not have been involved. This is not conceit. It's true. The countless hours I'd spent in the Chamber, in Cabinet, and above all at PLP meetings, listening, explaining our position, meant that we'd secured both understanding and support for what we decided to do.

In a joint interview to celebrate fifty years of Radio 4's *Today* programme, John Humphrys expressed frustration about the way I repeatedly quoted the text of Resolution 1441. I was, and am, unapologetic. Infuriating though it always was to those many who claimed that we had invented the menace posed by Saddam's Iraq, that we had deliberately lied about his WMD, the international community, hard-nosed negotiators from Paris, Moscow, Berlin and Beijing, all concluded in that resolution that Saddam's 'proliferation of weapons of mass destruction', and 'non-compliance' with Security Council resolutions, was a 'threat to international peace and security', the key prior test for the authorization of military force under Chapter VII of the UN's Charter. The Russians, the French, the Germans, the Chinese, all those so intensely negotiating the text of 1441, were grown-ups. They knew what was at stake, the enormity of what was riding on any resolution; after seven weeks of poring over every word, they agreed the text, every one of them. They didn't have to. No one forced them to do so. But they agreed it.

That was still their view four months later. In that last electrifying Security Council meeting on 7 March, no one was arguing that Iraq had complied with its obligations under 1441. There were some, Robin Cook among them, who disputed the likely scale of Saddam's WMD holdings, but few disputed the fact of them.*

So the question then was what we did about this wilful refusal to comply after twelve years of trying. The alternative – pursued by France, Germany and Russia – was for 'more time' for the inspections. Fine. But what happened when time was up? A further discussion in the Council? Saddam was brilliant at playing that game. The French, German and Russian position allowed him to bet that he would escape serious international pressure and pretty soon re-establish himself as a malevolent regional power.

I thought that would be the more dangerous course for the world than the military action that 1441 clearly anticipated.

I've been asked a million times since the invasion whether, knowing then what I know now, I would have made the same decision. No, I wouldn't. How could we have agreed to invade Iraq if we had known that there were no WMD there? But the question serves no purpose. We made a decision based on what we believed to be the case at the time.

To paraphrase Kierkegaard, life can only be understood backwards,

---

* Robin said in the Commons for instance that 'Iraq probably has no weapons of mass destruction in the commonly understood sense of the term – namely a credible device capable of being delivered against a strategic city target. It probably still has biological toxins and battlefield chemical munitions, but it has had them since the eighties when US companies sold Saddam anthrax agents and the then British government approved chemical and munitions factories.' Hansard, 17 March 2003, col. 727.

but it has to be lived forward. The issue is whether I believe that I should have made a different decision on the basis of what was or could have been known at the time. I've thought about this endlessly, not least because of the profound intelligence failure that emerged, and because of the unanticipated chaos and loss of life that happened after the invasion – much of which could have been avoided with better post-invasion planning and execution. I gave three long sessions of oral evidence to the Chilcot Inquiry, and also submitted four lengthy written memoranda.[8]

We all thought that the intelligence was reliable. This assessment was widely shared by key agencies across the international community including Hans Blix.* The contemporaneous intelligence-gathering about Libya's nuclear programme had understated, not overstated, the reality. We did err in failing to recognize that to the public, and many parliamentarians and journalists, the intelligence was seen as Holy Writ, with none of the caveats that those within the net of secrecy automatically applied to the agencies' reports. But, as I've explained, the September 2002 dossier and the US 'nuggets' were each produced in good faith in response to public demand. The key point is that they were never the case for war. They were a case for taking Iraq seriously.

But I made my choice, on the best available evidence. I do not back away from it now. To do so would be contemptible.

We could have dealt with the political fallout of no WMD more easily if the post-invasion situation had been peaceful and benign. It was the two together that was so difficult to defend. In retrospect we should have insisted on a more central role in post-invasion planning. But we thought we had this. It wasn't only the UK out of the loop, but half

---

* '[I]n the papers we have read . . . the broad conclusions of the UK intelligence community (although not some particular details) were widely shared by other countries'. Butler Inquiry, 14 July 2004, HC 898, para 457.

of the US administration – mainly the half we were talking to. The other problem was that almost all my time and focus was spent on the international/UN dimensions of the conflict and on handling Parliament.

To pick up Condi's observation, democracy in Iraq is still taking a long time. After the elections in March 2010 the Iraqis were unable to form a government for 249 days (they were much quicker than the Belgians, who, though no one really noticed, were without an agreed administration for a world record 541 days). The security situation is still difficult, with al-Qaeda-inspired terrorists still operating. Violent civilian deaths in 2011 numbered 4,087.[9]

The inconvenient truth, however, is that Iraq is a better place. The Iraqi economy is estimated to have grown by 9.6 per cent last year, whereas its pre-war economy was contracting by around 7 per cent a year. Access to services has increased dramatically, with 22 million Iraqis now able to access clean water compared to 13 million in 2003. Infant mortality has fallen from over 100 per 1,000 live births in 2000 to 40 per 1,000 in 2012.

There are regular protests in Iraq against corruption, the state of public services and economic mismanagement, but no one is shot as punishment for demonstrating; and Iraq has not been on our television screens as yet another Arab nation demanding democracy.

The Iraq Survey Group (ISG) concluded that there were no WMD. That assessment is known around the world. But some other ISG conclusions are less well known. Their report found that Saddam's 'primary goal from 1991 to 2003 was to have UN sanctions lifted'. His plan, once this had happened, was to reconstitute his WMD capability, although 'with a different mix of capabilities to that which previously existed', They also found that Saddam 'aspired to develop a nuclear capability in an incremental fashion, irrespective of international pressure and the resulting economic risks – but he intended to focus on ballistic missile and tactical chemical warfare (CW) capabilities'.[10]

If we'd followed the alternative course being urged upon us in the

Security Council, Saddam would have remained, with his power and prestige enhanced. He would have re-established his weapons programmes too, to assert his position as a strong regional power.

How far a re-energized Saddam would have been able to help stall the Arab Spring in neighbouring countries is a matter of speculation; but he certainly wouldn't have helped.

What is beyond dispute is that, but for the Iraq War, we'd be worrying not about the nuclear ambitions of Iran, but about others – maybe Iraq itself; without question, Libya.

Towards the end of 2003, Libya's leader, Colonel Gaddafi, was confronted with painstaking (and accurate) intelligence developed by our SIS and the CIA about his WMD programmes. I have no doubt that what convinced Gaddafi peacefully to abandon these programmes was Iraq. But don't take that from me. On 19 December 2003 Libya finally agreed to have its WMD programmes dismantled under international supervision. Three days later CNN reported that 'Gaddafi acknowledged that the Iraq War may have influenced him' in his decision.[11] 23 tonnes of mustard gas, 3,563 unfilled chemical aerial bombs, 'hundreds' of SCUD-B, and five of the much more advanced SCUD-C missiles made up part of the haul.[12]

Libya had previously declared just one nuclear site. There were in fact twelve. In 2004 inspectors from the IAEA gave forensic detail of an extensive active covert programme for highly enriched uranium and for the production of nuclear weapons.[13] They were all dismantled.

The 2011 uprising in Libya and the resultant military action against Gaddafi would have involved far greater risks if he'd had nuclear weapons available. There is every prospect he would have, but for Iraq.

EIGHTEEN

The Sick Man Bites Back: Europe and Turkey

Turkey seems to be falling to pieces, the fall will be a great misfortune . . . We have a sick man on our hands.

Attributed to Tsar Nicolas I of Russia, 1853, in Harold Temperley,
England and the Near East (Longmans, Greens and Co., 1936)

For three brief months, 9/11 brought the world together. President Bush had an unrivalled opportunity to allay the fears and suspicions about him which had been prevalent in Europe since he had been elected by a whisker the year before. Within Europe, too, there was a new unity.

Guy Verhofstadt, the Flemish prime minister of Belgium, in the chair for Belgium's six-month presidency of the EU, certainly thought so.

Belgium was created out of confessional and linguistic conflict in 1830. Its monarch is king of the Belgians, not 'of Belgium'. As a single, cohesive nation, it scarcely exists. Linguistically and culturally split, it has six parliaments, six parties. Like other Belgian politicians, Verhofstadt had little direct emotional comprehension of what it meant to come from a nation with a strong and enduring sense of itself. His world was his region – Flanders – and then Europe, with not much in between.

During Belgium's presidency, Verhofstadt had been working on his place in history – the Laeken Declaration. The analysis – about the distance of European peoples from EU institutions – was spot on.[1] His prescription has, however, exacerbated the EU's problems, and made its democratic deficit with its citizens worse.

The Declaration established a Convention on the Future of Europe, with government and parliamentary representatives from across the EU, chaired by the former French president Valéry Giscard d'Estaing. The objective was to create a constitution for Europe. Discussions on this solemn project were punctuated by an hilarious row between the Italian prime minister Silvio Berlusconi and the European Commission (led by Berlusconi's long-time adversary, Romano Prodi) over the location of the European Food Agency – should it be in Italy, or Finland? ('There's no such thing as Finnish cuisine,' shouted Berlusconi. 'What does Finland have to teach the world about food?' Italy won its battle in the end. Finland got a clearer division of EU competences as a consolation prize.)

In the great arguments in the sixties and seventies about whether Britain should be in the Common Market, I was on the No side. I'd been sufficiently worried about the implications of the 1992 Maastricht Treaty (which, among other things, laid the ground for the single currency) to have argued in John Smith's Shadow Cabinet (without success) for Labour to vote for the whole treaty to go to a referendum.

However, we were in Europe, and staying. My view by now, as a 'practical European', was that whilst the processes of the EU could be mind-numbing in their tedium and banality, the EU was (and remains) a noble institution. It provides a political method for resolving the endless, fractious arguments between the nations of Europe – on any basis far better than the alternative, the killing fields.

But the Convention on the Future of Europe turned out to be a *folie de grandeur*. I was part of that *folie*. I added to it with a signed article in *The Economist* making the case for a constitution of Europe, complete with a cartoon casting the Convention in the manner of the Founding Fathers. When I think of it now, I cringe. I redeemed myself, in my own eyes at least, when in 2004 I persuaded Tony Blair to commit the UK to holding a referendum on the constitution.

In the decade since, Europe has faltered. The euro crisis remains fundamentally unresolved. The euro was founded on a false prospectus, that it is possible to have a single currency beyond a single country. As a consequence, the EU is almost bound to limp from crisis to crisis. Few things illustrate better the poverty of ambition now infecting the Continent than the failure of its natural leaders, France and Germany, to follow through the decision they helped make in 2005, and secure Turkey's full accession to the Union.

My expectation was that the Convention on the Future of Europe would do what it said on the tin – bring the EU 'closer to its citizens . . . [with] European institutions . . . less unwieldy and rigid . . . more efficient and open'. I was particularly pleased that the Declaration had recognized that it should not be 'intervening, in every detail, in matters by their nature, better left to Member States' and regions' elected representatives'. It started out well enough.

I thought it might be possible to reduce the fundamentals of the EU's operation from hundreds of pages to something as concise as the US constitution, and to deal with the need to change the way the EU now operated, with a membership up from six when it started to the twenty-seven members it would have by 2007.

Giscard d'Estaing proudly presented the recommendations from the Convention to a European summit in Thessaloniki in June 2003. The venue was much more an augury for the future of Europe than the high-blown conclusions of Giscard d'Estaing's Convention.

The summit was a shambles, a failure of Greek organization on a monumental scale.

Modern Greece has become notorious for doing everything at the last minute. Athens was at the time in complete chaos, with street after street dug up as part of the 'preparations' – by then months late – for the 2004 Olympics. We hadn't quite expected the same at the summit. In place of red carpets being rolled out in our hotel, floor tiles were being laid – in front of us. One of Tony's long-serving members of staff, the wonderful Kate Garvey, made the mistake of putting her trust in a recently tiled stairway. The cement wasn't dry, the tiles slipped, and so did Kate, severely spraining her ankle.

In my room I noticed that the cistern for the loo was swaying gently. I discovered that it was not fixed to a wall but to stiff wallpaper, and the odd batten. Tony had no hot water in his room the whole weekend. Kate's injury aside, we all made light of the hotel's hazards. But Greece's palpable inability properly to organize something as routine as a European Council meeting was a reminder that Germany had been right in trying to resist Greece's admission to EU membership in 1981, and France wrong in their insistence, over Germany's and others' objections, that in the interests of 'European unity' their membership had to go ahead. It was a nice irony that the president of France at the time had been . . . Valéry Giscard d'Estaing.

After this summit, there was the Inter-Governmental Conference (IGC), in which all the member states negotiated a final text of the constitution based on the platform of the Convention's proposals. We made good progress – and secured many protections for the UK. Despite this progress, handling the EU constitution became ever more difficult, a classic case of the best becoming the enemy of the good.

The euro-enthusiasts had had a field day, with one unnecessary, and inflammatory, section after another. Worse than its title of 'constitution' were the in-your-face references to a flag, anthem, motto and annual 'Europe Day' for the whole of the EU, together with a currency (the euro); and the killer (and unecessary) Article I-6: 'Union Law' – 'the Constitution and law adopted by . . . the Union in exercising competences conferred on it shall have primacy over the law of the Member States'.

Whatever the merits of specific parts of the text, we were comprehensively losing the bigger battle for the British citizen's support.

The Conservatives had resolutely refused a referendum over the Single European Act, and the Maastricht Treaty – between them, of much greater significance than this constitution – but were now much more

Eurosceptic. Iain Duncan Smith as leader, and Michael Ancram as Shadow Foreign Secretary, were on a mission for a referendum on the constitution – and correctly saw that this could be a serious Achilles heel for Labour at the next election. They were joined by the Liberal Democrats, who, though very pro-Europe, thought that a text of this significance required endorsement by the British people. Tony and I ploughed on making the case that a referendum was unnecessary.

Most visitors to the floor of the Commons Chamber are amazed how small it is – and how short is the distance between the two front benches. But it's one of many reasons why real debate takes place there. If you're a minister, an hour on a difficult wicket answering thirty-plus questions in quick succession will soon tell you whether your arguments are soundly based or not. In my case, the more I deployed my arguments against a referendum, the less convinced I became. I don't think anyone in the House – or outside – noticed my doubts at the time. I shared them only with a small circle of officials and my special advisers.

My difficulty was that whilst many of the substantive changes in the constitution were natural developments to ensure that the EU did not seize up as its membership expanded, the overall impression the document gave was that it would lead to a new relationship between member states and the Union, 'a country called Europe'. Having a president of the Council was genuinely intended to strengthen member states against the centralizing tendency of the Commission, but few were listening. The anthem, flag, motto and the rest of that pretentious nonsense made it nigh on impossible to argue that this was just another sensible treaty change.

In the early months of 2004, wading through the treacle of why we didn't need a referendum, I came to the view that we would have to have one. The EU had always been a project pushed ahead of public opinion by elites – a variation of Douglas Jay's famous observation that 'the gentleman in Whitehall really does know better what is good for people than the people know themselves'.* This was just about acceptable if the public could rapidly see the benefits of the decisions taken for them. But such consent for the EU project was wearing very thin.

With a British general election highly probable around the fourth anniversary of our 2001 victory, there was little prospect of passing legislation to ratify the constitution, and settling the issue, before the election. If we had not committed ourselves to a referendum well in advance of the polls, our denial of the 'British people's right to determine their own future' would fast become one of the most damaging issues in the election itself.

I did the sums. There were at least thirty Labour MPs, in safe seats, who would come out in favour of a referendum whatever our whips told them. Without a clear commitment to a referendum, two things would follow. Some Labour MPs, normally relaxed about EU issues, but desperate to hold on to their seats, would commit themselves to voting in favour of a referendum; and we would lose more marginal seats because of our refusal.

I wrote Tony a detailed, private minute in early April 2004 in which I spelt all this out.

Tony's heart had always been in a different place from mine on the EU. He was a true believer, in a way I had never been. But his head was in the same place. He agreed.

Announcing this 180-degree U-turn was going to be tricky. We planned to do it after Easter. However, we were scuppered by the ever-assiduous Trevor Kavanagh, the stridently Eurosceptic political editor of the *Sun*. Who he'd talked to I still do not know; but he managed to piece together an exclusive which he published on 6 April. Tony made a formal statement announcing our U-turn decision as soon as the House came back after the Easter recess.

---

* Douglas Jay, *The Socialist Case* (Faber & Faber, London, 1937). Jay limited this statement to 'In the case of nutrition and health, just as in the case of education' – but inevitably the qualification was omitted when used against him and Labour.

The Constitutional Treaty was duly signed by each member state on 29 October 2004 in Rome at an elaborate ceremony organized by Silvio Berlusconi. My signature is there on the sheet, alongside Tony's. Berlusconi gave us each a fountain pen (with the Italian flag on top of its cap), which I still have – though its filling mechanism defies all known laws of physics.

Early in the new year I introduced the ratification bill into the Commons. Since all three parties were now signed up to a referendum, the heat went out of the argument. It meandered, and finally fell when Parliament was dissolved in early April for the general election, to be reintroduced once we were back in power.

I was not looking forward to campaigning for a Yes vote in the referendum – though I would have done. Neither was Tony, since a likely No vote would have placed him in considerable, possibly terminal difficulties, given that Gordon and his people were now circling.

We were, however, miraculously spared that fate by the referendums in the Netherlands and France, held in May and June 2005, which both resulted in No votes.

I could not contain my delight, I'm afraid. I thought it was time to kill the constitution, which I did by calling for a 'period of reflection'.

The iron had set harder in my soul on the EU, not least because in the three and a half years since the Laeken Declaration had promised to reduce the way the EU was 'intervening, in every detail, in matters better left to Member States' and regions' elected representatives', the EU had moved in the other direction.

Nothing illustrated this better than the way the Working Time Directive was being used to disrupt the orderly training of junior doctors.*

---

* *Sindicato de Médicos de Asistencia Pública* vs *Conselleria de Sanidad y Consumo de la Generalidad Valenciana* [2000] and *Landeshauptstadt Kiel* vs *Jaeger* [2003]. The SIMAP judgment defined all time when the worker was required to be present on site as actual working hours, for the purposes of work and rest calculations. The Jaeger judgment confirmed that this was the case even if workers could sleep when their services were not required.

The justification was that employment conditions should be similar in each member state. But this was always nonsense, because of enormous variations in the way health care is delivered. Some member states were able to circumvent the directives because of the way their junior doctors were employed; others did so simply through lax enforcement. Neither dodge was available to us. In co-operation with health ministers we tried every avenue to secure amendments to the Directive; but without success. The cost to the NHS has been huge, at more than £750 million per year.* From my days working for Barbara Castle in the seventies I was alive to the need to reduce junior doctors' hours from their intolerable level. But this is an issue that by its nature should be left to individual member states. Whatever the argument for reform here, the result of the EU's interference was a result few wanted, and which would never have gone through if the UK Parliament had been able to make its own decisions.

As negotiations over the constitution trundled on, there was a more immediate issue for us to decide. Ten new members of the EU would join on 1 May 2004. Two – Malta and Cyprus – were very small, members of the Commonwealth, with long-standing connections with the UK. The other eight ('A8') were all in eastern Europe. With our economy doing well, and much higher wage rates, working in the UK was likely to prove very attractive to Poles, Hungarians, Czechs and nationals of the other accession states.

The other western European states with borders adjacent or close by – like Germany, Austria and France – were alive to this prospect too. All chose to make use of the transitional restrictions on the free movement of labour from the accession states, for up to seven years.

Some members of our government wanted to pursue a more open

---

* This, according to the Royal College of Surgeons in November 2010, is the cost of having to hire temporary staff as a result of the Directive.

approach. Tony wanted to deliver good news to the A8 at the December EU summit – a key objective to rebalance the EU away from Paris and Berlin, particularly after Iraq.

The Home Office published a detailed research paper, which indicated that the net migration effects if we had no transitional restrictions would 'be relatively small, at between 5,000 and 13,000 immigrants per year up to 2010'.[2] But this was another issue on a slow burn. It really only hit our political radar a few weeks before accession in April 2004, when the tabloids started running scare stories.

The Home Office estimates proved wrong – by around a factor of ten. Net migration here from eastern Europe to the UK reached close to a quarter of a million at its peak in 2010.[3]

Basing social and economic policy on research, and sound data, is crucial. But this is a case study in how good intentions, and apparently good research, can lead government in the wrong direction. It's hard to think now of how we might have improved the process to secure a more accurate outcome – except that if we had started earlier, and had a more open, public debate, with select-committee hearings, and greater arguments amongst the academics, we might have been able to spot what was wrong with the forecasts, and adopted the same restrictive approach as our partners across the Channel.

An abiding tension inside the EU is between those who want a deeper union and those who want a wider one. In the UK we've long come down on the wider side of the equation. A larger union suits us. One of the reasons we were in the vanguard for the east European states was that their free market and pro-NATO stances provided potential for us to strengthen a natural alliance within the Union, against that led by France and Germany. There was a bigger strategic argument too – the more that all of geographical Europe could be bound into the Union, the less the risk of violent conflict between states; the greater the prospect of planting the deepest roots for the democratic idea across the Continent.

This is why the EU is a noble project; why it is worth – most of the time – working round its irritations, frustrations, pomposities, and the ever-present efforts of a self-serving administration in Brussels to extend its powers at the expense of those of the nation state. When the Soviet bloc collapsed in the early nineties, there was no guarantee that the newly 'liberated' states would move to Western-style democracies; nor, later in the the decade, that the new Balkan states would stop resorting to extreme violence to resolve their ethnic and territorial arguments. That these new states have all moved in the right direction is a tribute to the European Union.

What about one of the largest European countries, second in population only to Germany – Turkey?

In 1952 Turkey became a key member of NATO, a fundamental bulwark against the Soviet Union, with whom it shared a border. Membership of the European Union was a natural next step. It first applied in 1959 and in 1995 reached a deal for a Customs Union, as a precursor to full membership.

A serious financial and economic crisis in 2001 led to a political earthquake in Turkey the following year. The parties of government, humiliated by their economic mismanagement, and by strong allegations of corruption, were voted out of office.

But the leader of the winning party, the AKP, Recep Tayyip Erdogan, was not able to take up his seat in Parliament, still less become prime minister. In 1998 his then party, the Welfare Party, had been shut down for the threat it allegedly posed to the secular order. Erdogan himself had been charged with incitement to religious or racial hatred – for reciting a poem. To this Anglican, brought up in the school of muscular Christianity, the words ('The mosques are our barracks, the domes our helmets, the minarets our bayonets and the faithful our soldiers') appear rather less seditious of the secular order than 'Onward Christian soldiers, marching as to war'. But then Britain is not a secular state.

For four months, until the law was changed, the co-founder of the AKP, Abdullah Gul, was acting prime minister. In 2003, Abdullah then became foreign minister. I quickly established a great rapport with him, which developed into a lasting friendship through the most dreadful tragedy.

On 20 November 2003, two large terrorist bombs exploded in Istanbul, at the headquarters of HSBC, and at Pera House, the British Consulate-General. Thirty-three people were killed, including Roger Short, the British Consul General, and eleven other Consulate-General staff. Hundreds were injured. Within a few hours the FCO and the police had put together a squad of fifty counter-terrorist and FCO officers, and chartered a plane. (The whole time I was Foreign Secretary I kept a bag packed.)

I arrived in Istanbul in the early evening, and went straight to Pera House, where I met Abdullah, saw the devastation, talked to the very shocked survivors and bereaved relatives, and held the inevitable press conferences. Not for the first or last time, the fact that back in 1973 I had been in a terrorist bomb blast myself prepared me for what I saw, and helped me to understand what those caught up in the atrocity would be feeling. The Turkish response was magnificent; Abdullah could not do enough.

I spent a long time trying to get inside the soul of the AKP. Some headline-writers presented the party, pejoratively, as 'Islamist'. But the people I met – Erdogan, Gul, Yasar Yakis who was foreign minister whilst Abdullah was acting prime minister, and hundreds more – are as far away from 'Islamist' jihadism as Western politicians are from being medieval crusaders.

It is not only insulting, but an abdication of analysis, to label the AKP in this way. The AKP does seek to modify the anti-clerical secularism of the deep state, and to show greater respect for the religion to which 98 per cent of its population formally adhere. But in the UK, religious ceremony is intertwined into the rituals of the state. The better clue to the AKP is that it is an associate member of the European People's Party – the centre-right grouping which includes all the Christian Democratic parties of the EU, who espouse economic liberalism and social conservatism.

And, for those who still like to label the AKP as 'Islamist', the confusing paradox is that, by conventional Western economic policy tests, Erdogan's government has been far and away the most successful of any post-war Turkish government. On taking power in 2002 it rebased the currency and rapidly settled the country's economic crisis. On current predictions, it will have the largest population in Europe by 2020, and will be the twelfth biggest economy in the world by 2050.[4]

The sick man has now recovered. With economic power has come diplomatic strength. After the US, Turkey has the largest armed forces in NATO. It remains an active member of this alliance, but these days shows less deference towards the US, especially with regard to the Middle East.

There's another paradox about Erdogan's AKP government. The more far-sighted of Turkey's AKP leadership have realized that one key way of naturally embedding social and economic reform into the structure of Turkish society is through the process of becoming an EU member.

In 2004, Turkey signed an Association Agreement with the EU, as a precursor to the Union agreeing formally to begin accession negotiations – almost as big a hurdle as membership itself. Reporting this to the Commons, Tony said this showed 'that those who believe there is some fundamental clash of civilizations between Christians and Muslims are wrong . . . Turkey's membership is therefore of fundamental importance for the future peace and prosperity of Britain, Europe, and the wider world.'[5]

In late 2004 and early 2005, Tony told me on two separate occasions that he intended to keep me on as Foreign Secretary if we won the 2005 general election. Aside from the fact that he appeared to believe that I could do the job, there was also the looming prospect of the UK's presidency of the European Union in the second half of 2005. It would have undermined our effectiveness to have had a new and untried minister in the job.

The timing of our presidency meant that Britain would be in the lead when decisions on Turkey's membership came to a head. Most would be made by the General Affairs Council of foreign ministers, chaired by me, at its meeting on 3 October 2005.

There's a laundry list of priorities for any presidency. This one was no exception, but enabling Turkey to tie its future firmly into Europe was at the top of my list. Achieving this took every political skill, high and low, I had ever learnt.

Crucially, France and Germany were then, at least, signed up to Turkey's EU membership. Although it caused them some domestic discomfort, both President Chirac and Chancellor Schroeder shared our view that it was in Europe's interest to have Turkey inside the EU. Joschka Fischer, not only German foreign minister but leader of the coalition's junior partner, was of immense help throughout. Led by its foreign minister Georgios Papandreou, Greece, one of Turkey's oldest adversaries, also wanted Turkey inside the EU.

But, with the exception of that near neighbour, the closer the country geographically, the greater its objections to Turkey's entry. For more than five centuries the Ottoman Empire had expanded throughout central and eastern Europe. For Hungary, Poland, Bulgaria, Romania and Malta, battles with the Turks were part of their national identity. For the Austrians, the Siege of Vienna in 1529, and for the Croatians, the Battle of Sisak in 1593, are almost as immediate as Dunkirk and the Battle of Britain are for us.

Then there was Cyprus, whose Greek-Cypriot government was in a league of its own in its opposition to Turkish membership.

Since 1974 the island has been divided, with the Greek Cypriots in the internationally recognized 'Republic of Cyprus' and the Turkish Cypriots concentrated in the self-proclaimed 'Turkish Republic of Northern Cyprus' (TNRC), recognized only by Turkey. Between 30,000 and 40,000 Turkish troops are stationed on the island to this day.

At the end of March 2004, the UN Secretary General Kofi Annan held intensive negotiations with Greek-Cypriot and Turkish-Cypriot leaders on a 9,000-page plan for political unity for the island.

Recommending the plan to both communities, he said: 'The plan is fair. It is designed to work. And I believe it provides Cypriots with a secure framework for a common future.'[6] Since the leaders of both sides had negotiated the plan there was a legitimate expectation that both sets of leaders would recommend the deal to their peoples. The Turkish-Cypriots did so. But the hardline Greek-Cypriot president, Tassos Papadopoulos, an unattractive partisan, vigorously campaigned against. The referendum in the south was lost.

This happened just a few days before Cyprus was due to come into full membership of the EU. At a General Affairs Council on 26 April 2004 there was a fury with the Greek-Cypriots' antics of a kind rarely seen in international diplomacy. But neither Papadopoulos, nor George Iakovou, the Greek-Cypriot foreign minister, was bothered. Their calculation was that the EU was not going to block their entry into the Union five days later. They were right. We should have, but getting a consensus would have been nigh on impossible at this stage.

Running a little ahead of Turkey's accession negotiations was Croatia. A decision on whether or not Croatia could become an accession state was due to be made on 17 March 2005. But the International Criminal Tribunal for the former Yugoslavia (ICTY)[7] had a warrant for war crimes on the Croatian former lieutenant general, Ante Gotovina. There was considerable evidence that elements of the Croatian security forces were actively shielding him from arrest.

This was sufficient to persuade the General Affairs Council to postpone any decision on Croatia, but only for a month or two. I was desperate to put it off until 3 October, and then place it second on the agenda, after Turkey. That would give me a trump card not least with Austria, hard-wired into Croatia, and dead-set against Turkey.

No Turkey, no Croatia.

One of the many reasons for the fading popular support for the EU is its wilful wasting of money, including on its two sites for the European Parliament, and two sites for the European Council. For three months each year – April, June and October – all ministerial meetings and parallel official groups meet in Luxembourg, rather than Brussels.

At least, at that time, no one could accuse the EU of squandering money on the European Council buildings themselves in Luxembourg.* They were on the outskirts of the city, off an industrial park, and indistinguishable from the light-engineering factories and warehouses on that strip. The architects had added soft padding on the exterior of part of the building – something I found very useful. When the frustration of the negotiations really got to me I ran my head into the padding a few times, and felt much better for doing so.

A detailed draft of the conclusions had been drawn up, of which all twenty-five member states, and Turkey, had to agree every word if there was to be a positive decision. Some parts of this document were too opaque and obscure even for me. But for someone, somewhere, its details were of existential importance. It was a multi-dimensional nightmare, a Rubik's cube without solution. Solve one country's difficulty, and another was created. The Austrian foreign minister, Ursula Plassnik, a tall blonde straight from a Wagnerian opera, was in a class of her own, throwing one objection after another.

Around two in the morning, I adjourned the proceedings until the following day. We also ensured that Ms Plassnik had a good deal of homework to keep her occupied overnight.

I managed to catch about four hours' sleep that night – which was rather more, so she told me through narrowing eyes the next morning, than she had. I meant her no harm; indeed I liked her; but a negotiation like this is as much a matter of who stays alert the longest as who has the better case. I judged that if I could get most delegates to a state of catatonic exhaustion then a consensus might follow.

---

* Although a new £500 million building for the EU Court of Justice was opened in 2008, and in 2010 the EU announced its plans to spend a further £850 million on a new building for its translators and lawyers.

In normal circumstances the applicant country's foreign minister would have been round the table too, negotiating in real time with the rest of us. But there was a high risk that the Turks might have to go away empty-handed and they did not wish to be humiliated. I didn't blame them. Over the previous months I'd spent much time trying better to understand Turkey's position, and had been helped greatly in this by our ambassador Peter Westmacott, who'd become completely trusted by the Turkish government. Abdullah Gul, and Prime Minister Erdogan, stayed in Ankara and we had repeated adjournments so that I could telephone Abdullah and bring him up to date. This would have been fine, but for the fact that the there was the most incredible feedback on the phone lines; they seemed to be in a gurgling echo-chamber.

Crab-like, we finally got to one last issue, a single paragraph dealing with Turkey's attitude to Cypriot membership of international organizations including NATO. All twenty-five were ready to sign up to it, but now Turkey was digging in. I offered Abdullah one form of words. No good. Then another. No good either. I asked Condi if she could work the phones for me, which she did. Meanwhile the Greeks and the French knocked the Greek-Cypriots into line and the Austrian Chancellor was squared, overruling Ursula Plassnik. I then asked Tony, in London, if he would call Erdogan, for one last push.

Tony could really do detail, when needed. In this call he managed to persuade Erdogan to accept the first, more difficult, wording that Abdullah had rejected. In truth, there wasn't much difference between the two sets of words. What Erdogan had to decide was whether he wanted a deal or not. Agree these words, and he had one; reject the wording, and a significant part of his overall 'offer' to the Turkish people, especially among his softer support in the business community and the more secular Istanbul, would be undermined. He went for it and Abdullah boarded a plane to Luxembourg.

It was 3 October, which had been set as the deadline for the deal, but Abdullah didn't arrive until after midnight. It was the British presidency and it was still 3 October by UK time, so we were fine. When I announced this, there was relief all round. Abdullah and I gave a joint press conference. I opened by saying, 'This is a truly historic day for Europe and for the whole of the international community. We have just made history.' We had. It was my proudest personal achievement of my time as Foreign Secretary, and has given me an enduring interest in Turkey.

On the way back to our hotel I asked one of the staff if they could find a packet of cigs for me. We had some Scotch but I wanted to celebrate. I had been a (genuinely) occasional smoker for years – mainly scrounging 'real' smokers' cigs on the self-deluded basis that if someone else had bought them they'd do me less harm. In my hotel room, with my ever-resilient and brilliant private secretary Caroline Wilson, and a couple of other officials, I smoked my last cigarette.

The years since that marathon negotiating session have not quite worked out as most of us had intended.

In Britain, despite some intense inter-party argument over the EU, there's been strong bipartisan support for Turkey's membership. Not so across the Channel. In 2005 Chancellor Angela Merkel reversed the approach of her predecessor, claiming that 'Turkey's accession would strain the EU politically, economically and socially, and endanger the European integration process.'[8] Then, in the French election campaign of 2007, Nicolas Sarkozy, desperate for support from the far right, announced baldly that, 'Turkey has no place inside the European Union.'[9]

Of thirty-three separate chapters in the draft accession treaty, seventeen have now been blocked. No other accession state has ever been treated in this way. Indeed, the reverse has been the case.* The

---

* The EU leaned over backwards to accommodate many inadequacies in Bulgaria's and Romania's alignment with the acquis, to lever them into membership – even though their GDP per head is much below Turkey's, and their governance and judicial standards fall below the EU's standards.

immediate problem is Cyprus. But that would be soluble if France, Germany and the UK act with one voice.

Behind this convenient excuse, there's a more profound, and altogether more distasteful reason why Turkey's progress into the EU is being blocked without good reason. It's Muslim. When former President Sarkozy said that Europe 'must give itself borders'[10] he didn't mean geographical borders. If he did, it's hard to see how Malta or Cyprus could have been allowed in. He meant religious borders.

The European Union, not Turkey, will be the loser from all this. The EU needs Turkey rather more than Turkey now needs the EU.

NINETEEN

The Inconceivable and the Incompatible: Israel, Iran and the Middle East

For a secure and hopeful life . . . [let] us build a coalition for peace instead of war and hostility.

PRESIDENT SEYED MOHAMMAD KHATAMI OF IRAN,
10 November 2001[1]

I can date it precisely – 25 September 2001. The day when the scales fell from my eyes; the day the Israeli hawks tried to bully me. It made me angry beyond belief. I did not appreciate it. I have not forgotten it. It didn't work.

It was all over a single word. One Israeli Cabinet minister described this word as an 'obscenity', and 'pornographic'. Israeli prime minister Ariel Sharon expressed 'anger, outrage, and disappointment'.[2] Israeli president Moshe Katzav cancelled a meeting with me. Israeli foreign minister Shimon Peres cancelled a formal banquet.

The word was: 'Palestine'.

I'd used the word in an article published in Tehran to coincide with my visit there the previous day. The resulting hysterical storm in a teacup was at one level just another day of jostling and politicking in the Middle East.

But for me, it was more significant. It highlighted two things: the incredible vulgarity that had become the currency for public debate about the Middle East; and the dangers posed to peace in the region by the axis between hawks in Israel and hawks in the US. I came to the job of Foreign Secretary with great goodwill towards the Israelis which they then squandered, as they have done with so many in the West.

Closer to home, the reaction from Number 10 was a tiny red flag – one I didn't see at the time – about the dangers for me personally.

Relations with the Islamic Republic of Iran, always tricky, had gone into the deep freeze in 1989 when the Supreme Leader, Ayatollah Khomeini, had pronounced a fatwa inciting Muslims worldwide to murder Salman Rushdie, author of *The Satanic Verses*. Ten years later, when the reformist President Mohammad Khatami announced that his government no longer supported Rushdie's assassination, relations began to improve.

After 9/11, and President Khatami's remarkable solidarity with the United States, I visited Tehran. With military action imminent against the Taliban in Afghanistan, securing the active co-operation of the Iranians – with their long border with that country and strong links to the Northern Alliance – was a serious prize. Tony was keen.

It would be the first trip to Iran by a serving British Foreign Secretary since the Islamic Revolution in 1979. Much was riding on it. It was to be combined with visits to Jordan, the Occupied Territories, Egypt – and Israel. In a more tranquil world, it might have been better to have separated the trips to Iran and Israel altogether. But we didn't have that luxury. In any case, the Israelis knew they had at least as much as anyone to gain from some normalization of relations with Iran.

On the way to RAF Northolt there was the usual panic in the back of the car. A red box had been filled to overflowing with urgent work, which the office wanted done before we took off. With my private secretary Simon McDonald sorting the papers in order of importance, I ploughed through.

One item was the draft of an article, for my signature, which would be published in an Iranian newspaper as I arrived in Tehran. I was only dimly aware of this arrangement; I'd never seen the draft before. I read it – so did Simon. The key passages said:

> The human understanding which Iran showed [in respect of 9/11] stands in stark contrast to the jubilant reaction of the regime in Baghdad, which underlined once again how isolated Saddam Hussein is from the decent leaders in the Islamic world.
>
> Whilst in the past Britain and Iran may not always have agreed on the definition of terrorism, or how to deal with it most effectively, I hope this can be the beginning of a dialogue which leads to much closer co-operation between us on this important issue . . .
>
> Tony Blair and other world leaders have made clear that this is not remotely a war against Islam. My own constituency in England has over 25,000 people of the Muslim faith (and twenty-three mosques). I know how outraged the vast majority of Muslims throughout the world were by the attacks on New York and Washington.
>
> Equally, I understand that one of the factors which helps breed terrorism is the anger which many people feel at events over the years in Palestine. Last week, Israel and Palestine ordered a cease-fire.
>
> They now have it in their power to bring about a permanent settlement which is acceptable and fair to both sides.[3]

I thought it was good and approved it without significant amendment, moving on to all my other work.

The first leg of the trip, on Monday 24 September 2001, took me to Amman in Jordan, where I met with King Abdullah, his foreign minister Abdul Ilah Khatib, and later with Yasser Arafat, the leader of the Palestine Liberation Organization (PLO), who happened to be in Amman. We then flew to Tehran and stayed overnight in the grand neo-colonial British Ambassador's Residence, where I was given a good briefing from our ambassador Nick Browne and his colleagues. The article, translated into Farsi, had duly been published in a Tehran newspaper.

Early on the Tuesday morning, we began to get an inkling that the Israelis had taken exception to it. When I got back from a breakfast meeting with the Iranian foreign minister, Kamal Kharrazi, Alice was on the line. She told me that the BBC news had been dominated by reports that I'd offended the Israelis. The Downing Street press machine was doing nothing to help; rather, I appeared to be subject to a classic operation in which I was to be left hanging out to dry.

I called Tony on a secure line, and expressed my intense irritation with the treatment I was getting both from the Israelis and from his office. My article had been completely unexceptional. To allow the Israelis to behave badly simply because I had chosen to use the noun 'Palestine' (obscene) rather than the adjective 'Palestinian' (clean) was absurd. Tony had said the same thing as me, often enough: that anger over the treatment of the Palestinians was one of the factors that helped breed terrorism. (He would say it on many occasions afterwards.) The suggestion made by an Israeli foreign-ministry spokesman that the FCO was 'pro-Palestinian' because I'd referred to the number of Muslims in my constituency was insulting to the FCO, and to me. My point had been to support Tony's assertion that the post-9/11 action was not 'a war against Islam'.

In these situations Tony was ambivalent. He often gave the impression that he was too willing to give Israel the benefit of the doubt, even when nothing was in doubt. But he could also see that it wasn't sensible to leave me hanging. He said he'd call Sharon and try to calm things down.

In the meantime, after a meeting with President Khatami and a press conference, I headed for Tel Aviv. I was met at Ben-Gurion Airport by Sherard Cowper-Coles, who'd just taken over as British ambassador to Israel, after his stint as Robin Cook's private secretary. Sherard was in a high state of excitement. Alongside him, virtually hysterical, was

Michael Levy, 'the Prime Minister's Special Envoy on the Middle East' since 1998.

If you wanted to be Tony's Foreign Secretary, Michael was part of the package. On the tent principle* I had had the FCO find Michael an office in the building which he felt was suitable (no easy task), at the same time as resisting some of his grander requests, such as for his own ministerial-style red box. Even so I was consistently bemused as to what Tony seriously thought Michael added to the peace of the Middle East. He was a good accountant who'd made his money in the music business managing Alvin Stardust, Chris Rea and many others. He was an effective fund-raiser for the Labour Party, especially with the UK's Jewish community. He had a home in Israel, as well as in London. Of Michael's loyalty to Tony I was never in any doubt. But when Michael was given this position the Israelis must have thought that they'd won the lottery. His unpredictable manner led to many difficult moments; one senior official aptly described him as a 'self-launching, semi-guided missile'. My feelings towards Michael, I think it is fair to say, were reciprocated.[†]

If you represent a foreign country, there is no such thing as a private conversation in Israel, or in the Occupied Territories, except out of doors with a lot of ambient noise, or in a secure room. Everywhere was wired for sound – cars included. Sherard and I had a hasty consultation on the tarmac, and then a more guarded one in the mandatory Israeli government 'courtesy car'.

---

* 'It's probably better to have him inside the tent pissing out, than outside the tent pissing in.' Lyndon Baines Johnson, on FBI director J. Edgar Hoover, *New York Times*, 31 October 1971.

† Michael, for instance, says in his memoirs that he, 'never formed as close a personal relationship as [I] had with Cook,' and that I was 'shunted aside' in 2006 because 'for months [Jack] had reverted to what one of Tony's inner circle described as "student politics"'. A bizarre accusation from him of all people. Michael Levy, *A Question of Honour* (Simon & Schuster, London, 2008) p. 186.

I was happy to make some ameliorative comments to help calm down this ridiculous, synthetic drama. But I refused to apologize for what I had said. I batted those calls away by saying that I was not going to get involved in any textual analysis.

With the formal banquet cancelled as part of my punishment, I had a working dinner with Shimon Peres. If political survival were an Olympic sport, Shimon would hold the gold medal. Then aged seventy-eight, he had been active in Israeli politics for sixty years. He was awarded the 1994 Nobel Peace Prize, jointly with Prime Minister Yitzhak Rabin and Yasser Arafat, for securing the Oslo Accords. Prime minister twice, Shimon was elected president of Israel in 2007 (and is still in office at the time of writing in 2012). Shimon is entertaining, wonderfully fluent, with an unending supply of one-liners, exactly the man to send into any situation where the Israelis were batting on a difficult wicket. He signalled delphically that he wasn't that bothered about my article.

Around 10.30 p.m., Prime Minister Sharon had evidently decided that the Israelis had beaten up on me enough, and it was time for him to see me.

The meeting took place in the original Cabinet Room of the first Israeli government, a rudimentary hut in a compound in Tel Aviv, the walls covered in photographs of the early days of this extraordinary country. The furniture was the same vintage as the room. After Sharon had made his entrance, and we had gone through the forced pleasantries, we all sat down to begin the meeting proper. Suddenly, two seats along from me, there was a resounding crash. All I could see were Michael Levy's legs in the air. His chair had disintegrated as he sat in it.

The Israeli fandango done, the last leg of my trip was to Cairo, to see President Mubarak, Amre Moussa, Secretary General of the Arab League, and then Sheikh Mohammed Sayyid Tantawi, grand imam of the Al-Azhar mosque.

In contrast to the hierarchies of the main Christian denominations, and of Shi'ism, Sunni theological authority is much more diffuse – one

19. With a ranter like that it is easy to see why the lady is taking her family off so fast. Open-air meeting, 1983.

20. Interviewing two constituents in an advice 'surgery', 1987.

21 (*above*). Alice, William, Charlotte, and me, Oisy, Nièvre, France, summer 1983.

22 (*below*). William, Charlotte and Alice, too interested in their ice creams to notice the camera, Clamecy, France, 1992.

23 (*above*). Our lives changed . . . a police armoured shed being delivered to our Oxfordshire home, 1997.

24 (*below*). Wandsworth Jail, 2000. Life was a lot better than when my father was a wartime inmate there.

25 (*above*). Awarding an honorary MBE to the caretaker of our Kabul Embassy, February 2002.

26 (*below*). A very public breakfast with Abdullah Gul, then Foreign Minister of Turkey, Greek EU Presidency Foreign Ministers' Informal, 2003.

27 (*above*). Colin Powell, our host Ron Lauder, Private Secretary Simon McDonald, and me, taking a break from discussing the UN route for Iraq, The Hamptons, New York, August 2002.

28 (*below*). 'J'ai perdu la France,' President Chirac had told me. I was pointing to the French delegation. European Council, 2002.

29 (*above*). Condi and me, Ewood Park, March 2006.

30 (*below*). Condi and me with pupils from the primary school she attended, Birmingham, Alabama, October 2005.

31 (*above*). Gordon and me at our last Cabinet before the 2010 election, April 2010.

32 (*right*). Greeting Doreen Lawrence – one of the most extraordinary women it will ever be my privilege to know.

33. My mother and me, State Opening of Parliament, 2007. She was in the gallery, watching as I walked backwards, having safely passed the speech to the Queen.

reason why it is easier for extremist groups to proclaim that they represent the true word of the Holy Prophet. But Al-Azhar is regarded as perhaps the foremost institution in the world for the study of Sunni theology and law. My conversation with the grand imam went quite beyond the formulaic. And there remains a special place in my heart for Al-Azhar.

Offending articles aside, my visit to Tehran had proved productive. I had done my best to develop some understanding of Iran's history, how it worked, how its system of government held together.

The simple view, especially amongst the American right, is that it is a monolithic autocracy arbitrarily ruled by its supreme leader, Ayatollah Khamenei. The way that the more brutal elements of the regime have behaved in recent years – the Revolutionary Guards, the *basiji* (non-uniformed thugs attached to the Revolutionary Guards), the vicious repression of the protests against the rigged elections in 2009 – has simply served to reinforce that impression.

Iran is a theocracy. Final authority is vested in the supreme leader, under the theological doctrine of *'velayat-e faqih'*, the 'regency of the jurist', which the founder of the Islamic Republic, Ayatollah Khomeini, had developed from long-standing tenets of Shi'ism while in exile.* In a modern Western context, the idea that *velayat-e faqih* should be a central principle of government is weird. Historically, however, it is close to the dogma of papal infallibility, and similar to the Stuart assertion of the divine right of kings.†

---

* See Michael Axworthy, *Iran: Empire of the Mind* (Penguin, London, 2007), p. 258. This was a 'regency' of the jurists (i.e. of Khomeini, and his successors), and not a monarchy, since it would only last whilst the faithful Shi'a were waiting for the 'occluded' or 'hidden' Twelfth Iman to reappear and establish his righteous rule on earth.

† The Shi'a also have an almost exact equivalent of the Jesuitical 'doctrine of equivocation' which justifies untruths in defence of the faith.

But as with European theocracies in previous centuries, there has never been anything like a complete consensus in Iran about how this clerical doctrine should be applied to the operation of temporal power. Many leading theologians have argued for a strong role for more democratic institutions, using doctrinal justifications based on sharia.

And there is some history of democracy in Iran, It was there in its 1906 constitution; it was one of the 1979 revolution's aims. 'The immediate outcome (if not the longer-term result) [of the 1979 revolution] was a genuine expression of the people's will.'[4]

In its institutional structure the 1979 constitution of Iran reflects the tensions between *velayat-e faqih* and the democratic ideal. The leader is supreme; the control of the armed forces, declarations of war, the appointment of the judiciary, of broadcasters, and many other senior positions are powers vested in him. Ultimately, in any struggle for power, the leader holds the trump cards. Day-to-day government is more secular. There is an elected parliament, or Majlis, with considerable powers over the elected president, including the power to block ministerial appointments (as they have done with a number of President Ahmadinejad's nominees). But a 'Council of Guardians' (of clerics and jurists, half appointed by the leader) has to vet and approve any candidate for elective office, and can veto legislation passed by the Majlis.

As events in recent years have shown, including the disqualification of candidates and the rigging of elections, Iran's system of government meets few norms of Western democracy. But the fact that the same constitution (with the same supreme leader) allowed for the election of the reformist President Khatami (in 1997, and again in 2001) suggests that at any one time the distribution of power in Iran is many-layered, and can be fluid.

Like so much else about Iran, the pervasive attitudes of Iranians towards Europe, and especially the United States, are paradoxical. This reflects their history, and their powerful sense of themselves.

From their perspective, it is easy to understand why suspicion of foreigners can be so intense – with Britain seen as the principal villain. The quip amongst British diplomats that 'Iran is the only country that still regards Britain as a superpower' is less of a joke among the Iranians. The BBC's Persian Service has extraordinary reach.

In the last three decades of the nineteenth century Britain and Russia competed for influence in Iran. Exorbitant concessions were granted to British companies, including, in 1890, a tobacco monopoly. This led to a national boycott, and mass protests – both organized by the clerics – and had to be withdrawn.

In the early years of the twentieth century Britain extracted a deal, profoundly disadvantageous to the Iranians, for the Anglo-Persian Oil Company (later BP) to exploit the newly opened oil fields in south-west Iran. Thereafter Iran's strategic position, as well as its direct importance to our military effort, made it imperative from Britain's imperial viewpoint that we maintained hegemony over that country. The sensibilities of the Iranian people were secondary.

After the First World War, an attempt formally to make Iran a British Protectorate collapsed in the face of overwhelming hostility. Undeterred, in 1921, local British commanders on the ground helped a former sergeant in the Persian Cossacks, Reza Khan, to mount a coup. Within five years, this sergeant had himself crowned as shah of Persia.

Representative government was set aside; worse, the Iranians were denied many of their public religious practices. A ban on women wearing the veil in public meant that generations of girls, especially in the rural areas, were kept at home, uneducated, rather than being allowed out.

Hitler was much impressed by developments under Reza Shah and the admiration was reciprocated. Worried that these pro-Nazi sympathies could disrupt the unfettered use of Iran, Britain and the Soviet Union simply invaded the country in August 1941, and occupied it for the following five years. Reza Shah was moved aside in favour of his more amenable son, Mohammad Reza, who ruled until the 1979 revolution.

Post-war, the West was all over Iran. In 1953, the nationalist prime minister, Mohammad Mossadeq, who had sought Iranian control over its oil and other national resources, was removed in a coup.[5] The CIA and Israel's Mossad trained up the shah's notorious secret police, SAVAK. We continued to do all we could to prop up his regime, until its bitter end. Then, in the eight-year Iran–Iraq War, we supported Iraq.

It is not an impressive story. I tell it because it is fundamental to an understanding of the Iranians today (and of the approach I took towards Iran). This history is their present and future. Whilst in the UK remarkably little is known about our role in Iran, it is burnt into Iranian consciousness. We would not have appreciated it if the roles had been reversed.

Iran has a strong sense of its exceptionalism – as strong as that of the United States. Its borders are long-standing; its ethnicity in the main distinctive. There is a melancholy in the central story of Shi'ism, which has reinforced the Iranians' sense that they have been humiliated by the West. Respect for both their nation and their ancient civilization is what they hunger for.

In June 2001 – before 9/11 – President Khatami, a political philosopher as well as a politician, had proposed a 'dialogue among civilizations', an idea taken up by the United Nations later in the year.

After 9/11, the reaction of the Iranians was completely different to that of their Iraqi neighbours (as I had spelt out in the article against which the Israeli government had protested). Saddam had organized jubilant demonstrations to celebrate al-Qaeda's attacks, whilst in Tehran there had been torchlit vigils in support of the terrorists' American victims. Khatami, with Khamenei's backing, had reached out courageously to the 'great Satan' – the United States – and to the West.

But they were still highly suspicions of 'perfidious Albion'.

We, for our part, often found the Iranians infuriating. They are famed throughout the Middle East for being very difficult to pin down in any deal. This in part is due to the ambiguity inherent in the poetry they so greatly revere. They have such a familiarity with their poets –

THE INCONCEIVABLE AND THE INCOMPATIBLE

their Chaucers, Miltons, Wordsworths – that conversation at any level can be interspersed with quotations, which makes for an extra layer of interpretation in any negotiations. Once, in 2004, the day after a clear agreement had been reached in the nuclear dossier, the foreign minister Kamal Kharrazi called me and tried to unpick it – whilst I was in the lavatory of a very crowded train. Later, when I expressed my irritation to him he said: 'It's no good complaining to me, Jack, about how hard it is to negotiate with the government of Iran. Just imagine what it is like negotiating *within* the government of Iran.'

However, for all their suspicions of us, and for all our frustrations with them, they were delivering the co-operation we sought. For the time being our interests coincided. It was as plain as a pikestaff as well, that if their historic adversaries – the Taliban to the east, the Saddam regime to the west – were weakened, Iran's regional influence would be strengthened.

I believed then – as I do today – that this was perfectly manageable and could have led to the gradual dissolving of Iran's diplomatic isolation, to the greater benefit of all.

But that was expecting rather too much of the Israeli right, and of their allies in Washington.

A couple of blocks away from the British compound in downtown Tehran is the former American Embassy. Its perimeter walls covered with graffiti, it has been empty since the 444-day siege ended in January 1981.

On taking over as Secretary of State in January 2005, Condi Rice said: 'I was stunned to learn that there was no independent Iran desk in the Department of State. It turned out that the department thought in terms of "relations" with countries. Since we had no "relations" with Iran, it didn't warrant its own desk. Amazing.'[6] She was right. Especially in the years immediately after 9/11, the absence of heavyweight policy input on Iran from the State Department meant that it was too easy for the neocons' view of Iran to hold sway. Whether the inclusion of Iran in the 'axis of evil' in President Bush's State of the Union speech in January 2002 was negligent or wilful I don't know, but from America's strategic point of view it was a disaster. If they had had a more subtle understanding of Iran's complex elites, rather than a two-dimensional view that this was a dictatorship, they would have seen that such a profound rebuff was bound to weaken the authority of the one man – President Khatami – who might deliver a new and better relationship with the West, and would strengthen those darker forces in Iran whose position depended on demonizing America, and Israel.

In September 2000, after the failure of President Clinton's Camp David talks, Yasser Arafat had begun the Second Intifada, or uprising, against Israel.

By late 2001 the Israelis were suffering almost beyond endurance from repeated suicide attacks. By the time of the first full-day Commons debate on the Middle East for some years, on 16 April 2002, 1,300 Palestinians and more than 450 Israelis had been killed. Arafat's compound in Ramallah was under siege from the Israeli Defence Force (IDF).

The situation deteriorated rapidly in the following two weeks. The Israelis moved into Palestinian areas in huge force, including Hebron, and a refugee camp in Jenin. Whilst the Israeli's rage at the continuous terrorist attacks was entirely understandable, their disproportionate response was not. There was an international outcry and, as a result, I was rarely off the phone. We sponsored UNSCR 1405 welcoming an initiative by the Secretary General Kofi Annan to send a fact-finding team into Jenin, but then had to spend days trying to persuade the Israelis to admit them. Colin Powell's efforts in this period were heroic, as he battled for common sense, not only from the Israelis, but also their outriders in the administration in Washington.

Tony was alive to the need for a stable settlement between the Israelis and the Palestinians. He knew that, more than any other issue, the plight of the Palestinians led to a profound sense of injustice across the Muslim world; a mood which was then ruthlessly exploited by extremist terrorist leaders as a recruiting sergeant. He sought to use the unquestioned confidence that President Bush and the Israelis had in him to push them towards the 'two-state solution' which had been the elusive goal of the peace process. He saw this as a crucial parallel track to our potential involvement in military action in Iraq.

Considerable progress was made, despite the continued spiral of terrorism against the Israelis and overreaction by the IDF against the Palestinians. In a speech at the end of June 2002 President Bush outlined his support for a Road Map towards a full settlement, which was developed over the next few months by the UN and the US, EU and Russia. Full details of the Road Map were announced on 30 April 2003. Its central commitment was for Israel and Palestine to live side by side. I allowed myself a wry smile that my 'obscenity' of eighteen months before was now an internationally agreed goal.

The Foreign Affairs Council of the EU spent more time discussing Israel/Palestine than any other issue – sometimes to the point of pure tedium. It was rarely said out loud – it would have been an admission of impotence – but we all knew that, even were the EU properly united on the issue (and we never were), we lacked power. There would be no change unless the United States were fully engaged, and ready to push the Israelis to positions they would never get to by themselves.

The United States has a population of over 300 million. Israel's is 7 million. The US accounts for a fifth of the world's GDP; Israel for 0.3 per cent. But a man from Mars might be forgiven for thinking that Israel has greater control over US politics than the US does over Israel's.*

Big money's hold over American politics is hard to conceive for anyone brought up in the British system. Here, there are strict

---

* Bill Clinton is said to have said exasperatedly during one negotiation, 'Who is the superpower here?'

expenditure limits, national and local, and a complete ban on political advertising on television. In the United States there are no limits on total spending; no bans on political advertising in any media; donation caps are easier to evade. Big money is a cancer on the American body politic. It can – and does – buy politicians, or send them into oblivion. No one does this better than the American–Israeli Public Affairs Committee (AIPAC).

In their critical study of its operation John Mearsheimer and Stephen Walt describe AIPAC as 'The most powerful and best-known component of a larger pro-Israel lobby that distorts American foreign policy. The bottom line is that AIPAC, which is a de facto agent for a foreign government, has a stranglehold on the US Congress. Open debate about US policy towards Israel does not occur there, even though that policy has important consequences for the entire world.'[7] Since its foundation in 1951, AIPAC's power has been remarkable. It has helped ensure that Israel has been the largest single recipient of US foreign aid since the war, both in cash and military hardware.

In a lull after an informal lunch on my one visit to Camp David I asked President Bush why he, as a Republican, did not take a more proactive stance over the Middle East Peace Process, even if it did offend some Israelis. He was very frank. 'My father tried that,' he said, 'and look where it got him. Bill Clinton mercilessly used it against him – and took the presidency from him. I can't afford the risk.' With an engaging ability to mock himself, he then made reference to the 'closeness' of his win against Al Gore in 2000, and the fact that the evangelical Christian movement, traditionally strong within the Republican Party, had now formed a strong foreign policy alliance with the Israeli lobby.

Given the frightening spell which AIPAC held over American politics, it was a considerable achievement for Tony to have helped persuade Bush to agree to sponsor the Road Map. Tony deserves great credit for this – as does President Bush for biting the bullet of the two-state solution.

The next challenge was to cajole the Israelis to take serious steps towards making that a reality. We might have had a chance. On a 'Nixon/China' basis, Sharon could have been the man to deliver the Road Map. With unsurpassed credentials as a military commander for thirty years before he entered politics, the ever-neurotic Israeli public trusted him in a way that no politician on the left could match.

But here, Tony's profound emotional support for Israel got in the way of his ability to deliver some hard messages to both President Bush and to Ariel Sharon – to the mounting frustration of Colin Powell and me. Ultimately, it led to his fall as prime minister.

After the Road Map had been announced in April 2003, and endorsed by the international community in November 2003, the focus shifted back to Washington. There were protracted negotiations between the White House, the State Department and the Israelis over the next steps. The vehicle was to be an exchange of detailed letters, between President Bush and Sharon, agreed word by word between the two sides.

In April 2004 Colin visited Jerusalem. He was humiliated by Sharon, left hanging in the wind by his own president. After that, we spoke more frequently than usual. Colin was very anxious that Tony should himself be firm with Sharon, and Bush.

But in the final agreed text of Bush's letter to Sharon, Sharon got everything he wanted. The president (with Tony behind him) were the supplicants; Sharon the *demandeur*. Colin was very irritated that Tony had, yet again, pulled his punches with Bush.

The publication of the letters at a joint Bush/Sharon press conference at the White House on 14 April 2004 caused consternation throughout the Middle East – all they heard was words which appeared to offer a legitimization of the Israeli settlements, and a rejection of the right of return for Palestinian refugees. Later in the summer I sent Tony a detailed note about the Middle East and the UK's role. I said that this April letter had been a 'major triumph' for the centre-right Likud party – "'if we [Israel] get out of Gaza, you [US/UK] will turn a blind eye while we continue to annex East Jerusalem and the West Bank". This was underlined, I am afraid, by the perception – unfair and inaccurate but there nonetheless – that not only Bush, but you, appeared to endorse this approach.' I went on to remind Tony that Sharon had been dissembling about the expansion of the settlements, contrary to the Road Map. Condi had complained to me when I saw her on 17 August that the US were having to rely on satellite imaging because of the unreliable figures they were being fed by the Israelis. I concluded by saying that in 'Sharon's view . . . he has a free ticket from Washington to do anything he wants.'

This was all further confirmation that Tony and I were moving into different places on the Middle East; not, at that stage, that anyone outside a small circle noticed.

For Iran, the diplomatic environment changed when, in August 2002, the Iranian dissident group the National Council of Resistance of Iran (NCRI), the political wing of the terrorist organization MeK (People's Mujahideen of Iran), published claims that Iran was building two nuclear facilities which they had not disclosed to the IAEA. These were a uranium enrichment plant at Natanz, and a heavy-water plant at Arak. The claims were correct. There then followed the familiar Iranian semantic dance, as to whether the Nuclear Non-Proliferation Treaty, which they had signed, did in fact require them to disclose these facilities. They finally did so in February 2003, just weeks before the invasion of Iraq.

Shortly after the invasion, Iran (or rather part of it) began to put out feelers, through the Swiss Government, for bilateral talks towards a 'Grand Bargain' with the United States regarding Iran's nuclear programme, Iran's possible recognition of Israel, and the lifting of US sanctions. The United States chose to rebuff this – another error to add to the catalogue.

At the end of June 2003 I went back to Iran for my fourth visit. By now we'd grown used to the routine. As we landed the women members of my staff had to don their black cloaks and hoods, with much teasing as they did so, normally led by me.

The traffic in Tehran is terrifying. I was OK – in an armoured limo, with police front and behind – but citizens there take their lives in their hands on the roads, whether they are in vehicles or on foot, as Christopher de Bellaigue brings out in his wonderfully evocative memoir of Iran, *In the Rose Garden of the Martyrs*.* Many of the cars were ageing Paykan Hunters – originally made by the long-dead British Rootes Motor Company, and shipped out for assembly. The pollution from vehicles like this, compounded by low-quality petrol, was worse than Beijing's.

The nuclear dossier was high on the visit's agenda, especially with Dr Hassan Rowhani, the secretary of the National Security Council, and the man with more influence on this issue than anyone else outside the supreme leader's immediate circle. I made some progress then headed off to Kabul, Kandahar, Kuwait and Iraq.

The Iranians' approach to us, after their brush-off by the Americans, led first to diplomatic discussions with the regime and then in July and early August to detailed negotiations between the German, French and British foreign ministries over the terms of a joint letter to Foreign Minister Kharrazi that Dominique de Villepin and I had originally devised. Although the letter would come from we three foreign ministers, our heads of government were closely involved in its terms; and we did our best to keep the US indirectly on board too. As soon as Parliament rose, Alice and I left for a hideaway in south-western France, where the FCO had installed a fax. After endless iterations, the final

---

* 'I've seen cars prostrate over advertising hoardings. I've seen a compressed pedestrian dead like a slug in the middle of the road. I've seen cars skittle mopeds – no helmets of course, that would be sissy – and drive on regardless. Drivers communicate by leaning on their horns and flashing their headlights. They use symbols: the thumbs-up (a rough equivalent of the finger), the clenched fist (a bit worse).' (HarperCollins, London, 2004.)

version was delivered by our three ambassadors in Tehran on 6 August. The letter sought to open a formal dialogue with Iran about restoring the international community's confidence in the nature of their nuclear programme.*

By early October 2003, diplomatic negotiations (ably led in London by my political director Peter Ricketts, succeeded by John Sawers, fresh from our embassy in Cairo (and Baghdad) and, in Tehran, by Richard Dalton) were well enough advanced for the three of us – Dominique, Joschka, and me – to agree to make a joint visit at the end of the month.

Of all my singular experiences as a minister, this trip to Tehran is one of the most extraordinary.

The week before I left, Tony and I had attended a routine European summit in Brussels. Normally Tony would have reported back to the Commons, but over the weekend he was taken ill, diagnosed with an irregular heartbeat. I had to do it instead. I didn't get out of the Commons until 4.30 in the afternoon of the day I was due to depart. With time differences, this meant that I did not arrive in Tehran until the small hours.

I snatched a few hours' sleep, then offered some advice about the plumbing in the Residence (if I'd had my tools with me, I could have improved it). I had an early breakfast with Dominique and Joschka at the German Residence, to prepare for our major negotiating session with the Iranians, led by Dr Rowhani.

The foreign ministry in Tehran, like most government buildings – and our embassy – is in the valley in the southern part of the city. The Iranian government had decided that this session should be held in the

---

* The letter sought full co-operation with the IAEA, requested that Iran sign and implement an Additional Protocol to its IAEA Safeguards agreement and the Comprehensive Nuclear Test Ban Treaty; and sought a cessation of any development in Iran's capability to produce fissile material. In return for the resolution of these concerns we were willing to recognize the Iranian right to generate nuclear power and to provide access to modern technology.

north, the healthier, middle-class hills of the capital, in a diplomatic centre surrounded by well-laid out gardens. The Iranians love their gardens. Indeed, the word 'paradise' derives from the Old Persian word for a park or enclosure.

The meeting took place in a large rectangular room, without any natural light. Much of the draft communiqué had been agreed by officials; only the most difficult issues were left. The debate batted to and fro across the table, the Iranians hoping that the textual gymnastics for which they are world famous might produce a crack in the very solid wall the three of us presented.

The plan was that after we had reached agreement, we would all go off to see the president. This had been optimistically pencilled into the schedule for 10.30 a.m., but 10.30 came and went and there was still no agreement, especially on the break-issue of Iran's enrichment of uranium. Suddenly, Dr Rowhani announced, 'It's time for us all to go and see the president.'

The three of us looked at each other. We knew each other very well by now. 'But there's nothing to go and see him about,' I said. 'Our planes are at the airport,' Dominique said. 'And we're perfectly happy to go and get on them,' said Joschka. We suggested an adjournment, and all got out of our seats.

Consternation was writ large on the faces of the Iranian side. This had not been in the script. We watched as the Iranians went into a huddle. Dr Rowhani and the other negotiators started working their phones – we assumed to the supreme leader and his staff.

We hung around, then went into the beautiful gardens for a breather. Finally, we were invited back. The verbal parrying was now replaced by some straightforward, tough old-fashioned negotiation. The result was the Tehran Declaration.

Under this, Iran agreed to co-operate with the IAEA, to sign and implement an Additional Protocol (on more intrusive inspections by the IAEA) as a voluntary, confidence-building measure, and to suspend its enrichment and reprocessing activities during the course of the

451

negotiations. In return we agreed to recognize Iran's nuclear rights and to discuss ways Iran could provide 'satisfactory assurances' regarding its nuclear power programme, after which Iran would gain easier access to modern technology.*

We then agreed that we'd all go off to see the president.

The road leading away from the diplomatic centre was quite narrow. Suddenly, the whole convoy came to a halt. The *basiji* had organized an impromptu demonstration, aimed much more at President Khatami and his government than at us. 'Stay in the car, boss. You're not to get out in any circumstances,' the lead detective instructed me. He knew me, and my ever-inquisitive nature, too well. 'De Villepin has got out, and tried to hit a demonstrator,' he reported. I did as I was told.

A huge press conference followed, with the journalists trying to succeed where the Iranian diplomats had failed, by opening up some differences between the three of us. But they failed, too.

What was striking about this 'E3' initiative was how closely the three foreign ministers, and their officials, worked together; there was confidence and trust of the highest order. We were all conscious of the prize if we pulled off a deal with Iran. It would reduce the nuclear threat and help bring them in from the cold. It would also be a clear demonstration that a 'European Foreign Policy' could be more than just circular discussions at summits and Foreign Ministers' Councils.

This was the last of my five visits to Tehran. No British Foreign Secretary has been there since. Instead, further negotiations have taken place in Brussels, Paris and Geneva, where the E3 were joined by the great Javier Solana, the EU's foreign policy 'High Representative'. Javier had been the Spanish Socialists' foreign minister in the nineties, then NATO Secretary General. As a distinguished nuclear physicist before he

---

* Iran signed an Additional Protocol on 18 December 2003, and agreed to act as if the protocol were in force, making the required reports to the IAEA and allowing the required access by IAEA inspectors, pending Iran's ratification of the Additional Protocol.

entered politics, he was as skilled at the science of nuclear proliferation as he was at its politics.

One of the Iranians' early demands under the Tehran Declaration was for access to equipment banned from export to Iran, including spare parts for the Rolls-Royce engines of their decrepit – and by now actively dangerous – fleet of American planes. I wanted to meet the Iranians' requests; so did the French, the Germans, and Javier; Rolls-Royce had no objection in principle, but their biggest export market was the United States. Under the terms of the Iran/Libya Sanctions Act, a foreign company selling to Iran would be banned from trading with the United States.[8]

Colin Powell was very sympathetic and put in an immense amount of work to try to gain agreement within the administration, but he ran into the usual difficulty with the forces of darkness. Don Rumsfeld, for instance, has revealed in his memoirs that he thought the E3 process a 'disaster'.[9] Colin asked for more and more detail (down to the individual part numbers), but even this did not satisfy those who did not want to do a deal with Iran – and who were becoming suspicious of me, as well as of the Iranians.

Those suspicions surfaced in July 2004 when *The Times* ran a front-page story highlighting concerns about my approach towards Iran. This story quoted an unnamed source in the Bush administration who claimed that I was known as 'Jack of Tehran'.

It wasn't hard to track down who source was. The US Undersecretary of State John Bolton had been in town. Bolton is one of the few people I've met in public life I'd be happy not to see again. I found him prejudiced, and rebarbative. His positions were the lowest common denominator of the neocons and the Israeli right.

My verdict on Bolton was mild, though, compared to that of his ostensible boss, Colin Powell. I called Colin, and told him that no senior official or politician from London had ever turned up in Washington to give anonymous and uncomplimentary briefings against him, or Condi Rice, or anyone else in the administration.

With some colourful language, Colin told me that Bolton had been 'the price' he'd had to pay for insulating himself from the neocons and avoiding having to take even more of them on board. But he added, with a chuckle, 'If you think Bolton's bad, Jack, you should meet two of the guys who work for him. They've got hair growing out of their knuckles and they sleep upside down at night.'

Colin also told me that he'd talk to Bolton. He did, and it made a difference to his public attitude towards me, though not, I am sure, to his private view.

The central issue aggravating Bolton – and many in Israel – was my attitude towards military action against Iran.

During the course of 2004, as we were painstakingly trying to bolt down agreement with the ever-difficult Iranians following the Tehran Declaration, a war party was gathering. Then, as now, there were messages coming from some in Israel that it would be only a short while before Iran was able to develop a functioning nuclear weapons system; and that Israel was considering a 'pre-emptive' strike against Iran.*

No one could claim that I had some kind of conscientious objection to military action. I'd quoted Kofi Annan often enough about the importance of backing diplomacy, if necessary, with a realistic threat of war; and prosecuted the case for the Iraq War on exactly that basis.

Of course, there could be circumstances in which war against Iran would be justified, as there could for any country, in principle at least. The 'inherent right of . . . self-defence' is guaranteed by Article 51 of the UN Charter. But we were a million miles away from that. Although Iran had failed to make proper disclosures to the IAEA and, as usual, was proving a very frustrating negotiating partner, there was no concrete evidence that it was developing a nuclear weapons capacity, still less was there even the tiniest 'smoking gun' that it was close to obtaining a

---

* As they had carried out against one of Saddam Hussein's nuclear weapons' facilities in 1981, and were to do successfully against Syria in 2007.

proper weapons system. This was not Iraq, where we knew for certain what Saddam had been up to; thought we had good evidence for what he was doing (even though that turned out to be wrong); and had seventeen UN Security Council resolutions, some of which explicitly authorized military action.

I had certainly supported the Iraq War and, as I've explained, I believe that I made the right decision on the basis of what I knew at the time. But no one with any sense of history can go through an experience like that without learning from it.

I had learnt that the doctrine of backing diplomacy with the threat of military action has to be applied sparingly, with a care for the consequences, for the lives destroyed, and for the aftermath. War is chaotic; chaos has effects that are by definition impossible to foresee. The potential outcomes need to be thought through all the more carefully.

'Diplomacy backed by the threat of military action' cannot simply be a mantra to be incanted for want of a better strategy. If it is, this mantra can quickly fulfil its own promise. If, at each step down this diplomatic path there is always an unlocked gate marked 'war', then the further one goes down the path, the more frustrating the attempts at peaceful diplomacy will become, and the more apparently inviting will be the gate marked 'war', with its sedulous opportunity to resolve by military action that which has been unachievable by other means. War, to echo the Prussian military theorist Carl von Clausewitz, can too easily become the continuation of politics by other means.[10]

Nor is there any historical basis for claiming that the only diplomacy which can succeed where there are threats to international peace and security is that which is backed by a threat of military action. Brazil and South Africa both abandoned their nuclear weapons programmes principally because of internal political changes. Pakistan, India and Israel each have operational nuclear weapons systems; each has refused to submit to any kind of international supervision under the Non-Proliferation Treaty (which Iran has), and none has been subject to serious international sanction. North Korea is one of the least predictable regimes in the world. It has a nuclear weapons system, and an obvious target in South Korea. The United States has not threatened war or 'surgical strikes' on North Korean nuclear facilities for one very good reason: China.

On the best assessment we had at the time, there were no grounds for the United Kingdom to attach itself to a strategy towards Iran which allowed for the possibility of war. In normal circumstances, the standard formula 'military action is not on the agenda, though no country can rule out that option in any circumstance', would have been enough to make that clear.

But these were not normal circumstances. We were already involved in two wars. The aftermath of one of them, Iraq – with the gratuitous chaos caused by infelicitous decisions by one part of the Bush administration, and the failure to find WMD materiel – had gravely undermined trust in government, in us. With the noises off from Israel and Washington, the usual formula wasn't going to work.

If we had had a formal (and statutory)* National Security Council, there would have been a forum to which I could have submitted, on paper, my concerns about the way our view about how to handle Iran might drift closer towards the military possibility.

But this was not the way Tony worked; nor was he going to change. I talked to him a bit about my worries, but he was in a rather different place. He wanted, absolutely, to keep his options open. So I waited for an opportunity to close off the risks to the United Kingdom.

Tuesday 2 November 2004 was the date of the United States' fifty-fifth presidential election – and the Queen's State Visit to Germany.

The results of the election didn't come through in Europe until Wednesday. Bush had won a second term, this time by a convincing margin. The *Today* programme asked to interview me the following morning, the Thursday. I obliged, from the BBC's studio in Berlin.

---

* See Chapter Twenty-two.

There had been much speculation that Bush would now be more hawkish on Iran, with Colin Powell leaving the administration. It was easy to guess that Iran would be high on Jim Naughtie's sheet of questions. He bowled his usual opening slow ball, the spin in his double negative:

NAUGHTIE: You talked about divisions in the world that followed 9/11. The reasons for the divisions of course was the invasion of Iraq. Bearing in mind what has happened in Iraq, at the time and since, it is inconceivable, is it not, that the world would support American military action, presumably some sort of bombing, possibly using Israelis as a proxy, who knows, against the Iranians over their nuclear programme, if indeed such a programme exits?

STRAW: Well not only is that inconceivable, I think the prospect of it happening is inconceivable—

NAUGHTIE: But you're quite clear that if, and you say it's a very big if, but if the United States decided to take action against Iran we would not be on their side? We wouldn't fight shoulder to shoulder with them?

STRAW: I don't accept it, what I'm saying to you is that I don't accept the assumption, I don't think that will arise, all right, but I don't see any circumstances in which military action would be justified against Iran full stop. I think I've made that clear.[11]

Too clear for some, not least the Bush administration, and Tony, who was inevitably sensitive that he would be asked repeatedly to use the same words as I had. He never did, falling back on the standard 'not on the agenda, no option off the table' formula. But, whether he appreciated it or not, I did him a favour. Aside from the fact that I believed that I had to say this, in unambiguous terms, closing down the question of whether the UK could be involved in a third war meant that it was not an issue in the general election just six months away.

A week after my interview with Naughtie, on 11 November, Yasser Arafat died in a Paris clinic, aged seventy-five.

Friday 12 November was his funeral – the strangest I have ever attended.

The plan was that all the visiting dignitaries should assemble at a holding centre, then solemnly march a few hundred yards to an Egyptian Air Force compound, where the service was to be held, before Arafat's body was taken by helicopter to Ramallah for another service, and burial.

Since I was representing the British Head of State, or Government, or both, I was directed into the really senior visiting dignitaries' tent. Anyone who was anyone in the Middle East was there – kings, crown princes, presidents – plus a few stray foreign ministers to lower the tone, including me.

After a long unscheduled wait, we were invited to form up for the parade to the Air Force compound.

As we began to shuffle up the tree-lined dual carriageway in this up-scale part of Cairo, chaos broke out. People from the tents for the lower orders, plus many who'd simply turned up on the off-chance, overtook us on the pavements on either side. But we could only move at the pace of the slowest dignitaries. Some of these very very important people I was with gave the impression of not having walked any further than across a room for some years. The *hoi polloi*, on the other hand, were moving fast.

When the entrance to the Air Force compound came into view, its large steel gates were being closed. Those right at the head of my pha-lanx did get in, but the lower orders had taken most of the places. The whole site was now so packed with 'mourners' that even the Egyptian authorities could see that they might have a disaster on their hands.

So there we were, stuck on a dual carriageway with nowhere to go. But the weather was lovely, and the company was great. Nabil Sha'ath, Saeb Erekat, senior members of Fatah, Natwar Singh the Indian foreign minister, with a group of Indian parliamentarians mainly from the various Communist Parties in India. Conversation ranged from the Peace Process to the finer points of Marxist-Leninism. The veteran Middle East columnist of the *Independent*, Robert Fisk, evidently overheard some of this impromptu seminar. In his story he described me as an 'old Trot'.[12] I had to write to the *Independent* to complain about this 'malicious libel'. 'There is a very long list of old Trots who really were Trots who will be as outraged as me by this calumny.'[13] I might have added that if my friend Joschka Fischer had been with us, Fisk would have a real old Trot to talk about. But whilst we were chatting in the sunshine, Joschka was circling Cairo Airport – fruitlessly. The Egyptians refused his plane permission to land. Too late, they said; all airspace was closed for fear of a terrorist attack.

At this 'funeral' few spoke at all about Arafat. Those who did – the ones who had known him best – seemed relieved, rather than sad, at his passing.

Yasser Arafat's death provided a significant opportunity for a fresh start to the peace process. Ariel Sharon described it as potentially a 'turning point'. Under American pressure Arafat had already appointed Mahmoud Abbas as prime minister. With Arafat's passing Abbas was elected head of the PLO.

The Israelis pulled out of Gaza in the summer of 2005. Sharon gained considerable international approval. But settlement-building on Palestinian land in the West Bank continued. The Israelis had meanwhile been continuing with the erection of their wall around the Occupied Territories. Given the level of terrorist killings earlier in the decade, the Israelis had decided that they could not guarantee the security of their people without it. While its erection has unquestionably been a major contributory factor in the sharp drop in terrorist incidents within the territory of Israel, it has further sharpened the communal incarceration of the Palestinians – most of whom simply want to get on with their lives. That might have been moderated if the Israelis had not adopted a policy of wilful humiliation of

Palestinians as they sought to travel between the Occupied Territories and Israel.

Under the Palestinian constitution, elections for the Palestinian Authority were years overdue. With US and Israeli encouragement, Abbas agreed to hold elections in January 2006. The electorate punished the Fatah party for its ineptitude and deep-seated corruption. Hamas had campaigned principally on welfare issues and piety. To its surprise – and everyone else's – it won, taking seventy-four seats to Fatah's forty-five.

There wasn't the least doubt that these elections had been free and fair. So there could be no wriggling about that. I did an interview with the BBC and said that you couldn't urge democracy on people and then tell them they'd got the wrong result. I added though that those who entered democratic elections had to recognize the commitment to non-violence that goes along with them. Considerable wrangling took place over whether the international community should refuse to recognize Hamas as a legitimate partner. The Israelis were adamant that they would never talk to Hamas, so long as they did not eschew terrorism and refused to recognize the state of Israel. The Americans agreed; so, of course, did Tony.

At first Sergei Lavrov, the Russian foreign minister, took the opposite view. Sergei, who had taken over from Igor Ivanov in March 2004, was straight out of central casting. He'd spent his life in diplomacy, for the Soviet Union and then Russia. He knew the United Nations inside out – he had been Russia's permanent representative there for ten years. His English was terrific. He was tough but you could do business with him. I had a number of entertaining dinners with him in Moscow and London – each most notable for the clouds of accompanying smoke. A chain-smoker, his favourite brand was Parliament, complete with a nice picture of Big Ben on the pack.

Under pressure from Condi, Lavrov finally agreed, within the 'Quartet', restrictions on aid and contact with Hamas, dependent on their commitment to non-violence, some recognition of Israel, and acceptance of the previous agreements that the Palestinians had signed.

Though I publicly endorsed this approach, I was uncertain it was right. Michael Ancram, who had shadowed me from 2001 until May 2005, and who had stood down from the front bench altogether in December, had similar strong reservations. I had developed a close and confidential relationship with Michael over the years (which still flourishes). He knew the Middle East well, and believed strongly that simply isolating Hamas made no more sense than refusing to talk to the Provisional IRA whilst their terrorist campaign was continuing. A key Northern Ireland minister from 1993–7, he'd been at the forefront of the initially secret talks with PIRA, whilst they were still killing and maiming innocents across the UK.

Few internal conflicts of this kind have ever been capable of resolution without negotiation with terrorist organizations. Britain was hardly in a position to stand on its dignity, given its own record. Tony had only been able to make his extraordinary achievement in Northern Ireland by continuing the strategy that Michael and John Major had started.

Then there were the Israelis. It was never to be mentioned in polite company; all reference had long since been airbrushed from the memory. But Israeli terrorist groups – Irgun, and the Stern Gang – waged a terror campaign against the British to secure their aim of an independent State of Israel.

One of the leaders of the Irgun had been Menachem Begin, later prime minister of Israel. Eitan Livni had been chief operating officer. His wife Sara Rosenberg had been heavily involved too. They are the parents of Tzipi Livni, who was foreign minister of Israel when we were deciding what to do about Hamas. I liked Tzipi, and felt that she had a more open approach than many Israeli politicians. I can also understand why so many Jewish people resorted to terrorism in their desperation to establish a Jewish homeland after the unspeakable horrors of the Holocaust. What was the surprise was the way the Israelis had now elevated 'not talking to terrorists' as some kind of issue of principle. Anyway, the Israelis knew, and we knew, that they were talking to Hamas pretty regularly. They simply weren't advertising this fact.

A couple of months after she had taken over as Secretary of State, in early 2005, Condi secured a welcome shift in the United States approach to Iran. The US formally joined the negotiating formation in an 'E3 + 3' group (the US, Russia and China, along with France, Germany and the UK), and put together a package of concessions meeting the requests the Iranians had made to us for spare airplane parts and so on more than a year before. But it was too late. In the intervening period, not least because the US had so systematically undermined the reformists in Iran ever since the 'axis of evil' speech, the market in Iran had hardened; the reformists were fighting for their political lives, whilst the hardliners were re-emboldened to strike against them. It was therefore no great surprise when Kamal Kharrazi dismissed the offer as 'chocolates, Jack, chocolates'.

A further meeting in Geneva was held in May 2005, but the omens were poor. Presidential elections were held in Iran in June. This time the balance of power among the elite had shifted decisively. Mahmoud Ahmadinejad, the hard-line mayor of Tehran, won, in an election that few claimed was free and fair. John Bolton and the other neocons had reaped what they had sown.

Nonetheless we were still anxious to engage with the Iranians, and they with us.

Amongst other preoccupations, the Iranians are obsessed with status and protocol. The E3 foreign ministers – by now Dominique and Joschka had been replaced by Michael Barnier and Frank Walter Steinmeier – wanted to meet the new president; but we needed some device to achieve this. Kofi Annan came to the rescue. As equivalent to a head of state or government, he would host the meeting in his office in the UN building in New York, during UN General Assembly week in September.

Ahmadinejad reminded me of Ken Livingstone, vintage the early eighties (but only fashion-wise). Sitting uncomfortably next to him was

Ali Larijani, their chief nuclear negotiator, from the opposite end of the sartorial spectrum: suave, wearing a carefully pressed Ralph Lauren polo shirt.

Not much progress was made at this meeting.

I had tried hard to build a relationship with Kamal Kharrazi's successor as foreign minister, Manouchehr Mottaki. At meetings with him that week in New York, we E3 foreign ministers sought to persuade him that his boss had a chance with his speech to the General Assembly to present a new and softer image to the world, without compromising his beliefs.

Mottaki said that he saw the point. He showed me parts of the draft of his president's speech. They were truly terrible. I suggested where some changes might be made.

My breath was not bated as I sat to listen to Ahmadinejad's speech. He did not disappoint his hard-line supporters at home, nor his hard-line opponents in Washington and Tel Aviv. He failed everyone else.

After the speech Mottaki came up to me with a copy of the speech. Part of it was highlighted in tracked changes. 'Look,' he said, 'see all the alterations we made following our conversations.'

Our frames of reference were just different.

In February 2006 the board of the IAEA voted 27–3 to refer Iran's continued non-compliance to the Security Council. Only Venezuela, Cuba and Syria voted against.

Ahmadinejad's inflammatory rhetoric was being matched in Washington. In early April 2006, Seymour Hersh, the distinguished journalist, published a piece in the *New Yorker* claiming that some in the administration were speculating about a nuclear strike on Iran.[14] I saw this in the British newspapers early on Sunday 9 April, on my way to do *The Andrew Marr Show* on BBC.

Inevitably, I was going to be asked about this. I thought carefully about my response. I said it was 'nuts'.[15] It was; and it was important to close down any suggestion that anyone in the British system had any sympathy with such a dangerous idea.

In mid-April I visited Saudi Arabia to attend a joint conference with my friend, the foreign minister, Prince Saud al-Faisal. There was the usual group of diplomatic correspondents with me.

At a briefing in the garden of the British Embassy, Anton La Guardia of the *Daily Telegraph* asked me about relations with Hamas. I spelt out the three conditions agreed by the Quartet,* but I added my own gloss that these conditions were pretty easy for Hamas to agree. They had to accept the reality of Israel's existence but they did not have formally to recognize the State of Israel.

This briefing was explicitly 'off the record', background only. All observed this condition, except La Guardia, who chose to run a piece in the *Telegraph* extensively quoting me.[16] The headline, and the contrast highlighted with Tony's approach in the Commons the previous day, were designed to excite: 'Straw softens tone as he offers Hamas financial lifeline'. They did so.

The government of Israel were on the phone to Number 10 in a flash.

I saw Tony later that day on my return. Normally very polite, he was acerbic. This was when he made the remarks to me about my 'Muslim constituents'. I resented it thoroughly. If I'd been kowtowing to my Muslim constituents I would not have supported the Iraq War. No constituent, Muslim or otherwise, had said a word to me about the Hamas issue. I felt like making some sharp comment back in equally pejorative terms, about his 'Jewish backers'; about not judging me by his standards. Wisely I decided to say nothing.

Local elections were coming up in early May. Labour was likely to do badly – by late April we were trailing the Tories in the polls by nine

* See p. 460 – above – a commitment to non-violence, some recognition of Israel, and acceptance of the previous agreements that the Palestinians had signed.

points.[17] Tony's habit in this situation was to have a reshuffle the day after, in the hope of trumping the otherwise poor headlines. There was much speculation in the air.

John Sawers, my political director, who had excellent antennae into Number 10, warned me that something was in the wind; so did Michael Jay, who by this time had spent four years as head of the Diplomatic Service. But both were in a difficult position, Michael especially. I could not expect our decades-long personal friendship to compromise his professional duties; and I didn't.

However, the chuntering seemed to subside. After Cabinet on Thursday 4 May, I travelled to Blackburn to help in the elections, in the naive belief that I would still be in post as Foreign Secretary the following day.

In the late afternoon my Private Office told me that Number 10 were insisting I met Tony at 8.30 a.m. the following day. I called Jonathan Powell. He said that Tony was anxious to see John Prescott and me 'to clear these matters up' before embarking on the rest of the reshuffle. When I told him that this sounded ominous, 'I hope not,' was his bland reply.

The results in Blackburn were no better than elsewhere. We lost three Asian wards to the Liberal Democrats; one white ward to the far-right 'England First'. I left the count about 11.45 p.m., was into my bed in London at 3.30 a.m., and into Number 10 at 8.30 a.m.

This was the fourth time I'd seen Tony at reshuffle time. The previous three I'd been lucky. It was obvious that this was going to be different.

'Well Jack,' he said, fixing me with his cold, blue eyes, 'the time has arrived. I want to move you on from the Foreign Office to become Leader of the House.' He then referred to the discussion we'd had a year earlier after the general election. He had said then that he would not be keeping me for the whole parliament as Foreign Secretary.

I had said, after the 2005 election, that I didn't expect to do the job for ever, and I had mentioned that I would find Leader of the House an interesting job. But, as I told Tony now, when we'd had that conversation the year before, he had said not once, but twice, that if he were intending to move me he would give me adequate warning, and discuss the matter with me well in advance. This had not happened.

The first time I said this there was no response. I said it again. 'Sorry,' he replied, 'but my experience is that if I do give warning it leads to endless unproductive arguments.' I could have retorted that, if so, why on earth had he volunteered the undertaking, twice, the year before?

I asked if Tony would give me a few minutes to phone Alice. She and I both agreed that there was no point trying to argue. The truth was that Tony's positions and mine, especially on the Middle East and Iran, were becoming incompatible.

It was off to the parking lot reserved for Foreign Secretaries with opinions of their own, the office of the Leader of the House of Commons.

TWENTY

The Breaks

Out of twenty colleagues (in the Cabinet) there was probably not more than one who thought he should be minister of labour and nineteen who thought they should be Foreign Secretary.*

STANLEY BALDWIN, prime minister 1924–5

You should always promote or demote for a purpose, not for effect . . . There was a case for keeping Jack Straw. He had done really well and was admired by his fellow foreign ministers. There was no compelling reason to move him, other than that he had been doing it for five years; but when I think about it, moving him for that reason was plain stupid.

TONY BLAIR[1]

In politics, the most important thing is to have a seat at the table. You never know what may be served up.†

ATTR. ENOCH POWELL

---

* Malcolm Rifkind, Foreign Secretary in the last two years of John Major's government, often quotes Prime Minister Eden, himself quoting Prime Minister Baldwin, saying this.

† Attributed – I think he may have said it to me.

There is never a shortage of colleagues coveting the post of Foreign Secretary.

Margaret Beckett, however, was not one of them. Her surprise (and her words) after getting the job in the reshuffle of May 2006 were similar to mine five years before. I called her, wished her well, and talked briefly about the job.

I was still unclear as to what had tipped the balance with Tony. We were certainly in different places over Iran and the Middle East; but after so many years in government it was perfectly common for senior people to hold differing points of view, yet still co-operate honourably together. There'd been suggestions in the press that Tony had been 'irritated by what he saw as Mr Straw's opportunism in shifting his loyalty towards Mr Brown'.[2] We had been seeing a bit more of Gordon and his wife Sarah, but I felt I'd been very loyal to Tony, not least on the most difficult and dangerous issue of all – Iraq. My loyalty had never been a problem; his next-door neighbour was another matter. If loyalty had been the key criterion for a reshuffle, Tony should have moved Gordon from the Treasury years before. One thing, however, kept coming back to me. My trips with Condi Rice to Alabama and then Blackburn and Liverpool, just a few weeks before the reshuffle, had received extensive and very positive coverage. Tony had made a tart comment to me about the 'Condi and Jack' show. His tone of voice had unsettled me.

But – and it's a very big 'but' – whatever his reasons, I still owed Tony a huge debt. Without his confidence in me, I would not have had the chance to do two extraordinary jobs for nine years. Whingeing would be wrong, undignified, and would quickly backfire. Best to close down the speculation. Tony was generous in what he said publicly at the time; and even more so in his memoirs. Privately he told me just days after the reshuffle that he felt he had made a mistake.

In Enoch Powell's wise words, I still had a seat at the table. What was served up in large part depended on me.

*

I'd got close to many people in the Home Office – my Private Office, the press office, many officials – but there was an added intensity to the relationships I formed in the Foreign Office: we had all been wrestling with issues of human conflict and natural catastrophe; we shared the all-consuming pressures; we were forever on the move together.

The office arranged a farewell reception for me, in the largest space in King Charles Street, the Durbar Court. It was packed. Hundreds of staff turned up. It was a very poignant occasion. I was sad when it was over; but happy too that the initial reservations which some in the Diplomatic Service had held about my competence had been replaced by mutual affection and respect. As I left the building, I reflected on a conversation I had had a year before with Geoffrey Adams, then my principal private secretary. I had asked him why he had joined the Diplomatic Service, and stayed, given the great toll it took on personal and family life. 'To serve my country,' he had replied. There was no pomposity or self-regard. It was true, as for so many others in the Service.

In big departments, the Private Office is at the apex of a vast super-structure. Tens of thousands worked for the Home Office, thousands for the Foreign Office.

The Leader of the House has no department. The Private Office – just twenty people – is it. I had a conveniently situated room in the Commons, close to the Chamber, with space for three staff; but the main office had for some reason been exiled across St James's Park. I quickly got us all moved to Dover House, overlooking Horse Guards Parade, a two-minute walk from Downing Street's back door. Location matters.

I'd been in love with Parliament from the first time I'd visited the place, aged about eleven. I'd never lost my affection for it through the sometimes debilitating eighteen years of opposition, nor through all the rowdy, sometimes high-wire debates I'd been involved in – quite the reverse. My time as a minister had confirmed me in my view that there was no conflict between an effective, reforming government, and a strong Parliament. The latter was an essential precondition for the former.

As Leader of the House, more than in almost any other Cabinet job, who you were and what you felt about Parliament made all the difference. Some simply saw the job as a staging-post, but others had seen the opportunities it offered to help strengthen Parliament, and above all the voice of the backbencher. Geoffrey Howe, Robin Cook and I had each been consigned to the role, but we were each completely committed to Parliament as an institution and to making the most of our time as Leader. Our experience in government had made us all the more determined to see a rebalancing of the power relationships between the executive and the Commons. In a democracy there are few more important tasks than ensuring that elected representatives really have the tools to do their job, and are not held back by process or patronage.

So at one level I relished the job. I would have felt completely positive about the move if it had happened a year later, and if Tony had given me decent notice. I could also see – and feel – that I needed a rest. I'd had a bout of pneumonia earlier that year, so severe that to Alice's amazement I had taken myself to bed, and called the doctor. I wanted to see more of my family – Alice, William and Charlotte ('time to be a normal person again, Dad').

Nonetheless, I was angry and upset about my forced move. I did not enjoy the 'Straw demoted' headlines. I had been on top of my work, really hitting my stride. And exhausting as it was, I thoroughly enjoyed being Foreign Secretary.

But although I was bruised by the move, it was time to get stuck in.

'Modernization' was a New Labour buzz word. Soon after the 1997 election, the House even set up a select committee of that name, aimed at reforming the institution and updating some of its more arcane ways. As Leader of the House I had to chair it. Leery though I was of its title (it aroused the same suspicions as 'People's Courts' and 'Democratic

Republics'), it had done some good work, and it was the vehicle I used to advance reforms aimed at strengthening Parliament.

A common criticism of the Labour government under Tony Blair was that it turned Parliament into a poodle. I always thought that charge was overblown. True, we had big majorities for much of that period, which meant the government was rarely defeated in divisions; but we suffered regular rebellions. By the end of Tony's premiership Labour MPs were defying the whip on a hitherto unknown scale. The notion that this was a peculiar period of executive dominance is a myth.

Nevertheless, becoming Leader of the House gave me the chance to promote some important reforms that empowered backbenchers and tipped the scales of power a little in Parliament's favour.

Public bill committees replaced the old standing-committee system, which was widely acknowledged to be an ineffective means of assessing proposed new laws. Critically, these new committees had the powers to call both ministers and expert witnesses to give evidence.*

I also introduced topical parliamentary questions (PQs) for each department, as an addition to oral PQs. This meant that Secretaries of State could be put on the spot, without notice, in the same way that the prime minister is held to account each week. Many of my ministerial colleagues were understandably sceptical at first, but it is now an accepted part of the scrutiny process. Part of the point of topical PQs was that Parliament could hardly complain at lack of media interest if the discussions in the Commons Chamber were always a week behind

---

* This measure was said by Professor Philip Cowley to have 'the potential to do more to improve the quality of parliamentary scrutiny of bills than any other Commons reform in the last twenty years.' (P. Cowley, 'Parliament', in A. Seldon (ed.), *Blair's Britain 1997–2007* (Cambridge University Press, 2007), p. 22.) Time will tell whether that potential is realized. But I can say categorically that the scrutiny of government today is far more substantial not just than it was when I first worked as a special adviser in the seventies, but than in 1997.

the pace. The press would have even less excuse for failing to report Parliament if its proceedings were topical.

Another key vehicle for strengthening the Commons was the weekly 'Business Statement' in which the Leader announces the Commons' business for the following week, and then has to field questions on every conceivable subject. (It meant a very early start to get myself briefed.)

The Commons Leader has a unique perspective – representing the government's interest in Parliament, and Parliament's interest in government. Part of the job was to pursue other ministers for answers which MPs had otherwise been unable to secure.

It's a wise Leader who does not act in a partisan way, unless provoked. And in any case my approach in all my jobs was to judge the merits of a question not by the side it came from – ours or theirs – but by its substance.

So if an MP was making a good point in the Leader's Questions session following the Business Statement, I'd chase it up, whatever the subject was.

That included flags.

Andrew Rossindell, the MP for Romford, was (and is) a Tory Eurosceptic bruiser. But he was a fellow Essex geezer, from an area I knew well, with that brand of patriotic chutzpah which my home county has made its own.

At one Leader's Questions in January 2007 he asked me why the Union flag was never flown from the flagpole on Portcullis House. It's an issue that some might categorize as trivial, but wrongly handled it could easily have become a large, symbolic knocking story against New Labour. I said I'd find out.

'Health and Safety' was the answer that came back. A risk assessment had shown that running up the flag would be too dangerous for the staff concerned, to whom the House of Commons owed a 'duty of care'. My questions as to why the flagpole had been put there in the first place, and my observation that from the road it looked like a simple and safe job, were met with glazed eyes and a re-incantation of the 'Health 'n' Safety' mantra.

I said I'd go up to inspect the flagpole myself.

'You can't do that, Leader. Health 'n' Safety.'

I told them that I was going anyway, taking one of my protection officers with me, a former professional rugby player who would be big enough to force an entry if they didn't show me the way.

The inspection itself was a hoot. A private secretary, the protection officer, a Commons official, me – and the Health and Safety officer who kept waving the multicoloured 'risk assessment' at me – all clambered over some pipes and machinery in the roof space, and finally got to the doors in the roof, which opened to reveal the naked flagpole.

'So, what exactly is the problem?' I asked.

'It's the doors. They're heavy and the angle means that in a gale they might swing back on the person running up the flag.'

'Woolworth's sell a small brass bolt for less than a quid. Shall I get one, or will you?'

The bolt was fitted. The flag still flies. One hole fewer for the government to fall into; a satisfied MP; and a cautionary tale about trusting jobsworth experts.

When Tony moved me, he had said that in addition to my duties as Commons Leader, he was giving me the 'hospital passes' of party funding and House of Lords reform. Mark Davies, my Special Adviser from the last year in the Foreign Office, came with me, and took on handling of Lords reform. I recruited the very bright Deputy General Secretary of the Hansard Society, Declan McHugh, who worked on the other hospital pass. And much else besides, in both cases.

Party funding has long been politically controversial. Until the late nineteenth century British politics was heroically corrupt – and very expensive. More money was spent fighting elections then than at any time since. In addition, £10,000 (£1 million in today's money) from the

Secret Service Vote used to be given to the government chief whip of the day to bribe MPs into the correct voting lobby, and reward them with financial support at elections.

Successive reforms over the last century have given the United Kingdom fairer elections, and less expensive politics, than in most comparable countries. Scandals can still erupt, though. Claims about 'cash for questions' had dogged the outgoing Major government so much that on coming into office in 1997 we had asked the Committee on Standards in Public Life for a major report on party funding. As Home Secretary I had incorporated almost all its recommendations in the Political Parties, Elections and Referendums Act 2000.

Sleaze scandals are not, however, a monopoly of the Conservatives. They are a hazard for any government.

Concern about Labour donors rumbled on from the Bernie Ecclestone affair in 1997, and then erupted in 2006 over large loans which the party had secured to help with the costs of the 2005 election. Just before I became Leader Tony had, with the agreement of the other party leaders, set up a review of party funding.

Hayden Phillips, a former permanent secretary whom Tony had asked to head the review, was perfect for the job – bright and feline, he quickly gained the confidence of all three parties. I made it clear that I would be sticking to one of my key principles, that any major constitutional change had to have a clear consensus behind it, either from bipartisan backing in the Commons and/or through the voice of the people in a referendum (a principle whose abandonment the Coalition will regret).

There are two fundamental problems with party funding. One is that the public, and the press, demand that our democracy functions properly, but do not want to pay for the parties, the bedrock of any democracy. The other is that the interests of the parties are not symmetrical. The Conservatives can command many large donations from a broad base of wealthy individuals; Labour receives some big donations from individuals, but is significantly dependent on the trade unions.

The Conservatives are thus resistant to proposals for a very low donation cap, which would hit their income, and to tighter spending limits, which would undermine their financial advantage. Labour, meanwhile, is opposed to a uniform donation cap that would break its historic link with the unions and cripple the party financially.

I strongly resisted the idea that our political opponents should try to define our relationship with our affiliated unions. It's not the business of the state to tell the parties how to organize. However, I did see that if a deal was ever to be reached it would require some movement on union funding. This comes in two forms: as affiliation fees paid on behalf of each levy-paying union member and one-off donations agreed by union executives. I argued that affiliation fees should be exempt from any cap, but accepted that one-off donations would have to be caught. I knew it would be tough to sell this to the party and especially to the unions, who were implacably opposed to any new interference with their political funds. But I felt it was a compromise we had to be prepared to make.

With an interim report in October 2006, followed by months of painstaking negotiations, Hayden brokered a deal between the three parties. In return for a substantial increase in public funds there would be a cap of £50,000 on all donations from individuals and organizations, including trade unions. Affiliation fees would be exempt from the cap provided there was greater transparency in the way they were collected.

That was in July 2007, by which time Gordon Brown had become prime minister and I had moved to the Ministry of Justice, taking this responsibility with me. When the talks resumed after the summer the Conservatives' position had unexpectedly hardened. David Cameron sent a wrecking letter to Hayden, leaked to the press, which effectively torpedoed the whole process. In its wake, the talks collapsed. As David Heath, the Liberal Democrat spokesman, commented at the time, 'For the Conservatives to now, in effect, walk away is a tragedy and very short-sighted on their part.'

What had gone wrong? Some reports suggested that Cameron had been forced into a harder line to shore up his position internally following a rocky period when he had been badly bruised by a Tory Party row over grammar schools. Another explanation was provided by David Heath, who said, 'It was interesting that their attitude changes on this subject markedly over the summer at about the same time that a certain Lord Ashcroft moved into Central Office.'[3]

Whatever the truth, the collapse of the talks meant reform was off the agenda. The whole subject seemed destined for the long grass.

Finally, after a tortuous process that tested my patience almost to destruction, and that of my Special Advisers, my Private Office under my talented principal private secretary Alison Blackburne, and the excellent civil servants who worked tirelessly throughout this saga, the Political Parties and Elections Act 2009 was agreed by all parties. It represented an improvement on the status quo, but it was a 'lowest common denominator' piece of legislation that didn't put the issue of party funding to bed.

At least the discussions on party funding were polite and pretty civilized. That could not be said for those on the other 'hospital pass' I was given, the future of the House of Lords.

I'd not previously given much thought to reform of the Lords. I'd been pleased when in 1999 we'd removed all but ninety-two of the hereditary peers. The Lords continued to give Labour governments a harder time than they ever gave Conservative ones, but I thought that we could live with the irritation. I had to acknowledge that some amendments forced into our bills (certainly into my bills) were improvements. Overall, I thought there were other more important issues for us to deal with, which was one reason why, in February 2003, when Robin Cook, then Leader, had organized a set of votes for the Commons to determine its attitude in principle to reform, I had voted against an elected Chamber. In mitigation I'd just flown in from the Anglo-French summit in Le Touquet, and was flying out that evening to New York for the second of the Iraq Security Council meetings. The chief whip, Hilary Armstrong, a close friend, muttering something about 'problems with Robin', asked me to vote against the key propositions – so I did.

This is not one of the prouder moments of my career. The whips' operation on 'free votes' (in which I was complicit) meant that the Commons made a fool of itself, voting down every single option from total abolition of the Lords, through an all-appointed Lords to an all-elected Chamber. We had no policy at all. The Lords, meanwhile, predictably, came out in favour of appointment.

What changed my ambivalent view of the Lords was my closer exposure to the place.

In June 2006 I set up a cross-party group to produce a White Paper, and another set of options for reform. I went to talk to the Labour peers – my 'colleagues' – about the group's work. It was a Pauline moment.

For one hundred years Labour had been committed to reforming the Second Chamber. These people were all Labour Party members. They owed their position, their place in the Lords, to the party. They had not arrived there by accident.

I set out what I was doing to implement the policy of the government and the party.

If I had proposed the slaughter of the firstborn, and the abolition of the NHS, I would have had a better reception. It was one of the worst meetings I've ever attended, for both bone-headedness and gratuitous rudeness. Speech after self-serving speech, they outdid the Duke of Wellington's arguments against the 1832 Reform Bill in their defence of the status quo.*

I began to pay greater attention to our peers. Some were

---

* This wasn't the unanimous view of those present – at least one came up to me afterwards to apologize for the behaviour of his colleagues – but it was the prevailing view.

distinguished former Cabinet ministers or senior backbenchers, or eminent in their own professional fields. Others were not. Among the most reactionary were those former Labour MPs who'd traded their seat in the Commons for a nice billet in the Lords. I didn't blame them, but I didn't think they should try to turn their good fortune into a major constitutional principle. Then there were those who'd never stood for elected office in their life; and who gave the impression that they considered activities like canvassing rather vulgar.

In contrast to the meetings of Labour peers, the work of the cross-party group went well. All three parties were committed to further reform of the Lords. For the Liberal Democrats this promise had been written in tablets of stone, ever since 1910 when they had had to fight two general elections in a year to force through changes to limit the Lords' powers over the Budget. The Conservatives had long been more ambiguous. Their senior member on the group, Tom (Lord) Strathclyde, epitomized that ambiguity. I always felt that he had his fingers firmly crossed behind his back as he advanced the case for a more democratic Lords. But advance it he did.

I was determined that my plans should not go the way of Robin's. I devised a scheme for voting on the various options by which the Commons would have to come to a positive conclusion on at least one of them, by use of the Alternative Vote. None but my fellow anoraks recognized its intrinsic merits. The proposal attracted a level of opposition that would baffle anyone outside Parliament. I could see the writing on the wall, and I dropped it.

That was one raspberry blown at me. The other was for my 'recommended option' – my personal Best Buy – for a fifty/fifty elected/appointed Lords. It was defeated in the Commons by 263 votes. My old friend Michael Jay, now in the Lords, voted in favour of fifty/fifty in the Lords more from loyalty than conviction, and quipped that we were such a select band we might form an exclusive dining club.

Nonetheless in March 2007 the Commons came to a clear conclusion – for the first time ever. Against a wholly appointed Lords; in favour of both an 80 per cent elected, and a 100 per cent elected Second Chamber. These decisions have formed the framework for all subsequent policy development on Lords reform.

I had more free time as Leader of the House than I'd had for nearly twenty years. With no operational responsibilities for a great Department of State, no urgent phone calls in the small hours, and lighter ministerial boxes, I had some space for reflection, and to recharge my batteries after nine years of punishing schedules. I thought about some of the trickier issues which were on people's minds, and in their conversations, but which were off the political agenda because they were difficult to handle. One such issue was the veil.

Researchers at Blackburn Council had for years produced a regular report called 'The Changing Face of Blackburn and Darwen'. In it, they charted the area's changing demographics, as the Asian-heritage population from India and Pakistan grew, and much of the white population moved out. Mosques replaced redundant chapels or churches; some Anglican schools were 100 per cent Muslim; the landmarks in the memory removed.

I've already discussed the impersonal economic forces, and the hangover from the end of empire, which led to such large-scale immigration into our area. Nor has the disruption been on one side alone. Very few migrations in history have involved people who have been enjoying great prosperity in their homelands. The post-war Asian migration to the UK was no exception.

If you represent an area like Blackburn, you have a responsibility to be alive to what people are thinking, what are the rubbing points in relationships between these differing communities, separated by cultures, and faith, too many living parallel lives.

I talked to my many Muslim friends about it, and in particular about the increasing use of the full veil by some women in town. Only a small minority, I conceded, but enough for people to notice, and to worry about. Some were defensive, referring me to the Holy Koran; some more candid, but anxious that I should not open a can of worms by speaking publicly about the matter. I told them that I was reflecting not just the concern of other white people, but my own feelings. I found it difficult properly to relate to people whose faces I could not see. I couldn't quite understand why this practice was increasing since there was no clear instruction in the Koran for women's faces to be covered – certainly not in my well-regarded translation.*

Iqbal Sacranie, the president of the Muslim Council of Britain (MCB), and a personal friend, had invited me to speak in June 2006 at an Islamic trade and economics conference.

Answering a question, I went 'wildly off script' – to quote Mark Davies, my special adviser – and gave a wider audience to the views about the veil which had been bubbling up in my brain for some months. There were a number of journalists present, mainly from the Islamic world, some with TV cameras. As we left, Mark warned me that my remarks were bound to get some coverage, and that this could be very big. Not one word of what I said was reported.

Four months later, in early October, I went to Brussels to make a speech on the first anniversary of the EU's decision to start accession negotiations with Turkey. Shortly after the Eurostar had left Brussels I remembered that I had to write my weekly column for the *Lancashire Telegraph*.

There are few things more terrifying than a blank sheet, a blank mind and a deadline. As the plains of northern France rolled by, I sat staring out of the window, trying to come up with a subject. Suddenly

---

* 'The Qur'an makes a few references to Muslim clothing, but prefers to point out more general principles of modest dress . . . For instance, "Say to the believing men that they should lower their gaze and guard their modesty." (24:30)' and 'When the Qur'an first mentioned the concept of hijab, it was not as a veil or headscarf. Hijab was used in the context of a barrier or screen as in this Qur'anic verse: "And when ye ask (the Prophet's wives) for anything ye want, ask them from before a screen: that makes for greater purity for your hearts and for theirs." (33:53).' (BBC website 3/9/2009.)

I thought – 'I know, I'll write about the veil. I tried it out at that MCB conference, and no one batted an eyelid, so it will be safe.'

The words flowed from my pen. I showed the finished article to Caroline Wilson, my former Foreign Office private secretary who had accompanied me on the trip. She offered some comments as a friend, not an official. I had it typed up when I got to the office the next morning.

The trigger was an interview I'd had at a constituency advice 'surgery' the year before.

'It's really nice to see you face to face, Mr Straw,' this pleasant lady said to me in a broad Lancashire accent. 'The chance would be a fine thing,' I thought to myself. She was wearing a full veil.

I didn't say anything at the time. Later I decided that when a lady next turned up in a full veil I'd explain that the meeting would be of greater value if I could see her face – seeing what someone means is better than just hearing what they say.

I said as much in the article. I reminded readers that women had their heads uncovered the whole time they were on their hajj – pilgrimage – in Mecca. I concluded by saying that 'the veil was bound to make better relations between the two communities more difficult. It was such a visible statement of separation and difference. I thought a lot before raising the matter a year ago and still more before writing this. But if not me, who? My concern could be misplaced. But I think there is an issue here.'

My special advisers, Mark and Dec, both warned me that if I published it would be a big story – 'Make sure your mobile phone is fully charged.' So did Des McCartan, the Leader's press officer, like Mark a journalist, who'd spent a lifetime in the Lobby before coming over to the other side.

'No, it won't,' I kept saying. 'Don't worry. It may get a bit of local coverage, but nothing more. It's much more carefully phrased than my ad lib comments at that conference; that was a Muslim audience, and no one even seemed to notice.'

They were right; I was wrong. The *Lancashire Telegraph* ran it on their front page, and whoosh, it went international. Partly this was because of the rather misleading implication of the *Lancashire Telegraph* splash: 'Take Off Your Veils'. I had never proposed banning the veil, nor did I believe that it should be banned. Partly, it was because the party conference season had just ended, and the papers wanted to move on to something else. Above all, though, it was a subject that people had been desperate to discuss openly; my intervention had made it safe to do so.

I have never before or since had such coverage for an opinion I've expressed. It was as though I'd unblocked a dam. The veil dominated the news for two days and was a media 'talking point' for a week.

On Friday 13 October, eight days after the article had first appeared, I was back in Blackburn for my usual round of engagements and advice surgeries.

I tried to have a 'normal' constituency day, but it proved impossible. I was followed around by a large press pack, many from overseas, including a Japanese TV crew who were broadcasting, live, from the car park of the Mill Hill Community Centre. There were demonstrations by veiled women outside the advice centres, delegations of veiled women inside the advice centres.

I'd arranged months before for the Russian ambassador Yuri Fedotov and his aide to spend the day with me. The concept of a 'constituency day' was in itself fairly baffling for them. But as they followed me from meeting to meeting, surgery to surgery, accompanied by an ever-growing retinue of film crews and protestors, they became really very confused. At one point Mark found the ambassador and his aide wandering off down a shopping street, as though in search of refuge.

My modest article generated great debate in Muslim countries. The Al-Azhar mosque in Cairo, where I'd spent such an interesting time five years before, came out in my support, with the senior religious authority there, Sheikh Sayyid Tantawi, asserting that the niqab (the full veil) had never been obligatory. Another leading scholar from Al-Azhar,

Dr Souad Saleh,* weighed in to say 'There is a significant difference between the hijab [head scarf] . . . and the niqab . . . The first is a religious duty, but the second is a sheer cultural convention, which has no *raison d'être* in Islamic sources.'

Caught in the midst of a media firestorm, I was reminded of how I had felt when my pamphlet on Clause IV had been published. I was getting it in the neck for saying something discordant. But there was an added dimension to these criticisms. Many of my close Muslim friends, who'd supported me so loyally through the Iraq War, and the 2005 election, felt hurt that I'd taxed their loyalty to me again – and exposed them to further taunts that they were Straw toadies.

There was also the cultural fact of life that within our Asian communities there can sometimes be the most alarming eruption of strong collective emotions. I had witnessed these before, during the Salman Rushdie protests in 1989. I would do so again when I spoke about the sexual grooming of white girls by some Pakistani men.[4] It takes a strong nerve when you're in the middle of it all, but it does normally subside – provided you take the time to explain yourself.

I spent days in meetings, in Blackburn and elsewhere, talking about what I had said in my article, and what I had not said (i.e. 'ban the veil'). We reprinted the article, in Urdu and Gujarati, with a commentary, not least to head off some quite scurrilous claims from local Liberal Democrats. I spoke to a national group of Islamic scholars, and established that the injunction to wear the veil was a much later interpretation of the message of the Koran by ordinary mortals from particular schools of thought amongst the scholars, and had not come from the Prophet Muhammad. Gradually the row died down; gradually many Asian women (and some Asian men) thanked me for raising an issue which had previously been taboo.

Despite predictions to the contrary, the veil issue did not feature in

---

* Former head of the Faculty of Female Religious Studies.

the local elections six months later, still less in the 2010 general election.

Some Asian women still wear the veil in Blackburn, including some who come to see me for advice. Some remove their veil; some don't. I'm glad that on that October Tuesday, faced with a blank sheet, a blank mind, and a deadline, my brain engaged and I wrote that column. What's the point of being in politics, and not saying what you think about the difficult issues, as well as the easy ones?

More than any other country in the Middle East, Lebanon's population captures the fractured, violent history of the region, divided as it is between large minorities of Sunni and Shi'a Muslims and Maronite Christians, and smaller but significant minorities of Greek Orthodox, Greek Catholics and Druze. The constitution aims to balance these profound faith differences, with a Maronite president, a Shi'a Speaker of the Parliament, and a Sunni prime minister.

Since it gained its independence in 1943, Lebanon has had stretches of peace, interspersed by periods of the most brutal civil war, the worst lasting fifteen years, from 1975 to 1990.

I'd rarely had such intense security as on the trip I made to Beirut in early 2006. I was accompanied by at least twenty vehicles full of well-armed Lebanese soldiers; I caused a huge traffic jam as they closed most of the road system from the airport until I'd passed.

It was not for show. Some of the ministers I met had to live in the parliamentary compound for fear of assassination. An arrangement for Walid Jumblatt, the leader of the Druze, to have dinner with me at the British Ambassador's Residence, had to be made by messenger, since no one could trust the phone system. Jumblatt told me that he had to use a different vehicle every day, for fear he'd be the next target of the Syrians, who had almost certainly been behind the massive bomb that had killed Rafik Hariri, the Lebanese prime minister in February 2005.

My arrival in Beirut, on 4 January, coincided with the news that Ariel Sharon, the Israeli prime minister, had suffered a catastrophic stroke which has left him in a deep coma ever since. Handling this news would have been easier in virtually any other capital in the world, such was the intense bitterness in Lebanon towards Sharon – and not just from Israel's obvious enemy, Hezbollah, the Iranian-backed Shi'ite political and military organization which controlled much of south Lebanon. The mild-mannered, moderate Sunni prime minister Fouad Siniora was just as outspoken in his condemnation of what he saw as Sharon's personal responsibility for much bloodshed of the Lebanese people. Fortunately, I managed to navigate round these difficulties, and express my sympathy with Sharon's family, without inflaming my hosts too much.

In late July 2006, three months after Tony moved me and six months after I had visited Beirut as Foreign Secretary, Hezbollah fired rockets from south Lebanon into Israel, killing several Israeli soldiers.

After this latest rocket attack, and as ever in the contested history of this region, each side blamed the other; but there's little doubt that the immediate provocation was from Hezbollah.

If Israel had reacted proportionately, they would have had most international opinion on their side. But, they over-reacted. It's what they do, believing that a display of massive force is the only answer to threats like this. The irony is that if Sharon had still been in post, he might have had the political space to calibrate the force needed with greater sensitivity. But his successor as prime minister, Ehud Olmert, had nothing like Sharon's reputation, and needed to show that he was just as tough. He responded very hard. The Lebanese coast was block-aded, and Beirut Airport bombed, causing massive explosions. Civilian casualties among the Lebanese were mounting. International sentiment rapidly swung against the Israelis.

In the last Prime Minister's Questions before the summer break Tony was asked by the Liberal Democrat leader Ming Campbell, 'How can we be even-handed if we are not willing to condemn Israel's dispropor-tionate response, which the prime minister of Lebanon has described as cutting his country to pieces?'

Tony's reply, in which he put the blame wholly on Hezbollah, caused consternation across the House, and an unusually scornful second question from Ming.[5]

I sat in the Leader's place on the front bench, one along from Tony, staring into the middle distance, hoping that no one would spot what I was thinking. Like the majority of the PLP, as well as most Liberal Democrats, and many Tories, I was appalled that, more than he'd ever done before, Tony was acting as a back marker for the Israelis. Gradually all the anger, which I'd managed to bolt down since Tony had moved me without good reason, welled up. I was also frustrated – if I'd still been in post I might have been able to contain some of the damage Tony was doing to himself, and to his government, by appeasing the Israelis in such a one-sided way; I might even have been able to persuade Tony that his stance was wrong.

My 'twin', Bob Ayling and I were having a joint sixtieth birthday party at the weekend, as we had had a joint fiftieth a decade before, both organized by Bob's wife Julia, and by Alice. This one took place in Minster Lovell, in the tithe barn in the grounds of the house owned by our great friend Jill Parker, widow of the industrialist Sir Peter Parker, former chairman of British Rail. The setting is idyllic; by the River Windrush, adjacent to a large medieval ruin and the fifteenth-century parish church.

In the three days since PMQs, the situation in the Lebanon had deteriorated, and so had Tony's response. As Julia and Alice were making preparations for the party on the Saturday afternoon, I called Tony. Walking round and round Jill Parker's garden, we spoke for three-quarters of an hour. He was polite, as ever, but immovable. He met many of my points with his oft-repeated mantra that 'Israel was a democracy'. This was a statement of fact, but higher standards should be expected of democracies than of tin-pot dictatorships. In any event, Tony knew that the particular form of democracy which Israel practised was part of its problem, since its completely proportionate system of voting led to highly unstable coalitions in which extremist parties called the shots.

The party that evening was great. Charlie Falconer, a friend to both Bob and me, made an immensely witty speech at our expense. But those guests who were involved in politics could be heard chattering about why on earth Tony had chosen to isolate himself in this way. All that his critics (me included) were asking was that Tony called for a ceasefire, and condemned the disproportionate use of force by the Israelis in terms similar to those he'd used about the Hezbollah.

With Parliament in recess I went up to Blackburn midweek, for my last set of constituency engagements before Alice and I took our summer break. Many party members, good and loyal, the ones who'd defended Tony and me over Iraq and much else besides, simply did not believe that their government could not bring itself to condemn what was going on, and were instead defending the indefensible. A group of Asian leaders, led by the chairman of the Lancashire Council of Mosques who was also a Labour councillor, Salim Mulla, came to press their case. They were hurt, rather than angry, and asked if I would issue a public statement expressing some of the views which they knew privately I held. I readily agreed.

I gave the statement to the *Lancashire Telegraph*, and briefed Bill Jacobs, an old friend who'd been the Blackburn paper's lobby man and was now working for the Edinburgh evening paper. The text of my statement had been created almost entirely by cutting and pasting language which Condi Rice, Margaret Beckett and Tony had each themselves used. But, whatever their provenance, I was aware that, for the first time in my many years on the front bench, my words would be taken as a shot across my party leader's bow. But I thought if Tony wouldn't listen in private, maybe he would if I used the megaphone of the press.

Alice and I flew out the next day for our holiday on Martha's Vineyard, off the coast of Massachusetts. As we left Boston Airport to drive, in thick traffic, for two hours, down the coast to catch our ferry, my mobile rang. It was Number 10, with Tony on the line. He'd got wind that the *Sunday Times* were splashing on my statement with a

'Cabinet revolt' story, and was mighty exercised about it. At least he's had to listen, I thought, as I committed various traffic violations, and scared Alice by paying more attention to the call than to our safety. I went through the motions of explaining that my statement used 'authorized' language. But we were both grown-ups. He knew what I was doing, and so did I. Meanwhile, Mark Davies, my special adviser, back in London with a tiny baby, had to field endless calls, including one from Kofi Annan's staff, anxious for further briefing about my views.

Part of my concern about Tony's position was that by legitimizing Israel's excesses, he was constraining our ability to apply the necessary diplomatic pressure to get them to move. As usual, Israel was using every device they knew to manipulate their allies. Condi was (and is) ever loyal to her boss, President George Bush, but in her memoirs she charts how furious she was when she realized that Vice President Dick Cheney might have been 'negotiating behind my back [with the Israelis] and suggesting that the United States might support an extension of the war'; and still more angry when she discovered (years later) that US ambassador to the UN, John Bolton, had been 'sharing [US] information with [the Israelis' UN] ambassador without permission to do so'.[6]

As well as being angry with Tony, I felt sorry for him, and perplexed. There was no good reason for him to dig such a hole for himself. It certainly wasn't helping to bring peace. It was weakening his domestic grip, and forcing an unwelcome choice on many of his supporters and admirers. But Tony had reached a clear conclusion: 'If I had condemned Israel, it would have been more than dishonest; it would have undermined the world view I had come to hold passionately.'[7]

The gap between Tony's 'world view' and that of most other people was now beyond conciliation. In my book, a 'world view' is a dangerous and misguided notion, its proselytization inevitably leading to the most simplistic categorizations – of the kind practised by the American right, and its intellectual leaders, the neocons.

But, to the extent that the mainstream of the Labour Party had a single 'world view', it wasn't Tony's. It was very sad, for him, and for the party; but looking back on this, it was as if he was willing his martyrdom.

At the beginning of 2004, after the cliff-edge vote on top-up fees in higher education, I had been to see Tony in his room at the Commons. With a notional majority of 160, we had scraped home by 5. Like most members of the Cabinet I had spent my weekend speaking for hours with potential rebels (I have a complete recall of the paintwork on one of our window frames which I studied throughout one forty-five-minute call with a particularly difficult colleague).

'Please don't do that again, Tony,' I said. 'Your luck will run out.'

'Jack,' he replied, with his blue eyes blazing, 'I'm always lucky.'[8]

Two and half years later, his luck had run out. Profoundly isolated on this fundamental issue of policy, and with no way back, Tony finally succumbed, as Gordon and his cronies closed in. It wasn't pretty. On 7 September 2006 he announced that he would leave Downing Street the following year.

The next eight months were surreal.

One of the many reasons I had been taken by surprise by Tony's decision to move me from the Foreign Office was that we had been fairly close. I agreed with his analysis of how the party had to change if it were ever to be elected again – indeed, my Clause IV pamphlet had laid the ground for much of this. I shared his approach to politics, his desire to get away from the patronising condescension which so many on the intellectual left exhibited towards our core voters, and instead to understand and articulate those voters' dreams and needs. We had different backgrounds and temperaments, and differences over policy, too (the EU or Iran, for example), but these had never appeared insuperable.

For much of my time as Foreign Secretary, I was – physically – in one place, Tony in another. EU Councils – the quarterly 'summits' – were different. The two of us formed the UK's delegation, so we had to work together very closely. My anorak tendencies meant I could watch the detail, while he concentrated on his 'big picture'.

Quite frequently, these meetings would be interrupted by unscheduled adjournments, as some deal over the language of the final conclusions was being brokered. If the UK wasn't directly involved, we'd just sit there, gossiping about our life and times – including his difficulties with his next-door neighbour.

On two occasions at least, Tony suggested – I put it no higher than this – that I should think about the leadership once he had gone. 'You could do it, you know, Jack.'

I had thought about it quite a bit – ever since that *Economist* article at the beginning of 1999 (which had, perhaps predictably, provoked the Gods into visiting one calamity after another upon me). I reckoned that I could do much of the job. I could certainly have run the government properly, and would have relished the chance to introduce better process into our decision-making. I had never been short of opinions; and I thought that my particular brand of politics, with its high emphasis on my constituents, might appeal to the British public. But I wasn't sure I could do it all. I understood the Commons, and had handled the House through some incredibly difficult issues; but none of these compared with the weekly half-hour of Prime Minister's Questions, a real frightener for any prime minister. I might screw up, as I had in that dreadful Michael Howard debate. Most people had completely forgotten about it; but its ghost was still there inside me.

I guess I could have overcome these fears. I knew how to survive, after all. But there was a bigger question in my mind – did I want it enough, was I willing to pay the price, of further pressures on Alice and the family, and myself? Living in our bubble was odd enough, but I had seen enough to know that our life was normal compared with that of any prime minister. Lastly, there was the simple calculation – what would be the point of my becoming a candidate? It would involve a huge effort, Iraq would be wrapped round my neck, and whatever my qualities, it was hard to see how I could possibly win against the man whose life had been consumed by this one ambition – Gordon Brown.

'When folk put their money in the "Name the Leader" machine, the ticket came out with my name on it – not Gordon's,' Tony commented to me wryly during one of our natters at an EU Council. It was true; a year before, a year after, the machine might have printed a different answer, but that was the answer it gave on 12 May 1994, and Gordon had never quite come to terms with this fact.

After the 2001 election, Tony quite often complained to me about how badly Gordon was behaving towards him, how he would come into his room in Downing Street and shout at him. Tony's staff echoed these complaints. Less often I'd be on the receiving end of some dark Delphic comment from Gordon, about his neighbour next door. But there was nothing I could do to resolve the tension. Tony didn't have to keep the guy there as Chancellor. As long as he did, he'd be a problem.

In 1997–8 Alice had worked briefly for Gordon, in her last months as a director of public spending in the Treasury, before she got promotion to the Department of Health. She liked him; and felt that Sarah was something of a fellow spirit. Our son Will worked in the Treasury from 2003 to 2007 and often remarked on the esteem in which Gordon was held by civil servants there.

Gordon had always been relatively indifferent toward my departments, which was in general a good thing. Whilst it took all my ingenuity, and Tony's support, to get the allocations I needed, it also made it relatively easy for us to work around each other; we did not get in each other's way.

When Gordon and Sarah came to dinner at our London home in June 2006, the man we saw then was the charming Gordon – engaged, funny and very bright. I had long admired his forensic skills, and I thought, at that point, that he had done pretty well as Chancellor, despite his inexplicable reluctance to give me more money for prisons, and the Diplomatic Service, and more significantly, his unwillingness to engage when I had raised my concerns about our current account deficit, and the level of personal debt, in 2004.

Tony was going; Gordon was coming. One or two friends suggested that I should stand as leader, but by then, to Alice's great relief, I'd firmly decided not to do so. Quite apart from anything else, I knew I'd be beaten by some margin.

At some stage in early 2007 – and I now cannot remember exactly how this came about – Gordon asked me if I'd be his campaign manager. I knew why he had asked me – it tied me in. I knew why I had said 'yes' – Gordon was going to be the next prime minister, why wouldn't I accept? It caused a few raised eyebrows amongst some MPs closest to Tony, since I'd been his campaign manager in 1994, and the odd tease from some of my friends that I really was a political tart. But there was a vacancy. Tony was standing down. And I felt then, on the basis of what I had witnessed thus far, that Gordon would make a good prime minister.

On 8 May 2007, just after the local elections, Tony announced that he'd leave office six weeks later, on 27 June. By that time there were no obvious candidates likely to stand against Gordon. David Miliband toyed with the idea but (rightly, in my view) decided that the time was not ripe. The Cabinet's resident shooting star, John Reid, had a motive for fighting Gordon – they were long-standing adversaries from the incestuous village that is Scottish Labour politics – but his fortunes had waned as quickly as they had waxed. The only declared candidate was John McDonnell, the assiduous constituency MP for Hayes and Harlington who was a leading light in the hard-left Socialist Campaign Group.

Under the electoral college system, an MP needs the nominations of one-eighth of the PLP to get on to the ballot paper. In every election campaign in which I'd ever been involved, in the fifty years since I'd first been put, aged nine, outside a polling station to 'take numbers', there'd been other candidates to fight. This time was different. The task here was to sign up 291 Labour MPs so that no other candidate could stand. The Leader's office in the Commons was conveniently situated close to the Chamber. We had to be incredibly careful to ensure that the campaign incurred no cost whatever to government or Parliament, but using my room itself incurred no expense. So Mark Davies fixed regular meetings of Gordon's campaign group there, to work through the

PLP list. Gordon's guys came – Nick Brown, Ian Austin, Nigel Griffiths, Ann Keen, and Chris Leslie, then outside the House, running Gordon's campaign office. As well as Mark, I brought Sadiq Khan, and my PPS, Paddy Tipping. Paddy was an old and very loyal friend, who'd also been my PPS when I was at the Home Office.

These meetings were my first introduction to the cell-structure through which Gordon seemed to run his politics. Mark was trying to work from one central list; but Nick Brown had his own list, and Ian Austin a third in his head. A name would be called out; Nick would assert that he already had him lined up; there'd be a tiff between Nick and Ian, or anyone else asserting a greater knowledge of this MP's mind; and we'd go on to the next name. Paddy, whose loyalty was to the party not any one faction, but who was more 'Blairite' than 'Brownite', did most to persuade very reluctant New Labour believers to sign on the dotted line. The last few names were hard going. But we got there.

There's been much talk since that it would have been better, for Gordon as well as the party, if there had been a proper contest for leader. Maybe. It certainly would have strengthened his legitimacy. But life is not quite like that. I've never met any candidate for any office who wouldn't have preferred an unopposed win. There's enough risk in politics without manufacturing it. If I'd been the favoured candidate for party leader, not Gordon, and was within sight of blocking off other contenders by perfectly legitimate means, would I have tried to do so? Of course.

Gordon could have rested once the leadership was in the bag, but in the three weeks after nominations closed, he went on the campaign trail, his schedule woven into the (real) hustings for the deputy leadership. Occasionally, I went with him. The venues changed, as, sometimes, did the subject matter; the jokes stayed the same. Still, they worked to warm up his listeners, and he dealt with scores of questioners very well. I was reasonably confident that he had a plan, and that he would make a good fist of the job.

TWENTY-ONE

The Tights Come On

*I am in the bathroom. My wife is banging on the door. 'Jack?' she
says. 'Are you OK? What are you doing in there?'*

*'Just a minute!' I call, and I very slowly straighten my lacy cravat.
I am a modest man but some things are undeniable. I look magnificent. I should be on a five-pound note.*

*Tomorrow is the Queen's Speech. I am trying on my costume.
Again. Look at me. This is dignity. This is gravitas. This is how a
man should look.*

*'Jack?' calls my wife. 'I'm going to be late. Have you seen my
tights?'*

'My Week: Jack Straw' (as told by Hugo Rifkind),
The Times, 10 November 2007

I was writhing on the floor of the Lord High Chancellor's Commons
room with my big toe caught in one foot of the tights, the leg of the
other one twisted so firmly that iron ankle-manacles would have been
no more effective. Desperate not to ladder the tights, I wrestled with
myself for five minutes. I finally became free from my bonds, and
started again. I had been in the same room as Alice while she had been
dressing thousands of times, but I had paid no more attention to how
she put on a pair of tights, than she, I guess, had ever paid to how I

shaved. I then recalled that she always rolled them up first to get them safely over her feet. *Eureka!*

The remainder of the Lord Chancellor's court wear, unchanged since the eighteenth century, posed fewer challenges – knee breeches, wrist ruffs, buckled shoes, an incredibly heavy gold-embroidered gown – and that lacy cravat. Whether I looked 'magnificent' I'm far from sure; I certainly looked different. Should the People's Court have decided to try me for consorting with the enemy, my only defence would have been the old saw that 'nothing's too good for the working class'.

Gordon's first day as prime minister had been choreographed in minute detail. We were each given instructions about when to arrive in Downing Street for the first Cabinet meeting – and with whom. I was paired off with Alistair Darling and Geoff Hoon. We were Wisdom; behind us, Youth – Andy Burnham, and another young gun. All this whilst 'the end of spin' was being spun. After these jollifications, it was over to the new Ministry of Justice.

I returned for one last time to to my old offices on the ground floor of Dover House. Before leaving I gathered on the hall steps with all of my Private Office, my two special advisers, and the protection officers on duty that day to have our photograph taken – the entire staff of the Leader of the House fitting into one camera shot. I then travelled the short distance to Selborne House on Victoria Street, home of the Ministry of Justice, a department of 90,000 staff.

The story of this ministry's birth in 2007 speaks volumes for the capricious way in which government departments can be reorganized, without a proper assessment of the costs (usually high), and benefits (often unclear), and without prior approval by Parliament or Cabinet.

Back in 2001, Tony (and I) had resisted John Birt's eccentric (and unconstitutional) idea for an ever-bigger Home Office through a takeover of the Lord Chancellor's Department, and the Law Officers. The machinery of government changes he made then had not exactly been a success. Key amongst these had been the transfer of responsibility for licensing, alcohol, gaming and betting, and film and video censorship from the Home Office to the Department of Culture Media and Sport (DCMS).

What connects these issues is social control – how best to regulate individuals' freedom to drink themselves silly at any hour or squander their money on gambling, against the effect of such un-regulated behaviour on society as a whole. This is core business for the Home Office. They have the people, and the experience. DCMS, a small department, has neither. Partly because of this, they have not been able sufficiently to resist the powerful vested interests of the industries concerned. There is no evidence that the public interest has been served by this; nor that Home Secretaries have had an easier ride in conse-quence.

Despite this, the idea persisted that the still-sprawling Home Office's problems could be moderated by yet another reorganization. The sub-text of John Reid's 2006 'not fit for purpose' sideswipe at the people working for him was that he would be performing better if he had a differently constituted department underneath him. He had hatched a plan to split the Home Office in two, merging one half with the Department for Constitutional Affairs.*

Personally I would not have wasted time and energy on the change, although a coherent case for separate interior and justice ministries can be made – it's the norm in many countries. But the way this re-organization was carried out, and, in particular, the manner of its announcement, was simply indefensible.

In late January 2007, whilst still Leader of the House, I had been due to appear on Sunday morning television. The evening before I had called John Reid (and a couple of other Cabinet ministers) to check on the issues that might be bowled at me. John told me that the *Sunday*

---

* The Lord Chancellor's Department had by this point become the Department for Constitutional Affairs following another badly handled change in 2003.

Telegraph would be running an article by him proposing that the Home Office be split in two, so it was likely to be a big story. John said that he had done this to knock off another, disobliging story about which they were concerned.

When asked the next morning, I therefore retreated into the helpful thickets of compound sentences and subordinate clauses to ensure that my reply was unmemorable, and the interview moved on to other issues. But I could not believe, and I still cannot, that Tony could have allowed John to operate in such a cavalier way. Charlie Falconer, then Lord Chancellor and so at the head of one of the two departments concerned, only learnt of John's intentions through a phone call on the Saturday night.

Nor had the senior judiciary been given any more warning. Lord Phillips, Lord Chief Justice, later commented acidly that the impetus for this proposal was 'anxiety by [John Reid] to clear the decks so he could make a concerted attack on terrorism. It was not a decision taken because it was thought a very good idea to have a Ministry of Justice.'[1]

The formal announcement of these plans, rather than their informal trailing in the press, came on 29 March 2007. The new ministry came into existence on 9 May 2007, with Charlie Falconer at its helm. The merger in practice went better than anyone could have imagined, thanks in large part to Charlie, Alex Allan, the permanent secretary, and Antonia Romeo, Charlie's principal private secretary (whom I happily inherited).

The ministry was responsible for the courts, the judiciary, civil and criminal law, criminal justice policy including sentencing, the probation and prison services, and constitutional reform.

I'd now been a Cabinet minister for nearly ten years. Apart from the courts and the judiciary, I had covered my new portfolio before, either as Home Secretary or Leader of the House. I didn't really feel the need to study the briefs for incoming ministers too closely. I had very clear ideas about what I wanted to achieve – implement a comprehensive programme of constitutional reform; repair fences with the judiciary; build a fully functioning new department; stabilize prison numbers and deal with the Prison Officers' Association; and continue to do more for victims of crime – and how to go about it.

Hitherto, Gordon had never shown much interest in Labour's programme of constitutional reform. But encouraged by Wilf Stevenson, then running the Smith Institute, and Michael Wills, the cerebral Labour MP for Swindon North who joined me in the ministry, he had become convinced that he should lead a major programme of reforms to strengthen Parliament's say over the executive, and the people's sway over Parliament. I was very keen on this programme. It was in tune with my approach to parliamentary reform, and I was delighted that I would have the task of implementing it.

What I had simply not bargained for was the endemically chaotic way in which Gordon chose to work, from which I'd been so insulated during my previous ten years in government.

This central truth had first begun to dawn on me during the leadership campaign, when Dec McHugh, Mark Davies and I had attended a series of meetings with Gordon's people about what the programme would contain. As ever, it was a changing cast, and thus a constantly shifting set of ideas.

We spent the first weekend of Gordon's premiership writing and rewriting endless drafts of the 'Governance of Britain' Green Paper, with a talented team of Ministry of Justice officials led by Clare Moriarty. The messages from Number 10 were many, varied and inconsistent. On the Sunday, I had to go Number 10 to rewrite the document with Jeremy Heywood and Ed Miliband (who was always very good to work with).

Gordon himself had to spend much of his time over that weekend dealing with two crises – the Glasgow Airport attack and foiled London nightclub bombing, and the continuing floods across the UK – which he handled well. Despite these distractions, and the birth pains, the finished Green Paper was a good piece of work, and well received. Gordon made it the subject of his first Commons statement as prime minister, signalling the importance he attached to this agenda: 'For centuries, [the prime minister and the executive] have exercised authority in the name of the monarchy without the people and their elected representatives being consulted, so I now propose that in twelve important areas of our national life the prime minister and the executive should surrender or limit their powers.'[2]

The process (or rather lack of it) for implementing the programme set the tone for those first summer months of Gordon's time at Number 10. The external picture of his calm under fire, built upon his reaction to that first weekend's crises, masked the underlying reality.

The contrast with Number 10 under Tony was striking. Dealing with the centre then had had its moments (as no doubt they had felt about dealing with a minister like me), but the place had been better organized, the staff generally knew what they were doing – in Jonathan Powell and Alastair Campbell (and later David Hill) Tony had senior people who were highly professional, on top of their work, and in charge. In Gordon's Number 10 there was no organization chart worth the name. Downing Street increasingly reminded me of the famous quip about the European Union attributed to Henry Kissinger – 'Who do I call if I want to speak to Europe?'

This was compounded by some of the factions in Gordon's HQ. The majority of those working for him were proficient, decent people (who were as distracted as his ministers were about the lack of organizational coherence). But there were also those whose specialism was crude machine politics, and who brought Gordon no credit whatever. So far as I am aware, those from this dark side never did me any harm; but they harmed others, and damaged Labour's collective reputation, and Gordon's.

Sooner or later, the wheels were going to come off. They did so more quickly than any of us could have imagined.

The position of Lord Chancellor is the oldest of all offices of state. Until 2005, the holder had been simultaneously a senior member of the Cabinet, Speaker of the House of Lords and head of the judiciary. In that capacity, the Lord Chancellor could even sit as a judge, as indeed Derry Irvine did in the highest court in the land – the Law Lords. This holy trinity of roles defied all modern concepts of a separation of powers, yet, in a typically British way, it had worked.

But the arrangement was long out of date. So a plan, perfectly sensible in principle, had been developed to create more modern and constitutionally defensible arrangements: to make Britain's senior judge, the Lord Chief Justice, the head of the judiciary; to replace the Law Lords with a UK Supreme Court; to establish a Judicial Appointments Commission – and to abolish the post of Lord Chancellor altogether. In future, the responsible minister would be a common or garden Secretary of State.

Relations with the senior judiciary had first become strained when, in 2003, they had learnt of the government's plans to recast the role of the Lord Chancellor – and therefore their relationship with the executive – from a press release, issued whilst they were all away at a conference. As well as feeling insulted (with good reason) that these plans had not been discussed with them first, they were extremely sensitive to the need to preserve both the constitutional principle of judicial independence and their own status. The relevant legislation was amended, and amended again. The proposal to abolish the post of Lord Chancellor was defeated. In its place were explicit statutory rules on the qualifications needed by the holder of this office, and the oath they would have to swear on taking office.* My first outing in my tights was to the Lord Chief Justice's court in the Strand, where, in an elaborate ceremony, I swore this new oath, and two older ones.

---

* 'I, do swear that in the office of Lord High Chancellor of Great Britain I will respect the rule of law, defend the independence of the judiciary and discharge my duty to ensure the provision of resources for the efficient and effective support of the courts for which I am responsible. So help me God.'

I was the first member of the Commons to be Lord Chancellor since Sir Christopher Hatton in the sixteenth century. The only other Commoner to have held the role was Sir Thomas More, whose fate was hardly a good augury. I was aware of the anxiety among the judiciary about having someone like me in the post. True, I'd done well in Bar Finals, I'd practised, I was a Bencher of my Inn, I enjoyed the law and its intellectual puzzles; but Barking and Guildford Magistrates' Courts, Inner London Sessions, Westminster County Court, and occasionally the Old Bailey, and all for just two years, were never the forums in which the reputations of great jurists were made. So I decided to play it safe. I dispensed with the Lord Chancellor's full bottom wig, on the grounds that I had never taken silk and it would therefore have been an impertinence to wear it, but I kept assiduously to the rest of the finery. Hugo Rifkind was not wrong – I do enjoy dressing up.

I also learnt to walk backwards down the steps in front of the Queen at the State Openings of Parliament. This is not easy. My fancy buckled shoes had very slippery soles. The heavy gold-braided gown, worn on top of three layers of court dress, was a trip hazard. The steps turned a corner. And I had to do this watched by millions of the TV audience – and my mother in the gallery.

More seriously, I decided that as the first Commons Lord Chancellor in modern times I needed to work hard to rebuild trust with the judiciary. In this I was greatly helped by Suma Chakrabarti who took over from Alex Allan as permanent secretary in early 2008.

Fortunately I knew a few of the senior judges anyway: The Lord Chief Justice, Nick (Lord) Phillips was a close friend of my 'twin' Bob Ayling, and had attended our joint fiftieth and sixtieth birthday parties. I'd got to know Tom Bingham (by then the Senior Law Lord) when he'd been Lord Chief for the first three years of my stint as Home Secretary; and Harry Woolf, his successor as Lord Chief, in my last year in that post.

By happenstance, the 'Senior Presiding Judge', who effectively runs the administration of the court system under the Lord Chief, was Brian Leveson, whom Alice and I had met some years ago on holiday. And I quickly developed a good friendship with Igor Judge, who took over as Lord Chief Justice from Nick Phillips when he became president of the new Supreme Court. It all helped.

By the end of my three years as Lord Chancellor the judiciary remained, as I would expect, determined defenders of both judicial independence and their own position. Their memories are long and the way the department was created will continue to rankle. But I hope they are at least reassured that their independence is under no threat from having a Commoner as Lord Chancellor.

If working with the judiciary was new, and working on the constitution worryingly different, some parts of the role were reassuringly the same.

'Seeing you three old lags, it's as if I'd never been away,' I remarked to three officials who turned up in my office in the new ministry in the first week. They'd all worked with me when I'd been Home Secretary. Here we all were again, six years later. The faces hadn't changed much – and nor had the issues.

Top of my 'immediate' pile was a mounting crisis over prison numbers. That took me back not six years, but ten. Prison places had increased from 60,000 in 1997 to 79,000 by 2007, but this still was not enough to cope with demand.

Forecasting prison numbers is an imprecise science. Judges and magistrates are human. They do subconsciously react to shifts in public sentiment. (For example, the horror over the Jamie Bulger killing in the nineties led to an immediate hardening in sentencing.) 'Tough on crime' had meant that there had been a significant rise in convictions, especially of serious and violent offenders, who were then also receiving longer sentences.

The pressure had built up so much in the early months of 2007 that hundreds of prisoners had had to be housed in police cells. But even that was not enough. Some prisoners would have to be released early. This had never happened before under our watch. It would be a grave embarrassment for a government which had invested so much in bringing crime down. Prompt decisions got caught up in the semi-paralysis which overtook government in the closing months of Tony's premiership, making things worse. It was not until Tony's very last week that Charlie Falconer, who'd inherited this poisoned chalice from John Reid just six weeks before, had been able to announce an early release scheme by which shorter-term prisoners would be released up to eighteen days before their normal release time.

The day after my appointment I told the BBC that this would continue 'for some time'. I was right about that. The scheme was in operation until March 2010. We were only able to abandon it then thanks to indefatigable work by prisons minister Maria Eagle. It was as a result of her terrier-like pursuit of additional accommodation that we avoided having 'early release' hung round our neck during the 2010 election campaign.

Nonetheless, I was alive to the fact that as long as the early release scheme continued, there'd be damaging stories of prisoners on the scheme committing further offences – and that we'd be to blame. Avoiding such stories would be impossible, so I proposed that we should collect as much data as possible, and publish it each month. I was not intending to burden Number 10 with this decision until it was a fait accompli. But somehow they found out, and I then had Gordon on the line fretting that I could be producing regular own goals. I dug in. My view was very clear. It was right to provide this information, up front, and it would save us much bother if we did.

There were many things I missed when I moved from the Home Office to the FCO in 2001. One thing I had not missed for a second was having to deal with the Prison Officers' Association (POA). I always worked hard for a constructive relationship with the unions, but the POA were in a category of their own. They desperately needed to merge with one of the mainstream unions, and benefit from their professionalism, but none was ever going to take them. Indeed when later I privately canvassed the leaders of three of the big unions about a merger with the POA, I was met with fruity, and negative, responses.

The fundamental problem with the POA was that it was in a constant state of turmoil. There were too many elected full-timers each jostling for position. They went in for impossibilist demands, and then cried 'betrayal' when these could not be met. Still, I wanted an improvement in relations with the POA, and had agreed that Ed Sweeney, a former senior member of the TUC General Council and then chair of the employment service ACAS, should hold a thorough review into industrial relations inside the Prison Service.

On the morning of Wednesday 29 August 2007 I was woken at 6.30 by my principal private secretary Antonia to tell me that the POA had, fifteen minutes before, given notice that they were to begin a nationwide twenty-four-hour strike there and then. They had 80,000 prisoners in their charge, who would be left to the mercies of other prisoners, and the few staff – governors, and non-uniformed – who were not in the POA. They were on a high that they'd taken us by surprise, but it was utterly irresponsible, made worse by the paucity of their excuse for the action – that a 2.5 per cent pay rise was going to be phased, giving (they said) a real terms increase of 1.9 per cent.

Although we had had no advance warning of the strike, nor any information on its probable scale, instinct told me it was likely to be extensive. I told Antonia to instruct officials to draw up an application to the High Court for an injunction against the union, requiring them to return to work.

I was due to make some visits to South London courts and a police station that morning, and decided that I would go ahead with them whilst the scale of the strike, and its damage, became clear; and to avoid the impression of panic.

We got the injunction, with the judge saying that there was an 'overwhelming case' that the POA had broken its legally binding agreement, signed in 2001, not to strike. I called Colin Moses, the POA's president.

I explained to him the consequences for his union if the strike continued, and told him that he'd get precious little support from other unions, beyond *Socialist Worker*-inspired resolutions of solidarity. Brendan Barber, TUC general secretary, was immensely helpful in persuading the POA leadership to pull back from the precipice on which they had placed themselves. It was invaluable too having a young prison governor, Amy Rees, working inside the Private Office – an improvement since I'd last been in charge of the Prison Service, and one so obvious that I kept wondering why it had never been thought of before.

The strike fizzled out – but not before it did a great deal of damage, including young prisoners at the large Lancaster Farms prison setting fire to their cells, and wrecking an entire wing.

The union had already given a year's formal notice that they were going to withdraw from the agreement not to strike that they had signed with David Blunkett, and which was due to run out in May 2008. They believed that it would be too difficult for a Labour government to reinstate the statutory ban, originally signed when Michael Howard was Home Secretary, and that they would therefore, with one bound, be free to indulge in the highly disruptive action which had caused so many problems in the past.

I decided that since they had ambushed me, I'd return the compliment.

During the autumn I got collective agreement to add a provision imposing a comprehensive ban on industrial action by prison officers to a bill already going through the House. There was remarkably little dissent from Cabinet colleagues; just as remarkable was the fact that not a word of my intention leaked. Everyone understood how high the stakes were. The ban went through with a thumping majority of 435.[3] The POA had only themselves to blame. No government would ever again trust them to enter into binding agreements and not break them.

In the previous spending round, Charlie Falconer had secured a reasonable settlement for his Department of Constitutional Affairs;

certainly, I'd have done no better. But the judiciary and the courts accounted for less than 20 per cent of the budget of the new Ministry of Justice. The rest was from the Home Office.

Charles Clarke had been Home Secretary at the time. I can still recall my utter amazement when it had been announced one Cabinet that Charles had 'settled early'. (There had been some cock and bull story from the Treasury that there would be a benefit to settling early.) The Treasury themselves could not believe that anyone had fallen for such a plainly bogus ploy.

The result was that there was insufficient money to pay for key services, such as probation and prisons. Discovering this when he took over responsibility for them, Charlie Falconer had wisely insisted that there be a fresh scrutiny of the Prison Service's resources. He and the Treasury had asked Patrick Carter to undertake this. Happily, given my very close friendship with Patrick, I'd had nothing to do with his appointment; and friend or not, one reason for his high reputation was the extreme rigour with which he approached any task.

His report, which came to me in the autumn of 2007, argued for a significant uplift in cash, principally to increase the number of available prison places. Gordon could see the 'big picture'. Complete meltdown in the prison system would not be clever. But as ever, the Treasury was unkeen.

There then followed some weeks of tough negotiation, dominated by a small group of very bright, young and opinionated Treasury officials. I knew the type. They were very hard work (i.e. they didn't want to agree with me).

'I had a dream about you last night,' was my opening line to one of these officials as the negotiations wound to their conclusion. 'Yes, I dreamt that I had killed you – by strangulation.'

I got my money.

Apart from the POA strike and wrangling with the Treasury, the relative quiet continued. Gordon had made me chair of the Domestic Affairs Committee of the Cabinet, which I enjoyed. As Gordon's first party conference as prime minister began in Bournemouth in late September 2007, we were riding high in the polls. The best polls were putting us in the low forties, typically ten points ahead of the Conservatives.[4]

I arrived in Bournemouth to find that the only question in which the journalists were interested was 'Will he or won't he go for an immediate election?' Gordon wasn't saying, so the speculation ran out of control. His own people were divided on the question. In the absence of any decision from on high, in the hothouse atmosphere of the party conference, it was inevitable that their views would spill out into the open. Ed Miliband, then Chancellor of the Duchy of Lancaster and responsible for drafting the next election manifesto, came to see me. He seemed to be in the cautious camp – which was a relief.

I'd been giving a good deal of thought to the issue. Colleagues with marginal seats were pretty clear that they would struggle to hold their seats. Seasoned campaigners in Blackburn, with a good nose for the electorate, were against it – and so was my mother. She'd had decades of experience door-knocking for the party. She'd held a tricky seat on the district and town council in my home town of Loughton, Essex, well into her eighties. 'You go for an election which isn't needed, and they'll punish you. Remember Ted Heath.' I did, of course – that February 1974 general election had been the first one I'd fought. 'What's more,' she said, 'by polling day the clocks will have gone back. It will be cold, wet and dark. Our opponents will turn out, for sure; but too many of our supporters will stay at home. So we'll lose.'

I told Gordon, and his team, my view – don't go.

There was an additional factor, in my mind – Northern Rock. There'd been a run on this bank just a fortnight before. TV footage of depositors queuing to withdraw their money had gone round the world. Alistair Darling had handled it with great skill – as he was to do with the much worse financial crises to come.

So far, Northern Rock had not affected our poll ratings, but these things are often a slow burn. However hypocritical the Opposition were

– they'd been demanding less regulation, not more – we were vulnerable to the charge that we – Gordon – had allowed this to happen.

In the febrile atmosphere of an election campaign, there'd be some leak, some indiscretion, from someone in Northern Rock, or among the regulators; we'd have strenuously to fight allegations that this was a 'cut and run' election because we feared much worse news to come.

I took the view that midterm changes of prime minister without a subsequent election were quite normal. We should simply get on with the job. If Gordon had decided to hold an election almost as soon as he'd taken over at the end of June (not that I ever urged this on him), he would have had a convincing story as to why he'd called the election ('new prime minister seeks new mandate') and almost certainly would have won. However, by late September, the 'new mandate' argument wouldn't wash.

Gordon could still have emerged with dignity – and public approbation – if he had said either yes or no as conference began, on Sunday 23 September, or in his leader's speech two days later. But he dithered and dithered. He went off to Afghanistan in the middle of the Conservative conference the following week, which, though it had not been his intention, looked like a cheap wheeze. It was not until Saturday 6 October, two weeks after we'd assembled in Bournemouth, that he announced that there would be no election after all.

By then, because of his vacillation, the polls had started to turn. What could have been a triumph had turned into a disaster. The Cabinet and the PLP's confidence in him was severely damaged – and never recovered. David Cameron worked him over mercilessly in the first PMQs after the conference break: 'He is the first prime minister in history to flunk an election because he thought that he was going to win it.' This point marked a change in dynamics for the rest of the Parliament. Gordon's confidence in himself took a battering – and that never recovered. At the turn of the year, it was the Tories who found themselves in the forties in the polls, with Labour in the low thirties.

It got worse. By the May 2008 local elections we had dropped another ten points. We lost hundreds of council seats. Boris Johnson won his first term as London mayor.

Two weeks earlier the redoubtable Gwyneth Dunwoody, the long-serving Labour MP for Crewe and Nantwich, had died aged seventy-eight. Gwyneth was a one-off and I loved her. She used to describe herself as an 'awkward old bat' and a 'battleaxe' ('they're very well made, very sharp and largely very efficient at what they do').

After the 1983 election we had both had offices on the same corridor in one of the Commons' outbuildings. 'Young Straw,' she'd yell if she saw me passing. 'Come here'. I always did, even though half the time it was to get my head scrubbed for some failing or another.

In the mid-eighties I plucked up courage to ask Gwyneth whether she'd vote for me in the Shadow Cabinet election.

'Clean my shoes and I'll think about it,' she replied imperiously.

It was a joke at my expense, of course. I knew that there was no way she'd trade her vote for anyone; but I cleaned her shoes, then and many times thereafter.

Gwyneth was a woman of wide and sometimes hidden talent. When I was Home Secretary, we faced a crisis with Italy over failed asylum-seekers and I had to speak urgently with an Italian minister. The arrangements to have an interpreter on the line had failed. I went out into the corridor at the back of the Commons Chamber. The first person I met was Gwyneth

'I'm desperate—' I began.

'You always are,' she interjected before I could complete my sentence. 'Know anyone who speaks Italian?'

'Me, of course. Fluent,' she replied. I explained my plight.

'Give me a kiss and I'll sort it out.' I did and she did. Crisis averted.

Gwyneth's death was a great loss to the party. The by-election, at the end of May 2008, could not have come at a worse time. Her seat was intrinsically marginal. She'd held it, and well, by reaching out to 'non-traditional' Labour voters. Her daughter Tamsin, our candidate, was a fine woman, but the campaign to which she was subjected was awful.

Marginal voters were driven into the Tory camp by us playing the class-warfare card, and banging on about 'toffs'. Unsurprisingly, we lost. Labour's 7,000-plus majority at the 2005 election became the Conservative's 7,000-plus majority – a 17.5 per cent swing. It was the first time the Conservatives had picked up a seat at a by-election in twenty-six years.[5]

Two months later, at the end of July 2008, we faced another by-election, this time in Glasgow East. It took place as the party hierarchy, me included, were assembling in Warwick for our National Policy Forum (NPF). This was to be our last big policy gathering before the general election, and was an important precursor to the development of the manifesto. The trade union general secretaries would be there. All Cabinet ministers were expected to attend.

In the weeks after the Crewe and Nantwich by-election most conversations in the PLP, and with journalists, were dominated by concern about Gordon's leadership. Things were not exactly going to plan. Those who had long ago fallen out with Gordon (if they had ever fallen in) conveyed an air of *Schadenfreude*. Two such were Charles Clarke and Stephen Byers.

Despite my irritation at times with Charles' waywardness, he was a friend. I'd admired the way he'd acted as Neil Kinnock's chief of staff in the eighties and early nineties. I had lunch with Charles. I was less close to Stephen Byers, but I'd always rubbed along with him. He asked to talk to me, which I did on three or four occasions.

When I'm faced with a really tricky problem, to which there is no obvious solution, I have always tended to chew the fat about it. This is fine when my conversations have been limited to those who know me very well – my family, my personal staff, and a few trusted colleagues. It has obvious dangers (as Alice has warned me on many occasions) beyond such a tight circle. With Charles and Stephen, I opened up too much, leaving them with the impression that my musings that Gordon would have to go were my settled conclusions. The truth was that I could not make up my mind what the best outcome for the party would be.

If the PLP had been offered a magic wand, then at almost any time in 2008 and 2009 its three wishes would have been: Gordon would leave Number 10 with dignity; 'X' (David Miliband, Alan Johnson, me) would replace him; and Labour would then sail to an easy victory at the election. There were many of us in the PLP (including most of the Cabinet) who had supported Gordon in 2007 but whose faith in his abilities as leader had been fatally undermined; those who would have voted not to wave the wand were diminishing by the week.

In real life, however, the distance between the will and the deed can be wide – sometimes so wide, so deep, with so many dragons down there, that it's hazardous to make the leap.

My profound anxiety – which was what held me (and others) back – was that the most probable result of a leadership challenge would be a dreadful, bloody mess, which would leave the party in an even worse state. Gordon was not going to go quietly. He believed only he could lead Britain through the financial crisis; he and the loyal group around him would fight; he'd get some trade unions onside; some of the press who'd been so vitriolic about him might well turn him into a victim or hero, just to make mischief. The party could be plunged into near civil war.

Gordon was, I think, so bruised and isolated by this time that he was probably not fully aware that he might bring the party down with him. The party's rules were so cumbersome that a new leadership election would take at least six weeks, compared to the ruthlessly quick execution, facilitated by the Conservatives' rules, of leaders surplus-to-requirements.

There were, too, personal factors. I was deeply frustrated with Gordon's failings. If someone had fetched up at my front door and said 'Sign here, Mr Straw, and you're prime minister,' I would have done so; but that wasn't going to happen. I love the Labour Party. It has been my life. I could not be the man to damage it.

On top of all this, the party's default setting in favour of the leader in situ had historically been almost impossible to shift. On only one occasion in Labour's fractious history had a coup against the leader been successful. One month before the 1935 general election, Ernest Bevin launched his heavy artillery on the vacillating Labour leader George Lansbury, accusing him of 'taking your conscience from body to body to be told what you ought to do with it'.[6] Lansbury resigned within the week, to be replaced by Clement Attlee. Labour won 108 seats in the election, bringing its total to 154.

Post-war, attempted coups had never worked. Not against poor Michael Foot, and he was only opposition leader. Not against Attlee, despite the best (or worst) efforts of that world-class plotter, Herbert Morrison.[7] They hadn't against Wilson. Tony's own resignation in 2006/07 was not the result of a putsch alone.

I was by no means the only one feeling wholly conflicted about this leadership decision. As Warwick approached, what we could and should do no longer just dominated the conversation, it had become an obsession.

The mood when we got there was close to suicidal.

Like so much else under Gordon's regime, the NPF had been arranged without proper notice. Alice and I always booked our summer holiday for the first three weeks of the recess. I had cleared that date with Number 10 months in advance. We were now due to fly off to Martha's Vineyard late on the Friday – the second day of the forum.

I arrived at Warwick Business School with Dec on the Thursday afternoon. Outside was blazing sunshine and blue skies. Inside the atmosphere was hot, dark and oppressive. Informal policy discussions were already under way. I sought out some of the key people to try to square off policy issues where I had an interest.

By the evening people were getting hungry, but there was no proper food available. My two protection officers said the local coppers knew a great Indian restaurant, and we escaped the cocoon and headed there. The owners had been tipped off that I was coming. As I walked in, the manager approached with his arms outstretched. 'Ah, Mr Prescott, welcome.'

I hadn't been mistaken for JP before. I was starting to feel in holi-day mood so I had a couple of Cobra beers with my curry and began to relax. Then Dec's phone rang. It was Labour's head of news. 'Can Jack do some media?'

'Why?'

'We've lost the Glasgow by-election.'

It was a sobering message. The SNP had won the rock-solid Labour seat, albeit by a short head. If we couldn't win there, we couldn't win anywhere. The opinion polls showed our worst ratings ever – worse even than under Michael Foot. Now it was translating into actual results.

It was a serious moment. Speculation about Gordon's position was going to become even more feverish.

Before leaving the next day to meet Alice at the airport I spoke to Mark and Dec and stressed the importance of keeping a lid on every-thing. Although I had the most serious misgivings about where the party was going under Gordon I still thought a leadership contest was not a good idea. I agreed some lines with Mark, essentially that while the Glasgow result was both disappointing and worrying, this was not the time for a period of internal discussion about the leadership. Nonetheless, I was flattered that the bookies were giving me the short-est odds to succeed Gordon – according to Sky News – and did not do enough actively to quash the speculation.

My close pal George Howarth had never been a fan of Gordon. I'd had to work hard for his signature on the nomination sheet. As a senior backbencher he had a better appreciation than I did of the desperation so many Labour MPs were feeling about their prospects at the election, whenever it might be called. Moreover they knew, and so did George, that although the government had been knocked sideways by the world financial meltdown, the party's decline had been triggered before that, by Gordon's fateful indecision at his first conference as leader. Unbeknown to me, George had been doing some canvassing of his own – for me.

Saturday's papers were full of stories that Gordon's future was uncertain, alongside rumours of 'Straw plotting . . .' In reality, I was 35,000 feet above the Atlantic and completely out of range. With press speculation mounting, Mark concocted a statement of support for Gordon, and put it out in my name. Its central line was that 'this is not the time for a summer of introspection'. Although this did not satisfy some media commentators – who simply asked 'what about autumn?' – the speculation about me ultimately subsided.

But the episode had significant consequences, both in the short and long term. The day after the NPF closed, David Miliband, perhaps jolted into action by all the speculation about me, penned an article for the *Guardian* that many saw as the precursor to a leadership bid. In the end it proved abortive, but a Rubicon had been crossed. A mood of suspicion and mistrust hung over the Cabinet, and from then on, Gordon's position was never secure.

'Ordinary people' is a term I try to avoid like the plague. It's patronizing. It reinforces the idea of a self-satisfied political elite who have disdain for their electors. In fifty years of knocking on the doors of total strangers and impertinently asking them to share their private opinions with me, I've yet to meet Mr and Mrs Ordinary.

Mrs Brown (this really was her name) lived on an average main road, in an average sort of terraced property in a respectable part of Blackburn. In her early fifties, she was married and worked as an administrative assistant.

In previous years she had said that she was a Labour voter. I knocked on her door one cold wet evening in early April 2007, just a week or so after Gordon Brown's final budget as Chancellor. Would she be voting Labour again, I asked?

'No,' came the emphatic reply. 'And I'll tell you why.'

She fetched some detailed calculations she'd already made. 'See, here. Your Mr Brown is abolishing the 10p tax rate. I'm going to be worse off. Why's he doing it?'

I made notes about her complaint in my little red book. Her

numbers clearly stacked up. When I got home I sent a handwritten letter to Gordon about what Mrs Brown had told me, asking for his early reply.

Mrs Brown was well ahead of 'public opinion' on the issue, and certainly of the press. This was yet another issue on a slow burn nationally, to which my constituents had alerted me.

From early 2008 there was mounting concern about the damage the 10p cut was doing to us. Alistair Darling had understood how toxic it was as soon as he'd taken over as Chancellor. But, as he records, he too was met with stone-walling from Gordon. After further months of indecision, Alistair got agreement from Gordon to announce a 'solution' – a tax rebate of £120 a year for everyone earning less than £40,000, at a cost of an eye-watering £2.7bn. This concession evened matters up for most of the original losers; but only partially compensated those whose losses were more than that. Mrs Brown had a right to be cross.

On Friday 29 August 2008 (the first anniversary of the POA's one-day strike – a date forever fixed in my mind, if no one else's) the *Guardian* led with a long interview with Alistair Darling. He warned that the economy was facing its worst crisis for sixty years; the downturn would be 'more profound and long-lasting' than many thought. When I read this I was surprised by the strength of Alistair's message. I'd known and admired him for years. He was as straight as a die – and a canny Edinburgh lawyer who chose his words with care. I'd never known him exaggerate and, as events were to show, he was terrifyingly accurate in his predictions.

However, Gordon – and especially his staff – decided to work Alistair over. It was disgraceful. The sensible approach would have been for Number 10 to have supported Alistair – since all he said was true – and make a merit of his frankness, but the weekend papers were full of 'Brown fury' stories, adding to the leitmotif of disorder and disunity at the heart of government.

That Sunday I filled the ministerial slot on *The Andrew Marr Show*, with Emily Maitlis as Marr's stand-in. I supported what Alistair had said, did body-swerves around the disobliging Number 10 comment, and added that there would be no leadership challenge to Gordon. Towards the end of the interview, I described Gordon and Alistair as the 'experienced pilot and co-pilot', in contrast to David Cameron and George Osborne 'who've had no experience of flying a large plane whatever'.[8]

Fortunately, Ms Maitlis moved on to my own predictions for the economy rather than asking how much confidence the passengers could have if the pilot and the co-pilot were arguing so volubly.

The irony is that this metaphor was not as misplaced as it might have appeared. I can think of no other contemporary politicians, and few in history, who would have done better than Gordon and Alistair in piloting Britain through what was the worst financial crisis not for sixty years, but at least eighty.

Gordon's many great qualities, which had made him such a towering figure in British politics, came to the fore as the Lehman Brothers collapse wreaked severe collateral damage on Britain's financial services, and two of our biggest banks, RBS and HBOS, were nearly bankrupted. He deployed those talents brilliantly at the April 2009 G20 summit which he chaired – and which he persuaded to take practical measures to avert an even greater catastrophe for the world.

Alistair complemented Gordon. He too had had immense experience, throughout his ministerial career, of dealing with difficult economic issues; with his wonderfully droll sense of humour, and no overpowering ego in the way, he was deft at handling a stroppy House of Commons or an even stroppier interviewer on *Today*.

Despite all the difficulties in their relationship, the net effect of the decisions which Alistair and Gordon made to help Britain weather the economic storm was good, not bad. But their effect would have been very much better, and public support for them on a different planet, if Gordon had not reacted so intemperately to Alistair's 'sixty years' observation, if he had not been in denial for so long over the 10p tax and the need to make spending cuts. Left to himself, Alistair would have been more cautious than Gordon (so would I); even so, at this distance after the 2010 election – a time when we had positive growth and falling unemployment – the Darling–Brown record for economic management is beginning to look significantly more credible when set against the dismal performance of the Coalition.*

The reasons why Gordon so frequently buried his head in the sand are complex. But the people he surrounded himself with, the disreputable conspirators at court who fed his suspicious tendencies and gradually separated him from the senior people in his Cabinet, always made things worse. How and why such an otherwise charming, witty, intelligent man (and one who never did me any harm) could have allowed this is quite beyond my analytical skills.

In October 2008, as the financial crisis deepened, and the government's position seemed to become ever more precarious, Gordon made one of the best decisions of his premiership – to bring Peter Mandelson into his administration, as Business Secretary. It was unexpected, given Peter's very close association with Tony, and shrewd. Peter was always a first-class departmental minister, on top of his brief, held in respect by his officials, and an excellent strategist. No one round the Cabinet table thought that his appointment presaged victory at the polls, but there was relief that he had joined us, not least in anticipation of some rapprochement between the two wings of the party.

Our poll ratings did improve in the latter part of 2008 and early 2009, with the Tories' lead down to single figures. In early April 2009, for example, there was just seven percentage points between us – sufficient to give us all hope.

---

* The current budget deficit was just 0.6 per cent on the eve of the crisis. The Tories supported Labour's spending plans until after Lehman Brothers collapsed. The deficit increased to around 11 per cent primarily due to collapsing tax revenues – which were narrowly focused on finance – and emergency spending measures which prevented a depression.

But a month later, on 8 May, details of MPs' expenses were published by the *Daily Telegraph*, which led directly to Michael Martin's resignation as Speaker less than two weeks later, and to a crisis which was to envelop the whole of the political class. There were miscreants in all the parties, but it was bound to hit the party of government the worst.

It is impossible to exaggerate the pall which fell over Westminster when the MPs' expenses scandal broke. Regardless of whether they had kept to the rules (and the great majority had), everyone felt tainted; it dominated all conversation. We had to clean the system up, very quickly. As the Cabinet minister with responsibility for constitutional issues, I chaired all-party talks in the airless 'Large Ministerial Conference Room', directly under the Commons Chamber, to reach agreement on the establishment of the Independent Parliamentary Standards Authority, and then handled the legislation. (Since then six MPs and peers have been sentenced to imprisonment for fraud.)

The local elections had been delayed a month, to coincide with the Euro elections on 4 June. In the two days before polling, first Jacqui Smith, Home Secretary, then Hazel Blears, Communities Secretary, announced their resignations from Cabinet.

The results on the day were dire. We lost control of all the shire county councils we had previously held. In the Euro elections we came third, behind UKIP, with the lowest share of the popular vote we had ever received, 15.7 per cent, fewer than one vote in six.

As the polls closed, news came in of James Purnell's resignation as Work and Pensions Secretary, which he coupled with a call for Gordon to go. James was a very talented minister, as well as being a straight-forwardly nice guy. His departure was a serious blow to the government.

The next day Gordon did what Tony had done three years before to try to change the script after dismal local elections – he carried out an immediate and wide-ranging reshuffle, designed to make him look strong and in charge. Six Cabinet positions changed hands, and plenty more junior ministers. Caroline Flint and Jane Kennedy both resigned in protest at Gordon's leadership. David Cameron's comment at the time that Gordon and his critics in the party were locked in 'a slow dance of political death' was exactly how it felt. He added, 'He can't seem to reshuffle his Cabinet but they can't seem to organize a coup.'[9] He was right about that too.

I talked frequently to other senior colleagues, in particular Alistair Darling and Harriet Harman, who had succeeded me as Leader of the House. We dearly prayed for divine intervention, but in its absence we continued to feel trapped into indecision. It was ever a case of 'ready to wound but afraid to strike'.

Whatever the exact arithmetic, all of us in the Labour Party believed that Rupert Murdoch had both the capacity to wound, and the will to strike. He also liked to back a winner. It had been clear to me that the *Sun* was not going to support Labour as it had in Tony's three elections, and was likely to revert to type, to give us the kind of kicking we – and I – had received in the 1992 election (and many elections before that). What I had not anticipated was the ruthless vulgarity with which that decision to switch sides would be announced.

News International customarily held court at the party conferences, throwing the best parties, and putting up its senior executives in the smartest hotels. Ed Balls and I had separately been invited to meet Rebekah Brooks, the *Sun*'s editor, in her suite in Brighton in the late afternoon, after Gordon's speech, which had been impressive – Gordon at his best. There, we were told what in fact we had already gleaned – that the following day the *Sun* would announce its support for the Conservatives.

The *Sun* was always a fair-weather friend to Labour (as all the other national papers have been – the *Guardian* included – with the single and honourable exception of the Mirror Group's papers). The Murdoch–Brooks decision was no surprise but, even by the distorted standards of our popular press, its handling was gratuitously nasty. News International paraded their pro-Tory posters on the backs of lorries up and down the Brighton seafront. Their timing was stupid. The *Sun* lost all the influence it might have had if it had kept its tinder dry until the last moment. It created great anger and contempt on the Labour side for everyone involved in this unpleasant decision. Gordon gained considerable sympathy within the party – though sympathy is not the emotion any leader seeks.

The desultory discussions amongst senior people in the government about Gordon's leadership continued during the autumn of 2009. In retrospect, they were therapy, not strategy. The Lib Dems were breathing down our necks. If we misplayed our hand, they could replace Labour as one of the country's two main parties. We'd seen how close to this brink we had come in the early eighties, and did not want to be the people who pushed the party over the edge this time.

By the turn of the year, with an election not more than four months later, the die would be cast. Most of us understood that, but two of our erstwhile Cabinet colleagues did not.

Patricia Hewitt had been a competent, if rather technocratic, member of the Cabinet, leaving the government when Tony did. Geoff Hoon was a friend, who'd been an effective Defence Secretary during my period as Foreign Secretary. Geoff had been badly treated by Tony in his last reshuffle. He'd been given a subsidiary Cabinet post as Europe minister and quasi-deputy to Margaret Beckett – which had placed him in a nigh-impossible position. He'd actively supported Gordon for the leadership, and became chief whip, but he'd (correctly) felt undermined in that job by his ostensible deputy, Nick Brown, who'd been hard-wired to Gordon forever. He was moved to Transport in October 2008, before leaving the Cabinet altogether in Gordon's post-Euro elections reshuffle.

The House came back after the Christmas break earlier than usual, on Tuesday 5 January 2010. That evening George Howarth came up to me and told me he'd heard that something was afoot, but had no more details to give me. I then bumped into Geoff, and we had a conversation about our impending evidence sessions before the newly established Iraq Inquiry. He told me of his frustration over getting proper access to all his papers in the Ministry of Defence. Whilst he had every opportunity to tell me of his and Patricia's plans, he said not a word. We parted.

The following morning it became clear that something was up. I called Mark and Dec into my office and said that while I didn't know what was going to happen, something was. Heading across to Parliament for Prime Minister's Questions, I told Mark to text me if any news broke. It did. Just as I was going into the Chamber my phone buzzed with an update about a letter from Geoff and Patricia, to be released imminently, urging colleagues to join them in declaring that enough was enough. Incredibly, this unlikely duo had launched an attempted coup but failed to arrange for any infantry (or other generals) to follow them.

As it happened, I was due to speak to Labour's Parliamentary Committee, which met in the prime minister's room behind the Speaker's Chair every Wednesday immediately after PMQs. As was my tendency when in the midst of a political meltdown, I got on with business as usual, while all around me people were speculating wildly on what might happen next. I was in Gordon's room in the Commons, speaking to Labour's parliamentary leaders about pleural plaques (an emotive issue concerning asbestos-related industrial injuries) while outside the media were hammering on every conceivable door seeking ministers to pledge their allegiance – or otherwise – to the prime minister.

While Geoff and Patricia had badly misjudged things, the affair had to be a wake-up call for Gordon. This time, just a few months before the election, he really had to listen. Leaving the Parliamentary Committee, I suggested that Harriet Harman and I should get together as quickly as possible with others to discuss how we could use the

Hoon–Hewitt affair as a way of persuading Gordon that things had to change.

Ducking requests from Gordon's staff, who had been hanging about outside the meeting, desperate to get us on air to support their boss, I went with Harriet to her room in the Commons – my old office as Leader of the House – where we were joined by Alan Johnson.

The Number 10 people – including Joe Irvin, the prime minister's political secretary – were now outside, along with Mark Davies who was doing his best, via text, to keep me up to date with developments. One of these was a call from David Miliband's team urging me not to go on television yet: 'We've marched the troops up the hill before, we can't let them down again' was the gist of the message delivered to Mark. When he relayed this to me as Harriet and I finished our meeting with Alan, my reaction was, 'regicide is not the answer'.

Harriet and I agreed that we should simply turn up in Downing Street, together, and insist that we saw Gordon, together. We bundled into my police van. The detectives took us in the back door, away from the media scrum at the front.

What happened next said a great deal about Gordon's style as prime minister. First we were headed off by Sue Nye, his gatekeeper, who insisted, ludicrously, that while Harriet had a scheduled meeting with Gordon, it did not include me. We could see Gordon separately, but not together. Harriet was clear – she wanted me to attend. Sue was equally, and robustly, clear: she didn't want me to see Gordon with Harriet. I have heard since the black fedora I was wearing sparked jokes that I was a hit man there to take Gordon out. But Harriet and I had already agreed it was too late for that. We simply wanted to spell out to Gordon how he had to change his ways if he was to avoid the most awful legacy of any post-war prime minister.

Farcically, we could see Gordon in the open-plan office, laughing and joking with colleagues as he prepared to go out on a visit to thank workers for clearing up London streets after a very heavy snowfall.

Eventually, Harriet and I did go in to see Gordon together. Harriet's central point to Gordon was that if he wanted to have any chance of winning the election, he had to start leading a team. She told him that teamwork was fatally undermined when his 'people' briefed against colleagues, including her. He had to put a stop to it.

Gordon responded with the usual 'little boy lost' look that he deployed for complaints like this, lamely claiming that he knew nothing.

I backed her up, telling him that he had to widen the political circle involved in election planning. He agreed he would.

We took him at his word, slipped out of Downing Street by a side door. I then did some interviews, body swerving when asked to explain why I'd been silent for some hours.

The Hoon–Hewitt attempted coup, and its aftermath, did have the paradoxical effect of ending all speculation about the leadership. The election was imminent. We were now, to coin a phrase, all in it together.

Before then, I had to salvage what I could from the constitutional reform programme which Gordon had announced with such a fanfare just thirty months earlier. The Constitutional Reform and Governance Act 2010, passed in the final hours of the parliament, contained some worthy measures – the Dacre Review, a proposal for reducing the time for the publication of official records from thirty to twenty years and parliamentary powers over the ratification of treaties, among them – but it was paltry stuff when compared to what had been promised. Key proposals, for example, to strengthen Parliament's supervision of the intelligence agencies, and to lay down in statute law that only the Commons could authorize military action – both of which I had long pursued – were caught up in the sort of interdepartmental wrangling that only a prime minister could resolve. But Gordon was too exhausted, too weakened by then.

Separately, progress had been made on Lords Reform – so much so that we were ready to publish the key clauses of a draft bill. But Gordon kept havering. He got spooked by the politburo of the Church of England, who were worried about the (necessary) reduction in the number of Anglican bishops in the Lords which was an inevitable consequence of the reform. I assured him that the Church's concerns were easily managed. But he continued to delay until it was too late.

During the election campaign, most of us simply held our breath – we needed to.

On the morning of 28 April I was driven off to meet Gordon in a windswept car park at the back of the Oldham Athletic football ground, to travel on together to a couple of events in Oldham, before he went on to Rochdale, and then spent the rest of the day preparing for the third of the leaders' televised debates, being broadcast from Birmingham.

After the first event – a discussion session which he handled well – Gordon and I got back into his car to move to the second event, the CCTV control room for the town. As the car moved off, the detective in the front spotted that Gordon was still wearing the radio microphone which a TV crew had fixed to his lapel. He took it off, and passed it to me. I took the whole thing to bits just to make sure that it couldn't work in any circumstances.

After the excitements of the CCTV control room we parted – me to Blackburn, he to Rochdale. Within the hour the whole country heard about his unguarded remarks after his encounter with Mrs Duffy, broadcast for posterity on another radio microphone which he'd forgotten to remove. I simply couldn't believe that he had done it again. Gordon did his best to repair the damage with Mrs Duffy (and, remarkably, Labour's excellent candidate in Rochdale, Simon Danczuk, won the seat from the Liberal Democrats); he got through the TV debate in one piece, though he looked, as he was, wrung out.

The remainder of the campaign for me was split between Blackburn and campaigning around the country for candidates in marginal seats – complete with soapbox. It always works, generating interest and publicity, raising the morale of party workers – and for a very simple reason. It's completely authentic. There's no 'spin' associated with a politician standing on a box, taking questions from all-comers. Provided people believe that they are being taken seriously (and, however eccentric their questions may be, treating them all with respect is imperative) they will stay, and listen – and perhaps be persuaded in the right direction.

In Blackburn, the soapbox, and the energy of a brilliant party built up over three decades, certainly worked. Phil Riley, who pursues all his objectives with utter single-mindedness, had taken over as agent from Bill Taylor. En route for marginal seats in our area David Miliband came along to one of our Sunday morning organization meetings and gave a great impromptu speech.

The result for me was wonderful. My local party had done me proud yet again. This time there was a swing to Labour – of 1.1 per cent – and the turnout was up too.

Nationally, the news was nothing like as good and many hardworking Labour MPs had been defeated; but when the final tally came through, I decided that the Almighty must have a party card after all. The Conservatives could not muster a majority; the breakthrough by the Liberal Democrats that we had all been fearing fizzled out (they lost five seats). We lost 91, taking us down to 258, but we'd be able to run an effective opposition on those numbers. The Conservatives had done so in the outgoing parliament on just under 200 seats.

Our national defeat was no surprise. It had been inevitable for at least two years. In a democracy parties have to lose sometimes. We'd had a good run.

The office had told me that I'd need to be back in London by lunchtime on Friday, to be ready to go to the Palace to hand back the Great Seal of Office, fully kitted out in my morning suit with the correct waistcoat. (After my first swearing-in, as a novice Home Secretary back in 1997, one of the staff at Buckingham Palace had taken me aside. 'Thank you very much, Home Secretary, for coming today. But there is just one thing you might wish to note. Generally speaking' – looking

at my midriff, emphasizing every syllable – 'grey waistcoats are for wed-
dings, or Ascot, only.')

On the Friday I was indeed back in London, morning suit (and black
waistcoat) at the ready.

It was a long wait.

TWENTY-TWO

The Tights Come Off

The tights came back from the office, neatly folded on a hanger, together with the rest of the Lord High Chancellor's official court dress. They were mine to keep. If my successor Kenneth Clarke had been a standard size, I could have passed them down, saving the public purse. But that's not Ken. So the full kit was carefully stowed in a liberally mothballed suit bag in the wardrobe outside my study: a family heirloom.

Along with the tights came my P60. Both were a week later than expected. I had thought that my last Cabinet would be in April, just before Parliament was dissolved and we all dispersed to fight the campaign. I was wrong about that, too.

The election had taken place on a Thursday, as usual. Throughout the weekend that followed, Gordon, Peter Mandelson and Transport Secretary Andrew (Lord) Adonis had been locked in discussion with Nick Clegg to see whether a deal to form a coalition with the Liberal Democrats was remotely possible. Gordon brought his Cabinet together at 6 p.m. on Monday 10 May, to report on progress. This 'Political Cabinet' was preceded by a short official Cabinet, at which Alistair Darling briefed us – ruefully – on the latest episode of the euro crisis, observing that there were some 'fundamental problems with a single currency without a political union'.

There has always been a strong element of New Labour hankering after a formal alliance or even a merger with the Liberal Democrats. They saw the inconclusive election result as their best chance in a generation. These folk, including Peter and Andrew (who'd been in the SDP), were emotionally at ease with the Lib Dems, and shared with them an enthusiasm for 'more Europe'. It wasn't my bag. It wasn't really Gordon's either, but he was anxious to hang on to power if he possibly could. In his opening remarks to Cabinet, Gordon went through the dangers to the country, and the party, if the Tories were to take power, whether in a coalition or as a minority government, claiming that '15 million people had voted for a progressive majority'. He hadn't quite come to terms with the fact that we had lost the election, comprehensively, even if we'd done a lot better than most of us had feared.

I'd also spent the weekend coming to a clear view that a coalition with the Liberal Democrats simply wouldn't work, which I had told Gordon in a phone conversation on the Sunday. It was partly a matter of political psychology. Although I got on well enough with some senior Liberal Democrats (notably Ming Campbell and Alan Beith), I'd seen too much of how they operated institutionally to be able to trust them as a party. I might just have swallowed hard, and put aside those reservations, if the arithmetic had been favourable, but it wasn't. Even with the Lib Dems, we'd still be eleven seats short of a bare overall majority in the Commons. I'd witnessed the hand-to-mouth existence of the 1974–9 Labour government, the constant crises, the grubby deals (with the Lib Dems, and the other minority parties), the grotesque spectacle of nearly dead Labour MPs having to be brought into Speaker's Court in ambulances so that their vote could be counted – and that was with sixty more seats than we'd won now.

Since I thought the talks with the Lib Dems would run into the ground at some stage anyway, I was careful not to say too much about my profound reservations in front of the rest of the Cabinet.

Gordon called me after the Cabinet, and asked me to think overnight about working with the Lib Dems. I did, but came to the same conclusion.

On Tuesday, Sadiq Khan, Andy Burnham and Bob Ainsworth gathered in my Commons room. We were all of one mind. A Lib-Lab coalition would not work. For the avoidance of doubt, I sent Gordon a detailed note setting out my view that a coalition with the Lib Dems would be doomed – on grounds of legitimacy, stability and the management of the economy and public finances. I took issue with the fanciful notion of a 'progressive alliance' saying that I thought it 'arrogant nonsense'. 'There was no "Progressive Alliance" on the ballot paper. Many of those who voted Lib Dem would have done so tactically to stop Labour, and probably despite, not because of, the Lib Dems' policy offer.'

By the time he received it, Gordon had announced that he would stand down as leader, which though a Lib Dem precondition, could only add to the instability of any arrangement with them, and provoke scorn from the electorate that they were being foisted off with a new prime minister who had been untested at the election.

In mid-afternoon I drafted a formal press statement for use in the unlikely event that a coalition deal was cooked up. In it, I said that I wished the arrangement well, but I did not want to be part of it, and I'd therefore 'told the prime minister that I wished to stand down from the Cabinet'.

It was never needed. Lib-Lab talks collapsed. At 7.20 p.m. on Tuesday 11 May Gordon announced that he was resigning as prime minister, and had recommended that the Queen invite David Cameron to form an administration. Cameron's deal with the Lib Dems was finalized overnight.

It was the end of thirteen years of Labour government.

I like work. For thirteen years I'd been on the conveyor belt of a decision-making machine, getting through the contents of at least one red box a night. Each box would contain six inches of detailed papers on policy proposals, draft memoranda in my name for Cabinet Committee, draft speeches, intelligence reports, security authorizations, reports on prison incidents, and lots of correspondence to sign. Since

Rule One of political life is survival, and every box might have contained an unexploded bomb, I'd paid careful attention to the small print of everything that was put in front of me.

Now there were no more red boxes. Not only that, but no more early mornings, days and evenings packed with engagements, meetings, phone calls, the diet of all senior ministers; no more weekends and holidays which were not weekends or holidays.

In a democratic society, we need single-minded journalists able relentlessly to pursue wrongdoing; we occasionally need formal inquiries to do so even more thoroughly. Few of those who forensically examine any particular sequence of events, however, can fully comprehend just how many different decisions, on widely different matters, senior ministers have to make during any eighteen-hour day.

This is not an excuse for unacceptable standards, which do sometimes occur, but it is an explanation about the daily pressure of events, the challenge of having to keep any number of balls in the air and not drop one, the imperative of having to shift one's concentration from long-term policy to a crisis requiring an immediate response, to a press story which could go wrong, to a statement in the Commons, and a tough interview on the radio, more or less all at the same time. I had a wonderful time as a minister (some days excepted). It was an astonishing privilege to serve in a government from its start to its finish. I was relieved to discover I could do it. But the only people available to do these jobs are human beings, with families, and with failings and infelicities too.

Whilst there were no more red boxes, the glide path to the opposition benches was perhaps smoother for me than for many of my colleagues. I had had a good innings, and opposition carried no fear for me. After all, I'd spent my first eighteen years – a whole generation – on the opposition benches. I knew what to do.* I love the business of

---

* Only 25 per cent of the 2010 intake of Labour MPs had ever been in opposition before.

the Commons and get a buzz from the building itself; I love representing Blackburn. I looked forward to spending more time in the Commons, and in my constituency, seeing what difference I could still make. I also looked forward to having more time being 'normal', with Alice, my family and friends.

With Gordon's resignation, Harriet Harman became acting leader and I agreed to act as her deputy in the Commons. I enjoyed working with her, but I'd decided that after thirty years on the front bench, including twenty-three in Cabinet or Shadow Cabinet, I'd come off the front bench as soon as a new leader was installed.

That took six months – longer than would have been ideal. In the leadership election I voted for David Miliband, as did most members of the Blackburn Labour Party. I knew David much better than I knew the other main candidates. I'd worked with him when he had been Tony Blair's Head of Policy in Downing Street between 1997 and 2001, and I considered that he had done an excellent job as Foreign Secretary. (Andy Burnham was a fellow North West MP; I gave him my second preference, from regional solidarity.)

I had seen little of either Ed Balls or Ed Miliband when they had been on Gordon's staff – a product of the fact that Gordon and I had tended to work around each other. As Justice Secretary, I shared responsibility with Ed Balls for youth justice policy. This was not an arrangement of choice for me, but we co-operated well, and I found Ed a very straightforward and proficient minister.

Ed Miliband and I had few departmental interests in common – Energy and Climate Change and Justice are not natural partners. I liked Ed a lot, and enjoyed his sense of humour – including when it was at my expense. Ed had had the whole of Cabinet in hysterics in response to a rather laboured comment from me when Sir Tim Berners-Lee had paid us a visit. I had opined that meeting Sir Tim, the inventor of the world wide web, was 'like meeting the man who invented the wheel'. Quick as a flash, Ed had interjected, 'And what was *he* like, Jack?'

Ed Miliband had asked me whether I would support him for the

Leadership. I declined to do so, partly from natural loyalty to his brother David, and partly because I thought that David was ready for the gruelling, thankless job of Opposition Leader – the worst job in British politics – and that Ed was not. When Ed beat David by a whisker I worried for a while about whether he would cope. I'm not worried any more. After a hesitant start, Ed has found his voice. He's shown himself to be decisive and he's made some difficult moves well. He forced an end to the ludicrous and distracting rigmarole of annual Shadow Cabinet elections, replacing them with appointment by the leader; and his policy shifts, for example on immigration, show a determination to recognize that we got some things wrong when we were in government. The 2015 election is far from being in the bag. But we are much better placed than I had feared.

'Colin, where exactly are we going?' I asked as Secretary Powell and I walked briskly along the corridors of the UN building, down the escalator, and into the bright sunlight on First Avenue, during a lull in the 2004 UN General Assembly week.

'I haven't a clue. I'm following that guy with a thing in his ear. He's one of yours, isn't he? What are you doing, Jack?'

'I'm following the same guy with a thing in his ear.'

'Where are you taking us?' I asked the British detective we were both following.

'We thought you and Secretary Powell knew, sir. So we're' – gesturing to the other ten security guys who had surrounded us – 'sort of following you, from the front, sir. You were both due at the Security Council family photo, but you marched out with such purpose we all thought you knew were you were going.'

'Not a chance,' I muttered. 'I've been comprehensively de-skilled.'

For nearly thirteen and a half years I was a 'principal' in the care of a squad of close-protection officers. They were professional, discreet, good-humoured, and they kept my family and me safe, which was the point. But it was an odd existence. This was not some special chauffeur service, to turn on and off at a whim. I never went out of the house without a police officer walking alongside me – or if I was in company, a few paces behind. The only exception was when Alice and I went for walks in the countryside – though we always spelt out our route in advance, and took a police radio with us.

One other reason why the transition from government to opposition was easier for me was that I still had protection for three months after the election. It finished the day after our daughter Charlotte's wedding on the last day of July 2010.

Those three months gave me time to reorient myself into the real world. For thirteen years I'd not been on a bus, I'd travelled on the Tube only to the occasional Rovers' away game, I hadn't owned a car, and I had barely driven one. I'm an incorrigible jaywalker, with only one ear that works. For thirteen years I had had a bloke with a thing in his ear to tell me when it was safe to cross the road. Now I was off the lead, on my own.

I bought a car. Next was driving the thing. On a couple of trips up and back to the constituency, one of the detectives, with advanced driving qualifications, came with me. For the next trip, the detectives went in their car behind. A friend who wanted to see Blackburn took a police radio and sat with me.

We did fine until the M42. I sailed past the slip road, and was on the way to Worcester. 'Next exit, boss, into the service station. We can turn round there. You need a break anyway.'

As we four were munching our paninis a man in a suit made a bee-line for me.

'Black saloon, sir? I think you'll find it's just rolled down the car park, and into another vehicle.'

There we found my nice shiny saloon nestling into the rear bumper of a large Vauxhall. Its two occupants, Australian tourists who'd just spent twenty-four hours on their flight here, looked incredulous that there could be drivers that stupid, especially as this particular stupid driver had two plain-clothes policemen with him – a source of further incredulity.

Happily, no damage was done. I made a grovelling apology, exhanged details, and was then given very strict instructions about the importance of applying the handbrake properly. 'You're not in the back of one of our cars, any more, sir.' Ah, but I still thought I was . . .

. . . I was dozing gently, half awake, half in another world. I felt for the seat belt. It wasn't in its usual position. I guessed it was time for *The Archers* – I'd ask the detective in front of me to turn on Radio 4, as he was programmed to do. Luckily I stirred from my torpor just in time. I was no longer in the rear seat of a police vehicle. The man in front was not a detective but a fellow passenger. I was on the 159 bus.

At least that day it was the 159. A week later I was sat on a bus congratulating myself on my new-found bus-riding skills. I looked out of the window in a smug sort of way. The street did not look right. Whichever bus I was on it wasn't the 159. It did have a '1' in its number, but with buses there's no room even for minor errors; and the 133 does NOT go to the Palace of Westminster. A nice disembodied lady told me that the next stop was Kennington Underground station. I jumped off, jay-ran across the road, flicked my old-crocks' card (aka Freedom Pass) at the barrier, and was off by Tube. Miraculously I wasn't late.

The errors continued for some months. 'Avril, can you tell me where the nearest Tube station is, please?' I asked Avril Riddell (Peter's wife) as we were leaving the *Economist* party in late September. She led me there. I spotted an escalator and was heading down it when Avril caught up with me. 'No, Jack, this isn't the way for you. This is the Piccadilly Line to Heathrow. You live on the Northern Line, going south. This way.'

I finally got myself re-skilled, and now enjoy my new freedom, the ability to be normal. Thanks to Ken Livingstone (for it was he), buses and rail services improved beyond recognition whilst I was locked up with policemen.

I have to keep my wits about me; there is the occasional difficult encounter, usually over Iraq, and usually accompanied by shouts of 'war criminal'. But these are far outweighed by the scores of people who simply want a chat. Occasionally I even receive back-handed endorsements for my work as a minister.

''Ere Jack!' shouted a large, fifty-ish South London geezer in beige shorts and a beer belly, from the pavement outside our local pub. 'I need to talk to you.' There followed a stream of the most disgusting invective about the judiciary (many of whom he knew by name), until his friend cut in. 'Shut up, Tony, this Jack 'ere wasn't bad when I was inside.'

When I first started reading about the 1945–51 Labour government I couldn't understand why Attlee had felt impelled to call the 1951 general election even though he still commanded a majority of six. The usual explanation given was that he and his government were simply tired out.

I understand that fully now. None of us who served in the 1997–2010 administrations had been under anything like the constant pressure which Attlee and his senior colleagues had experienced. They had been in office not for six years, but eleven, through the wartime coalition, and had then faced the most excruciating decisions about how to build a welfare state and an economy in a country which had been fatally weakened by the war.

But still, we had been under pressure, and we were human. By 2010 New Labour had run its course. Many of us were tired physically and our ideas were tired, too. Over time in government, the options narrow, the excuses become threadbare, the disaffection from the disappointed and the never-appointed mounts. Of course, I would have given my right arm for a victory; but it was never to be. We needed a spell in opposition to renew ourselves and our ideas.

Changing the weather from the opposition benches is more difficult, but it can be done. I thought that with my experience, and my affection for the place, I might be able to make a difference – and maybe show younger colleagues that opposition can be a creative time, that the cockpit of the Commons can be used to good effect wherever one sits.

The Conservative MP for Shipley, Philip Davies, for instance, had lobbied the Labour government astutely on law-and-order issues. On our side, Chris Mullin was an excellent minister, who worked for me in the Foreign Office, but Chris would probably argue himself that he achieved as much when out of office as when in: as a dogged campaigner on issues like justice for the Birmingham Six, and as a member, and then chairman, of the Home Affairs Select Committee. His judgement – always independent, always worth listening to and usually right – had a great influence on the framing and implementation of policy when I was Home Secretary.

In my last ministerial post as Justice Secretary I'd made many decisions about many things; but I'd also spent three years ensuring that the government took no decision in response to a judgement by the European Court of Human Rights that the UK's ban on convicted prisoners being able to vote was unlawful. I'd kicked the issue into touch, first with one inconclusive public consultation, then with a second. I am a strong supporter of the European Convention on Human Rights. I introduced the Human Rights Bill into the Commons. But I felt that the European Court had overreached themselves here. The Court was there to ensure basic human rights across Europe, fair trials, no torture, and so on. It was not there to tell elected national parliaments what they could and could not do, about individuals' civic rights when they broke the law. David Davis, former Shadow Home Secretary, suggested that he and I forge an alliance on the issue. I readily agreed. We secured a full day's debate on the floor of the Commons from the new Backbench Committee.* Our cross-party motion was carried by 234 votes to 22 –

---

* The Backbench Committee is an important innovation, brought in by the Coalition government to implement one of the key recommendations of the select committee chaired by Tony Wright MP in the months before the 2010 election, which had been established to make improvements to the working of the Commons in the light of the expenses scandal. The first Business Committee to be established by the House, it provides an opportunity for backbench MPs to bring forward debates of their choice. 'Second Special Report: Work of the Committee in Session 2010–12 – Backbench Business Committee', 26 April 2012.

a warning to the government that they would find it impossible to push through a change in our law for which there was no popular demand whatever. David and I went to Strasbourg in November 2011 to talk to the president of the Court about our concerns. My successor, Ken Clarke (though much keener on all institutions European than David or me), has weighed in. The message is gradually getting through to the Court, and its enthusiasts, that it must return to the important but limited purposes for which it was established, and not set itself up as a supra-national Supreme Court for which it has no authority.

Our system of parliamentary democracy is far from perfect, but one of its great strengths is the individual constituency base; one geographical area, one MP.* The executive is then drawn directly from Parliament. There is an intensity in the relationship between the elector and the elected which cannot exist in any other system. It helps keep ministers' feet on the ground and ensures that policies in general are informed by the experiences of people in particular.

In early autumn 2010 I began to receive complaints about the car insurance premiums being demanded of drivers in my constituency with impeccable driving and claims records. They were suddenly facing increases of 50–100 per cent in a single year. These complaints came to me almost incidentally, as a residents' meeting was winding down, or during one of my soapbox sessions. I'd had similar mutterings about NHS dental provision some years before, and had managed to resolve that. I reckoned I needed to take concerted action on this front too.

With my ever-assiduous Commons researcher, Dan Sleat, I started digging. The deeper we went, the murkier the story became. Initially the insurers told me that the high premiums in my constituency were all down to fraud – the so-called 'cash for crash' phenomenon, by which criminals fake accidents.

---

* The word 'Commons' comes from the French 'communes'.

However, the numbers didn't add up; fraud might be a factor, but it couldn't be the principal explanation. And how about my close friend, and Blackburn Labour Party secretary, Phil Riley? He'd been driving his car in Preston, when the car behind had run into him. Phil's car suffered only minor damage; Phil was not injured at all. The other driver quickly paid up for Phil's car. But Phil was pestered for over a year to make claims for 'whiplash', against the other driver's insurer, with promises of £3,000-plus in damages.

I asked the Association of British Insurers to lay on a confidential meeting for me with the chief executives of two large motor insurers. 'Who passed on Phil Riley's personal details?' I asked.

There was a silence. Then one of the chief executives replied, 'Mr Straw, we did. This is the insurance industry's dirty secret. We sell the information, and get a large "referral" fee back.'

When I asked how it could possibly be in the interests of motor insurers to sell information that was bound to lead to higher claims and costs, I was told that it was not in the interests of motor insurers generally, but 'in a dysfunctional system, everyone behaves badly. Everyone is gaming the system, to worst their competitor.'

Over the following months I built up a big dossier. I got some valuable publicity for my findings from a piece in *The Times* in June 2011,[*] and in September that year I brought in a Ten-Minute Rule bill.[†] The government (who are not to blame for this situation – it happened under our watch) agreed, after some hesitation, to abolish referral fees, and cut the maximum legal fees that can be claimed. They've started to look at my proposals to make it far more difficult to claim for 'whiplash' in any circumstances. And the campaign to end insurers' discriminatory practice of basing premiums on postcodes, another issue

---

[*] *The Times*, 27 June 2011: 'Dirty secret that drives up motor insurance; Companies are selling drivers' details to claims firms exploiting the no-win, no-fee system.'

[†] Motor Insurance Regulation Bill. First reading on 13 September 2012.

in many areas of the north-west, continues. I reckon I'll get there in the end. If I'd still been a minister I'd like to think that I would have sorted this out despite the other pressures; but being a backbencher has made the pursuit of truly dodgy practices in the motor insurance industry that much simpler.

I've got stuck into campaigning for investment in the local railway system, exposing the way property companies are abusing the planning system to overcome the restrictions on out-of-town developments,[1] working to get new industrial investment into Blackburn, and now, following Blackburn Rovers' takeover by an Indian firm of poultry producers, looking at the governance of professional football in England.

I also retain a strong interest in Turkey and Iran in particular, chairing the Anglo-Turkish Tatlidil forum, and the Iran APPG – which in the current climate has proved a vital UK–Iranian channel.

The day after he'd resigned as prime minister, Gordon sent me a two-page handwritten letter in which he was very generous about my contribution as a minister. Given everything else he'd had to cope with, I thought the fact that he'd found the time and the energy to write this (and no doubt similar letters to others) spoke highly of him. I responded expressing great appreciation for the remarkable contribution he had made as Chancellor and prime minister.

Tony and I had exchanged letters of equal generosity when he had left office three years before.

I meant what I said in both those letters, and I have no doubts that Gordon and Tony did too.

As with any intense relationships, conducted under the pressure of events and the spotlight of the media, my feelings about my colleagues swung around, especially my feelings for the men with the greatest power, the two prime ministers whom I served. I am sure theirs did about me. We all have complicated, sometimes contradictory, personalities. In the higher reaches of government the bad and the ugly parts, as well as the good, will all come hanging out.

In the two years which have elapsed since we left office, what's my assessment of Tony, and of Gordon, as prime ministers?

History will, I believe, be much kinder to Tony than the contemporary assessments suggest. His record is bound to be dominated by Iraq, but there is so much else to weigh in the balance. He is the most successful leader in the history of the Labour Party, winning three elections in succession, the last despite Iraq. On the European and international stage, he was able successfully to amplify Britain's influence, and – to a degree – its power. At home, he presided over a transformation of our education, health, law-and-order and transport services, which are now taken for granted. In 1997 just one in three youngsters was getting five or more good GCSEs; by 2010 it was three in four. Every school has had huge investment. In Blackburn, we have a University Centre offering high-quality degree courses from the University of Lancaster. After eighteen years of failed promises, the money was found for a brand-new hospital. That, along with other improvements, has led to a significant change in health outcomes. Crime was an issue on every street fifteen years ago. It still dominated my residents' meetings seven or eight years ago. Today at some of these meetings, there's little for the local police to answer, except on the perennial issues of parking and speeding.

As for transport – we've a new railway station in Blackburn. It's heaving. The services for the town still need investment, but nationally there's been an astonishing increase in the number of passengers, and freight carried.*

Tony also oversaw something of a constitutional revolution. His government devolved power to Scotland and Wales, introduced the Human Rights and Freedom of Information Acts and removed most of the hereditary peers from the House of Lords. Tony secured the enduring peace in Northern Ireland, was crucial in bringing the conflicts in

---

* Association of Train Operating Companies figures show that from 1997 to 2007 the number of rail journeys in the UK doubled.

Kosovo and Sierra Leone to successful conclusions, and was at the very forefront of the global fight against al-Qaeda after 9/11.

Above all, Tony was a good leader.

History's verdict on Gordon is likely to be less positive. He helped lay the ground for much of the social reform of Tony's premiership. His commitment to making our society fairer is profound. He came into his own at the G20 London Summit in April 2009, giving international leadership during the global financial crisis. Yet the truth we in his Cabinet had to face – as I think he did himself in the watches of the night – was that there is no necessary connection between an obsessive desire for a job and an ability to do that job. Many of us thought he would make a good prime minister. He certainly did himself. And in many ways he was good. But overall, he struggled with the burden of that office: he found the imperative of swift, clear decision-taking too difficult, he was not skilled enough at managing personal relationships, and he often resorted to behaviour that was simply unacceptable.

There is, however, a question above and beyond the verdicts on these two individuals. Can anyone do the job of prime minister, and emerge in one piece? The answer is yes, just, but only if we recognize one central flaw of our current constitutional arrangements: prime ministers have too much power, for their own good, as well as the country's.

When Gordon gave his landmark statement on constitutional reform just a few days after his appointment as prime minister, he majored on the exercise of 'authority in the name of the monarchy without the people and their elected representatives being consulted', and made proposals to remove the use of the royal prerogative from twelve areas of our national life.[2] However, he left untouched the most potent example of the royal prerogative – the powers of a modern prime minister. There were no proposals then to modify this power. There should have been. We need a Cabinet Government Act, to put into law the powers and duties that 'the people and their elected representatives' believe should be exercised by the prime minister, and by his or her Cabinet.

I held two of the Great Offices of State and was also Lord Chancellor, but I was never Chancellor nor prime minister. So some might dismiss what follows as a view through a distorted prism. I hope and believe that it is not.

In all three major offices I held, what I could and couldn't do was heavily constrained by law: by statute, and by the active approach of our senior courts to the judicial review of executive decisions.* There is no such legal framework for the prime minister and Cabinet. So little does the prime minister of the day, or his staff, have to think about legal constraints, that there is no legal counsel to the prime minister.†

Defenders of the current arrangement will claim that its very flexibility, the absence of powers and duties to tie down the prime minister, gives it strength. They will say that other 'Westminster' governments, typically in the Commonwealth, have little or no legislative base for their prime ministers and Cabinets either. But the claim that it's always been done this way, and that other Commonwealth countries have followed our example, does not answer the question of whether or not we need reform now. I think it is long overdue.

Tony's reputation has suffered because he used informal, 'sofa government' methods of decision-making, rather than ensuring that Cabinet (and its Committees) were proper, formal bodies where collective decisions were made. The criticism is justified. Look at Iraq.

I was fully involved in the decisions over Iraq, made informally and formally. Because Tony had agreed that any decision to take military action would have to go to the Commons, there had to be a high degree

---

* There had been a long period when part of the work of the Home Secretary and the Foreign Secretary in overseeing our intelligence and security agencies was beyond any legal control whatever. That changed in the eighties and nineties. These agencies, and their responsible Secretary of State, are now subject to detailed legal constraints, and rightly so.

† This is a defect that Daniel Bethlehem, outgoing Legal Adviser to the Foreign Office, has proposed must urgently be put right: BBC Radio 4, *Law in Action*, 5 June 2012.

of involvement by Cabinet (and the Parliamentary Labour Party) in the final decision. The end point of this decision chain was very formal indeed – a resolution of the House of Commons. But it would have been far better – for Tony and his reputation, as well as for good government – if he, and I, and the Defence Secretary, had had to discuss progress with, and seek decisions from, a National Security Council, in turn reporting to Cabinet – and on paper, not by way of oral briefing. I am absolutely clear that had these systems been in place, the substantive decisions on Iraq would have been the same.

I am also sure that Tony would have found proper process frustrating. It can be. Process can easily be parodied as unnecessary bureaucracy; but that's to miss its point. What proper process would have given Tony, in respect of Iraq, is much greater legitimacy for the actions he was proposing; and an absence of subsequent charges that there was some kind of subterfuge involved in what he (and by extension I) was doing.

More generally, proper process would have made for better, and often more radical, and certainly more sustainable reforms. Tony's justification for bypassing accepted procedures was that the reforms he wanted would have been blocked. I know of no evidence for this. Rather, fewer unnecessary errors would have occurred, because the decisions would have had to have been better thought through – not only by Number 10, but by headstrong ministers enjoying – for the time being – Number 10 support.

Tony was by no means the only prime minister to have used informal methods in place of proper Cabinet government. Clement Attlee kept the decision that Britain should develop an atomic bomb away from Cabinet, successfully concealing the £100 million to pay for the programme inside the Estimates.[3] Eden's decision to go to war over Suez was hidden from Cabinet until it was too late; Wilson (with Barbara Castle) tried to bounce Cabinet with a fait accompli over *In Place of Strife*; Ted Heath preferred to make decisions with Head of the Home Civil Service, William Armstrong, rather than with his Cabinet; and

Margaret Thatcher was famous for the patronizing way she treated many of her Cabinet colleagues, and made use of bilaterals rather than Cabinet for much of her work.

Apart from examples such as this, and his natural informality, Tony was much influenced by the stories of what had happened when Cabinets had been let off the leash. In 1951, Attlee's Cabinet had split (with Bevan and others resigning) when it had considered Chancellor Hugh Gaitskell's Budget proposals for health service charges. In the late sixties, Roy Jenkins, as Chancellor, had had to endure days of Cabinet debate about his plans for public spending cuts. Jim Callaghan and Denis Healey went through over twenty Cabinet subcommittee discussions before gaining approval for their strategy to handle the 1976 economic crisis.

What remains the case, however, is that the level of informality was greater under Tony than it had been in the past. Certainly there was a stream of papers to Cabinet Committees, but not to Cabinet, which was often reduced to briefing sessions based on oral presentations.

The irony is that had there been a Cabinet Committee on the Economy or National Economic Council, chaired by Tony, and with clear powers – including approval of Treasury proposals for the Budget and for public spending – he would have had significantly greater control over many of the decisions which Gordon kept from him until the last minute (not least because he was unwilling or unable to make up his mind until the last minute).

The Treasury and the Chancellor gain even more from the absence of proper statutory arrangements for the prime minister than does the prime minister himself. Take two examples: the acute issue of 10p tax, and the chronic matter of our balance of trade. If there had been a full Cabinet Committee discussion of the 10p tax proposal, with Department of Work and Pensions ministers and others able to challenge it, on an equal basis to the Chancellor, I doubt whether it would ever have got through. I am less clear what the outcome would have been of discussions on the big trade deficit we ran, but a full debate could have shifted Gordon's and the Treasury's opinions, leading to a much more proactive strategy, earlier on, to encourage our own manufacturers.

There are plenty of other examples where Gordon made and announced decisions costing hundreds of millions on what appeared to be his pet projects. In our time, Treasury dominance was also used to overrule a clear Cabinet consensus on a key social issue – alcohol abuse. During a Cabinet discussion in 2009 there was a majority in favour of minimum pricing. The discussion was terminated when Gordon declared that it was a matter for the Chancellor.

There will be much resistance to any proposal to have proper Cabinet-level discussion of key economic decisions. The bleeding stump of Budget secrecy and sole right of the Treasury to devise tax policy will be paraded. But Budget secrecy these days is no longer absolute and the principle (if there still is one) is blown apart by the stream of leaking and briefing that precedes any Budget, care of Number 10 and the Treasury itself.

Economic and Budget decisions continue to be made without proper resort to Cabinet. The best (and worst) recent illustration of this is the decision of Chancellor George Osborne in late June 2012 to cut the 3p fuel duty levy. Made without the knowledge of other Treasury ministers, and the Transport Secretary, and at a cost of £550 million, this capricious move highlights why no one individual should be allowed this degree of power. If Mr Osborne had been required by law to make his case to a National Economic Council, he would have had to show how and why this expenditure was justified, when set against his government's strategy.

Economic and Budget decisions aside, much of the informality of Tony's years as prime minister, and Gordon's (though he tried, in part, to use Cabinet better), has been corrected by the current Coalition government by necessity. There is now an operational National Security Council, a thoroughly welcome development, and the Cabinet Manual has been much strengthened.

But there are three fundamental objections to leaving the operation of Cabinet government, and the power of the prime minister, to non-statutory codes and manuals, and new custom and practice.

The first is that coalitions require a degree of formality that single-party governments do not. Governments with clear majorities have been the norm since the last war. That pattern is likely to continue, especially as the high point of Liberal Democrat support has now passed. The larger the majority, the greater the sense of power in Number 10, the more the need for constraints on the exercise of that power – ones which cannot be bypassed at will.

The second is that it's time for prime ministers and governments to practise what they preach. Over the last forty years, ministers have expressed increasing exasperation with self-regulation in the professions, the City, the operation of companies, and many other aspects of national life. Statutory regulation of the professions is now prescribed by law; local authorities operate within a tight legal framework; banking and finance supervision has been strengthened; and publicly quoted companies are subject to regulation to a level of detail unknown inside central government. Isn't sauce for the goose, sauce for the gander? The days of self-regulation of Cabinet government should be over.

The third is that the current immunity of the prime minister and Treasury from Cabinet government when it suits them, especially on economic matters, is dysfunctional. If Britain's economy had performed spectacularly well as a consequence of the Treasury's autonomy, the current arrangements might be justified. But it hasn't.

I believe, therefore, that there must be a Cabinet Government Act. This would prescribe the duties of the prime minister and the Chancellor, and the role of Cabinet; provide for a National Security Council and a National Economic Council, whose approval would be needed for national security and Budget and public spending decisions respectively; and require the Cabinet Secretary to report to Parliament each year as to whether Cabinet government was operating effectively.

Such an Act would also stop hasty and ill-thought-out changes to the machinery of government, and seek to reduce the high turnover of ministers.

There's plenty of academic evidence – some of it quoted with approval by ministers – which strongly suggests that the benefits of mergers, acquisitions and reorganizations by companies rarely match their promise and often destroy value. The same is true of changes in the machinery of central government. The absence of any serious constraints can lead to madcap schemes, or to the outrageous, casual way in which the decision to establish a new Ministry of Justice was announced. The Public Accounts Committee and the National Audit Office have both set out their assessments of the wastefulness of the current arrangement.[4]

From time to time, departments do need to be reorganized; sometimes agencies need to be spun from them. The single Department of Work and Pensions has brought considerable advantages, but the way the change was carried out was wasteful. There's no case for shrouding these decisions, which have an impact way beyond the term of any one government, in such secrecy. There should be statutory procedures requiring that proposals have to be published and considered in advance by parliamentary committees; these should include proposals by the Leader of the Opposition, to provide for the changes that may accompany a change of government.

Under the current Coalition government there has been considerable stability of ministerial teams. That may partly be due to a personal decision of David Cameron to conduct fewer reshuffles, partly another consequence of coalition, and partly because this is still (in 2012) a relatively young administration.

There was some early stability in the Blair administration, but turnover then accelerated. Both Tony and Gordon misused reshuffles as a way of turning attention away from bad news (like poor election results). For most of the individuals involved, the constant churn (especially of junior ministers) led to them, and government as a whole, functioning far less well than they could have done if they'd had the time and security to learn their jobs and get on with them.

The figures are astonishing.

There are twenty-three positions in Cabinet.* Sixty different MPs and peers were members of Cabinet at some stage over our thirteen years, occupying an aggregate 127 posts. There were nine Work and Pensions Secretaries in a nine-year period.

The position among junior ministers (including whips) was even worse, with 770 changes of post. This included thirty-nine changes at the FCO; forty-five changes at the Home Office. The median time spent in any ministerial post was 1.3 years.†

With the composition of the Commons due to be cut to 600 seats, and the growth of alternative careers in the Commons through the select-committee system, the number of ministers should be cut, by law. It's hard to legislate in a parliamentary system against a high turnover. Some resignations – like those of Ron Davies and Peter Mandelson in the closing months of 1998, for example – come out of the blue, but it might be worth establishing the principle that ministers could expect to stay in post for at least two years.

The level of parliamentary scrutiny of the executive has increased in the decades I have been in Parliament.[5] But control of the government Whips' Office over the agenda of the Commons remains too tight. The establishment of the Backbench Business Committee, which now determines the use of non-governmental time on the floor, has been an important advance. Legislation, however, remains in an iron government grip. Indeed, this grip has tightened in recent years, as a direct result of the programming of all government legislation.

Filibustering – running debates into the small hours of the morn-

---

* In 2010 there were twenty-three Cabinet positions; this has grown from nineteen in 1900: House of Commons Public Administration Select Committee, 'Too many Ministers?', Ninth Report of Session 2009–10.

† This is for all ministerial posts, Cabinet and non-Cabinet, between May 1997 and May 2010. The mean average was 1.7 years. HoC Library MP database: 'Ministers in the Labour governments, 1997–2010'.

ing, and sometimes into the next day – can be great fun, but does not achieve much else, as I saw in the eighties. A ritual developed of wasting time on the early clauses of a bill, forcing the government to introduce a specific timetable – a guillotine – and then having the rest of the bill go through without proper consideration at all. The introduction by Labour of timetables for every bill has made the process apparently more rational, and the Commons hours more family-friendly.

However, it's had a significant downside. Under the previous arrangements, backbenchers could not only table amendments to government bills (as they still can) but could also normally ensure that they were debated and voted upon. Timetabling, coupled with the pernicious rule that once time is up only government amendments can be voted on automatically, means that these opportunities have been greatly diminished.

Meanwhile, government whips, who over the decades have cut to zero the filibustering techniques available to delay government bills, have made every use of the very same techniques to ensure that Private Members' bills are blocked to the point of extinction, often preventing a vote on them. Worse still (and I was inadvertently complicit in one example), even where a Private Members' bill has been passed into law, its coming into force may be delayed for years.*

The solution is very simple – though government whips will fight the change. It is to introduce a system of timetabling for those Private Members' bills which come high in the annual ballot, and have them debated during the normal Monday to Thursday parliamentary week, rather than relegated to the occasional Friday sitting when many MPs are caught up with constituency engagements. Do this, and provide that

---

* The Prisoner Earnings Act 1996, passed with all-party support, did not come into force until 2011. When I was Home Secretary, I or one of my ministers had apparently agreed to shelve the Act.

such bills have to be brought into force within six months of their passing, and the role of backbenchers would be transformed.* Procedure may be boring to some, but it's about the distribution and exercise of power. It really matters.

I tried hard in government to persuade Tony, and later Gordon, of the merit of some of these reforms. I sent Tony long memoranda about them in March 2002 and September 2003, but his approach was by then set in concrete. Gordon had good intentions on the need for constitutional change, but was soon diverted from this agenda, and in any event did not see that we needed to start with the beam in our own eye before seeking to extract the mote from others'. All these changes are still to come, but come they must.

By tradition, the Lord Chancellor is the final office-holder in an outgoing administration to relinquish his post – and (for reasons buried in the mists of time) he has to wait until the courts have closed for the day, too. It was not therefore until 3.45 on the afternoon of Thursday 13 May 2010, a whole week after the general election itself, that I got to the Palace to hand back the Great Seal of my Office.

The new ministers were arriving as I did. They were taken to the usual suite of rooms used for such formal occasions. I was ushered down an unfamiliar corridor to the 'Belgian Suite' to take my leave of the Queen. She made some very gracious remarks about my service as a minister. I took my leave, the last man standing from Labour's longest period in government.

---

* I would also introduce a requirement that every clause of every government bill should be brought into force within six months, unless through a special procedure Parliament decided otherwise. This would concentrate the mind of the government machine, and ensure that measures were not put on the statute book unless there was a coherent, costed plan to implement them.

NOTES

Introduction
1 Enoch Powell, *Joseph Chamberlain* (Thames and Hudson, 1977), p. 151.

1: My Mother, Your Father
1 Epping Forest Act, 1878.

2: Boaters and Boiler Suits
1 D. R. Thorpe, *Supermac: The Life of Harold Macmillan* (Chatto & Windus, London, 2010), p. 26.
2 Cf. Matthew Parris, *The Times*, 20 August 2011.
3 *Essex Weekly News*, Friday 17 May 1963.
4 *Brentwood Gazette*, Friday 17 May 1963.
5 *Daily Mail*, 22 June 1995.
6 See Thorpe, *Supermac*, fn18, p. 726.
7 See Phillip Williams, *Hugh Gaitskell* (Jonathan Cape, London, 1979), pp. 734, 761.

3: Respected but not Respectable?
1 FCO telegram from Santiago to London, 1966.
2 Ben Pimlott, *Harold Wilson* (HarperCollins, London, 1992), p. 304.
3 Ibid. p. 230.
4 Roger V. Seifert, *Revolutionary Communist at Work: A Political Biography of Bert Ramelson* (Lawrence & Wishart, London, 2011).
5 *Times* Guide for 1966, p. 16.
6 *Daily Telegraph*, 3 February 1968.
7 *Daily Mail*, 13 March 1968.
8 *News of the World*, 3 November 1968.
9 *The Times*, 10 April 1969.

10 Philip Ziegler, *Edward Heath* (HarperPress, London, 2010), pp. 214–17.
11 Ibid., p. 215.
12 V. I. Lenin, '"Left-Wing" Communism, an Infantile Disorder', 1920, in V. I. Lenin, *Selected Works*, English edition (Foreign Languages Publishing House, Moscow, 1952), Vol. II, Part 2.
13 Jessel, Stephen, 'Communist president of NUS plans no revolutionary changes', *The Times*, 31 March 1971.

4: Guile and Low Cunning

1 Dominic Sandbrook, *State of Emergency: The Way We Were (Britain 1970–74)* (Penguin, London, 2011), chapter 15.
2 Alan Bullock, *Ernest Bevin* (Politico's, London, 2002), p. xv.
3 Anne Perkins, *Red Queen* (Macmillan, London, 2003), p. 406.
4 Williams, *Hugh Gaitskell*, p. 734.
5 For a fuller account of this extraordinary saga, see Perkins, *Red Queen*, pp. 429–34.

5: Essex to Acapulco

1 *Blackburn Times*, 27 January 1927.
2 'Blackburn and Darwen Labour Market' (University of Manchester, 1985), figure 2.2.
3 Letter from Brian Mcginnis to Alice, then principal, DHSS, August 1978.

6: Drawing the Poison

1 Hansard, 13 December 1982, cols. 17–20.
2 Quoted in Kenneth O. Morgan, *Michael Foot: A Life* (HarperPress, London, 2007), p. 373.
3 Patrick Cosgrave, *Independent*, 26 September 2001.
4 Hansard, 29 October 1980, col. 607.
5 Hansard, 13 July 1982, cols. 946–52.
6 Hansard, 2 February 1989, cols. 439–519.
7 Affidavit, 3 February 1983.
8 Letter to Jack Straw, 26 May 1982, from the deputy chairman of the Police Complaints Board.
9 See *Labour Weekly*, 3 February 1984, Bill Taylor, p. 15.
10 *Guardian*, 26 April 1984.
11 Martin Westlake, *Kinnock* (Little, Brown, London, 2001), p. 299.
12 For a wonderfully atmospheric account of Gaitskell's speech to the 1960 Scarborough conference, see Williams, *Hugh Gaitskell*, pp. 607–13.
13 1 October 1985, Bournemouth.

7: Other People's Children

1 William Woodruff, *Beyond Nab End* (Abacus, London, 2003), p. 143
2 Was it a skirt too far?: A cabal of middle-aged male MPs ambushed Labour's plans to promote women, the *Independent,* Sunday 24 October 1993.
3 Westlake, *Kinnock,* p. 404
4 The Plowden Report (1967): Children and their Primary Schools, para. 1234.
5 Ibid., para. 5.
6 Ibid., para. 418.
7 Ibid., para. 612.
8 Susan Crosland, *Tony Crosland* (Jonathan Cape, London, 1982), p. 148.
9 *Guardian*, 5 September 1987.
10 Kenneth Clarke, Education Secretary, *Conservative Press Notice*, 6 June 1991.
11 Hansard, 6 June 1991, col. 404.
12 *The Times*, 14 March 1992.

8: Relics and Reality

1 John Maynard Keynes, *The General Theory of Employment, Interest and Money* (Macmillan, London, 1936).
2 Clause IV, Part (4), Labour Party constitution, 1918–1995.
3 Interview with Lord Wilson of Rievaulx, Oxford, 12 May 1984 in 'Taking genesis out of the Bible': Hugh Gaitskell, Clause IV and Labour's socialist myth, Tudor Jones, School of International Studies and Law, Coventry University (2008).
4 Merits of our values, *Tribune,* 16 December 1994.
5 Harold Perkins, *The Rise of Professional Society: England Since 1880* (Routledge, New York, 1989), p. 229. Also referenced in Jack Straw MP, *Policy and Ideology* (Blackburn Labour Party, Blackburn, 1993), p. 21.
6 British Election Study, Heath, Jowell and Curtis, quoted in Mark Stuart, *John Smith* (Politico's, London, 2005), p. 346.
7 Ibid., p. 315.
8 Alistair Darling, *Back from the Brink: 1,000 Days at Number 11* (Atlantic Books, London, 2011), p. 242.
9 Tony Blair, *A Journey* (Hutchinson, London, 2010), p. 37.
10 *British Journalism Review*, issue 4 1993, and issue 1 1999.
11 Hansard, 27 January 1986, cols. 646-90.
12 Hansard, 19 October 1995, col. 502.
13 Burns Report, 9 June 2000, p. 15, para. 6.49.

9: Life in the Graveyard

1 Don Rumsfeld, *Rumsfeld's Rules* (first published 1974).

2 British Crime Survey 2010, table 2.3.
3 Coroners and Justice Act 2009.
4 F. M. Cornford, *Microcosmographica Academica: Being a Guide for the Young Academic Politician* (Metcalfe & Company, Cambridge, 1908), pp. 15, 16.
5 Antisocial Behaviour Act 2003.
6 Ministry of Justice statistical notice: Anti-Social Behaviour Order (ASBO) Statistics England and Wales 2010, 13 October 2011.
7 Home Office White Paper (Cm. 8367), 'Putting Victims First; More Effective Responses to Anti-Social Behaviour' (May 2012).
8 Lords Hansard, 22 July 1998, col. 939.
9 Hansard, 22 July 1998, col. 954.
10 Blair, *A Journey*, p. 255.
11 Public Expenditure Statistical Analyses 2002–2003, chapter 8, tables 1.2 and 1.3.
12 Political Parties, Elections and Referendums Act 2000.
13 *Daily Mirror*, 24 December 1997.

10: Stephen Lawrence

1 Hansard, 3 November 1964, col. 71.
2 Cato, 'The Guilty Men' (Gollancz, London, 1940).
3 Louise London, *Whitehall and the Jews* (Cambridge University Press, 2001).
4 The Race Relations Act 1965, Race Relations Act 1968 and Race Relations Act 1976.
5 Vancouver Commonwealth Summit, 17 October 1987.
6 BBC, *The Long View*, 17 January 2012.
7 *Evening Standard*, 18 March 1998.
8 The National Archives: 'Stephen Lawrence Inquiry': transcript; part 1, day 32 NT2/38.
9 Public Interest Disclosure Act 1998, later incorporated into the Employment Rights Act 1996.
10 Hansard, 22 February 1999, col. 22.
11 Hansard, 24 February 1999, col. 390.
12 Ibid., col. 393.
13 Home Affairs Committee report into the Lawrence Inquiry – Ten Years On, 14 July 2009.
14 Table 8, Home Office Statistical Bulletin HOSB 13/11, July 2001.

11: A Dictator Calls

1 Hansard, 9 December 1998, col. 214.
2 In Re Pinochet. Oral judgment 17 December 1998, reasons 15 January 1999.
3 Hansard, 15 April 1999, col. 312.

4 Hansard, 2 March 2000, col. 574/5.
5 'Pinochet: Straw may have misled MPs', the *Observer*, Sunday 16 January 2000.
6 See D. Sugarman, 'Courts, Human Rights and Transitional Justice. Lessons from Chile' (2009), *Journal of Law and Society* 36, pp. 272–82.

12: A Tale of Two Policies

1 See 'A Bill of Rights for the United Kingdon: a comparative summary', Francesca Klug, *European Human Rights Law Review* 5, 1997, pp. 50–7.
2 Rights Brought Home: The Human Rights Bill, Cm. 3782 paras 1.18 and 1.19.
3 See my Gareth Williams Memorial Lecture 12 July 2011 for more on this.
4 Hansard, 21 October 1998, col. 1362.
5 Letter from Maurice Frankel, 18 April 2012.
6 *Sugar* vs *British Broadcasting Corporation & Another (2)*, SC 15 February 2012.
7 'Supreme Court upholds BBC's refusal on Israel report', BBC website, 15 February 2012.
8 *Your Right To Know,* Cm. 3818.
9 The Constitution Unit's Commentary on the FoI White Paper (January 1998).
10 *Guardian*, 3 July 1998.
11 *Observer*, 5 July 1998.
12 Freedom of Information: Consultation on Draft Legislation, Cm. 4355, May 1999.
13 Steve Richards, *New Statesman*, 24 April 2000.
14 Information Commissioner's Report to Parliament [HC 218], *Ministerial veto on disclosure of the minutes of the Cabinet Sub-Committee on Devolution for Scotland, Wales and the Regions* (5 January 2010).
    Information Commissioner's Report to Parliament [HC 622], *Ministerial veto on disclosure of Cabinet minutes concerning military action against Iraq* (10 June 2009).
15 Zurich/Spectator Parliamentarian of the Year Awards, 8 November 2001.
16 Interview of Radio 4's *World at One*.
17 *A (FC) and others (FC)* (Appellants) vs *Secretary of State for the Home Department* (Respondent), 16 December 2004.
18 BBC, Friday 17 December 2009.
19 *A (FC) and others (FC)* (Appellants) vs *Secretary of State for the Home Department* (Respondent), 16 December 2004, para. 97.
20 Public Prosecution Service Annual Lecture 2009. See also Francesca Klug, 'Human Rights and Victims' in 'Reconcilable Rights? Analysing the tension between victims and defendants', Legal Action Group, 2004.

21 *R (on the application of Barclay and others)* (Appellants) vs *Secretary of State for Justice and others* (Respondents), judgment given on 1 December 2009 and *R (Barclay and others)* vs *Secretary of State for Justice and the Lord Chancellor and others.*

    Other examples where journalists have benefited from the HRA include *Reynolds* vs *Times Newspaper* [2001] 2 AC 127: *Jameel* vs *Wall Street Journal Europe* [2006] UKHL 44: *Mersey Care NHS Trust* vs *Ackroyd* [2007] EWCA Civ 101; *Malik* vs *Manchester Crown Court and Chief Constable of Greater Manchester et al.* [2008] EWHC 1362 (Admin); *R (BBC)* vs *SSHD 11.11.12* [2011] EWHC 13 (Admin); *R (BSkyB)* vs *Chelmsford Crown Court* [2012] EWHC 1295 (Admin).

22 R v (1) Secretary of State for the home Department (2) Two Electoral Registration Officers, ex parte (1) Pearson (2) Martinez : Hirst v HM Attorney-General (2001) LTL 4/4/2001.

23 Case of Hirst V. the United Kingdom (no. 2) *(Application no. 74025/01)* Judgment Strasbourg 6 October 2005.

24 Information Commissioner's Office guidance, 15 December 2011.

25 Memorandum to the Justice Select Committee, Post-Legislative Assessment of the Freedom of Information Act 2000, December 2011.

26 Blair, *A Journey*, p. 516.

13: Calamity Jack

 1 *Sunday Times*, 23 January 2000.

 2 Appearance before Home Affairs Select Committee, 23 May 2006.

 3 Article 1, as amended by the 1967 Protocol.

 4 As at April 2011.

 5 Asylum Statistics – House of Commons Library Standard Note, 22 June 2011, SN01403.

 6 The Report of the Committee on the Civil Service, Cm. 3638.

 7 *Express*, 1 September 1999.

 8 NAO, 24 March 1999, 'The Home Office: The Immigration and Nationality Directorate's Casework Programme'.

 9 Ibid., para. 1.

10 *Guardian*, 24 August 1999.

11 Public Accounts Committee evidence, Wednesday 23 June 1999.

12 Hansard HL Deb., 6 February 2001, vol. 621, col. 95-6.

13 *Guardian*, 16 February 2001.

14 *Daily Express*, 1 July 1999.

15 BBC *Today*, 29 June 1999.

16 *Guardian*, 30 June 1999.

17 Hansard, 29 June 1999, cols. 140 et seq.

18 Hansard, 19 April 1995, col. 218.

19 Hansard, 23 June 1999, col. 1176.

20 'Asylum pleas "will not be met"', BBC website, 10 February 2000.

21 BBC, 10 February 2000.

22 AA Petrol and diesel price archive figures.

23 Hansard, 2 November 2000, col. 839.

24 See para 5.49 of the Hammond Report, HC 287, 2001.

25 *Observer*, 21 January 2001.

14: Life in the Air

1 Robin Cook, *The Point of Departure* (Simon & Schuster, London, 2003), p. 8.

2 A. J. P. Taylor, *A History of World War Two* (Octopus, London, 1974), *The Origins of the Second World War* (Hamish Hamilton, London, 1961), *The First World War: An Illustrated History* (Hamish Hamilton, London, 1963).

3 An interview with Anthony Mukwita, news editor of Zambia's largest selling monthly magazine *Bulletin & Record* – October 2011 edition of *Bulletin & Record*.

4 Ibid.

5 Tony Blair, statement to TUC conference, Tuesday 11 September 2001.

6 *Responsibility for the terrorist atrocities in the United States*, 10 Downing Street, 4 October 2001.

7 UNSCR 1368.

8 UNSCRs 1378 (14 November 2001), 1383 (6 December 2001), and 1386 (20 December 2001).

9 Resolution 1386 (2001). Operative Paragraph 1.

10 Alastair Campbell, *The Blair Years* (Hutchinson, London, 2007), p. 584.

11 Sherard Cowper-Coles, *Cables from Kabul: The Inside Story of the West's Afghanistan Campaign* (HarperPress, London, 2011).

15: The War That Nearly Was

1 UNSCRs 38, 39, 47 and 51.

2 'Pakistan's woes feature at Labour conference', *Dawn*, 24 September 2008.

3 'Terrorists attack Parliament; five intruders, six cops killed', Reeliff news, 13 December, 2001.

4 'Pakistan forces put on high alert: Storming of parliament', *Dawn*, 15 December 2001.

5 12 January 2002.

6 *Disarmament Diplomacy* 65, July–August 2002.

7 Ibid.

8 'No Straw Snub', the *Birmingham Post*, 23 July, 2002.

9 Pakistan economic survey 2011–12.

16: Iraq – The War of Choice

1 'Cheney changed his view on Iraq', *Seattle Post*, Tuesday, September 28, 2004.
2 Quoted by me in the Commons, Hansard, 24 September 2002, col. 33.
3 Comprehensive Report of the Special Adviser to the DCI on Iraq's WMD, 30 September 2004 [Iraq Survey Group (Duelfer) Report] – Vol. I, p. 30.
4 Hansard, 10 April 2002, col. 22.
5 Quoted in Robert Skidelsky, *John Maynard Keynes; Fighting for Britain 1937–1946* (Macmillan, London, 2000), p. 115. Keynes also wrote that if there was one thing he learnt from his experience of 'stepping like a cat over the hot tiles of Washington' it was that the situation was 'fluid up to almost the last moment'. 'I liken them to bees who for weeks will fly round in all directions . . . providing both the menace of stings and the hope of honey; and at last, perhaps because the queen in the White Hive has emitted some faint, indistinguishable odour, suddenly swarm to a single spot.'
6 Foreign Affairs Committee evidence, 24 June 2002.
7 United Nations Security Council Resolution 1441 (2002).
8 UNSCR 1441 (2002). Operative Paragraph 4.
9 UNSC Update on UNMOVIC inspection, Hans Blix, 27 January 2003.
10 *The Times*, 4 January 2003.
11 Press conference given by Mr Dominique de Villepin, Minister of Foreign Affairs (20 January 2003).
12 8 September 2005 interview with ABC News' Barbara Walters for the *20/20* programme.
13 See: Peter Goldsmith transcript, Iraq Inquiry, Wednesday, 27 January 2010.
14 'Unresolved Disarmament Issues. Iraq's Proscribed Weapons Programmes', Cm. 5785, pp. 25–ff.
15 Cm. 5785, p. 13.
16 UNSCR 1441 (2002), Operative Paragraph 5.
17 Hansard, 18 March 2003, col. 902.

17: The Aftermath: The Wrong Choices

1 Interview on CNN, 30 April 2006.
2 Condoleezza Rice, *No Higher Honour* (Simon & Schuster, London, 2011), p. 192.
3 Ibid., p. 210 and p. 208.
4 Rice, *No Higher Honour*, p. 215.
5 See George W. Bush, *Decision Points* (Crown, New York, 2010), pp. 169–71.
6 *Iraq Casualty Count* figures.
7 *Iraq Body Count* figures.
8 Memorandum to Iraq Inquiry, January 2010; Supplementary memorandum to Iraq Inquiry, February 2010; Statement to Iraq Inquiry, January 2011; Additional statement on sanctions, May 2011.
9 *Iraq Body Count* figures.

10 Comprehensive Report of the Special Adviser to the DCI on Iraq's WMD, 30 September 2004, p. 30.
11 Gadhafi: Iraq war may have influenced WMD decision, CNN, 22 December 2003.
12 Disarming Libya: Weapons of Mass Destruction, CRS Report for Congress, 22 September 2006.
13 Implementation of the NPT Safeguards Agreement of the Socialist People's Libyan Arab Jamahiriya, IAEA Board of Governors (GOV/2004/12), 20 February 2004.

18: The Sick Man Bites Back: Europe and Turkey

1 Laeken Declaration, 14–15 December 2001.
2 Home Office paper, 'Impact of EU enlargement on migration flows', 25 March 2003, p. 58.
3 Net migration to UK in 2010 at record high, BBC website, 24 November 2011.
4 The World in 2050, HSBC Global Research, January 2011.
5 Hansard, 20 December 2004, col. 1919.
6 UN Press Release SG/T/2402.
7 Established by UNSCR 827 in May 1993.
8 Schroeder Pledges Support for Turkey's EU Membership, Assyrian International News Agency, 27/8/2005.
9 Sarkozy: Turkey has no place inside the European Union, Turkish Press, 14/1/2007.
10 Ibid.

19: The Inconceivable and the Incompatible: Israel, Iran and the Middle East

1 Statement by His Excellency Seyed Mohammad Khatami, President of the Islamic Republic of Iran, The 56th Session of the United Nations General Assembly, New York, 10 November 2001.
2 Daily Mirror, 25 September 2001; Guardian, 25 and 26 September 2001. The minister was Ephraim Sneh, according to the Guardian.
3 Guardian, 25 and 26 September 2001.
4 Michael Axworthy, Iran: Empire of the Mind (Penguin, London, 2007), p. 266.
5 See Stephen Kinzer, All The Shah's Men (John Wiley & Sons, London, 2003).
6 Rice, No Higher Honour, p. 313.
7 John J. Mearsheimer and Stephen M. Walt, The Israel Lobby and US Foreign Policy (Farrar, Straus & Giroux, New York, 2007).
8 Iran and Libya Sanctions Act of 1996.
9 Donald Rumsfeld, Known and Unknown (Sentinel, London, 2011), p. 639.
10 Carl von Clausewitz, On War, ed. Michael Howard (Oxford University Press, 2007).

11 BBC Radio 4 *Today* programme, 4 November 2004.

12 *Independent*, 13 November 2004.

13 *Independent*, 16 November 2004.

14 'The Iran Plans: Would President Bush go to war to stop Tehran from getting the bomb?' Seymour Harsh, *The New Yorker*, 17 April 2006.

15 BBC Sunday *AM* programme, 9 April 2006.

16 *Daily Telegraph*, 20 April 2006.

17 UK Polling Report, 30 April 2006.

20: The Breaks

1 Blair, *A Journey*, p. 594.

2 *Guardian*, 6 May 2006.

3 David Heath, quoted in *Pink News*, 3 January 2008.

4 *Newsnight*, BBC, January 2011.

5 Hansard, 19 July 2006, col. 314.

6 Rice, *No Higher Honour*, pp. 490, 492.

7 Blair, *A Journey*, p. 600.

8 JS contemporaneous note, 31 January 2004.

21: The Tights Come On

1 Evidence to Commons' Constitutional Affairs Select Committee, 22 May 2007.

2 Hansard, 3 July 2007, col. 815.

3 Criminal Justice and Immigration Bill (HL Bill 16 of 2007–8).

4 YouGov, 24 September 2007, Lab: 44 per cent; Con: 33 per cent.

5 Mitcham and Morden in 1982.

6 Bullock, *Ernest Bevin*.

7 Nicklaus Thomas-Symonds, *Attlee: A Life in Politics* (Tauris, London, 2010).

8 *The Andrew Marr Show*, BBC, 31 August 2008.

9 BBC, 8 June 2009.

22: The Tights Come Off

1 Hansard, 10 January 2012, col. 151, and 16 May 2012, col. 662.

2 Hansard, 3 July 2007, col. 815.

3 Kenneth Harris, *Attlee* (Weidenfeld & Nicolson, London, 1982), p. 286. See also Margaret Gowing, *Independence & Deterrence: Britain & Atomic Energy, 1945–52,* Vols I and II (Macmillan, London, 1974).

4 Public Accounts Committee – Seventy-Seventh Report – Reorganizing central government bodies (26 March 2012) [HC 1802]. National Audit Office – Reorganizing central government (18 March 2010) [HC 452 Session 2009–10].

5 LSE lecture, 'The Future for Democracy – Politics in a Spectator Society', 28 June 2006.

INDEX

INDEX

INDEX

Hakim, Ayatollah 396
Hamas 460, 461, 462, 464
Hamilton, John 157
Hamilton, Mary 122
Handley, David 310–11, 316
Hariri, Rafik 484
Harkat ul-Ansar (HuA) 351
Harman, Harriet 520, 522–4, 533
Harris, Peter 153
Harrison, Stephen 5, 202
Harrison, Walter 141
Harrods 298
Hart, Graham 95
Hart, Judith 106
Hassan, Margaret 398–400
Hattersley, Roy 190
Hatton, Sir Christopher 502
Hatton, Derek 157–8
Hawthorn, Jeremy 64
Hayward, Ron 136
Hazell, Robert 5, 273, 278
HBOS 517
Healey, Denis 62, 96, 105, 112, 113, 138, 139, 143, 146, 147, 154, 546
health and safety 472–3
Heath, David 475, 476
Heath, Edward 70, 71, 77–9, 82, 91–2, 95, 104, 105, 112, 142, 314–15, 508, 545
Heffer, Eric 103, 105, 154
Henderson, Arthur 187
Hersh, Seymour 463
Heseltine, Michael 95, 174, 179, 216
Hewitt, Patricia 161–2, 521–4
Heywood, Jeremy 499
Hezbollah 396, 485, 486, 487
Higginson, Anne 4, 194, 303
Higginson, Mike 124
higher education, top-up fees 489
hijacking 291, 305–7
Hill, David 404, 500
Hindle, Charlotte 120
Hindle, Frances 120
Hindle, Madge 120
Hindle, Michael 120–1
Hinduja, G.P. 316, 317
Hinduja, Prakash 317
Hinduja, S.P. 316, 317–8
Hirst, John 285
Hitler, Adolf 12, 131, 232, 441
Hoare, Sir Samuel 232
Hodge, Margaret 117
Hoey, Kate 74, 82
Hoffmann, Gillian 256–7
Hoffmann, Lord Leonard 256–7, 259, 284
Home Office: Straw as Home Secretary 201–325; as graveyard for ambitious

politicians 202; responsibilities of 204–5; charges of incompetence 291; Straw leaves 322–3; compared with Foreign Office 329–30, 335, 469; changes made under Blair government 496–7; plan to split in two 497–8
homosexuality: in boarding schools 34–7, 42; as criminal offence 34–5, 213; and spies 98–9; Jeremy Thorpe 108–9; attacks on gay politicians 149; age of consent 213–14; public attitudes to 213; Straw's work for equality 213–15
Hoon, Geoff 336, 496, 521–4
Hoover, J. Edgar 437
Hornby, William Henry 133
house arrest 284
House of Commons 550–2
House of Lords, reform of 275, 473, 476–9, 524–5, 542
Houses of Parliament 131, 132
housing: demolition of Victorian 89; Straw's interest in 133, 184, see also council housing
Howard, Michael 196–8, 202, 203, 205, 206, 210, 211, 212, 216, 271, 272, 294, 296, 301, 490, 506
Howarth, Alan 162
Howarth, George 4–5, 160, 161, 194, 206, 514, 521–2
Howe, Geoffrey 133, 470
Howells, Kim 74, 194
Howells, Ros 234
Huddleston, Trevor 65
Hughes, Simon 149
human rights 205, 214; in Chile 252–3, 255, 257, 263, 264, 266; in post-war Europe 270; and asylum-seekers 292–3; in Kashmir 358; US handling of terrorist suspects 397–8
Human Rights Act (2000) 269–75, 278, 282–5, 287, 542
Human Rights Bill (1987) 270–1, 538
Humphrys, John 409
Hungary 65, 422, 427
Hunt, Alan 64
Hunter, Anji 194, 325
hunting 199
Huntley, Ian 284
Hurd, Douglas 328–9
Hussain, Akhtar 4, 124, 402
Hussain, Shaukat 402
Hussein, Saddam 342, 361, 371, 435, 443; western backing against Iran 361; First Gulf War 362, 381; and weapons inspectorate 363, 367, 380; no evidence of link with al-Qaeda 364, 384; Straw's view of 367–8, 372, 388, 409, 410, 412–13; and banned weapons 375–6, 377, 378, 409, 410, 412–13,